HELEN BARR read English at Oxford University. She is currently Fellow and Tutor in English at Lady Margaret Hall, Oxford. Her teaching interests include Old and Middle English language and literature, and the study of the English language up to the present. She has published articles on *Piers Plowman* and poems in the *Piers Plowman* tradition, and is preparing a book on the language of the *Piers Plowman* tradition.

THE PIERS PLOWMAN TRADITION

A Critical Edition of
Pierce the Ploughman's Crede,
Richard the Redeless,
Mum and the Sothsegger
and
The Crowned King

Edited by Helen Barr
Lady Margaret Hall, Oxford

Consultant Editor for this title
Malcolm Andrew
Professor of English Language and Literature
The Queens University of Belfast

J.M. Dent
London
Charles E. Tuttle Co., Inc.
Rutland, Vermont
EVERYMAN'S LIBRARY

Introduction, editing, notes and commentary
© J.M. Dent Ltd, 1993

Printed in Great Britain by
The Guernsey Press Co. Ltd,
Guernsey, C.I.
for
J.M. Dent Ltd
Orion Publishing Group
Orion House
5 Upper St Martin's Lane
London WC2H 9EA
and
Charles E. Tuttle Co., Inc.
28 South Main Street
Rutland, Vermont
05071, USA

First published in Everyman in 1993

British Library Cataloguing in Publication Data
for this title is available upon request

ISBN 0 460 87238 9

Everyman's Library
Reg. US Patent Office

CONTENTS

Introduction   I

I   Background to the *Piers Plowman* Tradition   I
II   *Pierce the Ploughman's Crede*   8
III   *Richard the Redeless*   14
IV   *Mum and the Sothsegger*   22
V   *The Crowned King*   30
VI   Editorial Procedure   35

Acknowledgments   46

Bibliography   49

Chronology of Historical Events   57

Pierce the Ploughman's Crede   59
Richard the Redeless   99
Mum and the Sothsegger   135
The Crowned King   203

Notes and Commentary   211

INTRODUCTION

I Background to the Piers Plowman Tradition

Late medieval England was a time of change and upset. In the last quarter of the fourteenth century, and continuing into the fifteenth, institutions and those prominent within them were exposed to challenge and reform. Confidence in the secular government of the realm was shaken by the scandals and military defeats of Edward III's dotage, and by the insecurity of Richard II's underage accession. In the great uprising of 1381, the Archbishop of Canterbury was murdered and the boy-king of England left to negotiate single-handedly with a crowd of rebels. Richard II presided over a kingdom which became increasingly lawless. Court culture and extravagance could not conceal the bitter feuds amongst the nobility, which, exacerbated by Richard's misrule, led in the closing months of the century to the deposition of England's anointed king.[1]

Henry Bolingbroke's accession in 1399 was initially promising. However, civil disturbances were characteristic of his reign from the Cirencester rebellion in 1399–1400 to the Battle of Bramham Moor in 1408. The Scots continued to harass the Northern Borders, the Welsh were in open rebellion under the leadership of Owen Glendower and there was the continuing threat of French invasion. Partly as a result of these military

---

1 The issues and events covered here are treated in more detail in the introduction and notes to the individual poems. To avoid duplication of annotation, references will be given only for critical works or particular points of information not otherwise discussed. These references will be by short title, with full details in the bibliography. A single citation of a work will be fully annotated *in situ*.

pressures, Henry's government repeatedly threatened to collapse into insolvency.

Throughout this time, the Church was attempting to counter the spread of heretical ideas stemming from the subversive teachings of John Wyclif, the Oxford philosopher. Some of his ideas were condemned by Papal bulls in 1377, and in 1382, when the Council of London examined twenty-four propositions drawn from Wyclif's writings, it declared ten heretical, fourteen erroneous. Nonetheless, support for Wyclif's ideas was not eradicated. His followers promulgated aspects of his teaching on matters such as the Eucharist, dominion and predestination, and the corruption of the contemporary church with dedication and enthusiasm. In 1395, *The Twelve Conclusions of the Lollards*, which called for ecclesiastical disendowment, were fixed to the doors of Westminster Hall.[2]

Stiff legislation, beginning with the 1401 statute *De Haeretico Comburendo* (which made provision for the burning of proved heretics) was passed in an attempt to curb this dissent. The laws had a direct impact on growing literacy and literary production. Archbishop Arundel's *Constitutions* of 1409 forbade the translation of the Bible into English and increased provision for the investigation of books. But this was not sufficient to prevent a civil rebellion in 1414 led by the Lollard knight Sir John Oldcastle, and although the rebellion was swiftly quelled, the Wycliffite movement was not quashed.

Henry IV had died in 1413. His rapid decline is often attributed to the illness which came upon him soon after he acquiesced in the execution of Archbishop Scrope for his part in the 1405 uprising. The accession of Henry V, like that of his father, promised new hope. War was renewed with France and success in battle deflected attention from continuing pressures at home. Military glory was bought at a price, however, with an already tax-burdened nation asked to dig ever further into its pockets to support the campaign.

Underlying these events were important demographic changes. The effects of successive plagues and increasing urban-

2 For the text of these, see *SEWW*, pp. 24–9. Throughout the present edition the names 'Lollard' and 'Wycliffite' will be used synonymously. Hudson (1988[1]), pp. 3–4 notes that the only distinction between the words in usage during the period 1385–1450 appears to have been that initially 'Lollard' was a clearer mark of disapproval. See further notes to *Crede* 532 and *Mum*, 417–19.

isation resulted in a gradual move away from a feudal, manorial economy to one which was cash-based. Traditional bonds and groupings in society were challenged, and as social mobility increased, especially amongst merchants, lawyers and small landowners, a new role emerged for the commons. Accompanied by growing literacy, these social changes increased the commons' awareness of their role in political events.[3] In 1376, the Commons petitioned for an annual parliament to correct the errors and faults in the realm,[4] and their growing confidence to question fiscal policy is seen in the tussles between king and parliament in the first decade of the fifteenth century over grants of taxation.[5]

The Lollard movement also stimulated new roles for some members of the Commons. There was powerful support for Wycliffite ideas from members of the gentry and aristocracy,[6] but also from those excluded from institutionalised positions of power. One of the foundations of Lollardy was that the Bible should be translated into English and made accessible to all, a proposal which weakened the male, clerical stranglehold on Christian belief and defied traditional educational patterns. The belief that the true Christian church consisted of the souls predestined for salvation bypassed the structures and ceremonies of the hierarchical, material Church. The Lollard John Purvey maintained in 1401 that all good Christians are made true priests by God and that the laity can legitimately administer all the sacraments necessary for salvation.[7] In 1409, the first victim of *De Haeretico Comburendo* was John Badby, a tailor from Evesham.[8]

A new age of political verse written in English accompanied these changes.[9] *Piers Plowman* stands at its centre. In both its themes and its exploration of genre, it is one of the most

3 These changes receive further discussion in Simpson (1990[1]), pp. 33–7.

4 *Rot.Parl.*, II. p. 335.

5 See further Rogers (1969).

6 See further McFarlane (1972) and A. Tuck, 'Carthusian Monks and Lollard Knights: Religious Attitudes at the Court of Richard II', *SAC* Proceedings, 1 (1984), pp. 149–61.

7 Cited in Hudson (1988[1]), p. 325.

8 This event and its political and religious significance is discussed fully by McNiven (1987).

9 This phenomenon is discussed further in Coleman, Harriss, Maddicott, Middleton (1978), Robbins and Scattergood.

expansive poems written in Middle English, and as such, it is
small wonder that its author, William Langland, spent nearly a
quarter of a century (c. 1362–86) composing and revising it. It
derives its title from an enigmatic ploughman figure who commands the highest voice of authority in the poem. *Piers* documents the quest of its narrator, Will, to learn what he must do
to save his soul, and conducts simultaneously an urgent investigation into contemporary fourteenth-century society, most
especially its secular government, the church, and economic
structures. It was one of the most popular poems of the English
Middle Ages, as the survival of over fifty manuscripts of its
three, or four, versions testifies. Of the works of the contemporary poets Chaucer and Gower, only *The Canterbury Tales* was
more popular.[10] The audience of *Piers* was wide; it was copied
throughout the South and the Midlands, and found particular
favour amongst relatively humble clerics and members of the
literate laity.[11]

Piers not only commented on matters of church and state, but
was itself caught up in them. Even while Langland was still
engaged in its composition, *Piers Plowman* was used as a
watchword for serious civil disobedience. John Ball was one of
the leaders of the 1381 uprising popularly known as the
'Peasants' Revolt'. Under a variety of pseudonyms, he sent
letters to his confederates to rally to the cause. A number of
phrases used within them refer to *Piers* and show knowledge of
Piers beyond mere familiarity with its title. Alongside references
to 'Peres Ploughman' are quotations of key phrases from the
poem: John Schep's letter bids the rebels to 'dowelle and bettre,
and fleth synne' and 'chastise welle Hobbe the robber'; Jakke
Carter's letter promises that he and Piers Ploughman will
provide food; John Ball's contrasts 'trewthe' with a catalogue
of the deadly sins, which, like the list in the A text of *Piers*,
omits mention of wrath. So confused became fact and fiction

---

10 All these points are discussed further by Simpson (1990[1]).
11 The audience of *Piers* is discussed by J. A. Burrow, 'The Audience of *Piers
Plowman*', *Anglia*, 75 (1957), pp. 373–84, reprinted with a postscript in *Essays
on Medieval English Literature*, (Oxford, 1984), pp. 102–116, and Anne
Middleton, 'The Audience and Public of *Piers Plowman*', in Lawton (1982), pp.
101–123.

that in the *Dieulacres Abbey Chronicle* (p. 164), 'Per Plowman' is listed as one of the leaders of the Revolt.[12]

Piers also became entangled in religious controversy. Although there were owners, annotators and compilers of *Piers* who saw in it material to uphold the true Catholic church, scarcely a decade after the completion of the C text, the poem was also appropriated to endorse opinion compatible with Lollard ideas. *Piers Plowman* itself, so far as records indicate, escaped examination for heresy, but its own examination of the contemporary church inspired later readers to write new works which radically questioned the church in a religious climate which increasingly branded reform as heresy. Two of the earliest of these new works form part of the *Piers Plowman* tradition. The appeal of *Piers* to religious sectarianism continued into the sixteenth century: Reformation propagandists found in *Piers* material to fuel their cause and indeed Robert Crowley's 1550 printed edition hailed the author of *Piers Plowman* as a disciple of John Wyclif.[13]

*

There must be few works which have been used to authorise both civil and religious dissent and which have also spawned a literary tradition. *Piers Plowman*, whatever the intentions of William Langland, is one. *Pierce the Ploughman's Crede, Richard the Redeless, Mum and the Sothsegger,* and *The Crowned King* were written between 1393 and 1415. All four poems, though in different ways, and to differing degrees, were inspired by *Piers Plowman* and form the substantial part of what has been termed 'the *Piers Plowman* tradition'.[14] Their literary indebtedness to *Piers* is shown in the recall of key words and

---

12 The texts of these letters were preserved in contemporary chronicles written by Thomas Walsingham (*H.A.* II, pp. 33–4) and Henry Knighton (*H.A.* II, pp. 138–40). R. B. Dobson, *The Peasants' Revolt of 1381* (London, 1970) collects these together, pp. 390–3. For further discussion see Hudson (1988²), pp. 251–52 and Helen Cooper, 'Langland's and Chaucer's Prologues', *YLS*, 1 (1987), pp. 71–81.

13 See further Hudson (1988²), pp. 254–63 and Hudson (1985), pp. 227–48.

14 See Derek Pearsall, *Old English and Middle English Poetry* (London, 1977), pp. 150–8, especially p. 153. Turville-Petre, pp. 32–3 and Lawton (1981). The fifteenth-century alliterative poems *Death and Liffe* and *Scottish Feilde* have been claimed as part of the *Piers Plowman* tradition but the evidence is inconclusive; see further, Hudson (1988²), p. 254.

phrases and in the reminiscence of important episodes. Like their great exemplar, all four poems are written in alliterative long lines, and, in keeping with *Piers*, in the plain alliterative register as distinct from the rich, ornamental style of poems such as *Sir Gawain and the Green Knight* and *The Alliterative Morte Arthure*.[15]

It is clear that the authors of all four poems had substantial knowledge of *Piers*, though of which version, or composite versions, it is hard to tell. With the exception of *Richard*, it is clear that the poets knew a long text of *Piers*. The most extensive acquaintance with the earlier poem is seen in *Mum*: echoes of *Piers* range from the Prologue to its closing lines.

The poems in the tradition respond to *Piers* primarily as a social document. Will's urgent, spiritual quest is scarcely reflected. Unlike John Ball's reading of *Piers*, however, none of the poems in the tradition is radical in a secular sense: indeed, all are stalwart supporters of a hierarchically maintained society directed by a strong secular power. *Richard*, *Mum* and *The Crowned King* show support for a limited monarchy and *Mum* in particular criticises the kind of civil disobedience which took place in 1381 (see note to lines 1374–7). That said, all the poems scrutinise the foundations of Christian authority in their criticism of recent events, the legal system, the church, the nature of kingship and decisions of government.

Although this scrutiny never compromises civil allegiance, two of the poems, *Crede* and *Mum*, overstep the bounds of orthodoxy in their analysis of the church. *Crede* is overt in its declared support for Wyclif and Wycliffite criticism of the church. *Mum*, influenced no doubt by the anti-Lollard legislation passed since the completion of *Crede*, is much more guarded. Nonetheless, to a reader familiar with Wycliffite ideas and terminology, the anticlericalism bears witness both to Lollard ideas and to their suppression.

The four later poems display a range of ideas and literary techniques. *Crede* is the earliest and adopts the name and figure of Piers Plowman to write an urgent and vigorous polemic against the friars. The poem utilises literary strategies characteristic of *Piers* to contrast the fraudulence of the fraternal orders with the simple sanctity of a true-living ploughman. *Richard the*

15 See Turville-Petre, p. 51.

Redeless was written directly after the events following Richard II's deposition. In keeping with the remaining members of the tradition there is no explicit mention of Piers Plowman by name, but the new poem takes up many of the concerns about government explored in *Piers*. *Richard* uses the errors of Richard II's reign, most especially the king's choice of unwise counsellors and his disregard for law and order, to write an 'advice to princes' poem which is of benefit for future rulers.

In many ways *Mum* continues where *Richard* left off; the exploration into government is widened and updated. The poem's concerns include the civil disturbances of Henry IV's reign, the corruption of the contemporary church, and a sweeping review of the estates of society which weighs them all in the balance and finds them wanting. Many of the narrative strategies familiar from *Piers* are adopted in this later poem, which in its investigation of the foundations of secular and religious authority, comes closest of the poems in the tradition to the more transcendental concerns of *Piers*. *The Crowned King* also continues the analysis of kingship and the roles of members of society, but in a much more restricted way. The poem was written in response to the start of Henry V's military campaign against the French, and while *Crowned King* falls a long way short of the technical and imaginative achievements of *Piers Plowman*, the echoes of the earlier poem are deft in their sober questioning of the cost of military pomp and circumstance.

All the poems in the *Piers* legacy bear witness to the emergent voice of those literate members of society who may have been excluded from key positions of sacred or secular authority, but who were keen in this time of flux and unrest that their voices be heard. In this, they, like *Piers*, take their place amongst the plethora of political poems which this increasingly literate age produced. Here, it is interesting to consider the illustration on the front cover.[16] It dates from the early years of the fourteenth century and depicts the symbolic ceremony of the king's coronation. The king is invested with crown, rod and orb, the bishops are represented by their mitres and croziers, the chancellor by his large gold coin. On the margins to left and right

---

16 The illustration is also reproduced, with a commentary, in *The Flowering of the Middle Ages*, ed. Joan Evans (London, 1966), pp. 13–14.

are two lawyers in their coifs. A figure on the left with a pair of white gloves may represent a member of the nobility.

In the context of all this ritual, the artist has transformed the traditional chequered background of medieval illumination. In each of the squares there are faces of nameless observers excluded from the symbolic ceremony. They are not individualised, nor graced with symbolic garb. It is to such faces that *Piers* gives an individual voice. The poem questions the power of institutions to foster political harmony and direct individuals to salvation. At the end of the poem it is the individual Conscience who exits from the institutionalised structures of church and state, and who goes in search for Piers Plowman and for grace. The four poems in the *Piers Plowman* tradition take up this quest of the individual conscience. In so doing, they, like *Piers Plowman*, give body – and a voice – to some of those faces looking on at the ceremony of power from behind the bars.

II Pierce the Ploughman's Crede

Pierce the Ploughman's Crede is the only member of the *Piers Plowman* tradition to survive in more than one copy. A fragment, lines 172–207, is preserved in British Library MS Harley 78, fol. 3r. It was copied c. 1460–70. MS Harley 78 (designated H in this edition) is one of the historical and poetical collections made by the Elizabethan antiquary John Stow. The manuscript also contains poems by Chaucer, Wyatt and Surrey. The other surviving copies date from the sixteenth century: from the first half, British Library MS Bibl. Reg.18.B.XVII (designated B); from the second half, MS Trinity College Cambridge R.3.15 (designated A) on which the present text is based; and the printed edition (designated C) by Reyner Wolfe (London 1553, 2nd edn. 1561, STC. 19904; 19908). The edition, like A and B, appends *Crede* to a copy of *Piers Plowman*. In B, *Crede* forms an introduction to a C text of *Piers*.

In London in 1814, T. Bensley reprinted a black letter copy of the 1553 edition. Thomas Wright edited *Crede* in his *The Vision of Piers Plowman* (London, 1832; repr. London 1856). The standard modern edition has been that by W. W. Skeat, *Pierce the Ploughman's Crede* (EETS OS 30, London 1867). *Crede* has recently been included in a teaching volume of texts,

Six Ecclesiastical Satires, ed. James Dean (TEAMS, Western Michigan University 1991).

Skeat (and Dean) base their text on the Trinity manuscript. Skeat (p.v) judged Trinity to be the best copy, not because of date, but because of the care taken by the copyist. Doyle (1982) notes that A is a 'meticulous transcript of a late-fourteenth or early-fifteenth-century copy' of *Crede* (p. 98). The British Library Royal manuscript (B) is much more carelessly copied and so I have used Trinity (A) as the base text. Skeat (p.v) thought that the two manuscripts known to him and the printed edition all came from the same exemplar, now lost, but Doyle (1959) has shown that this is not tenable. Doyle observes that the page in Harley may have come from the same source as the Royal copy. Either it was a reject from a complete copy of the poem, or it excited interest because of the detailed description of the London house of Blackfriars. Both H and B contain readings which suggest that the scribe was copying at speed, or from memory (see variants to 172–207 and B's readings at 81, 559, 580, 618, 716).

None of the texts appears to have been copied from any of the others. There are two dozen mechanical copying errors in A which are not found in B or C, and both B and C contain distinctive readings at many points. C is generally closer to A than is B; there are nearly three times as many distinctive B readings as there are C. However some of C's readings differ substantially from A and B and suggest that the copy was 'doctored' for ideological reasons. The reading at line 288 introduces a new note of anticlericalism and at lines 748 and 756 C alone substitutes 'abbot' for 'bishop'. The most significant differences between the copies are seen in C's version of lines in the Creed narrated by Peres at the end of the poem. At two points, C omits lines which concern the Eucharist (817–18, 823–5), and interpolates five new lines into the passage. In contrast to Skeat and Dean, I have not included in the body of the text the extra five lines found only in the 1553 edition. For further discussion, see notes to lines 817–19 and 823–5.

Crede is the most obviously Lollard member of the *Piers* tradition. Peres Ploughman declares his sympathy for Wyclif (528–32) and also for the West Country Lollard Walter Brut (657–62). The reference to Brut is important in dating the poem. Bishop Trefnant of Hereford tried Brut for heresy in 1393. Line

657 refers to Brut's prosecution and hence 1393 may be considered a *terminus a quo* for the composition of *Crede*. The poem is unlikely to have been written later than the end of the century. Given the outspoken comments about prosecutions, one might expect a reference to the burning of William Sawtre (1401) had this event already happened. Moreover, the overt support for Wyclif and Brut is more likely to have been declared before the passing of anti-Lollard legislation in 1401.

Crede is often compared with *The Plowman's Tale*, a four-teenth- or fifteenth-century Lollard poem which acquired a sixteenth-century narrative framework linking it to Chaucer's *Canterbury Tales*.[17] Points of contact between the two poems are indicated in the notes. *The Plowman's Tale* criticises the hypocrisy of the church, but refrains from including the friars in the scope of his attack because the author has already written about them :

> Of freres I have told before,
> In a makynge of a 'Crede',
> And yet I coude tell worse and more,
> But men wolde werien it to rede !   (1065–69)

This appears to claim authorship of *Pierce the Ploughman's Crede* but because the style of the two poems is widely divergent, it seems more likely that the remark is simply a reference to the reputation of another Wycliffite poem in order to enhance the standing of a new work. *The Plowman's Tale* is written in stanzaic rhyme while *Crede* is composed in alliterative long lines, and there is no clear evidence that *The Plowman's Tale* was influenced by *Piers Plowman*,[18] especially in terms of the narrative strategies which *Crede* strives to imitate.

The narrative scheme of *Crede* is derived from Will's meeting with the friars in Passus VIII of *Piers*. In *Piers*, Will emerges from his discussion none the wiser in his search for truth and so proceeds on an inner quest, during the course of which his interlocutors condemn the corruption of secular and spiritual

---

17 Ed. W. W. Skeat. For criticism on *The Plowman's Tale*, see Lawton (1981), Andrew Wawn, 'The Genesis of *The Plowman's Tale*', *Year's Work in English Studies*, 2 (1972), 21–40; and 'Chaucer, *The Plowman's Tale* and Reformation Propaganda: The Testimony of Thomas Godfray and *I Playne Piers*', *Bulletin of the John Rylands Library*, 56 (1973–4), pp. 174–92.

18 cf. Hudson (1988²), pp. 257–60.

institutions. *Crede* adopts this quest strategy. The narrator is introduced as one who wishes to find instruction in the basic articles of Christian belief and, accordingly, he consults in turn the four orders of friars, hoping to find one of them prepared to teach him his creed. What he gets, however, is not instruction but slander. Each of the representatives of the four orders condemns one of the others. The narrator cleverly engineers this self-criticism by mentioning one of the rival orders each time he poses his question. Thus when he meets the Franciscan, he tells him that a Carmelite has promised to teach him his creed (38-9), which stimulates the Franciscan to wax lyrical about the faults of the Carmelites, and thereby expose the hypocrisy of all the orders.

Exhausted and disillusioned from his enquiries the narrator chances to meet a poor ploughman, his wife and three children. Like his namesake in *Piers*, Peres is introduced abruptly into the poem and immediately commands a position of authority. In *Piers*, at the end of the first episode in which Piers plays a part, the ploughman is seen to get the better of an argument with a parish priest (VII. 105-138). So too, in *Crede*, the simple ploughman is shown to have greater spiritual understanding and insight than any member of the institutionalised church.

The literary strategy of the poem contrasts the hypocrisy and selfishness of the friars with the sincerity and generosity of the abjectly poor ploughman.[19] It is Peres, not the friars denounced by him, who is able to teach the narrator his Creed. As in the fashion of other Wycliffite texts (see note to 487) *Crede* makes extensive use of Christ's denunciation of the Pharisees in Matthew, chapters 15 and 23. This is contrasted with the citation of the Beatitudes from Christ's Sermon on the Mount, Matthew, 5. The juxtaposition of biblical texts shows how the friars have departed from the ideals of their founders, particularly from the ideal of apostolic poverty (see note to 21-3). By contrast, comments about Wyclif (528-32) and Walter Brut (657-62) are preceded by references to the 3rd and 9th Beatitudes, those which extol the virtues of the poor in spirit, and the peacemakers. The implication is that it is only Wycliffites who follow the apostolic life laid down by Christ when he sent out his disciples into the world.

19 This is discussed in detail by Lampe.

Scriptural citation is important in the poem. Like Peres, the narrator, a literate layman, cites biblical texts to reprove the friars, e.g. 141–2. Peres, who resembles a Wycliffite true priest (see note to 638–40 and 794), practises what he preaches. The friars' citation of Scripture, however (e.g. 89–93) serves only to slander their fellows and expose the gap between their words and their deeds. In contrast to *Piers*, scriptural texts (with the exceptions of 458 and 691) are given wholly in English. This in itself is an index of the confidence of the laity to appropriate institutionalised texts to express their own meanings.

Crede is not the work of a Lollard on the extremes of the movement. Peres's discussion of the sacrament of the Eucharist may not be entirely orthodox, but it does not explicitly deny the doctrine of transubstantiation (see further notes to 824–5). The sacrament of penance is not questioned, though the faith in oral confession proceeds from the mouth of the narrator, not Peres (9–10). Much of the antifraternal satire – criticisms of gluttony ; lechery ; worldliness ; the treatment of the sacrament of confession as a financial rather than spiritual transaction – can be paralleled in orthodox works. So too can the denunciations of the friars' pretensions to learning, their elaborate buildings, their encumbrance of the church, and their departure from the ideal of apostolic poverty. But as the notes to *Crede* indicate, these criticisms are especially prevalent in Lollard works and the nuance of *Crede* is very close in tenor to them.

Moreover, it is interesting that of all the fraternal orders, the Dominicans receive the most damning criticism. Lines 505–6 single out the Dominicans as being founded by the devil, even though at line 510 Dominic's founding ideals are praised. Exposure of the hypocrisy of the fraternal habit cites the garb of the Dominicans as example (695–6), and there is simply more extensive criticism of the faults of the Dominicans than of the other orders. This is largely the result of the elaborate description of the Dominicans' convent and the corpulent friar whom the narrator meets there. The details of the description correspond to the architecture of the friary at Blackfriars, London (see notes to 172–207). Herein may lie the clue to the poet's uneven treatment of the four orders. It was at the Council of London held at Blackfriars in 1382 that key tenets of Wyclif's teaching were condemned (see notes to 528–32).

Where the antifraternalism of the poem is most clearly Lollard is in its vacillation between praising the founding ideals of the friars (575–80; 775–8), and suggesting that their very foundation was contrary to Christ's institution of Holy Church. Lines 483–7 state that the friars were founded by the devil. These more extreme comments question the institutionalised church in a manner identical to that common in Wycliffite texts. Von Nolcken has shown (pp. 90–5) how *Crede* vacillates between a temporal and archetypal vision. Ultimately, the criticism of the visible church as represented by the friars establishes an archetype of the church of Antichrist. The only stable picture of the archetypal Church of Christ is the portrait of Peres, a ploughman 'be the waie' (420).

In comparison to the nuanced and open-ended treatment of ecclesiastical issues in *Piers*, *Crede* is simplistic and dogmatic. Even though it is a friar who brings down the Barn of Unity in *Piers* through selling contrition, the final lines state Conscience's enigmatic wish for the friars to have a 'fyndyng' (XX.384) to save them flattering for need. While *Piers* scrutinises the foundations of the institutionalised church much more keenly than *Crede*, ultimately the poem begs questions rather than supplying the schematised and overtly heterodox answers we read in *Crede*.

On its own terms, however, *Crede* is a poem of some merit. Its narrative strategies are well handled and while its vision is more clear cut than that of *Piers*, *Crede* is sufficiently free of the anxiety of influence to have its own voice, one characterised by vigorous proverbialism, biting wit and energetic description. The portrait of the quiveringly corpulent Dominican, his face as fat as a full bladder, his jowl as large as a goose-egg grown all of fat, is the equal of any medieval example of grotesque. The poem's visual imagination is often much keener than that in *Piers*, whether the subject is the blood-shod family of Peres (420–42) or the cobbler filthy with grease, whose biting of leather has left his teeth as jagged as a saw (752–3). There are also subtle changes of tone. While there is plenty of vituperation, such as the charge that the Dominicans deal with divinity as dogs do bones (357), this is tempered by moments such as the Augustinian's woeful dissimulation of grief at Franciscan hypocrisy (280), the narrator's wide-eyed surprise at the cost of the ornamental pillar (169–70) and Peres's weary request to his children to cease their crying (442). *Crede* is an enduring example of the inseparability of the cultural from the literary. Even at this distance in time, it ably demonstrates that doctrine need not be dull.

III Richard the Redeless

Richard the Redeless survives in a single copy only – Cambridge University Library MS Ll iv 14, which dates from the second quarter of the fifteenth century. *Richard* follows on from a B text of *Piers Plowman*. The remainder of the manuscript contains treatises on arithmetic; philosophy and astronomy; physiognomy; a Latin verse table of the arguments of the Psalms; sayings of the Latin fathers with translations into English verse; glosses to words from *Piers Plowman*; a treatise on fowling and fishing, and a quatrain of prayer.

Richard has had several christenings. The poem was first edited by Thomas Wright under the title *Poem on the Deposition of Richard II* (Camden Society 1838), where it formed a sequel to *Piers Plowman*. Wright also included it in his collection of *Political Poems and Songs* (Rolls Series 1859). In 1873, Walter Skeat appended an edition of the poem to his C text of *Piers Plowman* (EETS OS 54) and in 1886, to the end of his parallel three-text edition of *Piers*. Skeat thought that the poem had been written before Richard's deposition and altered Wright's title to *Richard the Redeless*, taking the name from the address to Richard II in line 88. *Richard* was included in these editions of *Piers* because Skeat thought that it was written by William Langland.

That is a view which few would now uphold. But in the present century, the title and authorship of the poem have again been questioned. In 1928 a manuscript of a previously unknown alliterative poem came to light and when scholars examined it prior to sale, they concluded that it was part of a continuation of *Richard*. Mabel Day and Richard Steele edited the new poem for the Early English Text Society (OS 199 1936) on this basis, allowing for a loss of some 247 lines between the two parts.[20] *Richard* formed the first section of the new poem and the two parts became known together as the poem *Mum and the*

20 Day and Steele, p. xviii.

Sothsegger. Day and Steele took this title from a marginal note in the recently discovered manuscript. Both *Richard* and *Mum*[21] are incomplete: *Richard* peters out unexpectedly in the middle of an account of an incompetently argued parliamentary debate, and there are lines lost from the beginning and end of *Mum*.

There is interesting evidence which supports Day and Steele's decision to treat *Richard* and *Mum* as a single, once continuous poem. John Bale's *Index Britanniae Scriptorum*, relying on information supplied by one Nicholas Brigham, mentions a poem called 'Mum, Soth Segger' and gives a Latin précis of its opening lines: *Dum orans ambularem presbytris altari astantibus, Bristollensi in vrbe*. The Latin citation translates the opening lines of *Richard* but nowhere in this poem (as it is extant) do the words 'Mum' or 'Soth Segger' appear. They are, however, the names of major personifications in *Mum*. The two fragments seem further connected by an inscription on the cover of the *Mum* manuscript which reads: 'The lyff off kyng Rychard the ij'. Richard II is never mentioned in *Mum* but dominates the discussion of *Richard the Redeless*. These external links between the two fragments are matched by an internal consistency of language and themes.[22]

In 1975, however, Dan Embree examined the narrative techniques of *Richard* and *Mum* and argued that it was highly unlikely that the two fragments once formed a single poem. He pointed out that while the Bale evidence is attractive, it should not be thought conclusive because what Bale refers to was probably a codex containing more than one poem. Embree's views have found general acceptance.[23] My own view (for reasons rather different from Embree's) is that *Richard* and *Mum* are indeed separate poems, but that nonetheless their previous entanglement in the Bale reference and the inscription on the *Mum* manuscript is far from fanciful. On examining the minutiae of the poetic technique of the two pieces, including

21 Throughout this edition *Mum* refers to the second fragment. Day and Steele used the title to refer both to *Richard* and to *Mum*.

22 See Day and Steele, pp. ix–x. Connections between *Richard* and *Mum* in terms of ideas, diction and style are discussed in further detail in the rest of the introduction and notes to individual lines.

23 See Turville-Petre, p. 32; Lawton (1981), p. 788 and (1982), p. 157; E. Salter, *Fourteenth Century English Poetry* (Oxford, 1983), p. 200, and Wawn, p. 283.

subliminal habits of composition, I found the poems not only to be remarkably similar, but in distinct contrast to other alliterative poems, including *Piers* and *Crede*.[24] Furthermore the fragments' treatment of kingship, law and nature is idiosyncratic when compared with the expression of similar ideas in other works.[25] In my opinion, the most reasonable explanation for this situation (and probably the external links between them) is that the two poems are by the same author. *Mum* is written later than *Richard* and represents a broad revision and expansion of ideas in the earlier poem. This reflects both the changes in the political and religious climate between the dates of the two poems, and also, as set out in more detail below, a more extensive knowledge of *Piers Plowman*.

Richard was written later than Skeat, or Day and Steele, realised. The poem discusses issues arising from events during the reign of Richard II (1377–99). A reference to the Cirencester uprising in 1399–1400 (see note to II.17) shows that the poem was written at least three months after the accession of Henry IV. At the start the narrator claims to be writing a treatise for the benefit of Richard to comfort him in his misfortune. However, the true target of the narrator's comments is not the deposed king but 'euery Cristen kyng that ony croune bereth' (I.43), and all those responsible for the government of the realm who follow their own pleasures rather than wisdom (82–7). *Richard* is a fifteenth-century 'advice to princes' poem which uses a review of Richard's misrule to warn future rulers against making the same mistakes.

The mention of Bristol (2) suggests that the poet had links with the West Country, but the Edinburgh survey locates the CUL Ll iv 14 copy of *Piers*, which is in the same hand as *Richard*, in Cambridgeshire.[26] The poet's intimate acquaintance

---

24 Barr (1990²).

25 See Mohl and Barr (1992).

26 *LALME*, III.111, from an analysis of *Piers Plowman*, fols.1r–21r. suggest that the dialect of *Richard* belongs to the South West Midlands (p. xxx). A full discussion of the dialect of *Richard* falls outside the scope of the present edition, but a significant difference between the dialects of *Piers* and *Richard* in CUL Ll iv 14 is seen in the third person feminine singular pronoun. In *Piers*, the form is 'sche' (*LALME*, III.111) but in *Richard*, unless there is a scribal error, the form is 'hue' (III.50). 'Hue' appears commonly in the SW Midlands (*LALME*, I.309/17) but does not appear in the area around Ely (*LALME*, II.14).

with parliamentary affairs makes it likely that at the time of composition he lived in London. There is precise knowledge of the events of the 1398 Parliament held in Shrewsbury (see IV. 11–16) and details of some of Richard's financial transactions with the nobility (IV.7). Throughout the poem a keen interest in legal matters and an abundance of legal diction suggest that its author could have been a parliamentary clerk. There is no evidence of the advanced learning that would have come from a university education.

Richard is structured rather loosely. Passus divisions are marked in the manuscript but their authenticity is uncertain (see note to I.1), and new developments in the poem's argument and subject coincide only intermittently with formal rubrication. The style of the poem is digressive; e.g. III.36 where the narrator announces that he will return to a subject from which he was distracted. Such meandering is characteristic of *Piers* (e.g. XI.316), but in *Richard* this self-conscious narrative ineptitude is part also of the narrator's ploy to disengage himself from responsibiliity for discussing political matters – a technique he may have learned from *Piers*, where the fallible narrator allows persons and institutions to give voice to their own corruption.

Richard begins with cryptic allusions to Richard's deposition and the accession of Henry IV. The narrator's allegiances are not here stated openly, but close examination reveals guarded Lancastrian support for Henry (see notes to I.11–12; III.69; 92–3). The narrator announces his intention of writing a treatise to comfort Richard, a device which enables him to discuss matters of kingship candidly. To review the faults of a former king is an enterprise quite different from discussing the policy of the present monarch. The narrator assures his readership that his purpose is not slander but reform.

The poem continues by comparing Richard's woeful track record of government with the ideal of kingship symbolised by his coronation. The tenor of the remarks suggests that the poet knew of the accusations against Richard proclaimed at the parliamentary assembly which deposed him (I.98–106). The narrator accuses the former king of wilfully disregarding the welfare of his subjects through his cultivation of upstarts, and criticises his failure to punish his favourites for their crimes. A complaint voiced at the end of Passus I, and which recurs throughout the poem, is that Richard refused to employ judicious counsellors.[27]

Passus II castigates Richard's distribution of his livery of the white hart to his supporters (see further notes to individual lines). The narrator scorns the extravagance of these awards and inveighs against the way that such maintenance oppressed the realm by corrupting the legal system. Henry IV's return from the banishment imposed by Richard (see note to I.13) provides redress. The end of Passus II describes Henry's rout of Richard's followers by focusing on the execution of a trio of Richard's most hated ministers (II.152–175).

Passus III recalls Richard's treatment of three important members of the nobility, the duke of Gloucester and the earls of Arundel and Warwick. They were outspoken critics of Richard's misgovernment, and in 1387, they accused the most prominent of his followers of treason. In 1388, the Merciless Parliament condemned some of Richard's supporters to death, and imposed on others sentences of exile and forfeitures of land (see notes to II.57–8). Nine years later Richard took his revenge: five new Lords Appellant accused the three original Lords Appellant of treason and the September parliament of 1397 sentenced them to death (see notes to III.13–36). The poet documents the people's outrage at these events and how they flocked to Henry on his return to help him to redress this injustice.

Half way through the Passus, the narrator turns back to consider some of the other reasons for Richard's downfall, focusing once again on Richard's unwise choice of counsellors; youths who cared more for extravagant fashions of dress than mature consideration of the affairs of state. A dramatic scene witnesses the expulsion of an allegorical figure called Wit from the decadent court. This is followed by further comments on Richard's disregard for the law, particularly his recruitment of a private army of archers from Cheshire who terrorised the country by settling all disputes (including those aired in parliament) by brute force. The Passus concludes with an account of their downfall in a tone which verges on the apocalyptic.

Passus IV contains a satirical sketch of a parliamentary meeting. This breaks off after 93 lines with a cryptic reference

27 The theme of counsel in both *Richard* and *Mum* has been discussed by A. B. Ferguson (1955), and (1965), pp. 70–90.

to the failure of the representatives to 'Dowell'. Details correspond closely to the matters raised at the 1398 Shrewsbury
session. The narrator criticises Richard's excessive taxation, the
corruption of parliamentary procedure, and the sheer stupidity
and incompetence of the members of the assembly. Abruptly,
the meeting collapses into chaos – and the poem into silence.

As this summary shows, the coverage of topical events in
Richard is not chronological. Rather, the narrator alludes to
topical events as a means of focusing discussion on key areas of
political debate. Perhaps the most fundamental of these is the
extent to which the government of the king can be guided by his
counsellors, and by constructive advice issuing from other
members of the political community. *Richard the Redeless* is the
poet's own contribution to this debate. At one point the narrator
draws back from continuing with his poem, but the personification of Reason enters the poem abruptly and authorises him to
continue (II.69–72). In this interchange, authorial anxiety
springs not from aesthetic considerations but from concern over
the legality of practising politics in verse. In effect, Reason's
speech sanctions the author of *Richard* to supply the sane
counsel which Richard II's government lacked. And indeed, the
narrator of *Richard* continues afresh to do so. Exposure of
Richard's personal misrule is accompanied by criticism of the
official machinery of government which ought to have halted
the king's lawlessness and his wilful extravagance. The narrator
points out how the inefficiency and corruption of the parliamentary and legal systems causes them to fail in their function of
ensuring the well-being of all members of the community. In the
absence of any strong institutionalised corrective, reforming
poetry enters the political arena.

Richard's political vision is essentially pragmatic. Unlike
many other examples of occasional topical verse, the poet does
not frame his political analysis with Christian moralising.
Although Henry's return has faint apocalyptic overtones and it
is suggested that his accession is divinely sanctioned (III.352),
the political well-being of the state is seen to be dependent not
on Christian virtue, but on mature government, with wise
policies developed from shrewd advice (III.350–3).

This pragmatism, however, is not the whole story. Characters
in *Richard* are usually represented by their heraldic badges:
Richard and his supporters by the king's badge of the white

hart; Gloucester, Arundel and Warwick by their respective emblems of the swan, horse and bear. Coded narration of this kind is common in political poetry written at this time, but the *Richard*-poet is distinctive in using this code to sustain an ethical commentary on the events which the poem describes.

The poet capitalises on the fact that the badges are all animals and describes recent events in a mode of narration close in tenor to beast fable. Plentiful use is made of the characteristic behaviour of animals recorded in bestiaries: for instance, it is the nature of deer to feed on adders, but Richard and his deer pervert this ordinance by attacking instead a horse, bear and swan and thus bring about their own destruction (III.13–36). Throughout the poem, there are vignettes, proverbial phrases, uses of figurative language, and explicit statements which show how Henry, in contrast to Richard, complies with natural law.

In Passus III the narrator states explicitly that the most iniquitous crime is that which offends against this authority (III.9–10). Behaviour which complies with natural order and harmony is shown to be founded on principles of law. The converse is also true. What links together the various episodes of *Richard* is an ethical vision based on the principle that if human beings follow reason rather than will, then they will behave in accordance with the rational principle discernible in all natural organisms and in the natural world as a whole. If individuals follow the principles of natural reason, then the state will also function harmoniously. It is a vision based ultimately on ideas of natural law (see further Barr 1992).

This unqualified belief in nature as a repository of political rectitude and harmony is unusual, though a conviction shared also by *Mum*. *Piers Plowman* may have exerted some influence here. Most of the echoes of *Piers* in *Richard* (both of episodes and phraseology) are from the Visio (*Piers*, Prol.-VII) which depicts a king who banishes corruption and self-interest from his realm. He preserves the integrity of the legal system against self-seeking individuals by listening to the shrewd advice of his counsellors. *Richard*'s response to *Piers* is to take up these issues and relocate them more precisely in topical events. The formulation of the Visio-kingdom in *Piers* (Prol.114–22) includes a key role for 'Kynde Wit', the personification responsible for creating clerks to counsel the king, devising crafts for the good of the community and establishing law and justice. The passage is usually interpreted as an expression of faith in a natural human faculty capable of forming and maintaining a political community which works for common good.[28] Further, it is the advice of the personification of Reason, supported by Kynde Wit (IV.157–8) which persuades the king to banish Mede. The treatment of nature and law is much more complex in *Piers* than this brief discussion suggests. Nonetheless echoes of these scenes in *Richard* suggest that a reading of this section of *Piers* was partly responsible for the later poet's distinctive view of nature and law.

This ethical vision grants a universality and timelessness to *Richard*'s localised comment. Although the poem's precise bounding in time and place requires a close knowledge of historical events to glean its full import, *Richard* is not simply a political pamphlet in verse. We do not find the vivid visual imagination of *Crede*, but there is plenty of verbal energy and wit. For instance, the thumbnail sketch of parliamentary chaos can be relished without recourse to the Rolls of Parliament. Here, as elsewhere, the writing is energetic, mainly from the use of characteristically dynamic verbs[29] (see especially lines IV.71–80), coupled with acidic proverbial wit: the dull knights of the shire sit like a zero in arithmetic; they mark a place but signify nothing (IV.53–4). Here, as elsewhere, the narrative is always teetering on the brink of metaphor.

Choice of vocabulary is frequently telling, often ingenious. For example, Wit is expelled from court by the porter's 'pikis' (III.232), a word which puns on the senses of weapon and piked shoes. These forerunners of winklepickers were only supposed to be worn by the nobility, and, to add injury to the porter's impertinence, he actually kicks Wit out of court! As the notes record, the poem is full of clever wordplay which, whilst it does not aspire to the transcendent heights of some examples in

---

28 Kynde Wit is translated variously as 'Native Intelligence', or 'Natural Reason'. In this episode in *Piers*, Myra Stokes sees the role of Kynde Wit as stressing the need for society to be based on principles of natural law (pp. 69–70). Hugh White (1988) suggests that its role is to suggest the naturalness of the good society, to make the point that it is within humankind's reach through natural endowment (pp. 18–21).

29 The energetic diction of *Richard* and *Mum* is discussed by Blamires.

Piers,[30] is nonethless a habitual and often devastatingly witty mode of composition. And while the poem has an apparently scatty narrator, one who occasionally muddles his information to the point of needing to go back over it to unscramble the sense (e.g. III.62–79), behind this façade there is a poet with a clear-headed understanding of current affairs and political ethics, capable of encapsulating his views in a poetic style that is both vigorous and wry.

IV Mum and the Sothsegger

The only surviving copy of *Mum and the Sothsegger* was discovered by a West Country bookseller in 1928 and is now preserved in British Library MS Additional 41666. The manuscript dates probably from the third quarter of the fifteenth century. The copy is defective: the opening of the poem is missing; it ends abruptly at line 1751 and many of the margins are torn. There are numerous corrections to the text, probably from a second exemplar in preparation for recopying. These appear to be in the same hand as the main copyist, though in a more informal mode; the ink in which they are written fades, like that of the main hand, on fol.5a. The corrections are discussed more fully in Part VI of this Introduction. The only printed edition is that by Mabel Day and Richard Steele (EETS OS 199 1936) where *Mum* forms a sequel to *Richard the Redeless* (see Part III). The title of the poem refers to its two major personifications: Mum (self-interested silence) and Sothsegger (truthtelling). Lines 841–991 are anthologised in John Burrow, *English Verse 1300–1500* (London, 1977).

Mum, like *Richard the Redeless*, is a poem principally concerned with the analysis of contemporary affairs. It was written later than *Richard* and discusses events and issues current in the first decade of the reign of Henry IV (1399–1409). The narration of events is less direct than in *Richard*. *Mum* considers events which concern people who currently held positions of power. Given the persistent unrest during the early years of Henry's

---

30 Wordplay in *Piers* is discussed by A. V. C. Schmidt, *The Clerkly Maker* (Woodbridge, 1987) and M. C. Davlin, *A Game of Heuene* (Woodbridge, 1989).

reign – resulting in laws to regulate the production of political verse (see note to *Mum*, 128) – the poet probably had to exercise more caution. The restraint may also be attributable to his religious views (see below).

Nonetheless, there are clear topical references in the poem. The earliest in date is to the 1402 hanging of a group of Franciscan friars for their part in spreading treasonable rumours that Richard II was still alive and was preparing to wrest back his throne from Henry (417–21). There are also references to the business of the 1406 parliament. Before the assembly would accede to Henry's demands for taxation, they presented the king with 31 articles of constitutional reform. There are allusions to one of these articles at lines 120 and 1672 (see notes and Barr 1990[1]). The latest dateable reference is in lines 408–14 where the poet criticises a statute which gave the friars sole preaching rights. This is in a section of the poem where the criticism of the church is Lollard in temper. The target of these lines is likely to be Archbishop Arundel's *Constitutions* of 1409 which prevented anyone from preaching who did not have a licence. Arundel's subsequent letter of March 1409, issued to the provincial clergy, exempted the friars from the terms of the *Constitutions* (see notes to 408–13). From the timespan of these allusions, I would suggest that *Mum* was composed shortly after 1409.

The narrative schemes in *Mum* are more tightly regulated than those of *Richard*. Situated in the context of a review of the king's officers, the poem opens with a discussion of how to protect the taxation revenues from their appropriation by greedy individuals. The narrator leaves until last the officer who is most worthy to serve a king. It is a 'soothsegger', one who will speak up honestly about the affairs of state. Such a man is seldom seen, however, for there are few lords who are prepared to employ his services. Instead, flattery and self-interest rule supreme.

In the midst of this passage, the narrator muses on the lawfulness of truthtelling, as in the interchange between the narrator and Reason in *Richard*, justifying the composition of his own poem, as well as stating the need for lawful criticism within the state. The poem then adopts the quest motif familiar from *Piers* and used also in *Crede*; for having established the necessity of a sothsegger, the narrator then wishes to know where he can find one (99–100). A nameless clerk interrupts to tell him that such people are scarce. The narrator marvels that truthtellers are kept from the king, rendering him ignorant of the grievances of the people. But since truthtellers have been punished (152–5), people are too afraid to voice their grievances in case they are put to death or imprisoned. The narrator restates his belief that truth will prevail and, having concluded his survey of Henry's household, launches into a brief encomium of the king's personal qualities (211–20) and hopes that his rule will be one of peace and stability.

Mum then bursts abruptly into the poem and ridicules the narrator for his naivety. A short debate establishes that flattery is more profitable than constructive criticism. The narrator is left pondering inconclusively on the altercation. He resolves to take his question of whether it is better to be Mum or a Sothsegger to the universities. His meeting with the Seven Liberal Arts and a Doctor of Philosophy leaves him (in true Langlandian fashion) none the wiser. The episode (322–91) satirises the uselessness of academic learning in a fashion reminiscent of Wycliffite polemics.

Admitting that he is unable to help him, the Doctor of Philosophy suggests the narrator take his question to the friars. He does; but the debate between Mum and the Sothsegger is temporarily submerged (as the narrator admits in lines 520–1) beneath a deluge of antifraternal criticism which reflects Lollard ideology (see notes to lines 392–535). Predictably, the friars are of no help in the narrator's quest, nor are the monks, nor the parish clergy whom he visits next. His travels, however, which include listening to a sermon preached on the distribution of tithes, give the narrator scope for further Wycliffite criticism of the established church (see notes to individual lines 534–673).

At this juncture, Mum bursts back into the poem to warn the narrator against the consequences of criticising the church. The narrator's rejoinder reminds Mum that priests are merciful by nature and are prevented by law from taking any part in a sentence of death. Rather curiously, Mum then makes a speech which plays into the narrator's hands. He exposes his own hypocrisy by stating that anyone who sees a crime and does not report it is guilty as an accessory (713–66). Mum refuses to admit that he has justified the practice of truthtelling and tells the narrator, if he still wishes to discover whether it is worth being a truthteller, to visit secular lords and towns. The narrator takes up this advice only to find himself at a mayoral banquet which demonstrates all the self-interested greed that Mum had warned him about. Weary and disillusioned, the narrator goes out onto the street where he catches a glimpse of a sothsegger sitting alone in a shop salving his wounds. The narrator realises his search is futile and that Mum was right all along. At the end of his tether, and according to time-honoured medieval literary practice, the narrator falls asleep.

In the dream-vision which follows, the narrator finds himself in a beautiful landscape, full of fruits, plants and joyfully bounding animals. He walks to a garden where he finds a gardener tending a hive of bees. The beekeeper's explanation of the workings of the hive uses the habits of the bees as an exemplum of a perfect political state. Having listened to this exposition, the narrator asks the beekeeper his question about the relative merits of Mum and Sothsegger. The beekeeper replies that Mum is the cause of all the disharmony in the realm. In effect, the beekeeper is the sothsegger for whom the narrator has been searching. He tells the narrator that the dwelling of the truthteller is in man's heart (1224–5) and bids him that when he wakes, he should remember his words and make a book of criticisms of faults in the realm to present to the king and members of the nobility.

The conclusion of the poem takes the beekeeper at his word. Rather than writing a book, however, the narrator opens a bag full of books which contain criticisms of contemporary faults. He provides a bibliography of the bag's contents, and in so doing, gives fresh impetus to his exposure of contemporary corruption. The targets include truant priests, civil disturbances, the greed of certain members of the nobility, various abuses of the legal system and the dissemination of inflammatory political prophecies. We never learn whether the narrator gets to the bottom of the bag, or if Mum reappears to whisk it from his clutches, for in the middle of criticising worldly bishops, the copy ends.

While some of the criticism is repetitive, *Mum* has a clear political vision. The poem upholds a strong monarch who governs in accordance with wise advice from his counsellors. Members of the nobility who infringe the king's regality are sharply rebuked. Throughout the poem, there are allusions to lords who have siphoned off the king's revenue and caused civil unrest. The target of these remarks are members of the Percy family: the earl of Northumberland, his son Hotspur, and Thomas, earl of Worcester. They were prominent amongst Henry's supporters on his return in 1399 but quarrelled with the king over financial remuneration for their support. The disputes led to open insurrections: the Battle of Shrewsbury in 1403; Archbishop Scrope's uprising in 1405 and the Battle of Bramham Moor in 1408 (see further notes to lines 1; 727–42; 1466–70; 1654–62 and 1731–3). The story of Genghis Khan, which is told at 1414–55, contrasts the supreme loyalty of Khan's subjects with the self-interested greed of the English nobility.

According to the political vision of *Mum*, a strong monarch is also a king who listens to the grievances of his subjects. But these must be voiced in their proper place, namely parliament. Unlawful criticism, particularly the grumbles of the labourers, is harshly criticised because it leads to civil unrest and distracts the nobility from defending the realm against external attack (1460–83). However, the cause for such dissent (1118–40) is that the members of parliamentary assemblies are too timid and too corrupt to speak truthfully. As in *Richard*, this failure of institutionalised correction leaves a gap which is filled by poetry. Awareness of the potential unrest caused by illicit criticism causes the narrator grave anxieties about the propriety of writing his own poem. *Mum* like *Richard*, is rich in legal diction, and like the earlier poem, this legal vocabulary is often used in passages which defend the lawfulness of writing satirical poetry (see especially notes to lines 72–94, and 1270–87, where the beekeeper, who commands the voice of highest authority in the poem, commissions the narrator to write a book of political comment).

This cautious confidence in the power of poetry to address affairs of state characterises the criticism of the contemporary church in *Mum*. Because of the anti-Lollard legislation that had been passed since the writing of *Crede*, the *Mum*-poet is much less overt in his support for Wycliffite ideas. Nevertheless, the tenor of the antifraternal criticism is similar to that of *Crede*, especially the identification of the friars with the church of Antichrist, which is brought out clearly by the marginal annotation to lines 519–20. As in *Crede* there is no Wycliffite

teaching on the sacraments, but the slant of the criticisms of
parish priests and private religions, especially its verbal
expression, is identical to that regularly found in Wycliffite
tracts. Given the dangers of voicing any comment about the
contemporary church at the time when *Mum* was written, we
must conclude that its author was either sufficiently sympathetic
to some Lollard ideas to make guarded use of them to frame his
criticisms of the church, or more simply, that he was a fool. His
informed stance on current affairs makes the latter rather
unlikely. It is perfectly compatible for a poem which shows
sympathy for Lollard ideas to demand unflinching loyalty to the
secular powers of authority. There are a number of demonstr-
ably Lollard texts which contain exactly *Mum*'s blend of church
reform and support for a strong, well-advised monarchy.[31]

In a number of places in *Mum*, echoes of *Piers Plowman*
signal criticism of the church which is far more radical than
Langland's position. Again, this is largely a question of date. It
is one thing for Anima to urge the secular lords to disendow the
clergy and let them live on tithes (*Piers*, XV.562–3) before the
passing of *De Haeretico Comburendo* in 1401. It is quite
another for the narrator of *Mum* to quote the tearing of the
Pardon scene from *Piers*, VII.109 before offering an unlicensed
sermon which not only contradicts one just preached by a parish
priest, but moreover, proposes a distribution of tithes compatible with Wycliffite ecclesiology (*Mum*, 657–62). The suppression of the bag of books may reflect the contemporary restraint
of ecclesiastical criticism. We learn that the bag had previously
been stolen by Mum and his confederates; Mum twice appears
in the poem as a bishop (see note to 1341–7).

Although not so fully dramatised a personification, Mum
bears strong resemblance to Mede in *Piers*, especially in his
corruption of the legal system. There are passages in the later
poem which recall particular criticisms in *Piers*, for instance, the
account of Mum's influence over the mayor (*Mum*, 802–22/
Piers, III. 76–103). But it is probably in its treatment of law and
nature that *Mum* is most indebted to *Piers Plowman*. As the
notes to individual lines emphasise, the *Mum*-poet was well

---

31 See *Plowman's Tale*, 677–84, *Thirty Seven Conclusions of the Lollards*
(ed. J. Forshall (London, 1851) under the title *Remonstrance against Romish
Corruptions*) and *Tractatus de Regibus*, ed. J.-P. Genet, pp. 1–19.

versed in common law and in legal theory. As in *Piers*, actual
fourteenth-century laws are cited,[32] and at one point the narrator
criticises a loophole in the legal system which contributes to its
inefficiency (1617–25). This legal knowledge, as in *Richard*,
fashions an ethical vision based on ideas of natural law which
underlies the topical criticism. Lawless behaviour, especially that
which transgresses natural hierarchy, is roundly condemned.
Actions which are fully in accord with legal principles are also
in agreement with the laws which regulate the natural world. In
keeping with *Richard*, *Mum* makes extensive use of bestiary lore
to show whether behaviour conforms to natural ordinance or
violates it. Often this takes the form of proverbial asides or
figurative diction, such as the talking birds of lines 152–5 who
have been unlawfully caged and thus deprived of their natural
voice, but there is an especially full exposition of this stance in
the dream-vision sequence.

The landscape which the narrator sees is of a natural world
fully in harmony with the laws which regulate its existence. The
narrator explicitly draws attention to the political significance
of the allegory (931). The model of the hive of bees takes an
example from the natural world to show how a human political
state should work. The bee-analogy is also found in the works
on the art of government by Aquinas and Giles of Rome (see
note to 877–943). The beekeeper stresses how the work of the
bees is entirely in accordance with the law and with nature
(997–1000; 1036) and in an echo of *Piers*, the bees are said to
be able to detect the wiles of the drones 'as kindely as clerc
doeth his bokes' (1016).

The influence of *Piers* in *Mum*'s political stance is more
pronounced than in *Richard*. *Mum*'s panoramic vision of
Middle Earth recalls Kynde's exposition of the workings of
nature in *Piers*, Passus XI.320–403, and the poem contains a
number of echoes of 'kynde' and 'knowyng' (109; 1016; 1063
and 1065). Further, the beekeeper's explanation of the dwelling
place of Truth is a collage of episodes drawn from Piers's
exposition of the route to Truth in *Piers*, V.595–629; the
description of the Castle of Caro (IX.1–59) and the siege of the
Barn of Unity (XX.212–380). There are also reminiscences of

---

32 See Alford and W. J. Birnes, 'Christ as Advocate: The Legal Metaphor of
Piers Plowman', *Ann. Med.*, 16 (1975), pp. 71–93.

the literary techniques of *Piers*. In Passus XVIII. 328–404,
Langland's description of the Harrowing of Hell uses actual
fourteenth-century laws and legal terminology to fuse the spiritual significance of the event with the social implications for his
own time, particularly in Christ's role as an exemplary king. In
Mum, the description of the battle between vice and virtue in
the human heart (1254–66) employs a similar synthesis. The
citation of common law draws an analogy between the breaking
of the law of God through sin and the breaking of the law of
the land by criminal acts. It is here that a poem of the *Piers*
tradition comes closest to the spirit and technique of Langland's
poem.

Mum is the most ambitious of the four poems in literary
terms. It catches something of *Piers*'s explorations of genres. In
addition to dream-vision, *Mum* uses the quest motif, debate,
personification allegory and extended allegorical narrative
sequences. The use of the bag of books as a narrative strategy to
deflect the consequences of writing topical criticism away from
the poet must rank as one of the most overtly bookish moments
in Middle English literature. It is a self-conscious proclamation
of the political significance of literacy.

The lively language of *Mum* continues the characteristic
raciness of the diction in *Richard*. Dynamic verbs are often used
in telling alliterative patterns, e.g. the friar who lies and licks to
save losing his office (441). There is plenty of epigrammatic
diction coupled with plain-speaking common-sense. People who
fail to foresee the political consequences of their actions are
likened to those who see from the clouds that a storm is
imminent, but choose not to take shelter. And so, when the
heavens open and they and their companions are soaked 'dung-
wete', they only have themselves to blame (732–39). Rather like
Chaucer's parish priest, the narrator is well able to 'snybben
sharply', often in somewhat gritty language, for instance, at
lecherous priests who, instead of tending their flock, play 'lille
for lalle with many a levde kitte' (1357). Delight in wordplay is
also continued. One of the wittiest examples is the caricatures
of the academics who are cartooned with puns drawn from the
terms of their useless learning. For all of Geometry's elaborate
diagrams, for instance, the narrator is left simply baffled (see
346–50). Despite the more adventurous experiments with genre

and narrative strategies, *Mum* still manages to preserve the vivacious and energetic diction so pervasive in *Richard*.

V The Crowned King

The only copy of *The Crowned King* is in Bodleian MS Douce 95 fols. 4a–6a, where it forms part of a mid-fifteenth-century[33] miscellany of Latin and English prose and verse. Its contents have explicit connections with Westminster and London (Doyle 1982, p. 99). *The Crowned King* has been printed twice: by Skeat at the end of his edition of the C text of *Piers* and *Richard the Redeless* (EETS OS 54 1873); and by R. H. Robbins in *Historical Poems of the XIV and XV Centuries* (New York 1959). As *Richard* and *Mum*, *Crowned King* contains precise discussion of recent events. The poem is set in the reign of Henry V, who succeeded to the throne after the death of his father in 1413. Two years after his accession, he renewed the Hundred Years War with France, thus ending the truce that had been sealed by Richard II's marriage to Isabella of France in 1396.

At the beginning of the century, the French political scene was one of disorder. Charles VI suffered increasingly prolonged bouts of insanity and in the ensuing political vacuum, other members of the royal family vied for power. Louis of Orleans favoured ejecting the English from Gascony and Calais by force, but was opposed by John the Fearless. John contrived to have Louis murdered in Paris in 1407. This precipitated a bloody civil war in which both sides sought English help. There was an expedition in 1411 to help the supporters of John the Fearless and protracted negotiations over English claims to French territory. Ultimately, the negotiations came to nothing and with propagandists expounding the dynastic claims of Henry in France, public opinion moved behind Henry's decision to settle the disputes by force.[34] The parliament held in November 1414 awarded Henry a very large grant, and although war had not yet started, it was understood that the money would be used to support an invasion of France. It is clear from the use of the

---

33 On fol. 12 the date 1439 is written.
34 See further Jacob, pp. 134–43 and Scattergood, pp. 47–59.

word 'solyen' in line 36 (see note) that the *Crowned King*-poet knew that such a grant was unprecedented.

Popular history (stimulated no doubt by Shakespeare's play) now imagines Henry v as a national saviour figure because of his victories against the French. In his own time, however, Henry had to take thought about securing his own position and was careful to engineer support for himself and his policies. In 1412, when he was still Prince of Wales, he commissioned John Lydgate to write *The Troy Book*[35], and Green has argued that Hoccleve's poem on the rising of John Oldcastle was sponsored by Henry as counter-propaganda against Lollardy while he was away in France. The poem represents Henry as already fighting on the continent (499–501) but it seems likely that Hoccleve had actually written it before the king had embarked.[36] The famous story of the tennis balls is part of a similar process of propaganda. In all likelihood, the Dauphin never sent them, despite the fact that the story appears in a number of the contemporary chronicles. It was a story disseminated to enhance Henry's popularity and standing. In its recall of the literary analogue in which Darius sent a present of a child's ball game to Alexander the Great, the Dauphin became equated with Darius, a symbol of overweening pride, and Henry with the military glory of the conquering Alexander.[37] The story found its way into contemporary verse, the first example being the verses on *Henry V's Invasion of France* preserved in British Library MS Harley 656. The poem describes the king receiving the good wishes of all the people as he embarked on his expedition.[38]

Many poems, from *The Agincourt Carol*,[39] to John Page's *Siege of Rouen*[40] adulate Henry's military campaigns.[41] A series of poems contained in MS Digby 102 also gives its blessing to

---

35 John Lydgate, *Troy Book*, ed. H. Bergen (EETS ES 97, 103, 106, and 126, 1906–35).

36 Green, pp. 184–5. Hoccleve's *Address to Sir John Oldcastle* is in *The Minor Poems*, pp. 8–24.

37 Green, pp. 186–7.

38 N. H. Nicolas, *The Battle of Agincourt* (London, 1832), p. 302. Other examples are discussed by Scattergood, pp. 51–3.

39 Robbins, 27, pp. 74–7.

40 John Page, *Siege of Rouen*, ed. J. Gairdner in *Collections of a London Citizen* (Camden Society, 1876), pp. 1–46.

41 These are discussed in Scattergood, pp. 53–69.

Henry's expedition against the French. Poem XIII reminds the king that France was the heritage of Edward III and he had rightly sought to repossess his territories through military action. The writer dissuades Henry from negotiations and treaties: 'With word of wynd, mad neuere ende / But dent of swerd endid the dede' (Kail, XIII.127–8) and urges the king to war (159–60). The military patriotism of the poem is not the whole story, however. Preceding the triumphalist call to arms are over a hundred lines of pragmatic advice on kingship. The poet urges the profitable use of parliament; the maintenance of law and justice; concern for the views of the commons, especially by the nobility for their tenants'; the banishment of scoundrels from the court and the upholding of truth. Only when the king has made peace at home, and the realm is unified, should he then go to sea.

This pragmatism is exactly the tone of *Crowned King*. The writer is not openly hostile to the French invasion but neither is there the patriotic fervour of the propagandist literature, even of the more guarded Digby poem. What interests the writer of *Crowned King* is the cost of the war. This focus on the consequences of taxation is similar to the pragmatic tone of the political vision in *Richard* and *Mum*. At no point in the *Crowned King* is there mention of Henry's heritage, or of the rightfulness of his claim. The poem focuses on the king's relationship to his subjects at home.

War is viewed as an occasion to increase taxation (36–41), and instead of blowing military fanfares, the poem urges the king to consider the welfare of his subjects. It is hard to gauge the tone of some of the lines. The king is urged to cherish the allegiance of his subjects because it will profit him more than 'mukke' (64), i.e. wealth. For all the castles which can be gained through military conquest, the most precious plant is what the poor people dig out of the earth (72). Henry should not be greedy for gifts; rather he should give them to those who have grievances (125–6). These warnings to favour the allegiance of subjects rather than acquiring wealth and property sit rather curiously in the context of war; they seem to suggest that Henry should focus on the day-to-day problems of government at home before contemplating military glory abroad.

It is significant that these comments do not issue straightforwardly from the mouth of the poet. In contrast to the Digby poem, there is a narrative framework to *Crowned King* which is noticeably influenced by *Piers Plowman*. The poem opens with an address to Christ and then recounts a journey which the narrator took to Southampton (for the topical significance, see note to line 20). The narrator falls asleep and the poem moves into dream-vision, a device which creates a distance between narrator and poet, and one which is furthered by a speaker within the dream taking over the narrative of the poem. A nameless clerk kneels down before the king, asks if he may offer him advice and receives royal assent. Responsibility for comments about greed and allegiance are thereby transferred to the anonymous clerk.

There are clear echoes of the Prologue of *Piers*. The clerk recalls the 'lunatik' who, kneeling 'clergially' before the king, urges him to rule his kingdom justly to earn allegiance (123–5). In *Piers*, the pragmatic advice issues from a speaker excluded from the symbolic part of the ceremony of coronation. Similarly, in *Crowned King*, the speaker is shown to have no part in framing the ordinance for taxation that has just been passed but, like the lunatic in *Piers*, he points out its serious consequences for the commonwealth as a whole. The opening scene of the dream-vision in *Crowned King* (31–52) recalls the Prologue of *Piers*, with echoes of the Field of Folk, the panoramic view of society, the king's coronation, and the formation of the political state.[42] These links are appropriate. In *Crowned King* the context of a military invasion is used to focus broad questions about the function of government and the relationship of a king to his commonwealth.

None of the advice offered to the king is exceptional. The clerk urges his sovereign to keep the law and uphold justice, to maintain the allegiance of his poorer subjects by looking after their interests, to unite the nobility in parliament, to shun flattery, to appoint efficient officers, to cultivate the personal qualities necessary for kingship such as learning and military skill, and to disdain the vices of avarice. These are points that can be paralleled at length in *Piers*, *Richard*, *Mum*, and occasional verse and prose tracts written throughout the Middle Ages. It would be fair to say that *Crowned King* is the least original of the poems in the *Piers* tradition but it is by no means

---

42 The parallels are annotated in the commentary.

the least interesting example of a very common type of political verse.

David Lawton (1982), has described *Crowned King* as 'bland and mercifully brief . . . in which "speculum regale" barely rises into sense through unintelligent Langlandian pastiche' (pp. 9–10). To my mind, the echoes of *Piers* are appropriate and not unintelligent. For instance, the description of what the labourers dig from the earth as the 'most precious plant' (71) recalls Holy Church's description of love as the most precious plant of peace (*Piers*, I.152). Such intertextuality, with its allusion to 'love' and 'peace' in the context of urging a king not to overlook the contribution of his labourers at a time of war, comes close to creating a pacificist subtext for this section of the poem.

Although Lawton's comment that *Crowned King* fails to transmit the transcendental concerns of *Piers* is indisputable, the poet has perceived the significance of the narrative strategies that he has borrowed. Further, like *Richard* and *Mum*, there is some influence from *Piers* of the importance of 'kynde' in political affairs. There are references to 'kynde' at lines 2, 26, 28, 107, 121 and 132; those at 2, 26 and 107, which refer explicitly to the course of nature, set up a framework of natural ordinance against which human conduct is measured. It is significant that the narrator should focus on the natural sequence of the sun before he falls asleep and should view the political scene below him from a hill (31). The scene is reminiscent of Nature's meeting with Will in *Piers*, XI, where Kynde leads Will to a mountain called Middle Earth (XI.323) from which he can regard the works of nature. The discussion of kingship in *Crowned King* is framed by this sketch of the course of the natural world, and the clerk himself urges the king to follow the 'kynde' of kingship (121) in more than name, and particularly to shun covetousness which is out of 'kende' for a king (132). While discussion of the political significance of 'kynde' is hardly extensive, *Crowned King* hints at the more expansive treatment of law, nature and kingship characteristic of *Richard* and *Mum*.

Crowned King also bears resemblances to *Richard* and *Mum* in its frequent use of legal diction. Terms drawn from the law, as in *Richard* and *Mum*, are used to authorise the legality of offering constructive advice to one's superiors (see notes to 46, 55, 106 and 135). This is another aspect of the poem which shows that its poet had understood some of the larger concerns of *Piers*. This self-consciousness about the practice of writing reforming poetry is common to all the poems of the *Piers* tradition. *Crowned King* lacks the energy of the other three poems, but is far from being merely a flaccid and thoughtless imitation. The poem's narrative strategies cut through the public triumphalism surrounding the preparations for Henry v's military campaigns, and the astute parallels to *Piers* frame a standard, but far from routine, 'advice to princes' poem. As in all the poems in the *Piers* tradition, *Crowned King* questions institutionalised, public issues in terms of what they mean both for the community – and for anonymous individuals.

VI Editorial Procedure

TEXTUAL POLICY

Given that all four poems arise from topical events and issues, the aim of this edition has been to produce texts that could conceivably have been read at the time. Editorial policy has therefore been conservative, and the texts have been altered only if their readings are deficient in sense and there is obvious evidence of routine scribal error. *Richard*, *Mum* and *Crowned King* each survives only in a single copy. In the absence of any further manuscript witness, manuscript readings have been retained where possible. This has sometimes resulted in restoring manuscript readings which previous editors emended e.g. *Richard*, I.113 and *Mum*, 417. There are a few instances where a manuscript reading unaltered by previous editors has been emended, but these are in places where I have felt that the sense is untenable, or words or phrases have been translated differently from previous editions, e.g. *Richard*, I.300, *Mum*, 1563 and *Crowned King*, 58.

In a number of places *Richard* and *Mum* have been emended in light of the evidence provided by corrections marked in the manuscripts. (There are no corrections marked in *Crowned King*.) Those in *Richard* usually substitute common vocabulary for less familiar words, e.g. 'caught' for 'laughte' at II.159, or alter spelling; there is frequent alteration of 'e' to 'y', e.g. 'by' for MS 'be' at III.41. A correction has been adopted if it restores sense, e.g. III.74. The corrections marked in the manuscript

which contains *Mum* are extensive. Day and Steele suggest that
the annotations were the work of at least two correctors, and
they design an elaborate scheme of classification to account for
the different ways in which the corrections were made. I propose
that even though the corrections are marked in different ways –
e.g. a dot in the margin and over a word for a small grammatical
change, or a curl to mark several words in need of correction –
a single hand is responsible for them all. The difference in
annotation is simply to mark alterations distinctively, to ensure
that the emendations are followed accurately. Doyle (1982, p.
98) has suggested that the corrections were made from another
exemplar of the poem in preparation for recopying, and that
they could be the work of the main hand in a more current
script.

Some of these corrections are straightforward linguistic or
grammatical alterations. At line 108 for instance, 'dwellyn' is
substituted for the more unfamiliar 'lendith'. The pattern of
corrections is not consistent.[43] More substantially, some corrections emend obvious scribal errors. This edition usually follows
Day and Steele in incorporating these, e.g. 272, 720, 1472 and
1505. Occasionally I have emended the text on the basis of these
corrections where Day and Steele do not emend, e.g. 1593
'statutz'. Elsewhere, the manuscript reading has been retained
instead of a correction adopted by Day and Steele, e.g. 939 and
1305. Some of these corrections substitute whole b-verses, and
following Day and Steele, this edition sometimes employs them
when the MS b-verse makes inferior sense, e.g. 345. Whole lines
are also provided. At 1336, the corrector's addition ensures the
continuity of the passage. At other places, lines marked to stand
in the text, though compatible with the context, are not
obviously necessary, e.g. 180, 604 and 1606. For this reason
they have not been included but substantial corrections of this
order are recorded in the notes. At some places, additional lines
marked for insertion are incompatible with the context where
they are assigned, e.g. 116, 505 and 535. These are recorded in
the notes, along with all corrections which have been used as
the basis of emendations.

A number of these corrections affect the alliteration of the
lines. Hoyt Duggan has argued that in the classical corpus of

43 These corrections receive fuller discussion in Barr (1989), pp. 10–16.

alliterative verse, 'the poets wrote exclusively in the alliterative pattern aa/ax'.[44] Explained simply, the notation means that in each line of alliterative verse there are two stressed words in the first half (a-verse). Each begins with the same letter. These are called full staves and are designated 'a' in alliterative notation. In the second half of the line, there is one more full stave, which alliterates on the same letter as those in the a-verse. Finally, there is a blank stave, i.e. a fully stressed word which does not continue the alliterative pattern which the other staves have established (designated x). A representative example is:

$$x \quad x \; / \; x \; / \; x \qquad x \; / \; x \quad x \; / \; x$$
(A) In a blessid borugh/that Bristow is named (B)

(*Richard*, I.2) (aa/ax)

Permitted variations on the normative alliterative staple aa/ax, are aa/aa, aaa/aa and extended a-verses with three metrical prominences: aaa/, aax/, xaa/, and axa/.[45]

There are a number of critical variations on this prescription.[46] The studies which have framed rules for alliterative staples have generally been based on poems which are preserved in a number of copies. These provide a control on the examination of scribal contamination. It is exactly just such a control

44 H. Duggan, 'Alliterative Patterning as a Basis for Emendation in Middle English Alliterative Poetry', *SAC*, 8 (1986), pp. 73–104, p. 77 and pp. 82–3.

45 *ibid.* If a line has two alliterative patterns, the letter 'b' is used to designate
$$x \; / \; x$$
the staves in the second alliterating pattern, e.g. *Richard*, III.290: 'For ho-so
$$x \; / \; x \quad x \; / \; x \quad x \; /$$
thus leued:his lyff to the ende' (ab/ba). If a line contains two blank staves, i.e. words which carry full stress but which do not alliterate with each other, then
$$x \quad x \; / \; x \qquad / \; x$$
the second stave is designated 'y', e.g. *Mum*, 106: 'For no maniere mede:that
$$/ \quad x \quad x \; / \; x$$
thereto belongeth' (aa/xy).

46 Kane–Donaldson argue that the alliterative staples used by Langland were: aa/ax, aaa/ax, aa/aa, aaa/aa, aaa/xy, aaa/bb, and, in instances where the final stave is on the first syllable of a trisyllabic or polysyllabic word, aa/xa, pp. 135–8. The staples considered authentic by Schmidt are aa/ax, aa/aa, aaa/ax, aaa/aa, aax/ax, aaa/xx, aaa/bb, ax/ax, ax/aa, ab/ab, pp. 359–60. See further, H. Duggan and T. Turville-Petre, eds., *The Wars of Alexander*, (EETS SS 10 1989), pp. xvii–xxv, J. P. Oakden, *Alliterative Poetry in Middle English: The Dialectal and Metrical Survey* (Manchester, 1968), T. Turville-Petre, 'Emendation on Grounds of Alliteration in *The Wars of Alexander*', *ES*, 61 (1980), pp. 302–17.

which is lacking in the case of *Richard*, *Mum* and *The Crowned King*. The corrections in the manuscripts offer some guidance, but they are not entirely consistent. Just over a dozen of the numerous corrections marked in *Mum* restore aa/ax alliteration, e.g. 166; but some destroy it, e.g. 'witte' for 'mynde' at 634, and at 1315, while the corrector's substitution of 'the seuene sterres' for the MS reading 'the elleuen sterres' improves the alliteration of the line, it is hardly tenable because the Bible story from which the poem quotes clearly states that there were eleven stars, Genesis, 37:9.

The alliterative practice of *Richard*, *Mum* and *Crowned King*, as witnessed by the only copies of the poems which survive, falls some way short of the rules formulated by Duggan.[47] However, as the hybrid alliterative practices of Richard of Maidstone and *Jack Upland* bear witness,[48] there is no guarantee that alliterative poets wrote according to a uniform metrical scheme. On the other hand, recent metrical studies have made important contributions to enable us to distinguish what 'the poet wrote from what the scribe botched'[49] and have suggested that the alliterative patterns of a poem preserved in a single manuscript are likely to misrepresent the practices of the poet.[50] As Turville-Petre has asked, however, 'what is to be done to preserve them faithfully?'[51]

On examining the metrical practice of *Richard* and *Mum*, I found that 72% of the lines in *Richard* alliterated on aa/ax and 80% in *Mum*. In each poem there were lines which did not conform to any accepted alliterative staple. *Richard*, IV.15 is completely deficient in alliteration because it refers precisely to an ordinance of parliament. The unusually high scores for the

47 While much of Duggan's metrical study arose from editing *The Wars of Alexander*, he also analysed a wide corpus of alliterative poems which included lines from *Piers*, and the first 431 lines of *Mum*, 'The Shape of the B-Verse in Middle English Alliterative Poetry', *Speculum*, 61 (1986), pp. 564–92 and 'Langland's Meter', *YLS*, 1 (1987), pp. 41–70.

48 See E. Salter, 'Alliterative Modes and Affiliations in the Fourteenth Century', *Neuph Mitt*, 79 (1978), pp. 25–35. The paucity of aa/ax alliteration in poems such as *Joseph of Arimathie* and *Cheualere Assigne*, and the reduced rate of *Crede*, Oakden, I.168, are also significant.

49 Duggan, 'Shape of the B-Verse', p. 567.

50 Turville-Petre (1980), p. 302.

51 T. Turville-Petre, 'Editing *The Wars of Alexander*', in *Manuscripts and Texts*, ed. D. Pearsall (Cambridge, 1987), p. 160.

metrical patterns xa/ax and aa/xa in both poems present particular difficulty because they could represent either the omission of a stave in the a-verse or scribal inversion in the b-verse.[52] When I analysed each instance, I found it impossible to reproduce a consistent pattern of emendation. There are well over 500 lines which, apart from departing from normative schemes of alliteration, make perfectly acceptable sense.[53]

Consequently, I have emended lines solely on grounds of alliteration only if there are corrections in the manuscript which authorise alteration. Some of these corrections remove what are clearly errors, such as the miscopying of a letter. At *Mum*, 266, the scribe writes 'cafting' in error for 'casting'. This does not affect alliteration, but the same mistake at 244 and 1247 disrupts the alliterative pattern of the line. In both these latter cases, the corrector's annotations restore both sense and alliteration. Sometimes the corrector supplies alliterative staves to half lines which are clearly deficient in sense or syllables, e.g. 88 and 411. Elsewhere, the corrector supplies synonyms for individual words, e.g. 116, 166, 368, 560, 1006. In the last two examples, the corrections make clearer sense than the MS readings.

There are many instances where deficient alliteration is not corrected. For example at line 106 'Mede' is marked for 'soulde' in the a-verse, but while this restores aa/ alliteration, it still leaves the b-verse without alliterative staves. A conjectural emendation could alter 'that thereto belongeth' to 'that to mellyng belongeth', but no such alliterative reconstruction is ever undertaken by the corrector. Simpler instances of alliterative deficiency are also left unmarked, e.g. line 89, where there is no substitution of 'renke' (a word used at 1211 and 1635) for 'man'. Where such correc-

---

52 xa/ax is not a pattern considered authentic by Kane–Donaldson, Schmidt or Duggan. aa/xa is considered authentic in Langland by Kane–Donaldson only when the blank stave falls on the first syllable of a trisyllabic or polysyllabic word, p. 139.

53 For example, at *Richard*, II.175 and *Mum*, 721, the identical b-verses 'amonge all the peple' both alliterate on 'p'. In order to emend to produce aa/ax alliteration, 'amonge' would need to conclude the line, something which occurs only in the poems when 'amonge' does not take an object (*Richard*, I. 57, 70; *Mum*, 116). When 'amonge' takes an object, there is never inversion of natural word-order. 'amonge' + object is a common syntactical frame in b-verses in both poems (*Richard*, I.4, 77, III.113, 209; *Mum*, 630, 807, 844, 936, 1504, 1575, 1580, 1709). The problems of emendation of non-normative staples is discussed further in Barr (1989), pp. 213–17.

tions are wanting, I have not emended, even though Day and Steele sometimes did, e.g. *Mum*, 662, 1216 and 1534. The only places where emendations have been made and alliteration has been restored without the presence of a correction, are where the sense of the MS reading is in doubt, e.g. 1524, 1545 and 1697.

In *Richard*, the corrections do not affect the alliteration. An alliterative stave has been supplied at I.133 because the line is deficient in sense, and I followed Skeat and Day and Steele in substituting 'ladde' for 'hadde' in II.170 (cf. II.56). But I have not altered 'yuell' to 'lither' in II.40, even though the word appears twice in *Mum*, (969, 1069). In the absence of any corrections to the text of *Crowned King*, I have not emended where the alliteration is deficient because of the difficulty in remaining consistent. In line 41, for example, the scribe possibly substituted 'made' for 'ordeyned' and at line 86, 'kepe' for 'get' in the less familiar sense of 'watch out for'; Minot uses the word in a very similar context.[54] But elsewhere, e.g. lines 24 and 116, it is not so straightforward to restore a normative alliterative pattern.

Pierce the Ploughman's Crede presents a different situation. There are three complete witnesses to the poem and a fourth for the lines on Blackfriars, London. There are instances where it was tempting to have emended on alliterative grounds because the readings were attractive, e.g. 69 and 707. In the absence of support from the other witnesses, I refrained from emendation, though the possibility is recorded in the notes. In a few cases, alliteration has been improved on the strength of variant readings. At 183, I have adopted H's reading because there is clear evidence of scribal confusion. At 531 the combined BC reading corrects a mechanical copying error in A (cf. 669), and at 763 the combined BC reading restores aa/ax alliteration which the initial letter of A's 'randes' disrupts, cf. 706. These are my most radical examples of emendation on grounds of alliteration, but only minimal alteration was required, which was supported by the combined weight of the other readings.

A substantial number of lines appear to lack alliterative staves

54 Laurence Minot, *Poems*, ed. T. B. James and J. Simons, (Exeter, 1989), II.36: 'bot get for thair gile'. 'geten' MED v (2) is attested in other alliterative poems, including *William of Palerne*, 2407 and *Destruction of Troy*, 2113. It can be used both transitively and intransitively. In *The Knight's Tale*, 2755 some manuscripts read 'kepe' or 'have' for 'gete'.

e.g. 37, 40 and 545, and the alliterative patterns of many others are non-normative, e.g. 26, 266, 542 and 749. In none of these instances, nor in any others where variants are registered in BC, or in H, is there correction of the alliteration. Consequently, no emendations have been made to either these examples, or the many others similar to them.

Editorial procedure for *Crede* as a whole is also conservative. The variants have been used from BC to correct A's straight-forward mechanical copying errors, usually of single letters, e.g. 233, 415 and 544. There are some instances where all three witnesses are in error. These instances were corrected by Skeat, and this edition follows his practice, e.g. lines 6, 61, 71, 268, 279, 421, 629 and 659. At line 703, all three versions are in error in their use of a masculine third person singular pronoun instead of the required feminine. Perhaps for unconscious assumptions about gender, both Skeat and Dean retain the MS reading, despite emending singular and plural pronouns to restore grammatical concord at other points. For conscious assumptions about gender (and to restore sense) I have emended.

Because A is carefully copied, it has not been necessary to refer to other readings to make large-scale emendations. The most substantial emendation occurs at 637, where C's variant reading suggests that the awkwardness of the combined AB reading is scribal. At line 91, in contrast to Skeat, the combined AB reading has been emended in favour of C because it is more faithful to the paraphrase of the biblical passage. Elsewhere, substantial variants have not been incorporated, and this edition sometimes departs from Skeat in retaining the reading of the base text, e.g. 614. The texts of B and C often provide some attractive variants and these are commented on in the notes, e.g. 288 and 360. The significant difference in C's version of the Creed at the end of the poem is not incorporated in the body of the text; as the notes to 817 indicate, the passage is not congruent with AB's witness at this point.

TEXTS

Spelling

Obsolete ME letters have been given their appropriate modern equivalents: 'th' for 'þ'; 'gh', 'y' or 'z' for 'ȝ'. The letters 'u' and 'i' appear as they stand in the MSS, even when their values are consonantal and they represent 'v' and 'j'. Similarly 'v' and 'j' have been retained when they represent the vowels 'u' and 'i'. On a number of occasions in *Mum*, the scribe attaches 'þ' to the beginning of a word which commences with a vowel. I have rended such instances as 'th'ende'.

Punctuation

Capitalisation and punctuation are modernised, though this edition sometimes follows capitalisation in the MSS which places special emphasis on a word, e.g. 'Eyere', *Richard*, II.145. Abbreviations are silently expanded. In the manuscript, *Richard* is divided into Passūs. I have altered Skeat's, and Day and Steele's allocation of these, see note to *Richard*, I.1.

Latin quotations

In *Richard* and *Mum*, Latin quotations are written in the margins of the manuscripts. Skeat incorporated the five examples in *Richard* into the body of the text because they suited the context, and in the case of the citation of the *Institutes of Justinian* at III.32, it was preceded by a reference in the text to clerical authority: 'as clerkis me tolde'. The remaining quotations are not directly signalled by the text in this way but, as Skeat argued, they authorise the argument of the main text. In the preceding copy of *Piers Plowman* in CUL MS Ll iv 14, while many of the Latin quotations are incorporated in the body of the text and underlined in red, some are written in the margins instead. *Richard* is written in the same hand as *Piers* and this strengthens the case for seeing the quotations as an integral part of the text. Day and Steele printed the Latin quotations in the margins. This edition incorporates them in the body of the text and provides translations and references in the commentary.

This practice has been adopted partly because I hold the view that *Richard* and *Mum* had the same author. The quotations in *Mum*, although once again written in the margins, are clearly designed to authorise the argument of the main text. The quotations are written in the same hand as the main text, and the ink in which they are written fades, like that of the main hand, on folio 5a. On seven occasions, these citations are prefaced by an appeal to authority in the text, e.g. 76, 289, 421,

519, 520, 1224 and 1585, and at 745 a Latin quotation is worked into the alliterative line. At other points, quotations clearly authorise the arguments of speakers in the poem, e.g. 641 and 712. Day and Steele placed these quotations in the margins. This edition incorporates them in the text and translates and references them in the commentary. This citation of authority is an important example of the imitation of the poetic practice of *Piers*. The situation is not relevant to *Crowned King* and does not arise in *Crede* because with two exceptions, biblical citations are paraphrased in English in the text of the poem. Where the Bible is quoted in Latin the citation is incorporated into the alliterative line (458 and 691).

APPARATUS

Emendations from the base texts, whether of individual words and phrases, or transposed lines, are signalled in the texts by square brackets. At the foot of each page of text the variations from the base texts have been recorded. In the cases of *Richard*, *Mum* and *Crowned King*, the emended word or phrase is enclosed in a square bracket which is then followed by the MS reading. In *Crede*, the emended reading from the text is likewise enclosed by a square bracket. If the emendation is adopted without alteration from another witness, the appropriate sigla of that witness, or witnesses, then follow. If the emendation is adapted from the reading of another text, then the unaltered reading of that text is given, accompanied by the appropriate sigla. The order of the citation is determined by the closeness of the reading to the emendation in the text. Where texts B, C and H differ materially from A's reading, the variants are recorded, even when A has not been emended. Spelling variants between the versions have not been recorded unless a difference in spelling suggests that the scribe understood a word in a different sense from A. If only one witness differs from A's reading, I have recorded that reading only and not supplied the spelling variants from the other version or versions. With the exception of the five lines inserted in the Creed, all the variants appear at the foot of the page. In all four texts, any editorial commentary necessary in recording a variant, such as 'omitted' or 'not in' is italicised. Manuscript readings within italicised comment are enclosed in speech marks.

GLOSSES AND TRANSLATIONS

The marginal glosses explain individual words likely to cause difficulty because of sense or spelling. These are often glossed more than once within a single poem and across the four poems as a whole. Where the meaning of a word is too complex to be recorded in the margin, the sign [c] is used to indicate that it receives further explanation in the commentary. Where necessary, the commentary translates lines where the syntax is likely to cause difficulty. There is often fuller discussion of the meanings of the lines in the commentary, even when this is not directly signalled in the margin of the text. All Latin citations are translated in the commentary.

NOTES AND COMMENTARY

Each poem is accompanied by a full commentary on matters of textual editing, and literary and historical significance. There is discussion of individual words and meanings and cross-references between the poems. Detailed historical background, necessary for elucidation of the topicality of individual lines, has been dealt with here rather than in the introduction. Where this explains a particular point of information, references to primary and/or secondary sources are given. Where notes summarise mainstream historical events, or issues current over a number of years, and the information has been drawn from a number of sources, individual references have not always been given. Standard works of reference are included in the bibliography. Cross-reference to other Middle English or medieval literature has been given to provide comparative examples of the treatment of standard themes, or to elucidate distinctive phraseology. I have not attempted to provide an exhaustive account of verbal similarities between poems in the *Piers* tradition and other works in Middle English. Instances where the poems appear to quote *Piers*, or where passages or verbal collocations are reminiscent of *Piers* are given where they occur. In each case, quotations from *Piers* have been provided to bring out the nature of the parallel. All quotations from the B text of *Piers* are from the Everyman edition by A. V. C. Schmidt. Quotations from A are from G. Kane's edition and from C, from the edition by D. Pearsall. Departures from this are recorded in the notes.

Plentiful use has been made of J. A. W. Bennett's edition of the Visio of the B-text. All quotations from Middle English are in the normalised spelling which I have used for the text of the poems in the *Piers* tradition, even when this departs from the editorial practice of the editions which are quoted.

BIBLIOGRAPHY

This includes all books referred to by short title in the introduction and commentary unless the reference is to a particular point of detailed information and is given only once. A selection is also included of the main works consulted, particularly on historical material, which have not specifically been mentioned. Abbreviations used in the commentary, other than surnames of authors or editors, appear in brackets after the relevant entry.

ABBREVIATIONS

For periodicals the standard abbreviations have been used. For reference books and publication series, the following: OED Oxford English Dictionary; MED Middle English Dictionary, ed. H. Kurath and S. M. Kuhn (Ann Arbor, Michigan); EETS The Early English Text Society; CS Camden Society; RS Rolls Series; SS Selden Society; *Cal.Pat. Rolls. Calendar of Patent Rolls*; Pl Tale, *The Plowman's Tale*, ed. W. W. Skeat (Oxford, 1897); *Rot.Parl.*, *Rotuli Parliamentorum*, ed. J. Strachey et al. (London, 1783); PL *Patrologia Latina*, ed. J. P. Migne (Paris, 1841–); *LALME A Linguistic Atlas of Late Medieval English*, ed. M. L. Samuels, A. McIntosh, et al. (Aberdeen, 1986); STC *Short Title Catalogue of English Books 1475–1640*, ed. A. W. Pollard and G. R. Redgrave (London, 1926), 2nd revd. edn., ed. W. A. Jackson, F. S. Ferguson, and K. F. Panter (London, 1976). All references to the Bible are to The (1609) Douay Version (London, 1955).

Helen Barr
1992

ACKNOWLEDGMENTS

For permission to publish manuscripts in their possession I thank the following: The Master and Fellows of Trinity College, Cambridge, (Trinity College, Cambridge MS Reg. 3.15, fols. 317a–328a: *Pierce the Ploughman's Crede*); The Syndics of Cambridge University Library, (CUL MS Ll iv 14, fols. 107b–119b: *Richard the Redeless*); The Board of the British Library, (BL Additional MS 41666: *Mum and the Sothsegger*) and The Bodleian Library, Oxford, (MS Douce 95, fols. 4a–6a: *The Crowned King*). I also thank The Master and Fellows of Corpus Christi College, Cambridge for permission to use the miniature from MS 20 fol. 68a for the cover illustration.

I wish to thank Lady Margaret Hall, Oxford, for generous assistance towards research costs, especially in the provision of computer equipment.

In the course of preparing this edition I have been greatly indebted to the work of other scholars, especially to previous editors of poems in the *Piers Plowman* tradition. It has been a privilege to draw on the erudition and good sense of Thomas Wright, the indefatigable Walter Skeat, Mabel Day, Richard Steele and R. H. Robbins. My indebtedness to other scholars is, I hope, fully recorded in the apparatus to the edition.

A number of people have generously given of their time and expertise while I have been working on the poems in the *Piers* tradition. I should particularly like to thank Professor Douglas Gray and Professor Anne Hudson for their help and encouragement over a number of years. To Professor Hudson I owe the initial suggestion that these poems were a profitable area of study, followed by her supervision of my doctoral thesis and much assistance since. Cathy Swire read the texts and apparatus and I am very grateful for her careful checking, helpful suggestions and companionable discussion. I am also very grateful to Charmian Hearne of J. M. Dent for her meticulous editorial work. Without the expertise of Lorraine Da Luz Vieira with 'point of a nedle', I doubt whether this edition would have been started, let alone finished. It is a pleasure to acknowledge her help. To David, who must often have felt he was married to four poems rather than to me, I owe thanks for tidying up my prose style and much else besides.

BIBLIOGRAPHY

Unprinted Primary Sources

Bodleian Library MS Digby 233 : Giles of Rome, *De Regimine Principum*, transl. John Trevisa.

Printed Primary Sources

Annales: see under Johannis de Trokelowe.
The Anonimalle Chronicle, ed. V. H. Galbraith (Manchester, 1927).
Aquinas, Thomas, *Selected Political Writings*, ed. A. P. D'Entreves, with a translation by J. G. Dawson (Oxford, 1948).
Arnold, T., ed., *Select English Works of John Wyclif*, vol. III (Oxford, 1871).
Bale, J., *Index Britanniae Scriptorum*, ed. R. L. Poole and M. Bateson (Oxford, 1902).
Bartholomaeus Anglicus, *De Proprietatibus Rerum*, transl. John Trevisa as *On the Properties of Things*, ed. M. C. Seymour, et al. (Oxford, 1975), 2 vols.
Bennett, J. A. W., ed., Langland, *Piers Plowman : The Prologue and Passus I–VIII of the B Text* (Oxford, 1972).
The Riverside Chaucer, ed. L. D. Benson et al. (Oxford, 1988).
Davies, J. S., ed., *An English Chronicle of the Reigns of Richard II, Henry IV and Henry V* (Camden Series, 1856).
Davies, R. T., ed., *Medieval English Lyrics* (London, 1963).
Death and Liffe, ed. J. Donatelli (Cambridge, Mass., 1989).
The 'Gest Hystoriale' of the Destruction of Troy, ed. G. A. Panton and D. Donaldson (EETS OS 39 1869 and 56 1874).
Dieulacres Chronicle, ed. M. V. Clark and V. H. Galbraith, *BJRL*, 14 (1930), 164–81.

Dives and Pauper, ed. P. H. Barnum (EETS OS 275 1976 and 280 1980).

English Medieval Lapidaries, ed. J. Evans and M. J. Serjeantson (EETS OS 190 1933).

English Wycliffite Sermons, vols. I and III, ed. A. Hudson, vol. II, ed. P. Gradon (Oxford, 1983, 1988 and 1990). (*EWS*)

Eulogium Historiarum, vol. III, ed. F. S. Haydon (RS 1863).

Evesham: see under *Historia Vitae*

Historia Vitae et Regni Ricardi Secundi, ed. T. Hearne (London, 1727). (Evesham)

Fitzralph, R., *Defensio Curatorum*, in *Trevisa's Dialogues*, ed. A. J. Perry (EETS OS 167 1925).

Freidberg, E., ed., *Corpus Iuris Canonici* (Leipzig, 1879–81), 2 vols.

The Chronicles of Froissart, transl. J. Bourchier, ed. G. C. Macaulay (London, 1913).

Gawain and the Green Knight, ed. J. R. R. Tolkien and E. V. Gordon, 2nd edn. ed. N. Davis (Oxford, 1967).

Genet, J.-P., ed., *Four English Political Tracts of the Later Middle Ages* (CS 4th Series, 18 1977).

The Complete Works of John Gower, ed. G. C. Macaulay (Oxford, 1899–1902), 4 vols.

The English Works of John Gower, ed., G. C. Macaulay (EETS ES 82 1901), 2 vols.

The Major Latin Works of John Gower, ed. and transl. E. W. Stockton (Seattle, 1961).

H. A.: see under Walsingham, T.

Hardyng, J., *Chronicle*, ed., H. Ellis (London, 1812).

Hoccleve, T., *The Regement of Princes*, ed. F. J. Furnivall (EETS ES 72 1897).

——, *The Minor Poems*, ed. F. J. Furnivall and I. Gollancz, revd. J. Mitchell and A. I. Doyle (EETS ES 61, 73 1970).

Jack Upland, Friar Daw's Reply and Upland's Rejoinder, ed. P. L. Heyworth (London, 1968).

Kail, J., ed., *Twenty Six Political and other Poems* (EETS OS 124 1904).

Lydgate, J., *Minor Poems*, ed. H. N. McCracken (EETS 107 1911 and OS 109 1934), 2 vols.

——, *Fall of Princes*, ed. H. Bergen (EETS ES 121–4 1918–19), 4 vols.

——, *Troy Book*, ed. H. Bergen (EETS ES 97, 103, 106 and 126 1906–35), 4 vols.

Kane, G., ed. *Piers Plowman: The 'A' Version* (London, 1960).

Kane, G., and Talbot Donaldson, eds., *Piers Plowman: The 'B' Version* (London, 1975).

King Arthur's Death, ed. L. D. Benson (Exeter, 1986).

Knighton, H., *Chronicon*, ed. J. R. Lumby (RS 1889–95), 2 vols.

The Lanterne of Light, ed. M. L. Swinburne (EETS OS 151 1917).

Matthew, F. D., *The English Works of Wyclif Hitherto Unprinted* (EETS OS 74 1880, 2nd revd. edn., 1902).

Mum and the Sothsegger, ed. M. Day and R. Steele (EETS OS 199 1936). (D&S)

The Parlement of the Thre Ages, ed. M. Y. Offord (EETS OS 246 1959).

Pearl, ed. E. V. Gordon (Oxford, 1953).

Pearsall, D., ed., *Piers Plowman by William Langland: An Edition of the 'C' Text* (London, 1978).

Pierce the Ploughman's Crede, ed. W. W. Skeat (EETS OS 30 1867).

The Plowman's Tale, ed., W. W. Skeat, in *Chaucerian and other Pieces, The Complete Works of Geoffrey Chaucer* (Oxford, 1897), pp. 147–90. (Pl Tale)

Robbins, R. H., ed., *Historical Poems of the XIVth and XVth Centuries* (New York, 1959).

A. V. C. Schmidt, ed., *The Vision of Piers Plowman: A Complete Edition of the 'B' Text* (London, 1987).

Scott, S. P., ed., *The Civil Law* (Cincinnati, 1932), 17 vols.

Select Cases in Chancery, 1364–1471, ed. W. P. Baildon (SS 1896).

Select Cases in the King's Bench, ed. G. O. Sayles (SS 1971).

Selections from English Wycliffite Writings, ed. A. Hudson (Cambridge, 1978). (*SEWW*)

The Siege of Jerusalem, ed. E. Kölbing and M. Day (EETS OS 188 1932).

The Simonie, ed. D. Embree and E. Urquhart (Heidelberg, 1991).

Skeat, W. W., ed., *Langland's Vision of Piers the Plowman, Text C, together with Richard the Redeless and The Crowned King* (EETS OS 54 1873).

——, *Piers Plowman and Richard the Redeless* (London, 1886), 2 vols.

The Tale of Beryn, ed. F. J. Furnivall and W. G. Stone (EETS ES 105 1909).

Chronique de la Traison et Mort du Richart Deux Roy Dengleterre. ed. B. Williams (London, 1846). (*Traison*)

Johannis de Trokelowe et Henrici de Blaneforde, *Chronica et Annales*, ed. H. T. Riley (London, 1886). (*Annales*)

Chronicon Adae de Usk, ed. and trans. E. M. Thompson (London, 1904) (*Usk*)

Walsingham, T., *Historia Anglicana*, ed. H. T. Riley (RS 1864), 2 vols, (*H.A.*)

The Westminster Chronicle, ed. L. C. Hector and B. F. Harvey (Oxford, 1976).

Wilkins, D., ed., *Conciliae Magnae Britanniae et Hibernae* (London, 1737), 4 vols.

The Romance of William of Palerne, ed. W. W. Skeat (EETS ES 1 1867).

T. Wright, ed., *Political Poems and Songs* (RS 1859–61), 2 vols.

——, *Alliterative Poem on the Deposition of Richard II*, (CS 3 1838).

Wynnere and Wastoure, ed. S. Trigg (EETS OS 297 1990).

Secondary Sources

Alford, J. A., *Piers Plowman: A Glossary of Legal Diction* (Cambridge, 1988).

Baker, J. H., *An Introduction to Legal History* (London, 1979).

Baldwin, A., *The Theme of Government in 'Piers Plowman'* (Cambridge, 1981).

Barr, H., *A Study of 'Mum and the Sothsegger' in its Literary and Political Contexts* (unpublished Oxford D.Phil thesis 1989).

——, 'The Dates of *Richard the Redeless* and *Mum and the Sothsegger*', *N&Q*, 235 (1990), 270–5. (1990[1])

——, 'The relationship of *Richard the Redeless* and *Mum and the Sothsegger*', *YLS*, 4 (1990), 105–33. (1990[2])

——, 'The Treatment of Natural Law in *Richard the Redeless* and *Mum and the Sothsegger*', *LSE*, 23 (1992), 49–80.

Bean, J. M. W., 'Henry VI and the Percies', *History*, 44 (1959), 212–27.

Bennett, J. A. W., *Middle English Literature*, ed. and completed by D. Gray (Oxford, 1986), esp. 55–59.

Blamires, A. '*Mum and the Sothsegger* and Langlandian Idiom', *Neuph Mitt*, 76 (1975), 583–604.

Brown, A. L., 'The Commons and Council in the Reign of Henry IV', *EHR*, 79 (1964), 1–29.

Coleman, J., *English Literature in History 1350–1400: Medieval Writers and Readers* (London, 1981).

Cunnington, C. W. and P., *A Handbook of Medieval English Costume* (London, 1969), 2nd edn.

Curzon, L. B., *English Legal History* (Plymouth, 1979).

Doyle, A. I., 'An Unrecognised Piece of *Pierce the Ploughman's Crede* and other Work by its Scribe', *Speculum*, 34 (1959), 428–36.

——, 'The Manuscripts' in Lawton (1982), 88–100.

Du Boulay, F. R. H., *The England of 'Piers Plowman'* (Woodbridge, 1991).

Eckhardt, C., 'Another Historical Allusion in *Mum and the Sothsegger*', *N&Q*, 225 (1980), 495–7.

Embree, D., '*Richard the Redeless* and *Mum and the Sothsegger*: A Case of Mistaken Identity', *N&Q*, 220 (1975), 4–12.

Ferguson, A. B., 'The Problem of Counsel in *Mum and the Sothsegger*', *Studies in the Renaissance*, 2 (1955), 67–83.

——, *The Articulate Citizen and the English Renaissance* (Durham, North Carolina, 1965), pp. 70–90.

Given-Wilson, C., *The Royal Household and the King's Affinity: Service, Politics and Finance in England 1350–1413* (London, 1986).

Goodman, A., *The Loyal Conspiracy* (London, 1971).

Green, R. F., *Poets and Princepleasers: Literature and the English Court in the Late Middle Ages* (Toronto, 1980).

Harriss, G. L., ed., *Henry V: The Practice of Kingship* (Oxford, 1985).

Hudson, A., *Lollards and their Books* (London, 1985).

——, 'Wycliffism in Oxford', in *Wyclif in his Times*, ed. A. J. P. Kenny (Oxford, 1986), 67–84.

——, *The Premature Reformation* (Oxford, 1988). (1988[1])

——, 'The Legacy of *Piers Plowman*', in *A Companion to Piers Plowman*, ed. J. A. Alford (Berkeley, 1988), 251–66. (1988[2])

Hutchison, R. F., *The Hollow Crown* (London, 1961).
——, *King Henry V* (New York, 1967).
Jacob, E. F., *The Fifteenth Century 1399–1485* (Oxford, 1961).
Jones, R. H. *The Royal Policy of Richard II: Absolutism in the Later Middle Ages* (Oxford, 1968).
Kane, G., 'Some Fourteenth Century "Political" Poems', in *Medieval English and Ethical Literature: Essays in Honour of G. H. Russell*, ed. G. Kratzmann and J. Simpson (Cambridge, 1986), 82–91.
Kendall, R. D., *The Drama of Dissent: The Radical Poetry of Nonconformity 1380–1590* (North Carolina, 1986).
Kenny, A., *Wyclif* (Oxford, 1985).
Kirby, J. L., *Henry IV of England* (London, 1970).
Lampe, D., 'The Satiric Strategy of *Pierce the Ploughman's Crede*', in *The Alliterative Tradition in the Fourteenth Century*, ed. B. S. Levy and P. S. Szarmach (Ohio, 1981).
Lawton, D., 'Lollardy and the *Piers Plowman* Tradition', *MLR*, 76 (1981), 780–93.
——, ed. *Middle English Alliterative Poetry and its Literary Background* (Cambridge, 1982).
McFarlane, K. B., *Lancastrian Kings and Lollard Knights* (Oxford, 1972).
——, *England in the Fifteenth Century*, ed. G. L. Harriss (London, 1981).
McKisack, M., *The Fourteenth Century* (Oxford, 1959).
McNiven, P., *Heresy and Politics in the Reign of Henry IV: The Burning of John Badby* (Cambridge, 1987).
Maddicott, J. R. L., 'Poems of Social Protest in Early Fourteenth Century England', in *England in the Fourteenth Century: Proceedings of the 1985 Harlaxton Symposium*, ed. W. M. Ormrod (Cambridge, 1986), 130–44.
Mann, J., *Chaucer and Medieval Estates Satire* (Cambridge, 1973).
Mathew, G., *The Court of Richard II* (London, 1968).
Middleton, A., 'The Idea of Public Poetry in the Reign of Richard II', *Speculum*, 53 (1978), pp. 94–114.
Mohl, R., 'Theories of Monarchy in *Mum and the Sothsegger*', *PMLA*, 54 (1944), 26–44.
Pantin, W. A., *The English Church in the Fourteenth Century* (Cambridge, 1955).

Robbins, R. H., 'Middle English Poems of Protest', *Anglia*, 78 (1960), 193–203.

Rogers, A., 'Henry IV, the Commons and Taxation', *Medieval Studies*, 31 (1969), 44–70.

Scase, W., *'Piers Plowman' and the New Anticlericalism* (Cambridge, 1989).

Scattergood, G., *Politics and Poetry in the Fifteenth Century*, (London, 1971).

Shepherd, G., 'The Nature of Alliterative Poetry in Medieval England', *PBA*, 41 (1970), 57–76.

Simpson, J., *'Piers Plowman': An Introduction to the B-Text* (London, 1990).

——, 'The Constraints of Satire in *Piers Plowman* and *Mum and the Sothsegger*', in *Langland, the Mystics and the Medieval English Religious Tradition*, ed. H. Phillipps (Cambridge, 1990), 11–30.

Steel, A., *Richard II* (Cambridge, 1962).

Stokes, M., *Justice and Mercy in 'Piers Plowman'* (London, 1984).

Swanton, R. N., *Church and Society in Late Medieval England* (Oxford, 1989).

Szittya, *The Antifraternal Tradition in Medieval England*, (Princeton, 1986).

Taylor, R., *The Political Prophecy in England* (New York, 1911).

Tuck, A., *Richard II and the English Nobility* (London, 1973).

Turville-Petre, T., *The Alliterative Revival* (Cambridge, 1977).

Von Nolcken, C., '*Piers Plowman*, the Wycliffites and *Pierce the Ploughman's Crede*', *YLS*, 2 (1988), 71–102.

Wawn, A., 'The Genesis of *The Plowman's Tale*', *YES*, 2 (1972), 21–40.

——, 'Truth-Telling and the Tradition of *Mum and the Sothsegger*', *YES*, 13 (1983), 270–87.

White, H., *Nature and Salvation in 'Piers Plowman'* (Cambridge, 1988).

Whiting, B. J., *Proverbs, Sentences and Proverbial Phrases from English Writings mainly before 1500* (Cambridge, Mass., 1968).

Wylie, J. H., *The History of England under Henry IV* (London, 1884–1895), 4 vols.

——, and W. T. Waugh, *The History of England under Henry V* (Cambridge, 1919–29), 3 vols.

Ziepel, C., *The Reign of Richard II and Comments upon an Alliterative Poem on the Deposition of that Monarch* (Berlin, 1874).

CHRONOLOGY OF HISTORICAL EVENTS

1377   Death of Edward III. Accession of Richard II. Pope Gregory condemns various propositions of Wyclif's teaching in a Papal Bull.

1381   'Peasants' Revolt'.

1382   Blackfriars Council, London condemns ten of Wyclif's propositions as heretical.

1386   'Wonderful' Parliament. Impeachment of chancellor, Michael de la Pole.

1387–8   Challenge of Lords Appellant to Richard II.

1387   Appeal of treason against the king's advisers. Battle of Radcot Bridge. Defeat of de Vere.

1388   'Merciless' Parliament. Execution of those supporters of the king who had not fled abroad.

1390   Statute against livery and maintenance.

1394–5   Richard's first Irish campaign.

1395   Lollard manifesto calling for clerical disendowment affixed to the doors of Westminster Hall.

1396   Twenty-eight-year truce with France.

1397   (Jan) Haxey's bill complaining about the costs of the royal household. (July) Arrest of the duke of Gloucester, earls of Arundel and Warwick. (Sept) Gloucester murdered, Arundel executed. Warwick exiled to the Isle of Man.

1398   Shrewsbury Parliament grants unprecedented taxation to Richard. Exile of dukes of Norfolk and Hereford.

1399   (Feb) Death of John of Gaunt. (May) Richard's second Irish campaign. (July) Return of Henry of Lancaster. Surrender of Richard. (Sept) Deposition of Richard. Accession of Henry IV.

1400   (Jan) Magnate revolt to restore Richard quashed at

Cirencester. (?Jan) Death of Richard, probably murdered. (Sept) Revolt in Wales led by Owen Glendower.

1401 Execution of William Sawtre for heresy. Statute *De Haeretico Comburendo*.

1402 Defeat of Scots at Homildon Hill.

1403 Battle of Shrewsbury: defeat of the Percy Revolt.

1405 Northern uprising: execution of Archbishop Scrope.

1406 Long Parliament demands 31 articles of Constitutional Reform before agreeing to the king's demands for taxation.

1408 Defeat of the earl of Northumberland at Bramham Moor.

1409 Publication of Archbishop Arundel's *Constitutions*. Burning of John Badby for heresy.

1410 Outbreak of Civil War in France.

1413 (Mar) Death of Henry IV. Accession of Henry V.

1415 Henry V's voyage to France to commence military campaign.

PIERCE THE PLOUGHMAN'S CREDE

PIERCE THE PLOUGHMAN'S CREDE

f.317a Cros, and Curteis Crist this begynnynge spede,

courteous ; assist

For the faderes frendchipe that fourmede Heuene,   *formed*

And thorugh the speciall spirit that sprong of hem tweyne,

sprang ; both

And alle in on godhed endles dwelleth.   *one*

5 A. and all myn A.b.c. after haue y lerned,

And [patred] in my pater-noster iche poynt after other,

[c] ; *Lord's Prayer ; clause*

And after all, myn Aue-marie almost to the ende;   *Ave Maria*

But all my kare is to comen for y can nohght my Crede.

do not know

Whan y schal schewen myn schrift schent mote y worthen,

confess ; made to do penance

10 The prest wil me punyche and penaunce enioyne;

punish ; enjoin

The Lengthe of a Lenten flech moot y leue

meat ; must ; give up

After that Estur ys ycomen and that is hard fare;

state of affairs[c]

And Wedenes-day iche wyke with-outen flech-mete.   *week*

And also Jesu hym-self to the Iewes he seyde,

15 'He that leeueth nought on me he leseth the blisse.'

believes ; loses

Therfor lerne the byleue leuest me were,   *faith ; desirable*

And if any werldly wight wille me couthe,   *man ; know*

Other lewed or lered that lyueth therafter,

illiterate ; learned ; lives

---

6 patred] patres AC ; partes B.   17 And if] Yf B ; Gif C; werldly] wordly C.

And fulliche folweth the feyth and feyneth non other;

fully ; faith ; pretends

20 That no worldliche wele wilneth no tyme,   *prosperity ; desires*

But lyueth in louynge of God and his lawe holdeth

And for no getynge of good neuer his God greueth,

acquiring ; wealth ; grieves

But follow[e]th him the full wey as he the folke taughte.

whole

But to many maner of men this matter is asked,   [c]

25 Bothe to lered and to lewed that seyn that the[y] leueden

say ; believed

Hollich on the grete god and holden alle his heste[s];

wholly ; commandments

But by a fra[y]nyng for-than faileth ther manye.

examination[c]

For first y fraynede the freres and the[y] me fulle tolden

That all the frute of the fayth was in here foure ordres,

fruit [c]

30 And the cofres of cristendam & the keye b[o]then,   *coffers*

And the lok [of beleue lyeth] loken in her hondes.

lock[c] *; locked*

Thanne [wende] y to wyten and with a whight y mette,

went ; know ; man

A Menoure in a morow-tide and to this man I saide,

Minor ; morning

'Sire, for grete god[e]s loue the graith you me telle,   *truth*

35 Of what myddelerde man myghte y best lerne   *earthly*

My Crede ? For I can it nought, my kare is the more;

do not know it

And therfore, for Cristes loue, thi councell y praie.

counsel [c] *; beg*

A Carm me hath y-couenaunt the Crede me to teche;

Carmelite ; covenanted

20 no tyme] at no tyme B.
23 followeth] followth A ; followth
   B ; folweth C.
25 they] theth A ; they BC. leueden]
   leveden B ; lieuden C.
26 hestes] C ; hesteg A ; hestys B.
27 fraynyng] BC ; frathnyng A.
28 they] C ; theth A ; themfull B.

30 bothen] C ; bethen AB.
31 of beleue lyeth] B ; lock of byleue
   lieth C ; an lene his A.
32 wende] wend B ; wennede C ;
   witcede A.
34 godes] BC ; gods A ; graith] truith
   B.
38 the Crede] AB ; ye nede C.

f.317b But for thou knowest Carmes well thi counsaile I aske.'

40 This Menour loked on me and lawghyng he seyde,   *laughing*

'Leue Cristen man y leue that you madde !   *dear ; believe*

Whough schu[l]de thei techen the God that con not hemselue ?
   How ; know

Thei ben but yugulers and iapers, of kynde,
   [c] ; *jesters ; by nature*

Lorels and Lechures and lemmans holden;
   rogues ; lechers ; lovers

45 Neyther in order ne out but vn-nethe lybbeth,
   [c] ; *singularly ; live*

And byiapeth the folke with gestes of Rome.   *fool ; stories* [c]

It is but a faynt folk i-founded vp-on iapes.
   deceitful ; founded

Thei maketh hem Maries men (so thei men tellen),
   claim to be ; Mary's

And lieth on our Ladie many a longe tale.   *lie* [c]

50 And that wicked folke wymmen bi-traieth,   *women ; betray*

And bigileth hem of her good with glauerynge wordes,
   flattering

And therwith holden her hous in harlotes werkes.
   maintain ; rascal's

And, so saue me God, I hold it gret synne

To gyuen hem any good swiche glotones to fynde,
   give ; wealth ; support

55 To maynteyne swiche maner men that mychel good

destruyeth.   *much ; destroy*

Yet seyn they in here sutilte to sottes in townes,
   subtlety ; fools

Thei comen out of Carmeli Crist for to followen,
   Mount Carmel

And feyneth hem with holynes that yuele hem bisemeth.
   feign ; ill ; befits

Thei lyuen more in lecherie and lieth in her tales   *live*

60 Than suen any god liife ; but [lurken] in her selles,
   follow ; cells

---

41 madde] maid B.

42 schulde] shulde C ; shuld B ;
  schude A.

46 gestes] iestes B.

47 vp-on] vp on C.

48 so] and so BC.

49 lieth] leyth B ; leieth C.

59 lyuen] levyin B ; tales] tallys B.

60 suen] shewin B ; lurken] C ; lyrken
  A ; lurkyn B.

[And] wynnen werldliche god and wasten it in synne.

gain; *good*

And yif thei couthen her crede other on Crist leueden,

knew; *believed*

Thei weren nought so hardie swich harlotri vsen.

audacious; *wickedness*; *practise*

Sikerli y can nought fynden who hem first founded,   *surely*; [c]

65 But the foles foundeden hem-self freres of the Pye,

fools; *magpie* [c]

And maken hem mendynauns and marre the puple.

mendicants; *injure*

But what glut of tho gomes may any good kachen,

glutton; *men*; *seize*

He will kepen it hym-self and cofren it faste,   *coffer*

And theigh his felawes fayle good for him he may steruen.

[c]; *lack*; *starve*

70 Her money may bi-quest and testament maken,   *their*; *will*

And no obedience bere but don as [hem] luste.

bear; *do*; *please*

[And] ryght as Robertes men raken aboute,   [c]; *rove*

At feires and at ful ales and fyllen the cuppe,   *fairs*; *festivities*

And precheth all of pardon to plesen the puple.

preach; *people*

75 Her pacience is all pased and put out to ferme,

finished; *farm* [c]

And pride is in her pouerte that litell is to preisen.   *poverty*

And at the lulling of oure Ladye the wymmen to lyken,

lullaby [c]; *like*

And miracles of mydwyves and maken wymmen to wenen

miracle plays; *think*

f.318a That the lace of oure ladie smok lighteth hem of children.

pain of childbirth

80 Thei ne prechen nought of Powel ne penaunce for synne,

St Paul

But all of mercy and mensk that Marie maie helpen.   *honour*

---

61 And] But ABC; werldliche]
   werdliche C.
62 yif] Yef B.
68 hym-self] hem self C.
70 bi-quest] by quest C.

71 no] none BC; hem] hym ABC;
   luste] list B.
72 And ryght] BC; Tryght A.
79 ladie] ladys B.
81 mercy] mary B; mensk] melk B.

With sterne staues and stronge they ouer lond straketh
stiff ; *staffs* [c] ; *stride*
Thider as her lemmans liggeth and lurketh in townes, *lie*
(Grey grete-hedede quenes with gold by the eighen),
great-headed ; *harlots* ; *eyes* [c]
85 And seyn, that here sustren thei ben that soiourneth aboute;
sisters ; *travel*
And thus about they gon and godes folke by-traieth. *go*
It is the puple that Powell preched of in his tyme; *St Paul*
He seyde of swich folk that so aboute wente :
'Wepyng, y warne yow of walkers aboute ;
90 It beth enemyes of the cros that Crist opon tholede. *suffered*
Swiche slomerers in slepe slau[ght]e is her ende,
destruction [c]
And glotony is her God with g[l]oppyng of drynk, *gulping*
And gladnes in glees and gret ioye y-maked; *festivities*
In the schendyng of swiche schall mychel folk lawghe.
destruction ; *many*
95 Therfore, frend, for thi feyth fond to don betere; *try*
Leue nought on tho losels but let hem forth pasen,
believe ; *rogues*
For thei ben fals in her feith and fele mo othere.' *many more*
'Alas, frere,' quath I tho, 'my purpos is i-failed, *said* ; *then*
Now is my co[m]fort a-cast ! Canstou no bote
cast down ; *no remedy*
100 Where y myghte meten with a man that myghte me [wissen]
guide
For to conne my Crede Crist for to folwen ?' *know*
'Certeyne, felawe,' quath the frere, 'with-outen any faile.
Of all men opon mold we Menures most scheweth
earth ; *show*
The pure apostell[e]s life with penance on erthe,
105 And suen hem in saunctite and suffren well harde. *follow*
We haunten none tauernes ne hobelen abouten; *frequent*

86 they] the C.
90 tholede] tho lede C.
91 slaughte] C ; slauth AB.
92 gloppyng] gloppynge C ; gopping
  A ; golping B.
94 mychel folk] many B.
95 fond] found B.

99 comfort] BC ; counfort A.
100 wissen] wyssen C ; willen A ;
  whissen B.
103 Menures] Minorites C.
104 apostelles] apostylles B ;
  aposteles C ; apostells A.

At marketts and myracles we medleth vs nevere;   *associate*
We hondlen no money but menelich faren,
                                        behave abstemiously
And haven hunger at [the] meate at ich [a mel] ones.
                                                food; meal
110 We hauen forsaken the worlde and in wo lyvveth,   *hardship*
    In penaunce and pouerte and precheth the puple   *poverty*
    By ensample of oure life soules to helpen;
    And in pouertie praien for all oure parteners   *pray; [c]*
    That gyueth vs any good god to honouren:
115 Other bell other booke or breed to our fode,   *bread; food*
    Other catell other cloth to coveren with our bones,   *goods*
f.318b Money or money-worthe, here mede is in heven.
                                        valuables; reward
    For we buldeth a burwgh – a brod and a large –   *convent*
    A chirche and a chapaile with chambers a-lofte,
120 With wide windowes y-wrought and walles well heye,
                                                very high
    That mote bene portreid and paynt and pulched ful clene,
                        decorated; painted; polished very brightly
    With gaie glittering glas glowing as the sonne.
    And myghtestou amenden vs with money of thyn owne,
                                            if you can help
    Thou chuldest cnely bifore Crist in compas of gold
                            should; kneel; surrounded by
125 In the wide windowe westwarde wel nighe in the myddell,
    And seynt Fraunces himself schall folden the in his cope,
    And presente the to the trynitie and praie for thy synnes.
    Thi name schall nobli[ch] ben wryten and wrought for the
        nones,   *nobly; fashioned; then*
    And, in remembrance of the y-rade ther for euer.   *read*
130 And, brother, be thou nought aferd; [bythenk in] thyn herte,
                                                think

---

107 medleth] medeley C.
108 menelich] monelich C.
109 the] BC; ther A; ich] ilche B; a
    mel] C; a mele B; amel A.
110 lyvveth] lybbeth B; libbeth C.
116 with] *crossed out in B.*
117 or] other BC.
118 a brod] abrod B.

119 chapaile] chapitre B; chapitle C.
121 portreid] porterid B; paynt]
    payntyd B; paint C.
125 windowe] wyndowes B.
126 seynt] sone B.
128 noblich] BC; noblith A.
130 bythenk in] C; by thenken A;
    by think in B.

Though thou conne nought thi Crede, kare thou no more.
I schal asoilen the syre and setten it on my soule,   *absolve*
And you maie maken this good thenk thou non other.'
                                        can provide; think
'Sire,' y saide, 'in certaine y schal [gon] and asaye.'   *try*
135 And he sette on me his honde and asoilede me clene,
And their y parted him fro with-outen any peine,   [c]
In couenant that y come agen Crist he me be-ta[u]ghte.
                                        agreement; commended
Thanne saide y to my-self, 'Here semeth litel trewthe:
First to blamen his brother and bacbyten him foule,   *backbite*
140 Theire-as curteis Crist clereliche saide,
'Whow myght-tou in thine brother eighe a bare mote loken,
                                                        see
And in thyn owen eighe nought a bem toten?   *beam; notice*
See fyrst on thi-self and sithen on another,   *first; then*
And clense clene thi syght and kepe well thyn eighe,   *guard*
145 And for another mannes eighe ordeyne after.'
                                        make provision
And also y sey coueitise catel to fongen,
                        saw; covetousness; property; receive
That Crist hath clerliche forboden and clenliche destruede,
                                        forbidden; condemned
And saide to his sueres forsothe on this wise:
                                        disciples; truly; way
'Nought thi neighbours good [couet yn] no tyme.'
150 But charite and chastete ben chased out clene.
But Crist seide, 'by her fruyt men shall hem ful knowen.'
Thanne saide y, 'Certeyn, sire thou demest full trewe.'   *judge*
Thanne thought y to frayne the first of this foure ordirs,
                                        examine
And presede to the prechoures to proven here wille.
                                        hastened; [c]
f.319a [Ich] highede to her house to herken of more;   *hurried*
And whan y cam to that court y gaped aboute.
Swich a bild bold, y-buld opon erthe heighte   *bold building*

---

134 gon] BC; gone A.   *147* destruede] AC; distrayid B.
137 be-taughte] BC; betaighte A.   *149* couet yn] coueyte in C; couetyn
141 myght-tou] myght thou BC;   A; coveit not at B.
    brother] AB; brothers C.   *155* Ich] C; ytche B; With A.
146 sey] saye B; see C.

Say I nought in certeine siththe a longe tyme.   *saw*; *since*
Y yemede vpon that house and yerne theron loked,
                                        looked; *attentively*
160 Whough the pileres weren y-peynt and pulched ful clene,
                                        How; *pillars*
And queynteli i-coruen with curiouse knottes,
                                elaborately carved; *bosses* [c]
With wyndowes well y-wrought wide vp o-lofte
And thanne y entrid in and even-forth went,
And all was walled that wone though it wid were,   *dwelling*
165 With posternes in pryuytie to pasen when hem liste;
                                gates; *secret*; *pleased*
Orcheyardes and erberes euesed well clene,
                                gardens; *trimmed*; *neatly*
[And] a curious cros craftly entayled,   *skilfully*; *sculptured*
With tabernacles y-tight to toten all abouten.
                                        niches; *set in*; *look*
The pris of a plough-lond of penyes so rounde
                                price; *plough-land* [c]; *pennies*
170 To aparaile that pyler were pure lytel.
                                decorate; *absolutely nothing*
Thanne y munte me forth the mynstre to knowen,
                                went; *church*; *discover*
And a-waytede a woon wonderlie well y-beld,
                                beheld; *dwelling*; *built*
With arches on eueriche half and belliche y-corven,
                                every side; *beautifully carved*
With crochetes on corners with knottes of golde,   *crockets* [c]
175 Wyde wyndowes y-wrought y-written full thikke,   *engraved*
Schynen with schapen scheldes to schewen aboute,
                                shining; *shaped shields*
With merkes of marchauntes y-medled bytwene,   *interspersed*

158 say]sawe B.
159 yemede] yemyd B; semed C.
160 Whough] How B; Whow C.
161 queynteli] queynely B.
166 euesed] vsyd B.
167 And] BC; A A.
171 munte] mount B.
172 a woon] it anon B; And a
    waited on that wold how wondirly
    bilt H.

173 and belliche y-corven] ekeliche I
    cornerd H.
174 crochetes] crochers B; on] on
    the B; corners] cornels H.
175 Wyde] With wyde H.
176 Schynen with schapen scheldes]
    A cheveron with sharpe shieldes H;
    schapen] sharpen B.
177 With] Mid H.

Mo than twenty and two twyes y-noumbred.   *more; twice*

Ther is none heraud that hath half swich a rolle,   *herald; such*

180 Right as a rageman hath rekned hem newe.   *just; catalogue* [c]

Tombes opon tabernacles tyld opon lofte,

                      canopied recesses; built off the ground

Housed in hirnes harde set abouten,   *corners; closely*

Of armede alabaustre [alfor] for the nones,

                      alabaster with coats of arms; then

[Made vpon marbel in many maner wyse,   *ways*

185 Knyghtes in her conisantes clad for the nones,]   *emblems*

All it semed seyntes y-sacred opon erthe;

And louely ladies y-wrought leyen by her sydes   *lay*

In many gay garmentes that weren gold-beten.

Though the tax of ten yer were trewly y-gadered,

                      year; collected

190 Nolde it nought maken that hous half, as y trowe.

                      would not; believe

Thanne kam I to that cloister and gaped abouten

Whough it was pilered and peynt and portred well clene,

.319b All y-hyled with leed lowe to the stones,   *covered; lead*

And y-paued with peynt til iche poynte after other;

                      painted tile; square

195 With kundites of clene tyn closed all aboute,

                      conduits; pure tin; enclosed

With lauoures of latun louelyche y-greithed.

                      basins; brass; exquisitely fitted

I trowe the gaynage of the ground in a gret schire   *yield* [c]

Nolde aparaile that place oo poynt til other ende.

                      decorate; one; to

Thanne was the chaptire-hous wrought as a greet chirche,

179 is] nys H.

180 rekned] I Rent H.

181 opon] with H.

182 in hirnes] in hernis B; in hornes C; and harneysed H.

183 armede] armed and H; alfor] H; clad ABC.

184–5 BC; *not in AH.*

185 conisantes] ther conisante C.

187 louely ladies] ladyes lovelich H; leyen] lyen B.

188 garmentes] garnemens C.

191 I to] I in to H.

192 portred] porteryd B; portreyd C; portrayed H.

194 peynt til] AH; paeintyles B; poynttyl C.

195 kundites] conduyte H.

198 Nolde] nold nat H; oo poynt til other ende] eche poynt after other H.

199 greet chirche] chirche H.

200 Coruen and couered and queyntliche entayled;

                        carved ; roofed ; elaborately sculptured

With semliche selure y-set on lofte;   *attractive panelling*

As a Parlement-hous y-peynted aboute.

Thanne ferd y into fraytour and fond there an other,

                                went ; refectory

An halle for an heygh kinge an housholde to holden,   *high*

205 With brode bordes aboute y-benched wel clene,

                                broad tables ;

With windowes of glas wrought as a chirche.

Thanne walkede y ferrer and went all abouten,   *further*

And seigh halles full hyghe and houses full noble,   *saw*

Chambers with chymneyes and chapells gaie;   *fireplaces*

210 And kychens for an hyghe kinge in castells to holden,

                                kitchens

And her dortour y-dighte with dores ful stronge

                          dormitory ; set out

Fermery and fraitur with fele mo houses,   *infirmary ; refectory*

And all strong ston wall sterne upon heithe,   *ground*

With gaie garites and grete and iche hole y-glased ;

                         garrets ; each ; glazed

215 [And othere] houses y-nowe to herberwe the queene.

                                enough ; lodge

And yet thise bilderes wilne beggen a bagg-full of wheate

Of a pure pore man that maie onethe paie   *scarcely*

Half his rente in a yer and half ben behynde.   *behind-hand*

Thanne turned y agen whan y hadde all y-toted,   *seen*

220 And fond in a freitour a frere on a benche,

A greet cherl and a grym, growen as a tonne,

                         lout ; grim ; barrel

With a face as fat as a full bledder   *bladder*

Blowen bretfull of breth and as a bagge honged

                       brimful ; breath ; hanged

200 couered] cornered H.

201 y-set] yseet C ; on] upon H.

202 aboute] al aboute H.

203 into] in to the H.

205 wel] ful H.

207 ferrer] ferre H.

208 seigh] AC ; see B.

209 chymneyes] chymbnais B.

215 And othere] BC ; To there A.

217 pure pore] pore B.

221 cherl] chorl C.

222 as] so C ; fat] fate B.

On bothen his chekes, and his chyn with a chol lollede,

jowl ; overhung

225 As greet as a gos eye growen all of grece; *goose-egg ; grease*
That all wagged his fleche as a quyk myre.

quivered ; quagmire

His cope that biclypped him wel clene was it folden,

covered ; neatly

Of double worstede y-dyght doun to the hele;

thick, spun wool ; fashioned

320a His kyrtel of clene whijt clenlyche y-sewed; *white*
230 Hyt was good y-now of ground greyn for to beren.

texture [c] ; *grain ; carry*

I haylsede that herdeman and hendliche y saide,

greeted ; shepherd [c] ; *politely*

'Gode syre, for Godes loue canstou me graith tellen *truth*
To any [worthely] wijght that [wissen] me couthe

person ; instruct

Whou y schulde conne my Crede Crist for to folowe,
235 That leuede lelliche him-self and lyuede thereafter,

believed ; faithfully

That feynede non falshede but fully Crist suwede ?

pretended ; followed

For sich a certeyn man syker wold y trosten,

steadfast ; certainly ; trust

That he wolde telle me the trewthe and turne to none other.
And an Austyn this ender daie egged me faste;

yesterday ; encouraged

240 That he wolde techen me wel he plyght me his treuthe,

pledged ; faith [c]

And seyde me, 'Serteyne, [sythen] Crist died *since*
Oure ordir was [euelles] and erst y-founde.'

without sin ; founded

'Fyrst, felawe,' quath he 'fy on his pilche ! *fie on his fur robe*
He is but abortijf eked with cloutes !

deformed ; patched up ; rags

---

224 chol] achole B.
225 As] So C; all] full B.
227 biclypped] be clepid B.
223 worthely] BC; wortheh A ;
  wissen] BC; willen A.
235 leuede] levid B; lenede C.

236 non] no C.
237 trosten] tresten B.
241 sythen] sythyn B; syghthen C ;
  syghen A.
242 euelles] C; yvellis B ; y eueffes A.

245 He holdeth his ordynaunce withe hores and theues,
                              religious foundation; *whores*
And purchaseth hem pryuileges with penyes so rounde;
                                        privileges [c]
It is a pur pardoners craft proue and asaye.
                              trade; *prove*; *test* [c]
For haue thei thi money a moneth therafter,   *month*
Certes, theigh thou come agen he nyl the nought knowen.
                              will not; *acknowledge*
250 But felawe, our foundement was first of the othere,
And we ben founded fulliche with-outen fayntise;
                                   completely; *deceit*
And we ben clerkes y-cnowen cunnynge in schole,
                              known; *learned*; *Schools*
Proued in procession by processe of lawe.   *proved*; [c]
Of oure ordre ther beth bichopes wel manye,
255 Seyntes on sundry stedes that suffreden harde;   *many places*
And we ben proued the prijs of popes at Rome,   *best*
And of gretest degre as godspelles telleth.'   *rank*; *Gospels*
'A syre,' quath y thanne, 'thou seyst a gret wonder,
Sithen Crist seyd hym-self to all his disciples: *since*
260 "Which of you is most, most schal he werche,
                              mightiest; *the most*; *work*
And who is goer byforne, first schal he seruen."
                                   goes ahead; *serve*
And seyde, "He sawe satan sytten full heyghe
And [ful lowe] ben y-leyd." In lyknes he tolde,   *laid*; *parable*
That in pouernesse of spyrit is spedfullest hele,
                              most profitable; *health*
265 And hertes of heynesse harmeth the soule.   *ambition*
And therfore frere, fare well; here fynde y but pride;   *only*
f.320b Y preise nought thi preching but as a pure myte.'   *mere*; *mite*
And anger[l]ich y wandrede the Austyns to proue,   *test*
And mette with a maister of tho men and meklich y seyde,

---

248 thi] the B.
249 nyl] wil C.
261 byforne] aforn B.
263 ful lowe] fullowe A; fullow
  BC.

264 spedfullest hele] the spedfullest
  heald B.
265 heynesse] heyne C.
267 preching] prechyns C.
268 angerlich] angerich AC;
  angreiche B.

270 'Maister, for the moder loue that Marie men kalleth,
                                                   love of the mother
    Knowest thou ought ther thou comest a creatour on erthe,
                                                   anywhere
    That coude me my Crede teche and trewliche enfourme,
    With-outen flaterynge fare and nothing feyne?   *behaviour*
    That folweth fulliche the feith and none other fables,
275 With-outen gabbynge of glose as the godspelles telleth?
                                                   lying; gloss [c]
    A Menour hath me holly by-hyght to helen my soule,
                                                   wholly promised
    For he seith that her sekte is sykerest on erthe,
                                                   most trustworthy
    And ben kepers of the keye that Cristendome helpeth,
    And pur[l]iche in pouerte the apostells they suweth.'
280 'Alas,' quath the frier 'almost y madde in mynde,   *go mad*
    To sen hough this Minoures many men begyleth.   *see how*
    Sothli, somme of tho gomes hath more good him-selue
                                                   truly; men
    Than ten knyghtes that y knowe of catell in cofers.
                                                   wealth; coffers
    In fraytour thei faren best of all the foure orders,   *fare*
285 And [vsen] ypocricie in all that they werchen,   *hypocrisy*
    And prechen all of parfitnes. But loke now, y the praye,
                                                   perfection
    Nought but profre hem in pryvite a [peny] for a masse,
                                                   only; give
    And, but his cnaue be prest put out myne eighe,
                                                   boy; ready [c]
    Though he hadde more money hid than marchantes of wolle.
290 Loke hough this loresmen lordes bytrayen,   *teachers*
    Seyn that they folwen fully Fraunceses rewle,
    That in cotynge of his cope is more cloth y-folden
                                                   cutting; folded
    Than was in Fraunces froc whan he hem first made.   *frock*
    And yet, vnder that cope a cote [hath] he furred,

---

273 feyne] fayne B.   287 peny] BC; pany A.
279 purliche] puriche ABC.   288 cnaue be prest] AB; name be
285 vsen] vson B; vsun C; vsune   Prest C.
    A.   294 hath] BC; hathe A.

295 With foyns, or with fitchewes other fyn beuer,
                       marten fur ; polecat fur ; beaver
And that is cutted to the kne and queyntly y-botend,
                                 skilfully buttoned
Lest any spirituall man aspie that gile.   *deceit*
Fraunces bad his bretheren barfote to wenden ;
Non han thei bucled schon for bleynynge of her heles,
                        buckled shoes ; blistering
300 And hosen in harde weder y-hamled by the ancle,
                      stockings ; cold ; cut short
And spicerie sprad in her purse to parten where hem lust.
                        spices ; spread ; distribute
Lordes loueth hem well for thei so lowe crouchen;
                               love ; crouch
But knewen men her cautel and [her] queynt wordes,
                          tricks ; deceitful
Thei wolde worchypen hem nought but a litel,
f.321a The image of ypocricie ymped vpon fendes.   *grafted ; devils*
But, sone, yif thou wilte ben syker seche you no ferther,
We friers be the first and founded vpon treuthe.
Paul primus heremite put vs him-selue
                     first hermit [c] ; *established*
Awey into wildernes the werlde to dispisen;
310 And there we leng[e]den full longe and lyueden full harde,
                      dwelt ; lived austerely
For-to all this freren folke weren founded in townes,   *friars'*
And taughten vntrulie; and that we well aspiede,   *saw*
And for chefe charitie we chargeden vs seluen   *chief ; charged*
In amending of this men. We maden oure celles   *with reform*
315 To ben in cyties y-set to styghtle the people,   *direct*
Preching and praying as profetes schulden ;
And so we holden vs the heued of all holy chirche.   *head*
We have power of the pope purliche assoilen   *purely ; absolve*
All that helpen our hous in helpe of her soules,
320 To dispensen hem with in dedes of synne;

---

295 fitchewes] fichen B.
299 bleynynge] AB ; blenyng C.
300 y-hamled] y-hamelid B.
301 sprad] speed B.
303 knewen] knowen C ; her] BC ;
   heir A.

310 lengeden] C ; longeden B ;
   lengden A ; lyueden] leueden C.
317 heued] hedd B ; hetheued C.
320 hem with] with him B.

All that amendeth oure hous in money other elles,   *or else*
With corne other catell or clothes of beddes,   *grain*
Other bedys or broche or breed for our fode.   *beads; brooch*
And yif thou hast any good and wilt thi-selfe helpen,
325 Helpe vs hertliche therwithe and here I vndertake,
Thou schalt ben brother of our hous and a boke habben
At the next chaptire chereliche ensealed;
                      chapter-meeting; cheerfully sealed
And thanne oure prouinciall hath power to assoilen
                               provincial [c]
Alle sustren and bretheren that beth of our order.   *sisters*
330 And though thou conne nought thi Crede knele downe here;
My soule y sette for thyn to asoile the clene,
In couenaunt that thou come againe and katell vs bringe.'
And thanne loutede y adoun and he me leue grauntede,
                          knelt; dispensation [c]
And so I partid him fro and the frere left.
335 Thanne seid I to my-self 'Here is no bote;   *remedy*
Heere pride is the pater-noster in preyinge of synne;
Here Crede is coueytise; now can y no ferther,
Yet will y fonden forth and fraynen the Karmes.'
                      go; examine; Carmelites [c]
Thanne totede y into a tauerne and ther y aspyede   *looked*
340 Two frere Karmes with a full coppe.   *cup*
There y auntrede me in and ai[s]liche y seide,
                      ventured; nervously
'Leue syre, for the lordes loue that thou on leuest,
                      dear; believe
321b Lere me to som man my Crede for to lerne,   *teach*
That lyueth in [lel] lijf and loueth no synne,   *faithful; life*
345 And gloseth nought the godspell but halt Godes he[s]tes,
                  glosses; keeps; commandments
And nether money ne mede ne may him nought letten,
                  reward; prevent
But werchen after Godes worde with-outen any faile.

322 other] or with B; of] to BC.
327 chaptire] chapiter B; chapitre C;
   chereliche] chyrlich B; clerliche C.
330 thi] the C.

341 auntrede] aventeryd B; aisliche]
   C; aillich B; ailiche A.
343 Lere] teache B.
344 lel] C; leele B; Lei A.
345 hestes] hestys B; hetes AC.

A prechour y-professed hath plight me his trewthe
To techen me trewlie; but woldest thou me tellen
350 [Yf] thei ben certayne men and syker on to trosten,

                steadfast; trust

Y wolde quyten the thi mede as my mighte wer.'

                requite; means

'A trofle!' quath he, 'Trewlie, his treuth is full litell.   *trifle*
He dyned nought with Domynike sithe Crist deide.

              St Dominic; since

For with the princes of pride the prechours dwellen;
355 Thei bene as digne as the devel that droppeth fro heuene.

                haughty

With hertes of heynesse wough halwen thei chirches

        haughtiness; how; consecrate

And deleth in devynitie as dogges doth bones.   *deal*
Thei medleth with messages and mariages of grete;

          meddle; [c]; nobility

They leeuen with lordes with lesynges y-nowe;   *live; lies; enough*
360 They biggeth hem bichopryches with bagges of golde;   *buy*
Thei wilneth worchipes, but waite on her dedes.

        desire; honours; examine

Herken at Herdforthe hou that they werchen,   *Hertford* [c]
And loke whou that thei lyven and leeue as thou fyndest.   *believe*
They [ben] counseilours of kinges Crist wot the sothe,

             knows; truth

365 Whou they [curry] kinges and her back claweth.

       curry favour with; [c] scratch

God lene hem leden well in lyvinge of heven,   *grant; lead*
And glose hem nought for her good to greven her soules. *flatter*
Y pray the, where ben thei pryue with any pore wightes,

          intimate; poor people

That maie not amenden her hous ne amenden hemseluen?

348 trewthe] trwethe C.
350 Yf] For ABC.
352 trofle] trefle BC.
355 as digne] so digne C.
356 wough] whough BC; thei] the BC.
358 medleth] medeleth C; meddeley B; messages] massages B.
359 leeuen] lyven B.

360 biggeth] beggen B.
361 her] eer C.
362 Herdforthe] Hartffourde B.
363 whou] when C; leeue] beleve B.
364 ben] C; bene B; beyn A.
365 curry] currey B; curreth C; carry A.
366 lene hem] leue hem C; leve hym B.

370 Thei prechen in proude harte and preiseth her order,
And wer[l]dliche worchype wilneth in erthe.

worldly honour; desire

Leeue it well, lef man, and men ryght-lokede,

believe; looked straight

Ther is more pryue pride in prechours hertes   *secret*
Than ther lefte in Lucyfer er he were lowe fallen;

remained; before

375 They ben digne as dich water that dogges in bayteth.

haughty; ditch; rummage

Loke a ribaut of hem that can nought wel reden   *rascal*
His rewle ne his respondes but be pure rote,   *responses* [c]
Als as he were a connynge clerke he [c]asteth the lawes,

learned; frames

Nought lowli but lordly and leesinges lyeth.   *humbly; lies*
380 For ryght as Menoures most ypocricie vseth,   *just*
Ryght so ben Prechers proude purlyche in herte.
.322a But Cristen creatour we Karmes first comen
Even in Elyes tyme first of hem all,   *Elijah's* [c]
And lyven by our Lady and lelly hir seruen   *faithfully*
385 In clene comun life kepen vs out of synne;   *communal*
Nowt proude as prechours beth but prayen full still

not; quietly

For all the soules and the lyves that we by lybbeth.   *live*
We connen on no queyntyse, Crist wot the sothe,   *falsehood*
But bysieth vs in oure bedes as vs best holdeth.   *prayers*
390 And therfore, leue leel man, leeue that ich sygge,

loyal; believe; say

A masse of vs mene men is of more mede   *humble; profit*
And passeth all praiers of thies proude freers.
And thou wilt gyuen vs any good y would the here graunten
To taken all thy penance in peril of my soule;
395 And though thou conne nought thy crede clene the assoile,
So that thou mowe amenden our hous with money other elles,

or else

---

371 werldliche] worldlich B ;
     worldliche C ; werdliche A.
372 Leeue] Ken B, *with 'leave' at end
     of* 371 ; and men] and yf men B.
374 er] or C.
378 casteth] BC ; hasteth A.

388 connen] cannon B ; couuen C.
390 leel man] leelman C.
393 would] woll B ; the] ye C.
394 in] on B.
395 conne nought] cannot B.
396 mowe] now B ; other] or B.

With som katell other corne or cuppes of siluer.'
property; grain

'Trewely, frere,' quath y tho 'to tellen the the sothe,

Ther is no peny in my palke to payen for my mete;   *bag; food*

400 I haue no good ne no gold but go thus abouten,

And travaile full trewlye to wynnen withe my fode.   *earn*

But woldest thou for Godes loue lerne me my Crede,   *teach*

Y schuld don for thy will whan I wele hadde.'   *prosperity*

'Trewlie,' quath the frere, 'a fol y the holde.   *fool; consider*

405 Thou woldest not weten thy fote and woldest fich kacchen !
fish; catch [c]

Our pardon and oure preiers so beth they nought parted.
shared out

Oure power lasteth nought so feer but we some peny fongen.
far; receive

Fare well,' quath the frere, 'for y mot hethen fonden, *go hence*

And hyen to an houswife that hath vs bequeathen
hurry; bequeathed

410 Ten pounde in hir testament. To tellen the sothe,

Ho draweth to the dethe-warde but yet I am in drede
she is on the point of death

Lest ho turne her testament and therfore I hyghe   *change; will*

To hauen hir to our hous and henten yif y mighte   *receive*

An Anuell for myn owen [vse] to helpen to clothe.' *annual* [c]

415 'Godys forbode,' quath [his] fellawe 'but ho forth passe
forbid

Wil ho is in purpose with vs to departen;   *share*

God let her no lenger lyuen for letteres ben manye.'   [c]

f.322b Thanne turned y me forthe and talked to my-selue

Of the falshede of this folk – whou feithles they [weren].

420 And as y wente be the waie wepynge for sorowe,

[I] seigh a sely man me my opon the plow hongen. *saw; poor*

His cote was of a cloute that cary was y-called,   *rag; cary* [c]

His hod was full of holes and his heer oute,   *hood; hair*

---

399 palke] pakke C.

403 thy will] the will BC; wele] well
    B.

406 parted] parten C.

407 so feer] soffer B.

414 vse] BC; vs A.

415 his] BC; this A.

417 letteres ben] lettes ther B.

419 they] the B; weren] C; werren
    B; werne A.

421 I] And ABC.

With his knopped schon clouted full thykke;
lumpy; *shoes*; *patched heavily*
425 His ton toteden out as he the londe treddede,
toes; *peeped*; *trod*
His hosen ouerhongen his hokschynes on eueriche a side,
stockings; *sinews* [c]; *each*
Al beslombred in fen as he the plow folwede;   *spattered*; *mud*
Twey myteynes, as mete, maad all of cloutes;
two mittens; *matching*
The fyngers weren for-werd and ful of fen honged.   *worn-out*
430 This whit waselede in the [fen] almost to the ancle,
man; *squelched*
Foure rotheren hym by-forn that feble were [worthen];
heifers; *become*
Men myghte reken ich a ryb so reufull they weren.
count; *every*; *pitiful*
His wijf walked him with with a longe gode,   *goad*
In a cutted cote cutted full heyghe,   *torn*; *cut very short*
435 Wrapped in a wynwe schete to weren hire fro weders,
winding sheet; *protect*
Barfote on the bare ijs that the blod folwede.   *ice*
And at the londes ende laye a litell crom-bolle,   *scrapbowl*
And thereon lay a litell childe lapped in cloutes,   *folded*
And tweyne of tweie yeres olde opon a-nother syde,
two; *two*
440 And alle they songen o songe that sorwe was to heren;   *one*
They crieden alle o cry a carefull note.   *miserable sound*
The sely man sighede sore, and seide 'Children, beth stille !'
sorely; *hush*
This man loked opon me and leet the plow stonden,   *let*
And seyde, 'Sely man, why syghest thou so harde ?
445 Yif the lakke lijflode lene the ich will   *sustenance*; *give*
Swich good as God hath sent. Go we, leue brother.'   *such*
Y saide thanne, 'Naye, sire my sorwe is wel more;

---

426 hokschynes] hock shynes B ; a side] side B.
427 beslombred] beslomered C.
428 mete] nettes B ; meter C.
429 for-werd] AC ; forweryd B.
430 fen] B ; fern A ; feen C.
431 worthen] B ; worthi AC.
432 reufull] rewfulle B ; rentful C.
435 wynwe] wynow B ; weren] AC ; waren B.
437 laye] lath C ; bolle] bole B.
439 olde] elde B.
445 Yif the] yf thou B ; Gif the C.
447 wel] myche B.

For y can nought my Crede y kare well harde;
For y can fynden no man that fully byleueth,
450 To techen me the heyghe weie and therfore I wepe.

                main path

For y haue [fonded] the freers of the foure orders,   *tried*
For there I wende haue wist but now my wit lakketh;

              thought; known; fails

And all my hope was on hem and myn herte also;
But thei ben fully feithles and the fend sueth.'   *devil; follow*
455 'A brother!' quath he tho, 'Beware of tho foles!   *those fools*
For Crist seyde him-selfe, "Of swiche y you warne."
And false profetes in the feith he fulliche hem calde,

f.323a   "*In vestimentis ouium* but onlie with-inne

            In the clothing of sheep [c]

Thei ben wilde wer-wolues that wiln the folk robben."
460 The fend founded hem first the feith to destroie,
And by his craft thei comen in to combren the chirche,

            encumber

By the coueiteise of his craft the curates to helpen;
But now they hauen an hold they harmen full many.
Thei don nought after Domynick but dreccheth the puple,

            behave; vex

465 Ne folwen nought Fraunces but falslyche lybben,
And Austynes rewle thei rekneth but a fable,   *count*
But purchaseth hem pryuylege of popes at Rome.
Thei couet[e]n confessions to kachen some hire,

         covet; gain; payment

And sepultures also some wayten to cacchen;   *burials; look*
470 But other cures of Cristen thei coueten nought to haue,   *cares*
But there as wynnynge lijth he loketh none other.'

            profit; lies; heeds

'Whough schal y nemne thy name that neighboures the
   kalleth?'   *who; call*
'Peres,' quath he, 'the pore man, the plowe-man y hatte.'

           Piers; am called

---

451 fonded] fondes ABC.
457 hem] hym B.
460 fend] fen C; destroie] distrie C.
468 coueten] C; couetun A;
    coveyton B.

469 sepultures] sepulturus C;
    cacchen] lacchen C.
472 the] ye C.
473 hatte] hott B.

'A Peres!' quath y tho, 'Y pray the, thou me telle
475 More of thise tryflers, hou trechurly thei libbeth.

treacherously; live

For ichon of hem hath told me a tale of that other,   *each*
Of her wicked lijf in werlde that hy lybbeth.
I trowe that some wikked wyght wroughte this orders

believe; created

[Thorughe] that gleym of that gest that Golias is y-calde,

subtlety; story [c]

480 Other ells Satan him-self sente hem fro hell
To cumbren men with her craft Cristendome to schenden.'

destroy

'Dere brother,' quath Peres, 'the devell is ful queynte;

devious

To encombren holy Churche he casteth ful harde,   *plans*
And fluricheth his falsnes opon fele wise,   *varies; many ways*
485 And fer he casteth to-form the folke to destroye.

far; plans ahead

Of the kynrede of Caym he caste the freres,

kindred; Cain [c]; *made*

And founded hem on Farysens feyned for gode;   *Pharisees* [c]
But thei with her fals faith michel folk schendeth,   *many*
Crist calde hem him-self kynde ypocrites;   *natural hypocrites*
490 How often he cursed hem well can y tellen
He seide ones him-self to that sory puple,   *wretched*
"Wo worthe you, wyghtes, wel lerned of the lawe!"

woe to you

Eft he seyde to hem-selfe, "Wo mote you worthen,   *become*
That the toumbes of profetes tildeth vp heighe!   *build*
495 Youre faderes fordeden hem and to the deth hem broughte.'

murdered

323b Here y touche this two twynnen hem I thenke.

mention; compare

475 tryflers] trvflers B.
476 that other] other B.
477 hy] he BC.
479 Thorughe] B; Trow ye A;
   Trowe ye C.
484 fele] sely B.
486 kynrede] kyndred B.

487 on] or B; Farysens] Sarysenes C;
   gode] good B; God C.
491 ones] ons BC.
493 hem-selfe] hymself B.
494 tildeth] AC; bildith B.
495 hem] hym B.
496 twynnen] and twynnen B.

Who wilneth ben wisere of lawe than lewde freres,

wishes; *unlearned*

And in multitude of men ben maysters y-called,   *masters* [c]
And wilneth worchips of the werlde and sitten with heye,

nobility

500 And leueth louynge of God and lownesse behinde ?

abandon; *humility*

And in beldinge of tombes thei trauaileth grete   *tax*; *nobility*
To chargen her chirche-flore and chaungen it ofte.

fund; *replace*

And the fader of the freers defouled hir soules,   *polluted*
That was the dygginge devel that dreccheth men ofte.

insidious; *harms*

505 The divill by his dotage dissaueth the chirche,

devil; *stupidity*; *deceives*

And put in the prechours y-paynted withouten.

painted; *outside* [c]

And by his queyntise they comen in the curates to helpen,
But that harmede hem harde and halp hem full litell.   *helped*
But Austines ordynaunce was on a good trewthe,
510 And also Domynikes dedes weren dernlich y-vsed,

practised inwardly

And Frauncis founded his folke fulliche on trewthe,
Pure parfit prestes in penaunce to lybben,   *perfect*
In loue and in lownesse and lettinge of pride,   *forsaking*
Grounded on the godspell as God bad him-selue.   *based*
515 But now the glose is so greit in gladding tales   *great*; *pleasing*
That turneth vp two-folde vnteyned opon trewthe,

ungrounded

That thei bene cursed of Crist y can hem well proue;
With-outen his blissinge bare beth they in her werkes.

exposed

For Crist seyde him-selfe to swiche as him folwede,
520 "Y-blessed mote thei ben that mene ben in soule";
And alle pouere in gost God him-self blisseth.   *poor*; *spirit*

---

498 in] a B.
499 worchips] worship C; sitten
        with heye] to sytten highe B.
508 hem] hym B.

515 tales] tallys B.
517 thei bene] they ben C; many
        bene B.
521 pouere] power C.

Whou fell freers fareth so fayn wolde y knowe !

> *how ; treacherous*

Proue hem in proces and pynch at her ordre,

> *prove ; [c] ; cavil*

And deme hem after that they don and dredles, y leue

> *without fear, I believe*

525 Thei willn we[xe]n pure wroth wonderliche sone,

> *grow extremely angry soon*

And schewen the a scharp will in a schort tyme, *show*

To wilne wilfully wra[thth]e and werche therafter.

> *wish ; wrath*

Wytnesse on Wycliff that warned hem with trewth ;

For he in goodnesse of gost graythliche hem warned

> *spirit ; truly*

530 To wayuen her wik[e]dnesse and werkes of synne. *abandon*

Whou sone this sori men [seweden] his soule,

> *wretched ; pursued*

And oueral lollede him with heretykes werkes. *accused* [c]

And so of the blessinge of God thei bereth litel mede.

> *carry ; reward*

.324a Afterward another onliche he blissede, *moreover ; only*

535 The meke of the [myddel-erde] thourugh myght of his fader.

> *earth ; power*

Fynd foure freres in a flok that folweth that rewle,

Thanne haue y tynt all my tast, touche and assaie.

> *lost ; discrimination*

Lakke hem a litil wight and here lijf blame, *fault ; bit ; life*

But he lepe vp on heigh in hardynesse of herte, *boldness*

540 And [n]emne the anon nought and thi name lakke

> *name ; nothing ; disparage*

With proude wordes apert that passeth his rule,

> *openly ; exceed*

---

522 Whou] how B ; fell] fele BC.
524 they] the C.
525 wexen] woxon B ; wexon C ;
 weyon A.
527 wraththe] wrath B ; wrathe C ;
 wrappe A.
530 wikednesse] BC ; wikdnesse A ;
 wayuen] waynen C.
531 seweden] BC ; lewden A.

535 myddel-erde] C ; myddel hertes
 A ; mydell herth B.
536 that rewle] the rewle B.
538 hem] hym B.
539 hardynesse] herdines B ;
 hardeness C.
540 nemne] BC ; memne A.
541 apert] apart B.

Bothe with "thou leyest, and thou lext" in heynesse of sowle,
                lie ; lie

And turne as a tyrant that turmenteth him-selue,
A lord were lothere for to leyne a k[n]aue
        more reluctant ; give money to a boy

545 Thanne swich a beggere the best in a toun.
Loke nowe, leue man beth nought thise i-lyke
Fully to the Farisens in fele of thise poyntes ?
           many ; charges [c]

Al her brod beldyng ben belded withe synne,   *broad ; built*
And in worchipe of the werlde her wynnynge thei holden;
            profit ; keep

550 Thei schapen her chapolories and streccheth hem brode,
         fashion ; scapulars [c]
And launceth heighe her hemmes with babelyng in stretes;
         slash ; babbling

Thei ben y-sewed with whight silk and semes full queynte,
          sewn ; white

Y-stongen with stiches that stareth as siluer. *pierced ; glare*
And but freres ben first y-set at sopers and at festes, *suppers*

555 Thei wiln ben wonderly wroth ywis, as y trowe; *indeed*
But they ben at the lordes borde louren they willeth,
          table ; glower

He mot bygynne that borde – a beggere – with sorwe.
          must ; head

And first sitten in se in her synagoges,   *see*
That beth here heyghe helle-hous of Kaymes kynde !
         Cain's nature [c]

560 For though a man in her mynster a masse wolde heren,
         church ; hear

His sight schal so [be] set on sundrye werkes, *various*
The penounes and the pomels and poyntes of scheldes
         pennants ; pommels

---

542 leyest – lext] lyest and the lixst
  B ; leyst and thou lext C.
543 turmenteth] turnnen C.
544 lothere] lether B ; leyne] beyne
  B ; knaue] BC ; kaue A.
550 schapen] sharpen B ;

chapolories] capolories B ; brode]
 abrode B.
551 launceth] lannceth C.
552 and semes] semes B.
557 that] the B.
559 hous] houndes B.
561 be set] B ; byset AC.

With-drawen his deuocion and dusken his herte;   *devotion ; darken*

I likne it to a lym-yerde to drawen men to hell,   *limed-stick* [c]

565 And to worchipe of the fend to wraththen the soules.   *anger*

And also Crist him-selfe seide to swiche ypocrites,

"He loueth in markettes ben met with gretynges of pouere,   *to be met ; poor*

And lowynge of lewed men in Lent[e]nes tyme."   *reverence*

For thei han of bichopes y-bought with her propre siluer,   *own*

570 And purchased of penaunce the puple to assoile.

324b But money may maken mesur of the peyne   *measure ; pain* [c]

After that his power is to payen, his penance schal faile.

(God lene it be a good help for hele of the soules !)   *grant ; health*

And also this myster men ben maysters icalled,   *craftsmen*

575 That the gentill Iesus generallyche blamed,   *noble ; altogether*

And that poynt to his apostells purly defended.   *forbade*

But freres hauen foryetten this and the fend [suweth],   *follow*

He that maystri louede, Lucifer the olde.

[Ner] Fraunceis or Domynik other Austen ordeynide   *neither*

580 Any of this dotardes doctur to worthe,   *fools ; become ; doctor of philosophy*

Masters of dyvinitie her matens to leue,   *matins ; abandon*

And chereliche as a cheueteyne his chambre to holden   *chieftain ; keep*

With chymene and chapell and chesen whan him liste,   *fireplace ; choose ; please*

And serued as a souereine and as a lorde sitten.   *lord*

585 Swiche a gome godes wordes grysliche gloseth;   *man ; wickedly*

Y trowe, he toucheth nought the text but taketh it for a tale.

---

567 ben met] tomet B.

568 Lentenes] C ; Lentnes A ; lentonys B.

572 After that] For as B ; payen] peye so B.

573 lene] leue B ; leue C.

574 myster] mynster B.

575 gentill] genltil C.

577 suweth] C ; sewith B ; fu luweth A *with 'fu' crossed through.*

579 Ner] Nor B ; Wher A ; Where C.

580 doctur to worthe] pryde for to ensewen B.

581 Masters] None maisters B.

583 chesen] chosen C ; him] hem BC.

585 grysliche] greislich B.

God forbad to his folke and fullyche defended
They schulden nought stodyen biforn ne sturen her wittes,

study ; *stir*

But sodenlie the same word with her mowth schewe

spontaneously

590 That weren yeuen hem of God thorugh gost of him-selue.

given ; *spirit*

Now mot a frere studyen and stumblen in tales,
And leuen his matynes and no masse singen,
And loken hem lesynges that liketh the puple,   *seek out lies*
To purchasen him his pursfull to paye for the drynke.

595 And brother, when bernes ben full and holly tyme passed,

barns ; *holy feast*

Thanne co[m]en cursed freres and croucheth full lowe;   *crouch*
A losel, a lymitour ouer all the lond lepeth,

wretch ; *limitour* [c]

And loke that he leue non house that somwhat he ne lacche;

get

And ther thei gilen hem-self and Godes worde turneth.

beguile ; *twist*

600 Bagges and beggyng he bad his folk leuen,   *forsake*
And only seruen him-self and hijs rewle sechen,   *his* ; *seek*
And all that nedly nedeth that schuld hem nought lakken.
Whereto beggen thise men and ben nought so feble;   *why*
Hem faileth no furrynge ne clothes at full,   *lack* ; *furs*
605 But for a lustfull lijf in lustes to dwellen ?   *pleasurable*
With-outen any trauaile vntrewliche lybbeth.

unfaithfully ; *live*

f.325a Hy beth nought maymed men ne no mete lakketh,   *maimed*
Y-clothed in curious cloth and clenliche arayed.

fancy ; *neatly dressed*

It is a laweles lijf as lordynges vsen,   *practise*
610 Neyther ordeyned in ordir but onlie libbeth.

ordained ; *singularly*

590 yeuen] given C; him-selue]
   hemselue C.
591 stumblen] stumlen C.
595 bernes] barnys B.
596 comen] BC; cornen A.
598 he] ye B; lacche] latche B; laiche
   C.

600 Bagges] to bagges B; leuen]
   lyven B.
605 dwellen] dellen B.
607 Hy] Thei C.
608 cloth] clothes B.
610 onlie] onethe BC.

Crist bad blissen bodies on erthe   *bless*
That wepen for wykkednes that he byforne wroughte.
                                             earlier ; committed
That ben fewe of tho freres for thei ben ner dede   *near ; dead*
And put all in pur clay with pottes on her hedes;   *earth* [c]
615 Thanne [he] waryeth and wepeth and wicheth after heuen,
                                             curses ; wishes
And fyeth on her falshedes that thei bifore deden   *curses ; did*
And therfore of that blissinge trewlie, as y trowe,
Thei may trussen her part in a terre powghe !
                                             pack up ; tar box [c]
All tho blissed beth that bodyliche hungreth;–   *those*
620 That ben the pore penyles that han ouer-passed
                                             penniless ; exceeded
The poynt of her pris lijf in penaunce of werkes,   *prime*
And mown nought swynken ne sweten but ben swythe feble,
                                             may ; labour ; very
Other maymed at myschef or meseles syke,   *mishap ; lepers*
And here good is a-gon and greueth hem to beggen.
                                             wealth ; grieves
625 Ther is no frer in feith that fareth in this wise;   *behaves ; way*
But he maie beggen his bred his bed is ygreithed;
                                             unless ; prepared
Vnder a pot he schal be put in a pryvie chambre,   *secret*
That he schal lyuen ne last but litell while after.   *nor exist*
Al-mighti god and man the merciable [blessed]   *merciful*
630 That han mercy on men that misdon hem here.   *misbehave*
But whoso for-gabbed a frere y-founden at the stues,
                                             criticised ; found ; brothel
And broughte blod of his bodi on bak or on side,   [c]
Hym were as god greuen a greit lorde of rentes.
                                             good ; great ; substance
He schulde sonner bene schryven, schortlie to tellen,
                                             sooner ; shriven

---

614 clay] cleye B ; purclath C.
615 he] BC ; ho A ; wicheth]
    whisshith B.
618 trussen] trullen B ; terre powghe]
    tree poghe B.
621 of werkes] and werkes B.

623 maymed] mayned C ; syke] lyke
    C.
624 good] God C.
626 bed] bede B.
627 pot] pote B.
629 blessed] and blessed ABC.

635 Though he kilde a comlye knyght and compased his morther,   *killed; planned; murder*

Thanne a buffet to beden a beggere frere.   *blow; bestow on*

[Crist the clene hertes] curtey[s]liche blissed,   *pure; graciously*

That [coueten] no katel but Cristes full blisse,   *covet; property*

That leeueth fulliche on God and lellyche thenketh   *believes; loyally*

640 On his lore and his lawe and lyueth opon trewthe.   *teaching*

Freres han foryeten this and folweth an other;   *forgotten*

That thei may henten, they holden, [and] by-hirneth it sone.   *receive; conceal*

Heir hertes ben clene y-hid in her highe cloistre,   *hidden*

f.325b As kurres from kareyne that is cast in dyches.   *curs; carrion; thrown*

645 And parfite Crist the pesible blissed,   *perfect; peacemakers*

That bene suffrant and sobre and susteyne anger.   *patient; steadfast; restrain*

A-say of her sobernesse and thou might y-knowen,   *examine*

Ther is no waspe in this werlde that will wilfullok[e]r styngen,   *more readily*

For stappyng on a too of a styn[c]ande frere.   *stepping; toe; stinking*

650 For nether souereyn ne soget thei ne suffreth neuer;   *subject; allow*

All the blissing of God beouten thei walken;   *outside*

For of her suffraunce, for sothe, men seth but litell.   *patience*

Alle that persecution in pure lijf suffren,

Thei han the benison of God blissed in erthe.   *blessing*

655 Y praie, parceyue now the pursut of a frere,   *see; persecution by*

---

635 morther] AB; mother C.
637 Crist the clene hertes] The clene hertes of Crist he AB; The clene hertes Crist he C; curteysliche] curteyliche ABC.
638 coueten] C; couetyne A; coveyten B; blisse] bles B.
642 and] B; *not in* AC.
643 y-hid] yhad B.
648 Ther is no] Ther ne is no BC;

that] the B; wilfulloker] wilfullokr A; wilfuller B; wil folloke C.
649 stappyng] stamping B; styncande] stynkande B; styncande C; styntande A.
650 soget] seget C.
651 the] thei C; beouten] bene outten B.
652 seth] say B; sey C.

In what measure of meknesse thise men deleth.

Byhold opon Wat Brut whou bisiliche thei pursueden   *busily*

For he seyde hem the sothe and yet syre, ferthere,

        furthermore

Hy may no more marren [hym] but men telleth   *harm*

660 That he is an heretike and yuele byleueth,   *falsely; believes*

And prechith it in pulpit to blenden the puple.   *blind*

Thei wolden awyrien that wight for his well dedes,

        curse; man; good

And so thei chewen charitie as chewen schaf houndes.

        chaff; dogs

And thei pursueth the pouere and passeth pursutes,

        persecute; exceed

665 Bothe they wiln and thei wolden [y]-worthen so grete

        desire; wish; become

To passen any mans might to mortheren the soules.

        power; murder

First to brenne the bodye in a bale of fijr,   *burn; blaze*

And sythen the sely soule slen and senden hyre to helle.

        then; poor; slay; it

And Crist clerlie for[b]adde his Cristene, and defended

        prohibited

670 Thei schulden nought after the face neuer the folke demen.'

        according to

'Sur,' y seide my-self, 'thou semest to blamen.

Why dispisest thou thus thise sely pore freres

None other men so mychel, monkes ne preistes,

Chanons ne Charthous that in chirche serueth ?

        Canons; Charterhouse [c]

675 It semeth that thise sely men han somwhat the greved

        grieved [c]

Other with word or with werke and therfore thou wilnest

---

656 thise] this B.
657 Wat] Water BC.
659 Hy] He B ; hym] hem ABC.
661 in] in the B.
662 awyrien] awyrene B.
663 thei] the B ; chewen] shewen B ;
    schaf] shaffen B.

664 pouere] power B.
665 y-worthen] BC ; th-worthen A.
669 forbadde] forbad BC ; forladde
    A.
670 face] faite B.
671 Sur] But B ; Sire C.

To schenden other [schamen] hem with thi sharpe speche,

                                    destroy ; shame [c]

And harmen holliche and her hous greuen.'

'I praie the', quath Peres, 'put that out of thy mynde.

680 Certen for sowle hele y saie the this wordes.   *health*

f.326a Y preise nought possessioners but pur lytel;   *possessioners* [c]

For falshed of freres hath fulliche encombred

Manye of this maner men and maid hem to leuen

                                kinds of ; abandon

Here charite and chastete and [chesen] hem to lustes,

                                devote ; pleasures

685 And waxen to werldly and wayuen the trewthe,

                                grow ; cast aside

And leuen the loue of her God and the werlde seruen.

But for falshed of freres y fele in my soule,

Seynge the synfull lijf that sorweth myn herte,   *seeing*

How thei ben clothed in cloth that clennest scheweth; *cleanest*

690 For aungells and arcangells all thei whijt vseth,

And alle aldermen that bene *ante tronum.*

                            before the throne [c]

Thise tokens hauen freres taken but y trowe that a fewe

Folwen fully that cloth but falsliche that vseth.

For whijt in trowthe bytokneth clennes in soule;

                            signifies ; purity

695 Yif he haue vnder-nethen whijt thanne he aboue wereth

                              underneath

Blak, that bytokneth bale for oure synne,   *misery*

And mournynge for misdede of hem that this vseth,

And serwe for synfull lijf ; so that cloth asketh.

                           sorrow ; requires

Y trowe ther ben nought ten freres that for synne wepen,

700 For that lijf is here lust and thereyn thei libben

677 other] or B ; schamen] shamen   waynen C.
    BC ; schenden A ; thi] the C.   689 clennest] clenenes B.
678 harmen] AB ; hannen C.   692–3] Folowyin fully that it
681 possessioners] pocessioners B ;   betokemthe : Butt fallslyche yey
    pocessioneres C.   vsythe B *in margin.*
684 chesen] schosen A ; chosen B ;   694 in] of B.
    shosen C.   695 wereth] wenith B.
685 werldly] werly C ; wayuen]   700 thereyn] thereby BC.

In fraitour and in fermori, her fostringe is synne.   *nurture*

It is her mete at iche a mel her most sustenaunce.   *every meal*

Herkne opon Hyldegare hou homlyche [ho] telleth

                          Hildegard [c]; *directly*

How her sustenaunce is synne; and syker, as y trowe.

                                        accurately

705 Weren her confessiones clenli destrued,   *completely put aside*

Hy schulde nought beren hem so bragg ne [belden] so heyghe,

                              boastfully; *build*

For the fallynge of synne socoureth tho foles,

                          transgression; *succours*

And bigileth the grete with glauerynge words,

                            nobility; *flattering*

With glosinge of godspells thei Gods worde turneth,   *distort*

710 And pasen all the pryuylege that Petur after vsed.

The power of the Apostells thei pasen in speche,

For to sellen the synnes for siluer other mede,

And purlyche *a pena* the puple assoileth,   *from pain* [c]

And *a culpa* also that they may kachen   *from guilt* [c]

715 Money other money-worthe and mede to fonge;

                        valuables; *reward*; *receive*

And bene at lone and at bode as burgeses vsithe.

                      lendings; *biddings*; *townsmen*

Thus they seruen Satanas and soules bygileth,   *Satan*

f.326b Marchantes of malisons, mansede wreches!

                      merchants; *curses*; *accursed*

Thei vsen russet also somme of this freres,

                        rough garments [c]

720 That bitokneth trauaile and trewthe opon erthe.

Bote loke whou this lorels labouren the erthe,

But freten the frute that the folk full lellich biswynketh.

                      devour; *loyally*; *produce*

With trauail of trewe men thei tymbren her houses,   [c]; *build*

And of the curious clothe her copes thei biggen,

                      fancy cloth; *buy*

---

703 opon] open B; ho] he ABC.

705 clenli] cleerly B; destrued]
   descryed B.

706 belden] BC; helden A.

707 tho] the C.

712 sellen] fellen C.

716 lone and at bode] love and at
   abode B.

722 freten] ferton B.

724 biggen] beggen C.

725 And [als] his getynge is greet he schal ben good holden.
                                            income ; considered
     And ryght as dranes doth nought but drynketh vp the huny,
                                            drones ; nothing
     Whan been withe her bysynesse han brought it to hepe,
                                            bees ; industry ; pile
     Right so, fareth freres with folke opon erthe;   *behave*
     They freten vp the fu[r]ste-froyt and falsliche lybbeth.
                                            first-fruit
730 But alle freres eten nought y-lich good mete,   *eat ; equally*
     But after that his wynnynge is is his well-fare,
                                            according to income
     And after that he bringeth home his bed schal ben graythed,
                                            prepared
     And after that his rychesse is raught he schal ben redy serued.
                                            obtained
     But see thi-self in thi sight whou somme of hem walketh
735 With cloutede schon and clothes ful feble,
                                            patched shoes ; threadbare
     Wel neigh for-wer[y]d and the wlon offe,
                                            worn out ; hems down
     And his felawe in a froke worth swiche fiftene,
     A-rayd in rede sc[h]on, – and elles were reuthe, –
                                            dressed ; otherwise ; pity
     And sexe copes or seven in his celle hongeth.   *six*
740 Though for fayling of good his fellawe schulde sterue,   *lack*
     He wolde nought lenen him a peny his lijf for to holden.
                                            lend ; preserve
     Y might tymen tho troiflardes to toilen with the erthe,
                                            compel ; triflers ; labour
     Tylyen and trewliche lyuen and her flech tempren.
                                            till ; temper
     Now mot ich soutere his sone setten to schole,
                                            cobbler ; school

---

725 als] BC; all A.   wlon] AC; wolne B.
727 hepe] haus C.   738 schon] scon A; stone BC;
728 freres] the freres B.   reuthe] renthe C.
729 freten] Fretton B; furste] C;   739 hongeth] hongid B.
     furst B; fuste A.   741 lenen] leuen C.
736 for-werd] AC; forweryd B;   744 schole] skale B.

745 And ich a beggers brol on the booke lerne,   *brat*
     And worth to a writere and with a lorde dwell,   *become*
     Other falsely to a frere the fend for to seruen.
     So of that beggers brol a bychop schal worthen,   *bishop*
     Among the peres of the lond prese to sitten,   *peers; eager*
750 And lordes sones lowly to tho losells aloute,
                       humbly; wretches; bow
     Knyghtes crouketh hem to and crucheth full lowe,
                       kneel; crouch
     And his syre a soutere y-suled in grees,   *father; soiled; grease*
     His teeth with toylinge of lether tatered as a sawe.
                       working; jagged
     Alaas that lordes of the londe leueth swiche wrechen,
                       believe; wretches
755 And leneth swiche lorels for her lowe wordes !   *give money to*
f.327a They schulden maken bichopes her owen brethren childre,
                       brothers'
     Other of some gentil blod and so it best semed,   *noble*
     And foster none faytoures ne swiche false freres
                  promote; false beggars [c]
     To maken fatt and full and her fleche combren.   *plump*
760 For her kynde were more to y-clense diches   *clean out ditches*
     Than ben to sopers y-set first and serued with siluer.   *placed*
     A great bolle-full of benen were betere in his wombe,
                  bowl-full; beans; stomach
     And with the [b]andes of bakun his baly for to fillen,
                     rinds; bacon; belly
     Than pertriches or plouers or pekokes y-rosted,
                  partridges; plovers; peacocks
765 And comeren her stomakes with curious drynkes,
                     burden; exotic
     That maketh swiche harlottes hordome vsen,
                  raqscals; lechery; practise
     And with her wicked worde wymmen bitraieth.
     God wold her wonynge were in wildernesse,   *dwelling*

---

745 brol] brawle B.
748 brol] brawle B ; bychop] an
   Abbot C.
749 prese] preise B.
751 full lowe] fullowe B.

755 leneth] levith B.
756 bichopes] Abbots C.
762 benen] beuen C.
763 bandes] BC ; randes A.

And fals freres forboden the fayre ladis chaumbres.   *forbidden*
770 For knewe lordes her craft, trewlie, y trowe,   *ploy*
They schulden nought haunten her hous so homly on nightes,
                       frequent ; intimately
Ne bedden swiche brothels in so brode schetes,
                       bed ; lechers ; wide
But scheten her heued in the stre to scharpen her wittes;
                       sheet ; head ; straw
Ne ben kynges confessours of custom ne the counsell of the
   rewme knowe,
                       realm
775 For Fraunces founded hem nought to faren on that wise,
                       behave ; way
Ne Domynik dued hem neuer swiche drynkers to worthe,
                       endowed
Ne Helye ne Austen swiche lijf neuer vsed,   *Elijah*
But in pouerte of spirit spended her tyme.
We haue sene our-self in a schort tyme,
780 Whou freres wolden no flech among the folke vsen;
But now the harlottes han hid thilke rewle,   *that*
And, for the loue of oure lorde haue leyd hire in water.   *laid it*
Wenest thou ther wold so fele swiche warlawes worthen,
                       think ; many ; liars
Ne were wor[l]dlyche wele and her welfare ?
785 Thei schulden deluen and diggen and dongen the erthe,
                       delve ; dung
And mene-mong corn bred to her mete fongen,
                     ordinary ; corn meal ; take
And wortes flechles wroughte and water to drinken,
                   vegetables ; meatless ; prepared
And werchen and wolward gon as we wrecches vsen;
                     labour ; wear wool
[An aunter yif] ther wolde on amonge an hol hundred
                   perhaps ; one ; whole

769 the fayre] fayre B.   785 diggen] dyken BC.
773 scheten] shottin B ; sheten C.   786 mene mong] mene mogg B ; to]
782 oure] the B.   and B.
783 Wenest thou] wenestow B.   789 An aunter yif] C ; Anauntergh if
784 worldlyche] worldlich B ;   A ; A Vanter yif B.
   wordlyche A ; werliche C.

790 Lyuen so for Godes loue in tyme of a wynter.'   *live thus*
    'Leue Peres,' quath y tho, 'y praie that thou me tell

        dear; then

    Whou y maie conne my Crede in Cristen beleue?'
f.327b 'Leue brother,' quath he, 'hold that y segge,   *mark; say*
    I will techen the the trewthe and tellen the the sothe:

CREDO

795 Leue thou on oure louerd God that all the werlde wroughte,

        believe; lord; created

    Holy heuen opon hey hollyche he fourmede,

        high; wholly; formed

    And is almighti him-self ouer all his werkes,
    And wrought as his will was the we[r]lde and the heuen;
    And on gentyl Jesu Crist engendred of him-seluen,

        noble; born

800 His own onlyche sonne Lord ouer all y-knowen,
    [That] was clenly conseued, clerlye in trewthe

        purely conceived

    Of the hey Holy Gost; this is the holy beleue;
    And of the mayden Marye man was he born,
    With-outen synnfull sede; this is fully the beleue.
805 With thorn y-crouned, crucified and on the crois dyede,
    And sythen his blissed body was in a ston byried,

        then; tomb; buried

    And descended a-doune to the derk helle,
    And fet oute our formfaderes and hy full feyn weren.

        fetched; forefathers; glad

    The thridde daye rediliche him-self ros fram deeth,

        third; readily; rose

810 And on a ston there he stod he st[e]igh vp to heuene, *ascended*
    And on his fader right hand redeliche he sitteth,
    That al-mighti God ouer all other whyghtes;

792 Whou] When B.
793 he] I C.
798 werlde] C; world B; welde A.
801 That] BC; It A.
802 the] thy B.

804 the] thy B.
810 steigh] C; stigh B; strigh A.
811 fader] faderes B.
812 whyghtes] whyght is B.

And is hereafter to komen Crist, all him-seluen,   *come*
To demen the quyke and the dede with-outen any doute.

                    living; dead

815 And in the heighe holly gost holly y beleue,
And generall holy chirche also hold this in thy mynde;

                    universal

And in the [sacrement] also that sothfast God on is,   *true* [c]
Fullich his fleche and his blod, that for vs dethe tholede.

                    suffered

And though this flaterynge freres wyln for her pride,   *will*
820 Disputen of this deyte as dotardes schulden,   *deity; fools*
The more the matere is moved the [masedere hy] worthen.

              discussed; more baffled

Lat the losels alone and leue you the trewthe,

            let; rascals; believe

For Crist seyde it is so, so mot it nede worthe; *must; needs be*
Therfore studye thou nought theron, ne stere thi wittes, *stir*
825 It is his blissed body, so bad he vs beleuen.
Thise maystres of dyvinitie many, als y trowe,
Folwen nought fully the feith as fele of the lewede.

              many; unlettered

Whough may mannes wijt thorugh werk [of] him-selue,

                intelligence

f.328a Knowen Cristes pryuitie that all kynde passeth?

              secrets; nature
830 It mot ben a man of also mek an herte,   *meek*
That myghte with his good lijf that Holly Gost fongen;

              receive

And thanne nedeth him nought neuer for to studyen,
He mighte no maistre [ben] kald, for Crist it defended,

              forbade

Ne puten [no] pylion on his piled pate;

           priest's cap; bald head

817–18 *not in* C. *Five new lines
  interpolated.*
817 sacrement] B; sacremens A.
819 And though] Al though C.
820 this] Godes C; deyte] diet B.
821 masedere hy] BC; mose dere by
  A.

823–5] *not in* C.
826 Thise] For these C.
828 may] many B; of] BC; or A.
831 that] the BC.
833 ben] C; bene B; then A; it] that
  B.
834 no] BC; on A.

835 But prechen in parfite lijf and no pride vsen.
But all that euer I haue seyd soth it me semeth, *true*
And all that euer I haue writen is soth, as I trowe,
And for amending of thise men is most that I write;
God wold hy wolden ben war and werchen the better ! *aware*
840 But, for y am a lewed man paraunter y mighte
ignorant; perhaps
Passen par auenture and in som poynt erren,
overreach; by chance; err
Y will nought this matere maistrely auowen;
masterly; authorise
But yif ich haue myssaid mercy ich aske, *mis-said*
And praie all maner men this matere amende,
845 Iche a word by him-self and all, yif it nedeth.
God of his grete myghte and his good grace
Saue all freres that faithfully lybben,
And alle tho that ben fals fayre hem amende, *graciously*
And yiue hem wijt and good will swiche dedes to werche
give; wit
850 That thei maie wy[nn]en the lif that euer schal lesten ! AMEN.
attain; last

840 paraunter] paraventure B.   aduenture C.
841 par auenture] paventur B; par   850 wynnen] BC; wymien A.

RICHARD THE REDELESS

RICHARD THE REDELESS

Passus One

f.107b And as I passid in my preiere ther prestis were at messe,
                    proceeded; *devotions*
   In a blessid borugh that Bristow is named,   *borough*; *Bristol*
   In a temple of the trinite the toune euen amyddis,
                        in the centre
   That Cristis Chirche is cleped amonge the comune peple,
                        called
  5 Sodeynly ther sourdid selcouthe thingis,   *arose*; *marvellous*
   A grett wondir to wyse men as it well myghth,   *great*
   And dowtes for to deme for drede comynge after.
                  fears; *judge*; *dread*
   So sore were the sawis of bothe two sidis :
                  bitter; *speeches* [c]
   Of Richard that regned so riche and so noble,
 10 That wyle he werrid be west on the wilde Yrisshe,
                  made war; *Irish*
   Henrri was entrid on the est half,   *east*
   Whom all the londe loued in lengthe and in brede,   *breadth*
   And rosse with him rapely to rightyn his wronge,
                 rose; *quickly*
   For he shullde hem serue of the same after.
 15 Thus tales me troblid for they trewe where,   *troubled*; *were*
   And amarride my mynde rith moche and my wittis eke :
                confused; *right*; *also*
   For it passid my parceit and my preifis also,
            exceeded; *perception*; *evidence* [c]
   How so wondirffull werkis wolde haue an ende.

But in sothe whan they sembled some dede repeute,

assembled ; consider

20 As knowyn is in cumpas of Cristen londis,   *extent ; lands*

That rewthe was, if reson ne had reffourmed   *pity*

The mysscheff and the mysserule that men tho in endurid.

mischief ; misrule

I had pete of his passion that prince was of Walis,

pity ; suffering

And eke oure crouned kynge till Crist woll no lenger;

will ; longer

25 And as a [liage] to his [lord] though I lite hade,   *subject ; little*

All myn hoole herte was his while he in helthe regnid.

whole [c]

And for I [wuste] not witterly what shulde fall,

knew ; certainly ; happen

Whedir God wolde [g]eue him grace sone to amende,

whether ; give

To be oure gioure a[g]eyn or graunte it another,   *ruler*

30 This made me to muse many tyme and ofte,

For to written him a writte to wissen him better,

book ; advise

And to meuve him of mysserewle his mynde to reffresshe

move ; misrule

For to [preie] the prynce that paradise made,   *beseech*

To fullfill him with feith and fortune aboue,   *fill*

35 And not to grucchen a grott ageine Godis sonde,

grumble ; jot ; decree

But mekely to suffre what-so him sente were.

f.108a And yif him list to loke a leef other tweyne   *please ; look ; two*

That made is to mende him of his myssededis,   *reform*

And to kepe him in confforte in Crist and nought ellis,

40 I wolde be gladde that his gost myghte glade be my wordis,

spirit ; be gladdened

And grame if it greued him be God that me boughte !

displeased ; grieved

(Ther nys no gouernour on the grounde ne sholde gye him the
    better);   *is no ; rule*

---

25 liage to his lord] lord to his liage.   29 ageyn] ayeyn.
27 wuste] woste.   33 preie] preise.
28 geue] yeue.

And euery Cristen kyng that ony [croune] bereth,   *bears*
So he were lerned on the langage my lyff durst I wedde,
        dare; pledge
45 Yif he waite well the wordis and so werche ther-after,
        consider
For all is tresour of the trinite that turneth men to gode.
And as my body and my beste oute to be my liegis,   *beast*
So rithffully be reson my rede shuld also,
        rightfully; reason; advice
For to conceill, and I couthe, my kyng and the lordis;
        counsel; could
50 And ther-for I [fondyd] with all my fyue wyttis   *endeavoured*
To traueile on this tretis to teche men ther-after   *labour*
To be war of wylffulnesse lest wondris arise.   *aware*
And if it happe to youre honde beholde the book onys,   *once*
And redeth on him redely rewis an hundrid,
        straightaway; lines
55 And if ye sauere sum-dell se it forth ouere,
        enjoy; some part; look over the rest
For reson is no repreff be the rode of Chester !   *reproof; cross*
And if ye fynde fables or foly ther amonge,   *falsehoods*
Or ony fantasie yffeyned that no frute is in,   *fiction; feigned*
Lete youre conceill corette it and clerkis to-gedyr,
        wisdom; correct
60 And amende that ys amysse and make it more better :
For yit it is secrette and so it shall lenger,
Tyll wyser wittis han waytid it ouere,   *minds; perused*
That it be lore laweffull and lusty to here.   *teaching; pleasing*
For witterly, my will is that it well liked   *truly*
65 You and all youris and yonge men leueste,   *best*
To be-nyme hem her noyes that neweth hem ofte.
        rid; troubles; renew
For and they mvse thereon to the myddwardis,   *muse; middle*
They shall fele fawtis foure score and odde,   *discover; faults*
That yough[th]e weneth alwey that it be witt euere.
        youth; imagines; wisdom
70 And though that elde opyn it other-while amonge,
        old age; sometimes

43 croune] grounde.   69 youghthe] youghe.
50 fondyd] fordyd.

And poure on it preuyly and preue it well after,
pore; *privately*; *prove*

And constrewe ich clause with the culorum,
construe; *meaning* [c]

It shulde not apeire hem a peere a prynce though he were,
harm; *jot* [c]

Ne harme nother hurte the hyghest of the rewme,   *realm*

f.108b But to holde him in hele and helpe all his frendis.   *health*

And if ony word write be that wrothe make myghte   *angry*

My souereyne, that suget I shulde to be,   *subject*

I put me in his power and preie him, of grace,

To take the entent of my trouthe that thoughte non ylle,
intention [c]; *loyalty*

80 For to wrath no wyght be my wyll neuere,   *man*; *desire*

As my soule be saff from synne at myn ende.   *safe*

The story is of non estate that stryuen with her lustus,
class; *struggle against*

But tho that folwyn her flessh and here frelle thoughtis;
those; *follow*; *frail*

So if my conceyll be clere I can saie no more,

85 But ho be greued in his gost gouerne him better,
aggrieved; *spirit*

And blame not the berne that the book made,   *man*

But the wickyd will and the werkis after.

Now, Richard the redeles reweth on you-self,
advice-less; *take pity*

That lawelesse leddyn youre lyf and youre peple bothe;   *led*

90 For thoru the wyles and wronge and wast in youre tyme,
wiles; *waste*

Ye were lyghtlich ylyfte from that you leef thoughte,
easily removed; *dear*

And from youre willffull werkis youre will was chaungid,

And rafte was youre riott and rest, for youre daiez   *removed*

Weren wikkid thoru youre cursid conceill; youre karis weren
newed,   *cares*

95 And coueitise hath crasid youre croune for euere !
covetousness; *crashed*

Radix omnium malorum cupiditas.

Of alegeaunce now lerneth a lesson other tweyne,
allegiance; *two*

Wher-by it standith and stablithe moste —   *endures*; *stands firm*

By dr[e]de, or be dyntis or domes vntrewe,
dread ; blows ; judgments

Or by creaunce of coyne for castes of gile,
credit ; money ; tricks ; guile

100 By pillynge of youre peple youre prynces to plese,   *robbing*

Or that youre wylle were wroughte though wisdom it nolde;
carried ; would not wish

Or be tallage of youre townnes without ony werre,
taxation ; war

By rewthles routus that ryffled euere,   *pitiless mobs ; pillaged*

Be preysinge of polaxis that no pete hadde,
appraising ; pole-axes

105 Or be dette for thi dees deme as thou fyndist, –   *debt ; dice*

Or be ledinge of lawe with loue well ytemprid.
conducting ; favour [c]

Though this be derklich endited for a dull nolle,
darkly ; indicted [c] *; head*

Miche nede is it not to mwse ther-on,   *much ; muse*

For as mad as I am though I litill kunne,   *know*

f.109a I cowde it discryue in a fewe wordys.   *describe*

For legiance without loue litill thinge availith.

But graceles gostis gylours of hem-self,   *people ; self-deceivers*

That neuere had harnesse ne hayle-schouris,
harness ; hail-showers [c]

But walwed in her willis forweyned in here youthe,
wallowed ; pampered

115 They sawe no manere sighth saff solas and ese,
sight ; except ; comfort ; leisure

And cowde no mysse amende whan mysscheff was vp,

But sorwed for her lustus of lordsch[i]pe they hadde,
grieved ; pleasures

And neuere for her trespas oo tere wolde they lete.
crime[c] *; one ; tear*

Ye come to youre kyngdom er ye youre-self knewe,

120 Crouned with a croune that kyng vnder heuene

Mighte not a better haue boughte, as I trowe;   *believe*

So full was it filled with vertuous stones,   *of virtue* [c]

With perlis of pris to punnysshe the wrongis,   *pearls ; price*

With rubies rede the right for to deme,   *red ; justice*

98 drede] dride.   117 lordschipe] lordschpe.

125 With gemmes and juellis joyned to-gedir,	*jewels*
And pees amonge the peple for peyne of thi lawis.	*penalty*
It was full goodeliche ygraue with gold al aboughte;	
	engraved
The braunchis aboue boren grett charge;	*carried; weight*
With diamauntis derue y-douutid of all	*strong; feared*
130 That wroute ony wrake within or withoute;	
	committed; offence
With lewte and loue yloke to thi peeris,	*loyalty; locked*
And sapheris swete that soughte all wrongis,	*sapphires*
Ypouudride wyth pete ther it [pounced] be oughte,	
	powdered; pity; embossed
And traylid with trouthe and treste al aboute;	
	decorated in a trailing pattern; tressed
135 For ony cristen kynge a croune well ymakyd.	
But where this croune bicome a clerk were that wuste;	*knew*
But so as I can declare it I thenke,	
And nempne no name; but tho that nest were,	
	name; those; nearest
Full preuyly they pluckud thy power awey,	*secretly*
140 And reden with realte youre rewme thoru-oute,	*rode; royalty*
And as tyrauntis, of tiliers token what hem liste,	
	tillers; took; pleased
And paide hem on her pannes when her penyes lacked.	
	heads; pennies
For non of youre peple durste pleyne of here wrongis,	
	complain [c]
For drede of youre dukys and of here double harmes.	
f.109b Men myghtten as well haue hun[t]yd an hare with a tabre	
	tabour
As aske ony mendis for that thei mysdede,	*compensation* [c]
Or of ony of her men though men wulde plete,	*plead at law*
For all was felawis and felawschepe that ye with ferde,	*dealt*
And no soule persone to punnyshe the wrongis;	*single*
150 And that maddid thi men as thei nede muste.	
For wo, they ne wuste to whom for to pleyne.	*knew*
For, as it is said by elderne dawis,	*olden sayings*
'Ther gromes and the goodmen beth all eliche grette,	
	servants; rich; equally

133 pounced *omitted*.   *145* huntyd] hunyd.

Woll wo beth the wones and all that woneth ther-in !'
        woe betide ; dwellings ; live
155 They ladde you with loue that youre lawe dradde *led ; feared*
To deme youre dukys myssdedis so derue thei were   *strong*
Thus was youre croune crasid till he was cast newe, *crashed*
Thoru partninge of youre powere to youre paragals.
         sharing ; peers
Thus lacchide they with laughinge and lourid longe after,
        grasped ; glowered
160 But frist sawe they it not ne youre-self nother ;
For all was wisliche ywroughte as youre witte demed,
       wisely conducted
And no fauutis yffounde till fortune aperid. *faults ; worsened*
But had youre croune be kepte that comons it wiste,
        protected ; knew
Ther nadde morder ne mysscheff be amonge the grette.
       would not have been
165 Thus youre cautell to the comoune hath combred you all,
       deceit ; ruined
That, but if God helpe youre heruest is ynne. *harvest ; in*
Wytteth it not youre conceill but wyte[t]h it more youre-self,
        blame
The fortune that fallyn is to feitheles peple ;
And wayte well my wordis and wrappe hem to-gedir,
       consider ; weigh them up
170 And constrwe [clerlie] the clause in thin herte *construe*
Of maters that I thenke to meve for the best *move* [c]
For kyngis and [kayseris] comynge here-after. *rulers*
Whane ye were sette in youre se as a sir aughte, *see*
Ther carpinge comynliche of conceill arisith,
       discussion ; commonly
175 The cheuyteyns cheef that ye chesse euere,
       leaders ; chief ; chose
Weren all to yonge of yeris to yeme swyche a rewme ;
       govern ; such ; realm
Other hobbis ye hadden of Hurlewaynis kynne,
       yobs ; Hurlewain's kin [c]
10a Reffusynge the reule of realles kynde. *royalty's nature*

167 wyteth] wyteh.   172 kayseris] kayseceris.
170 clerlie] clergie.

And whane youre conceill i-knewe ye come so at ones
180 For to leue on her lore and be led be hem,   *believe*; *teaching*
For drede that they had of demynge ther-after,
And for curinge of hem-self cried on you euere,   *protection*
For to hente hele of her owen greues,   *obtain*; *redress*; *griefs*
More than for wurschepe that they to you owed.
185 They made you to leue that regne ye ne myghte   *believe*
Withoute busshinge adoun of all youre best frendis,

                                             striking [c]

Be a fals colour her caris to wayve,

                       excuse [c]; *troubles*; *remove*
And to holde hem in hele if it happe myghte.   *health*
For trostith rith treuly and in no tale better,

                                       trust; *account* [c]

190 All that they moued or mynged in that mater   *spoke*
Was to be sure of hem-self and siris to ben y-callid;   *lords*
For that was all her werchinge in worde and in dede.
But had ye do duly and as a duke oughte,   *done*; *rightfully*
The frist that you formed to that fals dede,   *informed*
195 He shulde haue hadde hongynge on hie on the forckis,

                                                   gallows

Though youre brother y-born had be the same.
Than wolde other boynardis haue ben abasshyd   *rascals*
To haue meved you to ony maters that myssheff had ben ynne.
But for ye cleued to knavis in this cas I avowe,   *case*; *declare*
200 That boldid thi burnes to belde vppon sorowe,

                             encouraged; *men*; *build*
And stirid you stouttely till ye stombled all.

                                       spurred; *vigorously*

Passus Two

But moche now me merueilith and well may I in sothe,

                                                   marvel

Of youre large leuerey to leodis aboughte,   *livery*; *men*
That ye so goodliche [g]af but if gile letted,

                             gave; *guile*; *prevented*
As hertis y-heedyd and hornyd of kynde,

                             harts; *antlered*; *nature*

3 gaf] yaf.

5 So ryff as they ronne youre rewme thoru-oute,   *rife ; ran*
 That non at youre nede youre name wolde nempne *name*
 In fersnesse ne in foltheed but faste fle awayward;
           fierceness ; folly ; fled
 And some stode astonyed and stared for drede, *astonished*
 For eye of the egle that oure helpe brouute.   *brought*
10 And also in sothe the seson was paste   *over*
 For hertis yheedid so hy and so noble
 To make ony myrthe for mowtynge that nyghed.
          moulting ; approached
110b That bawtid youre bestis of here bolde chere;
          bolted ; appearance
 They seuerid and sondrid for somere hem faylid,
        separated ; scattered ; summer
15 And flowen in-to forest and feldis aboughte,   *fields*
 All the hoole herde that helde so [to]-gedir;   *whole*
 But yet they had hornes half yere after.
 Now liste me to lerne ho me lere coude, *whoever ; teach*
 What kynnes conceyll that the kyng had,   *kind of*
20 Or meued him most to merke his liegis, *moved ; mark* [c]
 Or serue hem with signes that swarmed so thikke
 Thoru-oute his lond in lengthe and in brede, *breadth*
 That ho-so had hobblid thoru holtes and tounes, *woods*
 Or y-passid the patthis ther the prynce dwellyd,
25 [Of] hertis or hyndis on hassellis brestis, *retainers'*
 Or some lordis leuere that the lawe stried, *livery ; destroyed*
 He shulde haue y-mette mo than ynowe. *more than enough*
 For they acombrede the contre and many curse seruid,
         harassed ; district [c]
 And carped to the comounes with the kyngys mouthe, *spoke*
30 Or with the lordis ther they belefte were,   *lived*
 That no renke shulde rise reson to schewe.   *man*
 They plucked the plomayle from the pore skynnes, *plumage*
 And schewed her signes for men shulde drede
 To axe ony mendis for her mys-dedis. *ask ; compensation*
35 Thus leuerez ouere-loked youre liegis ichonne;
         despised ; each one
 For tho that had hertis on hie on her brestis,
 For the more partie I may well avowe,

16 togedir] gedir.   25 Of] Or.

They bare hem the bolder for her gay broches,
And busshid with her brestis and bare adoun the pouere
                    pushed [c]; *bore down on*; *poor*
40 Liages that loued you the lesse for her yuell dedis.   *evil*
So, trouthe to telle as toune-men said,
For on that ye merkyd ye myssed ten schore
                   one; *marked*; *score* [c]
Of homeliche hertis that the harme hente.   *received*
Thane was it foly in feith, as me thynketh,
45 To sette siluer in signes that of nought serued.
I not what you eylid but if it ese were: *afflicted*; *leisure*
For frist at youre anoyntynge alle were youre owen,
f.111a Bothe hertis and hyndis and helde of non other;
No lede of youre lond but as a liege aughte,   *man*
50 Tyl ye, of youre dulnesse deseueraunce made   *separation*
Thoru youre side signes that shente all the browet,
                crooked; *spoilt*; *broth*
And cast adoun the crokk the colys amyd.
                pot; *amongst the coals*
Omne regnum in se diuisum desolabitur: luoe xi c.
Yit am I lewde and litill good schewe   *unlettered*
To coueyte knowliche of kyngis wittis,   *covet*
55 Or wilne to witte [what] was the mevynge
                wish; *know*; *motivation*
That [ladde] you to lykynge youre liegis to merke,
That loued you full lelly or leuerez beg[a]nne,   *loyally*
And as redy to ride or renne at youre heste   *command*
As wyghte myghte wilne wonnynge vppon erthe,
                man; *wish*; *living*
60 Tyll leuerez hem lette and lordyns wrongis,
                hindered; *of lords*
As youre-self fonde well whane fortune you [fayled].   *found*
For whan ye list to lene to youre owen lymes,   *lean*; *limbs*
They were so feble and feynte for faughte of youre lawe,
                default

And so [wankel] and wayke wexe in the hammes
              unsteady; *weak*; *grown*; *thighs*

55 what] how.
56 ladde] *omitted*.
57 beganne] begynne.

61 fayled] folwyd.
64 wankel] feble.

65 That they had no myghte to amende youre greues
   Ne to bere byrthen youre banere to helpe.   *burden ; banner*
   But it longith to no liegeman his lord to anoye   *belongs*
   Nother in werk ne in word but if his witt faile.
   'No, redely,' quod Reson 'that reule I alowe :
                                          advisedly ; uphold [c]
70 Displese not thi demer in dede ne in wordis
   But if the liste for to lede thi lyf in dissese.   *wish*
   But yif God haue grauntyd the grace for to knowe
   Ony manere mysscheff that myghtte be amendyd,
   Schewe that to thi souereyne to schelde him from harmes;
                                                    shield
75 For and he be blessid the better the betydyth
                                 it will be better for you
   In tyme for to telle him for thi trewe herte.'
   Now for to telle trouthe thus than me thynketh,
   That no manere meyntenour shulde merkis bere,
                                    maintainer ; badges
   Ne haue lordis leuere the lawe to apeire,   *damage*
80 Neither bragger ne boster for no breme wordis.
                                          boaster ; fierce
   But ho-so had kunnynge and conscience bothe   *learning* ; [c]
.111b To stonde vnstombled and stronge in his wittis,   *resolute*
   Lele in his leuynge leuyd be his owen,
                       loyal ; faith ; living on his own income
   That no manere mede shulde make him wrye,
                              kind of payment ; swerve
85 For to trien a trouthe be-twynne two sidis,   *judge a dispute* [c]
   And lette for no lordschep the lawe to susteyne
                                    hinder ; maintenance
   Whane the pore pleyned that put wer to wrongis,
   And I were of conceill by Crist that me boughte,
   He shuld haue a signe and sum-what be yere
                                    badge ; something
90 For to kepe his contre in quiete and in reste.   *district*
   This were a good grounde so me God helpe !   *basis* [c]
   And a trewe tente to take and to yeue,   *intention ; give*
   [For] ony lord of this [londe] that leuerez vsith.

93 For] and; londe] lonnde.

But how the gayes han y-gon God wotte the sothe
                              nobles; behaved; knows
95 Amonge myghtffull men alle these many yeris,   *powerful*
And whedir the grounde of [g]ifte were good other ille,
                              whether; or
Trouthe hathe determyned the tente to the ende,   *decided* [c]
And reson hath rehersid the resceyte of all.
                              recited; receipt [c]
Yit I trowe youre entente at the frist tyme   *believe; intention*
100 Was, as I wene, yif I well thenke in multitude of peple,
                              imagine
That ye were the more myghtier for the many signes
That ye and youre seruantis aboughte so thikke sowid;
And that they were more tristi and trewer than other   *trusty*
To loue you for the leuere that legaunce stroied;   *destroyed*
105 Or ellis for a skylle that skathed youre-self,   *reason; injured*
That comounes of contre in costis aboute
Sholde knowe by hir quentise that the kyng loued hem   *device*
For her priuy prynte passinge another.
                              secret; device; exceeding
Yif that was youre purpos it passith my wittis   *purpose*
110 To deme discrecion of youre well-doynge.
                              judge discretion [c]
Thus were ye disceyued thoru youre duble hertis,
                              deceived; [c]
That neuere weren to truste so God saue my soule !
But had the good greehonde be not agreued,
                              greyhound; aggrieved
But cherischid as a cheffeteyne and cheff of youre lese
                              leader; chief; leash [c]
115 Ye hadde had hertis ynowe at youre wille to go and to ride.
                              enough
And also in serteyne the sothe for to telle,   *certain*
f.112a I wondir not hyly though heed-dere thou failid;
                              highly; head-deer
For litill on youre lyf the list for to rewe   *you pleased; pity*
On rascaile that rorid with ribbis so lene,
                              young deer; cried out
120 For faughte of her fode that flateris stelen,   *lack; food*

96 gifte] yifte.

And euere with here wylis and wast ofte they hem anoyed,

      wiles; *waste*

That pouerte hem prickid full preuyliche to pleyne,

     urged; *secretly*; *complain*

But where, they ne wyste ne ho it wolde amende.   *who*

Thus ye derid hem vnduly with droppis of anger,

     afflicted; *unlawfully*

125 And stonyed hem with stormes that stynted neuere,   *stopped*

But plucked and pulled hem anon to the skynnes,

That the fresinge frost freted to here hertis.   *freezing*; *gnawed*

So whanne youre hauntelere-dere where all ytakyn,

     antlered-deer [c]

Was non of the rasskayle aredy full growe   *ready*

130 To bere ony breme heed as a best aughte,   *bear*; *strong*

So wyntris wedir hem wessh with the snowis,   *washed*

With many derke mystis that maddid her eyne.   *vexed*; *eyes*

For well mowe ye wyttyn and so mowe we all,   *must*; *know*

That harde is the somer ther sonne schyneth neuere.

     summer; *sun*

135 Ye fostrid and fodid a fewe of the best,   *fostered*; *fed*

And leyde on hem lordschipe a leyne vppon other,

     laid; *layer* [c]

And bereued the raskall that rith wolde thei hadde,

     dispossessed; *justice*

And knewe not the caris ne cursis that walkyd;   *troubles*

But mesure is a meri mene though men moche yerne:

     moderation; *mean*; *yearn*

Deus exaudit clamorum pauperum, et iudicat causam eorum;

  David in psalmis

140 Thus [rend] be the rotus youre raskall endurid,

     torn; *roots*; *survived*

Tyll the blessid bredd brodid his wyngis   *bird*; *extended*

To couere hem from colde as his kynde wolde.   *cover*; *nature*

Rith as the hous-hennes vppon londe hacchen   *hatch*

And cherichen her chekonys fro chele of the wynter,

     cherish; *chickens*; *chill*

145 Ryth so the hende Egle the Eyere of hem all,

     noble; *Mother* [c]

Hasteth him in heruest to houyn his bryddis,

     brood over; *birds*

140 rend] *omitted.*

And besieth him besely to breden hem feedrin,
cover them with his feathers

Tyll her fre fedris be fulliche [vn]-y-pynned,
noble; feathers; loosened

That they haue wynge at her wyll to wonne vppon hille;
dwell

150 For venym on the valeye hadde foule with hem fare,
venom; badly; dealt

Tyll trouthe the triacle telde somme her sothes.
healing remedy; told

Thus baterid this bred on busshes aboughte,   *battered; bird*

f.112b And gaderid gomes on grene ther as they walkyd
gathered; men; grass

That all the schroff and schroup sondrid from other.
refuse; rubbish; separated

155 He mellid so the matall with the hand-molde
beat; metal; hand-crusher [c]

That [they] lost lemes the leuest that they had.   *limbs; dearest*

Thus foulyd this faukyn on fyldis aboughte,
hunted; falcon; fields

And caughte of the kuyttis a cartffull at ones,   *kites*

That rentis and robis with raveyn euere laughte.
revenues; ravine [c]; took

160 Yit was not the fawcon full fed at his likynge,
For it cam him not of kynde kytes to loue.   *became; nature*
Then bated he boldeliche as a brid wolde,   *flew down*
To plewme on his pray the pol fro the nekk;   *pull; prey; head*
But the blernyed boynard that his bagg stall,
blear-eyed; rogue; stole

165 Where purraile-is pulter was pynnyd full ofte,
rags of the poor; fastened

Made the fawcon to floter and flussh for anger   *flutter*
That the boy [nadd] be bounde that the bagge kept.
had not been

But sone ther-after in a schorte tyme,
As fortune folwith ech fode till his ende,   *man*
170 This lorell that [ladde] this loby awey   *rascal; bundle of rags*
Ouere frithe and forde for his fals dedis,   *wood; stream*

---

148 vn] *omitted.*   167 nadd] hadd.
156 they] *omitted.*   170 ladde] hadde.

Lyghte on the lordschepe that to the brid longid,
lighted ; *belonged*
And was felliche ylaughte and luggid full ylle,
cruelly ; *captured* ; *baited*
And broughte to the brydd and his blames rehersid   *crimes*
175 Preuyly at the parlement amonge all the peple.
Thus hawkyd this egle and houed aboue,   *hovered*
That, as God wolde that gouerneth all thingis,
Ther nas kyte ne krowe that kareyne hantid,
crow ; *carrion* ; *fed on*
That he ne with his lynage he louyd full sone.
kindred ; *humiliated*
180 For wher-so they ferde be fryth or be wones,
went ; *wood* ; *dwellings*
Was non of hem all that him hide myghth,
But cam with him a reclayme fro costis aboughte,
at the call [c]
And fell with her fetheris flat vppon the erthe,
As madde of her mynde and mercy be-soughte.
185 They myghte not aschonne the sorowe they had serued,
escape
So lymed leues were leyde all aboughte,
And panteris preuyliche pight vppon the grounde,
snares ; *secretly* ; *set*
.113a With grennes of good heere that God him-self made
traps ; *hair*
That where-so they walkid they waltrid dounwardis.
stumbled
190 And euere houed the egle on hie on the skyes,
And kenned clerliche as his kynde axith,
perceived ; *clearly* ; *requires*
Alle the preuy poyntis that the pies wroughth.
secret moves ; *magpies* ; *made*

Passus Three

Now leue we this beu brid till I restore,
leave ; *beautiful* ; *return* [c]
For mater that my mynde is meved in now,   *moved*
That whi the hie hertis her hele so mysside,   *health* ; *failed*

That pasture axid rith to here pure wombis,   *grew* ; *right* ; *very* ; *stomachs*
5 I wolle schewe as I sawe till I se better;   *show*
And if I walke out of the wey I wolle me repente.   *will*
Now herkeneth, hende men how that me thynkyth,
                                                              courteous
Sauynge souereynes and sages avise   *knowledgeable* ; *teach*
That the moste myscheff vppon molde on   *earth*
10 Is demed the dede ydo ayeins kynde.   *committed* ; *nature*
Yit clereth this clause no thinge my wittis,
With-out more mater what it mene wolde.
I mene of the hertis [of] hautesse of yeris,   *stateliness*
That pasture prikkyth and her preuy age,   *spurs* ; *vigorous*
15 Whan they han hoblid on the holte an hundred of yeris,
                                                    hobbled ; *wood*
That they feblen in fleissh in felle and in bones.
                                              grow feeble ; *skin*
Her kynde is to keuere if they cacche myghth   *regain health*
Adders that [h]armen alle hende bestis;   *noble*
Thoru busschis and bromes this beste, of his kynde,
                                          bushes ; *brooms* ; *beast*
20 Secheth and sercheth tho schrewed worms,
                                          seeks ; *cursed snakes*
That steleth on the stedis to stynge hem to deth;
                                          steal upon ; *steeds*
And whanne it happeth the herte to hente the edder,
                                          chances ; *seize* ; *adder*
He putyth him to peyne as his pray asketh,
                                    inflicts pain ; *hunting requires*
And fedith him on the venym his felle to anewe,
                                          venom ; *skin* ; *renew*
25 To leue at more lykynge a longe tyme after.   *pleasure*
This is [clerlie] hir hynde coltis [not] to greue,
                                          clearly ; *colts* ; *harm*
Ne to hurlle with haras ne hors well atamed,
                                      contend ; *stallions* ; *tamed*
Ne to stryue with swan though it sholle werre,
                                          strive ; *should* ; *war*

13 of] that.   26 clerlie] clergie; not] *omitted*.
18 harmen] armen.

Ne to bayten on the bere ne bynde him nother,
       set dogs on ; *bear* ; *neither*
30 Ne to wilne to woo that were hem ny sibbe,
       destruction ; *closely related*
Ne to liste for to loke that her alie bledde; *desire to see* ; *allies*
This was ayeins kynde as clerkis me tolde; *against nature*
Propter ingratitudinem liber homo reuocatur in seruit[u]tem ut in
  stimulo compunccionis, et in lege ciuili.
.113b And ther-for the hertis here hele so myssid, *recovery*
And myghte nat passe the poynte of her prime age. *condition*
35 Now constrew ho-so kunne I can saie no more,
       whoever is able
But fare I wolle to the fowle that I beffore tolde. *go* ; *bird*
Off all billid breddis that the bough spareth,
       beaked ; *birds* ; *shuns*
The propirte of partriche to preise me lustith,
       nature ; *partridge*
That in the somer seson whanne sittinge nyeth,
       incubation ; *approaches*
40 That ich foule with his fere folwith his kynde,
This brid be a bank bildith his nest,
And heipeth his [eiren] and hetith hem after.
       heaps up ; *eggs* ; *warms*
And whane the dame hath ydo that to the dede longith,
       done ; *pertains*
And hopith for to hacche or heruest begynne, *hatch*
45 Thane cometh ther a congion with a grey cote, *rascal*
As not of his nolle as he the nest made, *head*
Another proud partriche and precyth to the nest,
       forces his way
And preuylich pirith till the dame passe,
       secretly ; *watches* ; *goes*
And sesith on hir [sete] with hir soft plumes,
       occupies ; [c] ; *seat*
50 And houeth the eyren that the hue laide,
       broods over ; *eggs* ; *hen* [c]
And with hir corps keuereth hem till that they kenne,
       body ; *covers* ; *hatch*

32a seruitutem] seruititem.   49 sete] cete.
42 eiren] heires.

And fostrith and fodith till fedris schewe,
nurses; feeds; feathers
And cotis of kynde hem keuere all aboughte.   *coats; cover*
But as sone as they styffe and that they steppe kunne,
grow strong
55 Than cometh and crieth hir owen kynde dame,
natural mother [c]
And they folwith the vois at the frist note,   *voice*
And leueth the lurker that hem er ladde,
skulker; previously led
For the schrewe schrapid to selde for her wombis,
wretch; scratched for food; seldom
That her lendys were lene and leued with hunger.
loins; lean; weakened
60 But then the dewe dame dineth hem swythe,
rightful mother; immediately
And fostrith hem forthe till they fle kunne.   *fly*
'What is this to mene, man?' maiste thou axe,   *might; ask*
'For it is derklich endited for a dull panne;
darkly; composed; head
Wherffore I wilne yif it thi will were,   *wish to know*
65 The partriche propurtes by whom that thou menest?'
partridge's properties
A! Hicke Heuyheed! hard is thi nolle
Hick Heavyhead [c]; *head*
To cacche ony kunynge but cautell bigynne!
learning; unless; deceit
Herdist thou not with eeris how that I er tellde   *ears; earlier*
f.114a How the egle in the est entrid his owen,   *east; own* [c]
70 And cried and clepid after his owen kynde briddis,   *called* [c]
That weren anoyed in his nest and norished full ille,   *afflicted*
And well ny yworewid with a wronge leder?   *nearly destroyed*
But the nedy nestlingis whan they the note herde
Of the [hende] Egle the heyer of hem all,   *noble; superior*
75 Thei busked fro the busches and breris that hem noyed,
hastened; briars
And burnisched her beekis and bent to-him-wardis,
polished; turned
And folowid him fersly to fighte for the wrongis;   *fiercely*

74 hende] ende.

They bablid with her billis how thei bete were,	*beaten* [c]
And tenyd with twiggis two and twenty yeris.	*taxed* [c]

80 Thus lafte they the leder that hem wrong ladde, *left*
  And [tyned] no twynte but tolled her cornes,
  restrained; nothing; taxed; grain
  And gaderid the grotes with gyle, as I trowe.
  gathered; money

  Than folwid they her fre fader as good feith wolde, *noble*
  That he hem fede shulde and fostre forther,

85 And bringe hem out of bondage that they were broughth inne.
  Thanne sighed the swymmers for the swan failid,
  And folwid this faucon thoru feldus and tounes,
  falcon; fields

  With many faire [fowle] though they feynte were, *faint*
  And heuy for the hirte that the hors hadde. *sad; hurt*

90 Yit they ferkyd hem forth as faste as they myghte, *went*
  To haue the Egles helpe of harme that they hadde;
  For he was heed of hem all and hieste of kynde *head; highest*
  To kepe the croune as cronecle tellith. *chronicle*
  He blythid the beere and his [bond] braste,
  gladdened; bear; burst

95 And lete him go at large to lepe where he wolde. *at liberty*
  But tho all the berlingis brast out at ones, *bear-cubs*
  As fayne [as] the foule that flieth on the skyes *glad*
  That Bosse was vnbounde and brouute to his owen. *Boss* [c]
  They gaderid hem to-gedir on a grette roughte, *rout*

100 To helpe the heeris that had many wrongis; *heirs*
  They gaglide forth on the grene for they greued were
  cackled; aggrieved
  That her frendis were falle thoru felons castis.
  fallen; criminals' tricks
  They mornyd for the morthir of manffull knyghtis,
  murder; mature

114b That many a styff storme with-stode for the comunes;
  heavy

105 [They] monside the marchall for his myssedede,
  cursed; Earl Marshal [c]

81 tyned] tymed.	*97* as] was.
88 fowle] foole.	*105* They] The.
94 bond] brond.	

That euell [coude] his craft whan he [cloyed] the stede.

ill ; knew ; lamed

And euere as they folwide this faucon aboute,   *followed*

At iche mevinge fotte [venyaunce] they asked

each ; moving ; foot

On all that assentid to that synffull dede

110 Arere now to Richard and reste here awhile,   *turn back*

For a preuy poynt that persith my wittis,   *hidden ; pierces*

Of fauutis I fynde that frist dede engendre   *faults ; did*

Cursidnesse and combraunce amonge the yonge lordis,

oppressiveness

And the wikkid werchinge that walmed in her daies,

surged up

115 And yit woll here-after but wisdom it lette;   *prevent*

That were a lord of lond that lawe hathe in honde,

That to lyghtliche leueth or lewte apere,

believes ; before ; loyalty

The tale of a trifflour in turmentours wede,

trifler;tormentor's dress [c]

That neuere reed good rewle ne resons bookis !

120 For ben they rayed arith they recchith no forther,

costumed fittingly ; care

But studieth all in strouutynge and stireth amys euere;

strutting ; behave

For all his witte in his wede ys wrappid for sothe,

More than in mater to amende the peple that ben mys-led

For I say for my-self and schewe, as me thyn[k]ith,

125 That ho is riall of his ray that light reede him folwith;

royal ; dress ; advice

Yit swiche fresshe foodis beth feet in-to chambris,

people ; fetched

And for her dignesse endauntid of dullisshe nollis,

display ; cherished

And, if thou well waite of no wight ellis;   *consider ; person*

Qui mollibus vestiuntur in domibus regum sunt : in euangelio

Than waite mo wayes how the while turneth   *more ; wheel*

130 With g[uy]leris, joyffull for here gery jaces;

deceivers ; changing ribbons

---

106 coude] conude; cloyed] clothed.   *124* thynkith] thynthith.
108 venyaunce] venyanunce.   -   *130* guyleris] gyuleris.

And for her wedis so wyde wise beth y-holde.   *are considered*
They casteth hem to creaunce the courte for to plese,   *in credit*
And hopen to be hied in hast, yif they myghthe,   *promoted*
Thoru swiche stif strouutynge that stroyeth the rewme;
                                        stubborn; destroys
135 But here wey is all wronge ther wisdom is ynned.   *lodged*
[For] they lepith als lygh[t]ly at the long goynge,
                                        in the long run
    Out of the domes carte as he that throff neuere,
                                        tumbril; prospered
115a For they kepeth no coyne that cometh to here hondis,   *save*
    But chaunchyth it for cheynes that in chepe hangith,
                                        exchange; Cheapside [c]
140 And settith all her siluer in [seintis] and hornes,
                                        belts [c]; *drinking horns*
    And for-doth the coyne and many other craftis,
                                        weaken the currency
    And maketh the pep[l]e for pens-lac in pointe for to wepe;
                                        lack of money
    And yit they beth ytake forth and her tale leued,
                                        cultivated; believed
    And for her newe nysete nexte to the lordis,   *foolishness*
145 Now, be the lawe of Lydfford in londe [and] in water   [c]
    Thilke lewde ladde oughte euyll to thryue,   *stupid; thrive*
    That hongith on his hippis more than he wynneth,
                                        hangs; earns
    And doughteth no dette so dukis hem preise,   *fears*
    But beggith and borwith of burgeis in tounes
                                        borrows; burgesses
150 Furris of foyne and other felle-whare,
                                        beach-marten; fur-ware
    And not the better of a bene though they boru euere.
                                        bean; borrow
    And, but if the slevis slide on the erthe,
    Thei woll be wroth as the wynde and warie hem that it made;
                                        angry; curse
    And [but] yif it were elbowis adoun to the helis   *heels*

136 For] But; lyghtly] lyghly.   145 and] ne.
140 seintis] se + 4 *minims* + tis.   154 but] *omitted*.
142 peple] pephe.

155 Or passinge the knee it was not acounted.   *esteemed* [c]
     And if Pernell preisid the pleytis bihynde,   *Pernell* [c]; *pleats*
     The costis were acountid paye whan he myght.   *reckoned*
     The leesinge so likyde ladies and other   *diamond-patterning*
     That they ioied of the jette and gyside hem ther-vnder;
                                                          fashion; *disguised*
160 And if Felice fonde ony [faute] thenne of the makynge,
                                                              Felice; *fault*
     Yt was y-sent sone to shape of the newe.   *be re-done*
     But now ther is a gyse the queyntest of all.   *most extraordinary*
     A wondir coriouse crafte y-come now late,   *skill*
     That men clepith kerving the clothe all to pecis,
                                                     call; *carving*; *pieces*
165 That seuene goode sowers sixe wekes after   *seven*
     Moun not sett the seemes ne sewe hem ayeyn.   *might*
     But ther is a pr[o]ffit in that pride that I preise euere,
     For thei for the pesinge paieth pens ten duble   *joining together*
     That the clothe costened the craft is so dere.
170 Now if I sothe shall saie and shonne side tales,   *shun*; *oblique*
     Ther is as moche good witte in swyche gomes nollis,
                                                             such men's heads
     As thou shuldist mete of a myst fro morwe tyll euen.
                                                          measure; *morning*
f.115b Yit blame I no burne to be, as him oughte   *man*
     In comliche clothinge as his statt axith;
                                              suitable; *estate*; *requires*
175 But to ledyn her lust all here lyff-daies   *follow*; *pleasure*
     In quentise of clothinge for to queme sir Pride,
                                                            elegance; *please*
     And euere-more stroutynge and no store kepe,
                                                          strutting; *capital*
     And iche day a newe deuyse; it dullith my wittis   *outfit*
     That ony lord of a lond shulde leue swiche thingis,   *believe*
180 Or clepe to his conceill swiche manere cotis,
                                                     call; *council*; *coats*
     That loueth more her lustis than the lore of oure Lord.
     And if a lord his leuere lyste for to yeue,   *pleases*; *give*
     Ther may no gome for goodnesse gette ther-of but lite
                                                               man; *little*

_____

160 faute] ffaunte.   *167* proffit] prffith.

For curtesie, for comlynesse ne for his kynde herte,
185 But rather for his rancour and rennynge ouere peple,
                                             anger; *running*
For braggynge and for bostynge and beringe vppon oilles,
                                             boasting; *flattery* [c]
For cursidnes of conscience and comynge to the assises.   [c]
This makyth men mysdo more than oughte ellis,
                                             anything else
And to stroute and to stare and stryue ayeyn vertu.
                                             strut; *strive*; *against*
190 So [clerlie], the cause comsith in grette,   *nobility*
Of all manere mysscheff that men here vsyn.   *use*
For wolde they blame the burnes that broughte newe gysis,
                                             men; *fashions*
And dryue out the dagges and all the Duche cotis,
                                             dagged cloth [c]; *German*
And sette hem aside and sc[h]ort of hem telle,
                                             speak slightingly
195 And lete hem pleye in the porche and presse non ynnere,
                                             enter no further
Ne no proude peniles with his peynte sleve;
                                             penniless; *painted*
And eke repreue robbers and riffleris of peple,
                                             reproach; *plunderers*
Flateris and fals men that no feith vseth,
And alle deabolik deoris dispise hem ichone,
                                             diabolical; *each one*
200 And coile out the knyghtys that knowe well hem-self,   *select*
That were sad of her sawis and suffre well [couude],
                                             measured; *speech*
And had traueilid in her tyme and temprid hem-self,
                                             worked; *moderated*
And cherliche cheriche hem as cheff in the halle   *cheerfully*
For to ordeyne officeris and all other thyngis,   *appoint*
205 Men shuld wete in a while that the world wolde amende;
                                             know
So vertue wolde flowe whan vicis were ebbid.
f.116a But now to the mater that I be-fore meved

190 clerlie] clergie.   *201* couude] conude.
194 schort] scorte.

Of the gomes so gay that grace hadde affendid,   *offended*
And how stille that steddeffaste stode amonge this reccheles
  peple,   *giddy*
210 That had awilled his wyll as wisdom him taughte: *tempered*
For he drough him to an herne at the halle ende,
                                                drew ; corner
Well homelich yhelid in an holsum gyse,
                                          covered ; wholesome
Not ouerelonge, but ordeyned in the olde schappe,
                                          fashioned ; style
With grette browis y-bente and a berde eke,
                                  eyebrows ; arched ; beard
215 And y-wounde in his wedis as the wedir axith;
                                        wrapped up ; requires
He wondrid in his wittis as he [well] myghthe,
That the hie houusinge herborowe ne myghte   *high ; harbour*
Halfdell the household but hales hem helped;
                                    half of ; unless ; tents
But for crafte that he [couude] caste thenne or be-thenke,
                                        strategy ; devise
220 He myghte not wonne in the wones for witt that he vsid;
                                          dwell ; lodgings
But, arouutyd for his ray and rebuked ofte,
                                        reproached ; dress
He had leue of the lord and of ladies alle   *permission*
For his good gouernaunce to go or he drank.   *before*
Ther was non of tho mene that they ne merueilid moche
                                        company ; much
225 How he cam to the courte and was not y-knowe;
But als sone as they wiste that Witt was his name,
                                          knew ; Wisdom
And that the kyng knewe him not ne non of his knyghtis,
He was halowid and y-huntid and y-hotte trusse,
                                hollered at ; sent packing
And his dwellinge ydemed a bowe-drawte from hem,
                                        judged ; bow-shot
230 And ich man y-charchid to schoppe at his croune,
                                        ordered ; chop ; head

216 well] will.   219 couude] counude.

Yif he nyhed hem ony nerer than they had him nempned.
                                    came ; nearer ; named
The portir with his pikis tho put him vttere,
                                    piked shoes [c] ; *outside*
And warned him the wickett while the wacche durid :
                                    denied ; gate ; revelry
'Lete sle him !' quod the sleues that slode vppon the erthe,
                                    Let's kill ; slid
235 And alle the berdles burnes bayed on him euere,
                                    beardless men
And schorned him, for his slaueyn was of the olde schappe.
                                    coat

Thus Malaperte was myghtffull and maister of hous,
                                    Impudence ; powerful
And euere wandrid Wisdom without the gatis.   *outside*
'By him that wroughte this world !' quod Wisdom in wrath,
                                    made ; said
240 'But yif ye woll sumtyme I walke in amonge you,
                                    unless ; wish
f.116b I shall forbede you burnesse the best on this erthe   *men*
That is, gouernance of gettinge and grace that him follwith;
                                    good management ; revenue
For these two trewly twynned yet neuere.'   *separated*
And so it fell on hem, in feith for faughtis that they vsid,
                                    faults ; practised
245 That her grace was agoo for grucchinge chere,
                                    gone ; grudging ; behaviour
For the wrong that they wroughte to Wisdom affore.
For tristith, als trewly as tyllinge us helpeth,   *trust ; tilling*
That iche rewme vndir roff of the reyne-bowe
                                    realm ; roof ; rainbow
Sholde stable and stonde be these thre degres :
                                    stand firm ; ranks
250 By gouerna[un]ce of grete and of good age;
                                    nobility ; mature
By styffnesse and strengthe of steeris well y-yokyd,
                                    boldness ; oxen ; yoked
That beth myghthffull men of the mydill age;   *powerful*

250 gouernaunce] gouernanmce.

And be laboreris of lond that lyfflode ne fayle.

labourers; *sustenance*

Thanne wolde [right dome] reule if reson where amongis us,

justice [c]

255 That ich leode lokide what longid to his age,

man; *looked to*; *belonged*

And neuere for to passe more oo poynt forther,   *one*

To vsurpe the seruice that to sages bilongith   *usurp*

To be-come conselleris er they kunne rede,

counsellors; *know how*

In schenshepe of souereynes and shame at the last.   *disgrace*

260 For it fallith as well to fodis of xxiiij yeris,

pertains; *people*; *24*

Or yonge men of yistirday to yeue good redis,   *give*; *advice*

As becometh a kow to hoppe in a cage!

It is not vnknowen to kunnynge leodis,   *knowledgeable people*

That rewlers of rewmes around all the erthe

265 Were not yffoundid at the frist tyme   *first*

To leue al at likynge and lust of the world,   *live*

But to laboure on the lawe as lewde men on plowes,

unlettered; *ploughs*

And to merke meyntenourz with maces ichonne,

strike; *maintainers*; *each one*

And to strie strouters that sterede ayeine rithis,

destroy; *strutters*; *acted*; *justice*

270 And alle the myssedoers that they myghte fynde,   *criminals*

To put hem in preson a peere though he were;   *prison*

And [not] to rewle as reremys and rest on the daies,   *bats*; *dais*

And spende of the spicerie more than it nedid,   *spice-store*

Bothe wexe and wyn in wast all aboughte,   *wax*; *wine*; *waste*

275 With deyntes y-doublid and daunsinge to pipis,

dainties; *dancing*

In myrthe with moppis myrrours of synne.   *fools*

Yit forbede I no burne to be blithe sum while: *cheerful*

f.117a But all thinge hath tyme for to tempre glees: *temper*: *festivities*

For caste all the [countis] that the kyng holdith,

reckon; *accounts*

280 And loke how these lordis loggen hem-self,   *lodge*

---

254 right dome] *omitted.*
272 not] *omitted.*   279 countis] counntis.

And euere shall thou fynde as fer as thou walkiste,   *far*
[That] wisdom and ouere-wacche wonneth fer asundre.
        late hours; *dwell*; *apart*
But whane the gouernaunce goth thus with tho the hous gie
  shulde,   *guide*
And letith lyghte of the lawe and lesse of the peple
        thinks lightly
285 And herkeneth all to honour and to ese eke,   *attends*; *leisure*
And that ich wyght with his witt waite on him euere,
To do hem reuerence aright though the rigge brest,
        back; *break*
This warmnesse in welth with wy vppon erthe
        prosperity; *man*
Myghte not longe dure as doctourz us tellith.   *last*
290 For ho-so thus leued his lyff to the ende,   *whosoever*; *lived*
Euere wrappid in welle and with no wo mette,
        prosperity; *misfortune*
Myghte seie that he sawe that seie was neuere,   *say*; *seen*
That heuene-[gates] were vnhonge out of the hookis,
And were boun at his bidding yif it be myghte.   *ready*
295 But clerkis kne[w] I non yete that so couude rede
In bokis y-bounde though ye broughte alle
That ony wy welldith wonnynge vppon erthe;
        man; *subsists*; *living*
For in well and in woo the werld euere turneth;
Yit ther is kew-kaw though he come late.   *reversal* [c]
300 [But yit ther is a foule faute that I fynde ofte :]   *fault*
A new thing that noyeth nedy men and other,   *annoys*
Whanne realles remeueth and rideth thoru tounes,
        courts; *travel*
And carieth ouere contre ther comunes dwelleth,   *journey*
To preson the pillourz that ouere the pore renneth;
        imprison; *robbers*
305 For that were euene in her weye if they well ride;   *right*
They prien affter presentis or pleyntis ben yclepid,
        seek; *before*; *pleadings*
And abateth all the billis of tho that noughth bringith;
        cancel [c]; *nothing*

282 That] What.   295 knew] kne.
293 gates] *omitted.*   300] *follows* 305.

And ho-so grucche or grone ayeins her grette willes,

grumble; *groan*

May lese her lyff lyghtly and no lesse weddis.

lose; *pledges* [c]

310 Thus is the lawe louyd thoru myghhty lordis willys,

humiliated

That meyneteyne myssdoers more than other peple.

For mayntenance many day well more is the reuthe!

Hath y-had mo men at mete and at melis   *more*; *food*; *meals*

f..117b Than ony cristen kynge that he knewe euere;

315 For, as reson and rith rehersid to me ones,   *justice*

Tho ben men of this molde that most harme worchen.

those are; *world*

For chyders of Chester where chose many daies   *were chosen*

To ben of conceill for causis that in the court hangid,

causes; *were impending* [c]

And pledid pipoudris alle manere pleyntis.   *piepowders* [c]

320 They cared for no coyffes that men of court vsyn,   *coifs*; *use*

But meved many maters that man neuer thoughte,

And feyned falshed till they a fyne had,   *settlement* [c]

And knewe no manere cause as comunes tolde.

Thei had non other signe to schewe the lawe

325 But a preuy pallette her pannes to kepe,

strong; *headpiece*; *heads*

To hille here lewde heed in stede of an houe.

cover; *unlearned*; *coif*

They constrewed quarellis to quenche the peple,

contrived quarrels [c]

And pletid with pollaxis and poyntis of swerdis,

pleaded; *pole-axes* [c]

And at the dome-yeuynge drowe out the bladis,

judgment-giving; *drew*

330 And lente men leuere of her longe battis.   *gave*; *cudgels* [c]

They lacked alle vertues that a iuge shulde haue;

For, er a tale were ytolde they wolde trie the harmes,

damages[c]

Withoute ony answere but ho his lyf hatid.

answer [c]; *unless anyone*

And ho-so pleyned to the prince that pees shulde kepe,

appealed

335 Of these mystirmen medlers of wrongis,   *tradesmen* [c]

He was lygh[t]liche ylaughte and y-luggyd of many,
easily seized ; *baited*
And y-mummyd on the mouthe and manaced to the deth.
silenced ; *menaced*
They leid on thi leigis, Richard lasshis ynow, *laid* ; *subjects*
And drede neuere a dele the dome of the lawe. *part*
340 Ther nas rial of the rewme that hem durste rebuke, *noble*
Ne juge ne justice that jewis durste hem deme
dared pass sentence [c]
For oute that thei toke or trespassid to the peple. *anything*
This was a wondir world ho-so well lokyd,
That gromes ouere-grewe so many grette maistris;
lads ; *outstripped*
345 For this was the rewle in this rewme while they here regnyd.
rule ; *realm*
Though I satte seuenenyght and slepte full selde,
for a week ; *seldom*
[They wrought] many mo wrongis than I write couude;
committed ; *crimes*
For selde were the ser[gi]auntis soughte for to plete, *plead*
f.118a Or ony prentise of courte preied of his wittis,
apprentice ; *sought*
350 The while the degonys domes weren so endauntid.
bumpkin's judgments ; *esteemed*
Tille oure sire in his see aboue the vijne sterris
lord ; *seven* ; *stars*
Sawe the many mysscheuys that these men dede,
mischiefs ; *did*
And no mendis ymade but menteyne[d] euere *reparation* [c]
Of him that was hiest y-holde for to kepe *held* ; *protect*
355 His liegis in lawe and so her loue gette.
He sente for his seruantis that sembled many, *assembled*
Of baronys and baccheleris with many brighth helmes,
bachelor-knights
With the comunes [of] contres they cam all at ones;
And as a duke doughty in dedis of armes, *awesome* ; *feats*
360 In full reall aray he rood vppon hem euere, *royal* ; *rode*

336 lyghtliche] lyghliche.
347 They wrought] Of.
348 sergiauntis] serigauntis.

353 menteyned] menteyne it.
358 of] the.

Tyll Degon and Dobyn that mennys doris brastyn,
> [c] *doors* ; *break down*

And were y-dubbid of a duke for her while domes,
> *dubbed* ; *former*

And awakyd [fro] wecchis and wast that they vsid,
> *revelries* ; *extravagance*

And for her breme blastis buffettis henten.
> *fierce* ; *blows* ; *received*

365 Than gan it to calme and clere all aboughte,

That iche man myghte ho-so mynde hadde,   *each*

Se, be the sonne that so brighte schewed,   *see*

The mone at the mydday meve, and the sterris,   *move* ; *stars*

Folwinge felouns for her false dedis,   *criminals*

370 Devourours of vetaile that foughten er thei paide.   *provisions*

Passus Four

For where was euere ony cristen kynge that ye euere knewe,

That helde swiche an household be the halfdelle   *by half*

As Richard in this rewme thoru myserule of other,

That alle his fynys for faughtis ne his fee-fermes,
> *faults* ; *fee farms* [c]

5 Ne for-feyturis fele that felle in his daies,   *forfeitures* ; *many*

Ne the nownagis that newed him euere,
> *nounages* [c] ; *renewed*

As Marche and [Moubray] and many mo other,   [c] ; *more*

Ne alle the issues of court that to the kyng longid,
> [c] ; *belonged*

Ne sellynge, that sowkid siluer with faste,   *sucked*

10 Ne alle the prophete of the lond that the prince owed,   *profit*

Whane the countis were caste with the custum of wullus,
> *accounts* ; *reckoned* ; *wools*

Myghte not areche ne his rent nother,   *suffice* ; *income*

To paie the pore peple that his puruyours toke,   *purveyors*

f.118b Withoute preiere at a parlement a poundage biside,
> *petition* ; *subsidy* [c]

15 And a fifteneth and a dyme eke,   *fifteenth* ; *tenth*

---

363 fro] for.   7 Moubray] mounbray.

And with all the custum of the clothe that cometh to fayres ?

> customs

And yet, ne had creaunce icome at the last ende,   *credit*

With the comunes curse that cleued on hem euere,   *cleaved*

They had be drawe to the deuyll for dette that they owed.

> drawn ; devil

20 And whanne the reot and the reeuell the rent thus passid,

> riot ; revelry

And no thing y-lafte but the bare baggis,   *left*

Then felle it afforse to fille hem ayeyne,   *it was necessary*

And feyned sum folie that failid hem neuere

> feigned ; madness

And cast it be colis with her conceill at euene,   *devised ; tricks*

25 To haue preuy parlement for [proffitt] of hem-self,   *secret*

And lete write writtis all in wex closid,   *wax ; enclosed*

For peeris and prelatis that thei apere shuld,   *appear*

And sente side sondis to schreuys aboughte,

> crooked mandates ; sheriffs

To chese swiche cheualleris as the charge wold,

> knights ; mandate wished

30 To schewe for the schire in company with the grete.   *represent*

And whanne it drowe to the day of the dede-doynge,

> drew ; action

That souereynes were semblid and the schire-knyghtis,

> assembled

Than, as her forme is frist they begynne to declare

> procedure ; first

The cause of her comynge and than the kyngis will.

35 Comliche a clerk than comsid the wordis,

> appropriately ; began

And prononcid the poyntis aperte to hem alle,   *openly*

And meved for mony more than for out ellis,   *anything else*

In glosinge of grette lest greyues arise.

> flattery ; nobility ; griefs

And whanne the tale was tolde anon to the ende,   *straight*

40 Amorwe thei must, affore mete mete to-gedir,

> tomorrow ; food ; meet [c]

The knyghtis of the comunete, and carpe of the maters,   *speak*

With citiseyns of shiris ysent for the same,

---

25 proffitt] propffitt.

To reherse the articlis and graunte all her askynge.
But yit for the manere to make men blynde,
45 Some argued ayein rith then a good while,   *right*
And said, 'We beth seruantis and sallere fongen,
                           salary ; receive
And ysent fro the shiris to shewe what hem greueth,
f.119a And to parle for her prophete and passe no ferthere,
                           speak ; profit
And to graunte of her gold to the grett wattis   *people*
50 By no manere wronge way but if werre were;   *unless ; war*
And if we ben fals to tho us here fyndyth,   *those ; fund*
Euyll be we worthy to welden oure hire.'
                    scarcely ; receive ; payment
Than satte summe as siphre doth in awgrym,
                       cipher ; arithmetic
That noteth a place and no thing availith;   *contributes*
55 And some had ysoupid with Symond ouere euen,
                     supped ; Simony [c]
And schewed for the shire and here schew lost ;
And somme were tituleris and to the kyng wente,   *tale-tellers*
And formed him of foos that good frendis weren,
                     informed ; foes
That bablid for the best and no blame serued   *spoke*
60 Of kynge ne conceyll ne of the comunes nother,
Ho-so toke good kepe to the culorum.
                 paid attention ; meaning
And somme slombrid and slepte and said but a lite;
                     slumbered
And somme mafflid with the mouth and nyst what they ment;
                 mumbled ; knew not
And somme had hire and helde ther-with euere,
                 payment ; adhered
65 And wolde no forther affoot for fer of her maistris;
                 a-foot ; fear
And some were so soleyne and sad of her wittis,   *limited ; dull*
That er they come to the clos acombrid they were,
                 conclusion ; confused
That thei the conclucion than constrewe ne couthe,
No burne of the benche of borowe nother ellis,
                 man ; borough
70 So blynde and so ballid and bare was the reson.   *bald*

And some were so fers at the frist come,   *fierce; coming*
That they bente on a bonet and bare a topte saile
                                fastened; canvas; topsail
Affor the wynde fresshely to make a good fare.   *journey*
Than lay the lordis alee with laste and with charge,
                                to leeward; cargo; burden
75 And bare aboughte the barge and blamed the maister,
                                turned around; ship
That knewe not the kynde cours that to the crafte longid,
                                natural course; skill
And warned him wisely of the wedir-side.   *wind-ward side*
Thanne the maste in the myddis at the monthe-ende,   *middle*
Bowid for brestynge and broughte hem to lond;
                                bent; breaking
80 For ne had thei striked a strake and sterid hem the better,
                                taken in a reef
And abated a bonet or the blast come,   *lowered; sail; storm*
They had be throwe ouere the borde backeward ichonne.
                                each one
f.119b And some were acombrid with the conceill be-fore,
                                encumbered
And wiste well y-now how it sholde ende,   *knew*
85 Or some of the semble shulde repente.
Some helde with the mo how it euere wente,   *majority*
And somme dede rith so and wolld go no forther.   *did; would*
Some parled as perte as prouyd well after,   *openly; proved*
And clappid more for the coyne that the kyng owe[d] hem
                                clamoured; money
90 Thanne for comfforte of the comyne that her cost paied,
                                community
And were be-hote hansell if they helpe wolde
                                promised reward [c]
To be seruyd sekirly of the same siluere.   *served assuredly*
And some dradde dukis and Do-well for-soke;
                                feared; abandoned

*   *   *   *   *   *   *   *

89 owed] owen.   93] *rest of the page blank.*

MUM AND THE SOTHSEGGER

MUM AND THE SOTHSEGGER

f.1a Hovgh the coroune moste be kept fro couetous peuple

protected ; *covetous*

Al hoole in his hande and at his heeste eke,

whole ; *bidding* ; *also*

That euery knotte of the coroune close with other,   *interlock*

And not departid for prayer ne profit of [grete],

divided ; *favour* ; *nobility*

5 Leste vncunnyng [comyn] caste vp the halter

unlearned ; *commonality* ; *throw off*

And crie on your cunseil for coigne that ye lacke,

council ; *coin*

For thay shal smaicche of the smoke and smerte thereafter

taste ; *smart*

Whenne collectours comen to caicche what thay habben.

take ; *have*

And though your tresorier be trewe and tymbre not to high,

treasurer ; *loyal* ; *build*

10 Hit wil be nere the worse atte wyke-is ende;   *week's*

For two yere a tresorier twenty wyntre aftre

May lyue a lord-is life, as leued men tellen.   *unlettered*

Now your chanchellier that chief is to chaste the peuple

chancellor ; *correct*

With conscience of your cunseil that the coroune kepith,

15 And alle the scribes and clercz that to the court longen,

belong ?

Bothe iustice and iuges y-ioyned and other,

judges ; *appointed* [c]

Sergeantz that seruen for soulde atte barre,   *serve* ; *payment*

---

4 grete] other.   5 comyn] come yn and.

And the prentys of court, prisist of alle,
                               apprentices ; most precious
Loke ye reeche [not] of the riche and rewe on the poure
                               ensure ; care ; take pity
20 That for faute of your fees fallen in thaire pleyntes;
                               lack ; fail ; lawsuits
Haue pitie on the penylees and thaire pleynte harkeneth,
And hire thaym as hertly as though ye hure had,
                               hear ; sincerely ; payment
For the loue of hym that your life weldeth;   *rules*
And graunteth [thaym] for God-is sake and with a good chiere
                               cheer
25 The writing of writtz and the waxe eke;   [c]
And thay wil loue you for the lawe as liege men aughte,
                               subjects

More thenne for mayntenance that any man vseth,
Or for any frounting for faute of the coigne.
                               violence ; lack of money
Now ye haue y-herde of the haselle names   *retainers'*
30 Of officiers withynne and without eke,   *outside*
But yit of alle the burnes the beste is behinde
                               men ; still to come
Forto serue a souurayn in somer and in wintre,   *lord*
And most nedeful at eue and at morowe eke,   *morning*
And a profitable page for princes or for ducz
                               household officer ; dukes
35 Or for any lay lord, lettrid or elles,
That litel is y-take fourth or his tale lyeued;
                               advanced ; believed
And yf ye willeth to wite what the wight hatte,
                               know ; man ; is called
Hit is a sothe-sigger that seilde is y-seye
                               truthteller ; seldom ; seen
To be cherisshid of chief in chambre or in halle,
40 But for his rathe reasons is rebukid ofte,   *earnest ; arguments*
And yf he fable to ferre, the foote he goeth vndre.
                               speak [c] ; *far ; dismissed*
[T]here is no clerc with the king that clothid hym ones,

19 not] *omitted.*   42–6] *margin is torn.*
24 thaym] hym.

[B]ut clothid hym at cristmasse and al the yere after. [c]
[S]aunder the seruiselees shuld be his name,

Saunder the Serviceless

45 [For] he abidith in no household half a yere to th'ende
[But the] lord and the lady been loeth of his wordes,

averse to

f.1b And the meyny and he mowe not accorde, *retinue; agree*
But al to-teereth his toppe for his trewe tales.

tears out; hair; pleadings [c]

He can not speke in termes ne in tyme nother [c]; *neither*
50 But bablith fourth bustusely as barn vn-y-lerid;

boisterously; untaught child

But euer he hitteth on the heed of the nayle-is ende, *head*
That the pure poynt pricketh on the sothe
Til the foule flessh vomy for attre. *vomit; poison*
Thenne is this freke a-frountid for his feithful tale,

man; rebuked

55 And y-[ferked] vndre foote while falsenes goeth aboute

driven

With cautelle and with coigne forto caste deceiptz

tricks; contrive

Hough trouthe might be trauerssid and tournid of the weye.

contradicted [c]; *turned*

Thenne fareth fals fourth and flatereth atte beste *goes*
And lightly is y-lyved withoute long tale, *believed*
60 And euery gome of hym glad, so glorieusely he loketh *man*
Thorough the peynt[ur]e of the preynte that in the palme
  hongeth. *paint; print*
Right as the cockil cometh fourth ere the corne ripe,

cockle; grain

With a cleer colour, as cristal hit semeth,
Among the grayne that is grene and not ful growe,
65 Right so fareth falsnesse that so freysh loketh *fresh*
Thorough the colour of the crosse that many men incumbreth.

[c]

But whenne trouthe aftre tornement hath tyme forto kerne

reversal; form seed

And to growe fro the grovnde anone to th'ende,
Thenne fadeth the flour of the fals cockil.

55 y-ferked] y-filled. 61 peynture] preynte.

70 That lykne I to lyers, for atte the long goyng,
                                liken ; *in the long run*

Of euery segge-is sawe the sothe wol be knowe.
                                 man's speech ; *truth*

Yit is hit not my cunseil to clatre what me knoweth
                                 counsel ; *chatter*

In sclaundre ne scathe ne scorne of thy brother,
                                 slander ; *harm* [c]

For though thy tale be trewe thyn tente might be noyous,
                                 intention [c] ; *harmful*

75 For whiche thou mighte be harmed and haue that thou serues.
                                           [c]

For go to the gospel that grovnd is of lore,   *basis* ; *doctrine*
And there shal thou see thyself, yf thou can rede,
Whethir I wisse the wel wisely or elles.   *guide*
He seith that thou shuldes the synne of thy brother
80 Telle hym by tyme and til hymsilf oon,   *to* ; *alone*
Yn ful wil to amende hym of his mysse-deedes.
Si peccauerit in te frater tuus corrige etc.
And yf he chargeth not thy charite but chideth the agaynes,
                                 regards not [c]

Yit leue hym not so lightly though he lovre oones,
                     abandon ; *easily* ; *glower* ; *once*

But funde hym to freyne efte of the newe,
                        try ; *examine* [c] ; *again*

85 And haue wittenes the with that thou wel knowes,
And spare not to speke, spede yf thou mowe,
                                 prosper ; *may* [c]

And he that moost is of might thy mede shal quite
                    greatest ; *power* ; *reward* ; *pay*

For suche [soeth] sawes that sounen into good,
                      true ; *sayings* ; *resound*

And of a reasonable man rewarde to haue.
90 For whenne thy tente and thy tale been temprid in oone,
                           intention ; *harmonised*

And menys no malice to man that thou spekys,
                           you mean ; *speak*

But forto mende hym mukely of his misse-deedes,
                           amend ; *meekly*

88 soeth] omitted.

Sory for his synne and his shrewed taicches,   *cursed; vices*

f.2a And the burne be y-blessid and balys cunne eschewe

   man; know how to avoid trouble

95 And thrifty and towarde, thou shal thanke gete.   *promising*

Were I a lord of a lande that lawe aughte gouuerne,

Suche a siker seruant shuld haue robes,   *steadfast*

Though he seide euer sothe and seruyd of noon other.   *served*

But now wolde I wite of a wise burne,   *know; man*

100 What kynnes creature that me couthe telle   *kind*

Where to finde this freek, yf the king wolde   *man*

Haue hym in housholde as holsum were.   *wholesome*

'By Crist,' cothe a clerc that conceipte he had,

   said; clerk; understanding

'There is no wiseman, I wene, wolde be y-weddid   *think*

105 To suche a simple seruice, a-say where the liketh,

   try; it pleases you

For no maniere [mede] that thereto belongeth,

   manner; payment

Ne ferthryng ne frendship while flatryng helpeth.

   advancement

For alle the greet clercz that with the king lendith   *live*

Knoweth this as kindely as clerc doeth his bokes;   *naturally*

110 Hit is no siker seruice but for a somer saison,   *permanent*

But yf hit wer for a fool that wold not be ferthred.   *promoted*

He might sey sothe sum while among thaym

And shuld be holde fooly though hit feul after.'

   foolish; fell afterwards

But muche now I meruaille, and so mowen other,

   marvel; may

115 That oure corouned king is kepte fro tho ludes,   *those men*

Forto [saye] hym the sothe sum while among,

Hough he shuld grece the griefz er the woundz gunne festre

   anoint; hurts; before

And so to leede his life in loue of the royaulme.

For the poure peuple hath prece of thaym many   *multitude*

120 Forto telle thaym thaire toyes twyes a woke.

   trifles; twice a week

Et nunc reges intelligite erudimini qui iudicatis terram etc.

  David.

---

106 mede] soulde.   *116* saye] telle.

And any neighebourgh be nigh on eue or a morowe,   *near*
Hit wold not long be lefte, my life durste I wedde;   *pledge*
And that is grace and thaire good happe to gouuerne thaym
    better   *fortune*
And in welthe to be ware ere that woo falle.
                                        aware ; trouble happen

125 But the king ne his cunseil cunne not mete with thaym,
                                                        can ; meet

But cleerly the cause I knowe not for sothe
But dreede of the deeth dryveth thaym thens,   *unless ; fear*
Or elles looste of thaire likerous life vppon erthe.
                                        pleasure ; luxurious

Thus is the court accumbrid and knoweth not thaire happes;
                                        encumbered ; fortunes

130 Ne God neither goodman ne thaym-self nothir,
Til fortune for foolie falle atte laste,   *folly ; happen*
And al the world wondre on thaire wilde deedes.
But yf the king might knowe that the comune talketh
[H]ough grotz been y-gadrid and no grief amendid
                                        groats ; collected

135 [A]nd hough the lawe is y-lad whenne poure men pleyne,
                                        how ; manipulated

[I] bilieue loyally oure liege lord wolde
[Ha]ue pitie on his peuple for his owen profit
[A]d amende that were amysse into more ease.
[B]ut the cause why the king knoweth not the mischief
f.2b Is for faute of a fabuler that I bifore tolde of   *lack ; truthteller*
Forto telle hym the texte, and touche not the glose,   *gloss [c]*
How the worde walketh with oon and with other.   *one*
But whenne oure comely king came furst to londe,
Tho was eche burne bolde to bable what hym aylid
                                        then ; man ; speak ; afflicted

145 And to fable ferther of fautz and of wrongz,   *speak ; faults*
And romansid of the misse-reule that in the royaulme groved,
                                        spoke ; realm ; grew

And were behote high helpe, I herde hit myself
                                        promised ; redress
Y-cried at the crosse, and was the king-is wille   *proclaimed*

134–9] *Margin torn.*

Of custume [and] of coylaige the comunes shuld be easid.

customs; *taxation* [c]

150 But how the couenant is y-kepte I can not discryue,

promise; *held*; *describe*

For with the king-is cunseil I come but silde.   *seldom*

But piez with a papegeay parlid of oones,

magpies; *parrot*; *spoke* [c]; *once*

And were y-plumed and y-pullid and put into a cage.

feathered; *plucked*

Sith the briddes were y-bete the beke is vndre whinge

beaten; *wing*

155 But yf thay parle priuyly to thaire owen peeris.

unless; *secretly*; *lords*

But the king ne his cunseil may hit not knowe

What is the comune clamour ne the crye nother,   [c]

For there is no man of the meeyne, more nother lasse,   *retinue*

That wol wisse thaym any worde but yf his witte faille,   *advise*

160 Ne telle thaym the trouthe ne the texte nothir,

But shony forto shewe what the shire meneth,   *shuns*; *show* [c]

And beguile thaym with glose, so me God helpe,

And speke of thaire owen spede and spie no ferther,

profit; *look*

But euer kepe thaym cloos for caicching of wordes.

close; *overhearing*

165 And yf a burne bolde hym to bable the sothe

man; *brave himself*

And [mynne] hum of mischief that misse-reule asketh,

warn; *provokes*

He may lose his life and laugh here no more,

Or y-putte into prisone or y-pyned to deeth   *tortured*

Or y-[brent] or y-shent or sum sorowe haue,   *burnt*; *ruined*

170 That fro scorne other scathe scape shal he neure.

harm; *escape*

Thus is trouthe doune y-troode and tenyd ful ofte,

down-trodden; *harassed*

Y-bete and y-bounde in bourghes and in shires,

beaten; *imprisoned*; *boroughs*

And principaly of princes y-pyned thenne of other,   *than*

---

149 and] *omitted.*   169 brent] blent.
166 mynne] warne.

Y-[halowid] and y-huntid and y-hoote trusse,
     pursued with shouts; ordered packing
175 That he shoneth to be seye forto shewe his harmes,
           shuns; seen

But euer hideth his heede fro the hayl-stones,
And is ouer-woxe with wrong and wickid wedes, *overgrown*
And tenyd with tares and ill amisse temprid.
      strangled with tares; out of harmony
Yit wol he growe fro [greue] and his grayne bere, *grief*
180 And after sowe his seede whenne he seeth tyme.
For alle the gomes vndre God goyng vppon erthe *men*
Were neuer so slygh yit forto sle trouthe; *sly; slay*
Though thay batre hym with battz and bete on hym euer,
        batter; cudgels

Trouthe is so tough and loeth forto teere *loth; tear*
185 And so pryuy with the prince that paradis made *intimate*
f.3a That he hath graunt of his lyfe while God is in heuene, [c]
For though men brenne the borough there the burne loiggeth,
        burn; lives

Or elles hewe of the heede there he a hows had, *cut off*
Or do hym al the disease that men deuise cunne, *harm*
190 Yit wol he quyke agayne and quite alle his foes
       revive; pay back

And treede ouer the tares that ouer his toppe groued,
      tread; head; grew
And al wickid wede into waste tourne. *turn*
And therefore my cunseil (though the king knowe hit
And alle the lordz of this londe, right lite is my charge)
      small; responsibility

195 Ys to be at oone with trouthe and tarre hym nomore,
      one; vex

Leste he tucke at your tabart ere two yere been endid,
      tabard [c]

But ye suffre his seruant to be seye oones *unless; allow; seen*
Among you in the moneth (but yf ye more wil)
Forto saye you the sothe, though ye shame thenke. *think*
200 For hit wol sauere your mouthe swetely with-ynne short after
      savour

Whenne fortune you fleeth and falleth elles-where;

174 halowid] haulid.   179 greue] fro grayen.

And yf ye sauere on his sawe and serue thereafter   *speech*
And eke wirche by his worde, the whele wol tourne

             work ; wheel
And eke chaunge his cours of care and of sorowe,
205 And tourne into tidewel, terme of your lifes.   *good fortune* [c]
Now is Henry-is hovs holsumly y-made   *house ; wholesomely*
And a meritable meyny of the most greet,   *retinue ; noblest*
And next I haue y-named as nygh as I couthe,   *closely*
And the condicions declarid of alle,
210 Rehershing no rascaille ne riders aboute.   *rehearsing ; rabble*
But he hymsilf is souurayn, and so mote he longe,   *king ; may*
And the graciousist guyer goyng vppon erthe,   *ruler*
Witti and wise, worthy of deedes,
Y-kidde and y-knowe and cunnyng of werre,

           recognised ; known ; expert
215 Feers forto fighte, the felde euer kepith,

           fierce ; battlefield ; holds
And trusteth on the Trinite that trouthe shal hym helpe;
A doughtful doer in deedes of armes   *valiant ; performer*
And a comely knight y-come of the grettist,
Ful of al vertue that to a king longeth,   *belongs*
220 Of age and of al thing as hym best semeth.
But hit be wel in his dayes we mowe dreede aftre

           must ; dread
Lest feerelees falle withynne fewe yeres.   *marvels ; happen*
But God of his goodnes that gouuernith alle thingz   *governs*
Hym graunte of his grace to guye wel the peuple   *rule ; people*
225 And to reule this royaume in pees and in reste,   *realm*
And stable hit to stonde stille for oure dayes.   *make it firm*
But I dreed me sore, so me God helpe,
[L]este couetise of cunseil that knoweth not hymself

           covetousness ; council
([O]f sum and of certayn, I seye not of alle)
230 [Th]at of profitable pourpos putteth the king ofte,

           purpose ; deters
[Th]ere his witte and his wil wolde wirche to the beste –
f.3b Nomore of this matiere,' cothe Mum thenne   *matter ; said*
'For I meruaille of thy momeling more thenne thou wenys.

           mumbling ; think

228–31 MS is torn.

Saides [not] thou thyself, and sothe as me thoughte,
235 That thees sothe-siggers seruen noon thankes?
And thou knowes this by clergie, how cans thou the excuse
learning

That thou ne art nycier than a nunne nyne-folde tyme,
more foolish; times

Forto wite that thy wil thy witte shal passe?'
know; will; intelligence; exceed

I blussid for his bablyng and a-bode stille   *blushed; kept quiet*
240 And knytte there a knotte and construed no ferther;   [c]
But yit I thoughte ere he wente, and he wold abide,
wanted to stay

To haue a disputeson with hym and spie what he hatte.
see; was called

'I am Mum thy maister', cothe he 'in alle maniere places,
master

That [sittith] with souuerayns and seruyd with greete.
245 Thaire wille ne thaire wordes I withseye neuer,   *contradict*
But folowe thaym in thaire folie and fare muche the bettre,
folly

Easily for oyle, sire, and elles were I nyce.   *flattery* [c]; *foolish*
Thus leede I my life in luste of my herte,   *pleasure*
And for my wisedame and witte wone I with the beste;   *dwell*
250 While sergeantz the sechith to saise by the lappe
seek; seize [c]

For thy wilde wordes that maken wretthe ofte.   *cause anger*
Thow were better folowe me foure score wynter
Thenne be a soeth-sigger, so me God helpe,
Oon myle and nomore waye, I Mvm wol avowe.
twenty minutes [c]; *declare*

255 And therefore I rede, yf thou reste wilnest,
advise; peace; wish

Cumpaignye with no contra yn no kynnes wise,
keep company; contradiction; no way

But parle for thy profit and plaise more here-aftre.
speak; please

For there nys lord of this londe ne lady, I wene,   *is not; think*
Prince nether prelat ne peer of the royaulme,

---

234 not] *omitted.*   244 sittith] *fittith.*

260 Bachillier ne bourgoys ne no barne elles
　　　　　　　　　　　　　bachelor-knight; *burgess*; *man*
　　That yf thay wite what thou arte, that wil the desire
　　　　　　　　　　　　　　　　　know; *are*; *you*
　　Or coueite to [thy] cumpaignie while contra the foloweth'.
　　　　　　　　　　　　　desire; *contradiction*
　　'Now to this altercacion' cothe I, 'an answere behoueth;
　　　　　　　　　　　　　　is necessary [c]
　　For I fele by thy fabelyng thou art felle of werkes
　　　　　　　　　　　　　fiction-mongering; *wicked*
265 And right worldly wise of wordes and deedes,
　　And euer kepis the cloos for [casting] bihinde.
　　　　　　keep yourself close; *for fear of being left behind*
　　Thou wol not putte the in prees but profit be the more
　　　　　　　　　　　　　make a complaint [c]
　　To thy propre persone, thou passes not the bondes
　　　　　　　　　　　　　　　own; *bounds*
　　Forto gete any grucche for glaunsyng of boltes.
　　　　　　　　　　　　　ill-will; *shooting*; *arrows*
270 Thus me semeth that thou serues thy-self and no man elles,
　　And has housholde and hire to holde vp thy oyles,
　　　　　　　　　　　　　　　reward; *flatter*
　　And eke bouche of court for colte and for [cnaue];
　　　　　　　　　　　allowance of food; *horse*; *boy*
　　And [yit] thou suffris thy souurayn to shame hym-self
　　There thou mightes amende hym many tyme and ofte.
　　Facientis culpam habet, qui quod potest corrigere negligit
　　　　emendare in secretis etc.
275 Now suche a-nothir seruant, the same and noon other,
　　Mote dwelle with the deueil til Do Bette hym helpe.'
　　　　　　　　　　　　　must; *devil*; [c]
　　Thus after talkyng we twynned a-sundre　　*separated*
f.4a Bothe Mvm and I, and oure mote endid;　　*discussion*
　　But muche mervailled I, whenne Mvm was passid,　*had gone*
280 Of his opinion that he heulde euer,　　　*maintained*
　　And prouyd hit by profitable poyntz y-nowe
　　　　　　　　　　　　　proved [c]; *enough*
　　That better was a burne to abide stille　　*keep quiet*

---

262 thy] his.
266 casting] cafting.
272 cnaue] caue.
273 yit] yf.

Thanne the soeth to seye that sitteth in his herte,
Forto warne the wy that he with dwellith,   *man*
285 Or mynne hym of mischief that misse-rewle askith.
                              warn ; misrule ; provokes
And euer he concludid with colorable wordes   *fraudulent*
That who-so mellid muche more than hit nedeth   *spoke*
Shuld rather wynne weping watre thenne robes.
And cleerly Caton construeth the same,   *interprets*
290 And seyth soethly, I saw hit in youthe,
Nam nulli tacuisse nocet, nocet esse locutum
That of 'bable' cometh blame and of 'be stille' neuer,
                                        talk ; quiet

And a wise worldly worde, as me thenketh,
Of the whiche I was hevy and highly abawyd,
                              depressed ; very confused
And for the double doute as dul as an asse,   *difficulty* [c]
295 And troublid for the travers, and amisse temprid,
                              denial ; out of harmony
That I wente in a wyre a grete while after   *perplexity*
For woo I ne wiste who had the better   *woe ; knew*
Of Mvm and me, and musid faste,
Rehershyng the reasons of bothe two sides,
300 The pro and the contra as clergie askith.   *for and against*
But for witte that I wanne I wolde that he knewe;
                                    insight ; obtained
I was neuer the nyre, but as newe to begynne   *nearer*
As clerc is to construe that can not reede.   *explicate*
Thenne thoughte I on Sidrac and Salomon-is termes,   [c]
305 And Seneca the sage I soughte for the nones,   *then*
That whilom were the wisest wies vppon erthe   *once ; men*
Forto wise any wighte, what-so hym grieued.   *instruct*
I bablid on thoo bokes that thoo barnes made,
                              read aloud ; those men
And waitid on thaire wordes aswel as I couthe,   *studied*
310 But of the matiere of Mvm might I nought finde,
Ne no maniere nycete of the newe [iette],   *foolishness ; fashion*
But al homely vsage of the olde date,   *custom ; time*
How that [good] gouuernance gracieusely endith.   *ends*

311 iette] yette.   313 good] omitted.

But glymsyng on the glose, a general revle
                            glancing; universal rule
315 Of al maniere mischief I merkid and radde :   *noted; read*
    That who-so were in wire and wold be y-easid   *perplexity*
    Moste shewe the sore there the salue were.   *salve*
    Thenne was I wel ware what he wolde mene,   *aware; meant*
    That I shulde cunne of clergie to knowe the sothe,
                            learn; learning
320 Forto deme the doute that me so dul made.
                          adjudicate; question
    I was wilful of wil and wandrid aboute,
    Til I came to Cambrigge couthe I not stynte,   *could; stop*
    To Oxenford and Orleance and many other places *Orleans*
f.4b There the congregacion of clercz in scole   *school*
325 Were stablid to stonde in strengthe of bilieue.   *established*
    I moeued my matiere of Mvm, as ye knowe,   *moved*
    And of the soethe-sigger in fewe shorte wordes;
    To alle the vij sciences I shewed as I couthe   *seven* [c]
    And how we dwellid in dome [for] doute of the better.
                        judgment; doubt [c]
330 Sire Grumbald the grammier tho glowed for anger
                          grammar; then
    That he couthe not congruly knytte thaym to-gedre.
                       could; congruently
    Music and Mvm mighte not accorde,
    For thay been contrary of kynde, who-so canne spie.
                        nature; see
    Phisic diffied al [the] bothe sides,   *defied*
335 Bothe Mvm and me the soeth-siggre;
    He was accumbrid of oure cumpaignye, by Crist that me
       bought,   *vexed* [c]
    And as fayn of oure voiding as foul [of his make].
                glad; departure; bird; mate
    Astronomy-ys argumentz were alle of the skyes,
    He-is touche no twynte of terrene thinges.   *jot; earthly*
340 Rethoric-is reasons me luste not reherce,   *pleased*
    For he conceyued not the caas, I knewe by his wordes;
                        conceived; case

329 for] and.
334 the] y.   337 of his make] on the skyes.

But a subtile shophister with many sharpe wordes   *sophister* [c]
Sette [the] soeth-sigger as shorte as he couthe.
But he wolde melle with Mvm ner more ner lasse,
                         speak ; neither ; less
345 So chiding and chatering [as choghe was he euer].
                                chough

Ieometrie the ioynour iablid faste,
                  Geometry ; joiner ; gabbled
And caste many cumpas, as the crafte askith,
              set up ; compass ; skill ; requires
And laide leuel and lyne a-long by the squyre.
                 level ; line ; square [c]
But I was not the wiser by a Walsh note   *Welsh*
350 Of the matiere of Mvm that marrid me ofte,   *troubled*
And stoode al a-stonyed and starid for angre   *astonished*
That clergie couthe not my cares amende,   *could*
And was in pourpoos to passe fourth right in pure wreth.
                purpose ; go ; anger
But a semely sage that satte al a-bouue,
355 Y-chose to the chaire forto chaste fooles,   *chosen ; chastise*
Whom alle the vij. sciences seruyd at wille,
Bothe in werke and in worde weren at his heste,   *command*
And more bunne at his bede than boy til his maister.
              ready ; bidding ; to
He satte as a souurayn on a high siege.   *place*
360 A doctour of doutz by dere God he semyd,   *doubts*
For he had loked al that lay to the vij. artz;
             studied ; belonged to
He was as ful of philosophie and vertues bothe
As man vppon molde mighte perceyue.   *earth*
This comely clerc me called agaynes,
365 And cunseillid me so cleerly that I caughte ease,   *took relief*
And seide, 'soon, seest thou this semble of clercz,
              son ; assembly
How thay bisien thaym on thaire bokes and beten thaire wittz,
                          beat
And how thay loken on the levis the [letter] to knowe?   *look*

---

343 the] a.
345 as choghe was he euer] and   couche was he neuer.
                                  368 letter] better.

For whenne thay knowen the scripture thay construen no
   ferther   *interpret*

f.5a Forto soutille ne to siche no side-wayes.   *argue subtly; seek*
But as long as I haue lerned and lokid in bokes,
And alle the vij. sciences y-soughte to th'ende,
Yit knewe I neuer suche a caas, ne no clerc here,   *case*
As thou has y-moeued among vs alle.   *moved*

375 Hit is sum noyous nycete of the newe iette,
                       harmful; folly; fashion
For the texte truly telleth vs nomore
But how that goode gouuernance graciousely endith.
But and thou woldes be wise and wirche as I telle, *wish; work*
I wolde wisse the to wite where that thou shuldest
                       advise; know
380 Haue knowlaiche of thy caas cleere to thyn intent,
And thy cumberouse question quycly be assoilled.
                  vexing; relieved [c]
Now harke and holde and hye to th'ende.   *attend; continue*
Sum of this semble that thou sees here,   *some; assembly*
Whenne thay haue loked the lettre and the lyfez ouer   *leaves*
385 Of alle the vij. sciences or sum as thaym liketh,
Thay walken fourth in the worlde and wonen with lordes,
                           dwell
And with a couetous croke Saynt Nicholas thay throwen,
              covetous; crook; abandon
And trauaillen nomore on the texte, but tournen to the glose,
                       turn; gloss
And putten thaym to practike and plaisance of wordes.
                    deceits; pleasance
390 But thay cunne deme thy doute, by dere God in heuene,
I can not knowe of thy caas who couthe elles.'   *otherwise*
Thenne ferkid I to freres, alle the foure ordres,   *went; friars*
There the fundament of feith and felnesse of workes
                foundation; [c]; *wickedness*
Hath y-dwellid many day, no doute, as thay telle.
395 I frayned thaym faire to fele of thaire wittes,
          examined; courteously; sound out
And moeuyd my matiere of Mvm, as ye knowe,   *moved*
And of the soeth-sigger in fewe sho[r]te wordes.

397 shorte] shotte.

To euery couple I construed my caas for the nones,
Til the cloistre and the quyre were so accorded

quire; in agreement

400 To yeue Mvm the maistrie withoute mo wordes,

give; mastery

And shewid me exemples, the sothest vppon erthe,
Nad Mvm be a more frende to making of thaire houses
Thenne the sothe-sigger, so God shuld thaym helpe,
Hit had be vnhelid half a yere after.

unroofed

405 Now ne were thre skiles and scantly the ferthe,

reasons [c] ; *barely; fourth*

I wolde loue as litel thaire life and thaire deedes
As man vppon molde, til Amendes me prayed.

earth

The furst is a faire poynt forto wynne heuene,

point [c]

Whenne thay stirid a statute in strengthe of bilieue

enacted

410 That no preste shuld preche saue seely poure freres.

priest; holy

But this [deede] dide thay not, I do you to wite,

have you know

For no maniere mede that mighte thaym befalle,

reward

Ne forto gete the more good – God wote the sothe,

wealth [c]

But for good herte that thay haue to hele [men-is] soules.

heal

415 The secund is a pryvy poynt, I pray hit be helid;

secret; kept hidden

f.5b Thay cunne not reede redelles a-right, as me thenketh;

riddles; accurately

For furst folowid freres Lollardz manieres,

prosecuted [c] ; *manners*

And sith hath be shewed the same on thaym-self,

since; been the subject of a plea [c]

That thaire lesingz haue lad thaym to lolle by the necke;

lies; led; hang

420 At Tibourne for traison y-twyght vp thay were.

Tyburn; treason; strung

For as hit is y-seide by eldryn dawes,   *said; ancient days*
'That the churle yafe a dome whiche came by hym aftre'.

gave; judgment [c]

---

411 deede] *omitted.*   414 men-is] man is.

Patere legem quam ipse tuleris. Seneca.

The thrid is no lesing ne no long tale: *third*; *lie*

Thees good grey freres that mouche loue geten   *much*; *get*

425 For keping of thaire conscience clenner than other,   *cleaner*

Thay goon al bare abouue the foote and by-nethe double

2 layers underneath

With smale semyd sockes and of softe wolle,   *seamed*; *wool*

For the loue of oure lord harde life induren;

Thay mellen with no monaye more nother lasse,

concern themselves with; *money*

430 But stiren hit with a sticke and staren on hit ofte   *stir*

And doon thaire bisynes there-with by obedience of th'ordre;

business

But in the herte ne in the hande ne may hit not come,

For thenne thay shuld bee shent of the subpriour.   *punished*

The fourthe poynt is fructuous and fundid al in loue:

profitable; *grounded*

435 Whenne freres goon to chapitre for charite-is sake,

chapter-house; *holy love's*

Thay casten there the cuntrey and coostz aboute,

arrange; *district*; *areas*

And parten the prouynce in parcelle-mele,

divide; *into portions* [c]

And maken limitacions in lengthe and in breede,

begging districts

Til eche hovs haue his owen as hym aughte.   *house*; *ought*

440 Thenne hath the limitour leue to lerne where he cometh

licensed friar; *permission* [c]

To lye and to licke or elles lose his office;   *lie*; *extort*

But sum been so courtoys and kinde of thaire deedes

courteous; *noble* [c]

That with thaire charite thay chaungen a knyfe for a peyre,

exchange; *pair*

But he wol pille ere he passe a parcelle of whete

steal; *portion*

445 And choise of the chese the chief and the beste.

choice; *cheese*

He is so cunnyng in the crafte that where-so he cometh

skilful

He leueth the lasse for the more deele.

leaves; *lesser*; *greater part*

Thus with thaire charite and with thaire fayre chere
Thees good God-is men gadren al to thaym   *gather*
450 And kepen hit to thaire owen croppe clene fro other.
                                         reserve; separate
For though a frere be fatt and haue a ful coffre   *coffer*
Of gold and of good, thou getys but a lite   *get; little*
Forto bete thy bale, though thou begge euer.
                                         alleviate; distress
But that is no meruail, by Marie of heuene,
455 Forto begge of a begger what bote is hit   *help*
But who wolde balle [with] his [browe] to breke harde stones ?
                                         strike; forehead
Thus thaire conscience is y-knowe and thaire crafte eeke,
                                         known; profession
That hath be kepte cunseil and cloos many dayes,   *close*
Til al the world wote what thay wolde meene;
                                         know; intended
460 And that is this trevly, tende who-so wil,
                                         truly; attend; whosoever wishes
Thorough crafte of confession to knowe men intentz, —
f.6a Of lordz and ladies that lustes desiren,   *pleasures*
And with thaire wyly wittz wirchen on euer   *work*
And mulden vp the matiere to make thaym fatte,
                                         knead; matter
465 And gouuernen the grete and guilen the poure.
                                         govern; beguile
Now take my tale as my intent demeth,
And ye shal wel wite I wil thaym no mischief
                                         know; wish; harm
By my worde no by my wille as wissely [for] sothe   *surely*
As God that is oure gouuernour me gye at my nede.   *guide*
Honora dominum de tua substancia proph[eta]
470 For whenne thay come to your cote to craue that thaym nedeth,
                                         cottage
Gyfe thaym for God-is sake and with a good wille   *give*
Mete or monaye as ye mowe indure,   *food; can afford*
And yefe thaym sauce there-with of the sothe-sigger
                                         give; sauce [c]
Forto preche the peuple the peril of synne,

456 with] *omitted*; browe] heede.   468 for] *omitted*.

475 How symonie shendith al hooly church,   *simony destroys*
    And not forbere bisshop ne baron that lyveth   *spare; noble*
    That thay teche treuly the texte as hit standeth,
    And abide thereby with a bolde herte,
    And spare for no spicerie ne no speche elles,   *spices/bribery*
480 But telle oute the trouthe and tourne not a-side   *turn*
    How Couetise hath caste the knyght on the grene,
                                              covetousness; thrown
    And woneth at Westmynstre to wynne newe spores,
                                                     lives; spurs
    And can not crepe thens while the crosse walketh.   *thence* [c]
    He multiplieth monaye in the mote-halle   *council-chamber*
485 More for his mayntenance and manasshing of wordes
                                                         menacing
    Thenne with draughte of his swerde or deedes of armes.
                                                          drawing
    And telle the frere a toquen, that trouthe wote the sothe   *token*
    Why men meruaillen more on thaym thanne on othir, —
    That suche a cumpaignye of confessours cunne not yelde
                                                      [c]; *yield*
490 Oon martir among thaym in [vij] score wynter.   *one*; *martyr*
    Thay prechen alle of penance as though [thay] parfite were,
    But thay proue hit [in no] poynt there thaire peril shuld arise.
    Thaire clothing is of conscience and of Caym thaire werkes,
                                                           Cain
    That fadre was and fundre of alle the foure ordres,   *founder*
495 Of deedes thay doon deceipuyng the peuple,   *deceiving*
    As Armacanes argumentz, that thaire actes knewe,
                                                    Armagh's [c]
    Provyn hit apertly in a poysie-wise;   *prove*; *clearly*; *verse*
    For of Caym alle came, as this clerc tolde.
    For who writeth wel this worde and withoute titil,
                                              abbreviation mark [c]
500 Shal finde of the figures but euene foure lettres: *exactly*
    C. for hit is crokid [for] thees Carmes thou mos take,
                                        crooked; *Carmelites*; *must*
    A. for thees Augustines that amoreux been euer,
                                             Augustinians; *amorous*

490 vij] viij.
491 thay] *omitted*.   492 in no] not.
                                        501 for] *omitted*.

I. for thees Iacobynes that been of Iudas kynne,

          Jacobins ; Judas's kin

M. for thees Menours that monsyd been thaire werkes.

          Minors ; cursed

505 I seye of thaym that suche been and cesse agaynes other,

          cease

But wel I wote that wilful and worldly thay been sum,   *know*

And eeke spracke and spitous, and spices wel thay louen,

          brisk ; spiteful

f.6b For Symon-is sermons thay setten al to taske,

          Simony's ; enjoin as study

And feele other fautz fourtene hunthrid   *many ; faults*

510 Thay lepen ouer lightly, and lyen woundre thicke.

          lie ; amazingly

I can not deme deuely of what degre thay bee;

          judge rightly ; rank

Thay been not weddid, wel I wote, though thay wifes haue;

But knightz yit of conscience I couthe of thaym make,   *could*

For thay haue ioygned [in ioustes] agayns Ihesus werkes;

          joined ; jousts

515 And forto proue thaym prestes thees poyntz been agayne
    thaym.   *priests*

I can not reede redily of what revle thay been,   *read ; rule*

For hooly churche ne heuene hath not thaym in mynde,

Saue in oon place thaire office and ordre is declarid,   *one*

I sawe hit in a ympne and is a sentence trewe,

          hymn ; judgment [c]

520 And elles-where in hooly writte I herde thaym y-nempnyd.

          named

Auferte gentem perfidam. Credentium de finibus,

Deleantur de libro viuencium et cum iustis non scribantur.

But of the matiere of Mvm ne of the sothe-sigger

This is not to pourpoos the pare of oon pere,

          to the point ; peeling of a pear [c]

And therfore my wil is to walke more at large   *freely*

Forto fynde sum freeke that of feith were   *man*

525 Not double, but indifferent to deme the sothe,   *fraudulent* [c]

Whether Mvm is more better or Melle-sum-tyme

          speak-some-time

514 ioustes] iustice.

Forto amende that were amysse into more ease.   *wrong*
And for the fikelle freres were fully witholde

fickle ; supported
And alied to Mvm in many maniere wises,   *allied*
530 And eeke ful partie, as prouyd by thaire wordes,

completely biased [c]
I lyeued wel the lasse thaire lore and thaire deedes,

believed ; less ; teaching
And forto eschewe chiding I chalanged thaym alle,

escape ; challenged [c]
And lepte lightly fro thaym, leste I laught were;   *caught*
For thaire curtesie is crokid there thay caste ille,   *devise badly*
535 And that witen thay wel that han wrastlid with thaym.

know ; wrestled
Thenne passid I to priories and personages many,   *parsonages*
To abbeys of Augustyn and many hooly places,
There prestz and prelatz were parfitely y-closed

priests ; enclosed
To singe and to reede for alle cristen soules.
540 But for I was a meen man I might not entre;   *poor*
For though the place were y-pighte for poure men sake

founded
And eeke funded there-fore yit faillen thay ofte
That thay doon not eche day do beste of alle.
Mutauerunt caritatem in cupiditatem. Sapiencia.
For the [fundacion as] the fundours ment   *founders intended*
545 Was groundid for God-is men, though hit grete serue.

nobility
Thay koueiten no comers but yf thay cunne helpe

covet ; visitors
Forto amende thaire mynstre and to maynteyne thaire rente,

church ; income
Or in worke or in worde waite thaire profit,   *serve*
Or elles entreth he not til thay haue y-[sopid].   *dined*
550 Thus thaire portier for my pourete putt me thens,

porter ; poverty ; threw me out
And grauntid me of his goodnesse to go where me luste

pleased
And to wandry where I wolde without the gates.   *wander*

544 fundacion as] fundacions of.   549 sopid] sepid.

Thenne raughte I fro religion, redelees of wittes,
>   *went ; at my wits' end*
f.7a And caried to closes and cathedralle churches   *travelled*
555 There that pluralite was prisely y-stablid.
>   *[c] ; preciously established*
I queyntid me with the quyre for my questions sake,
>   *acquainted ; quire*
And moevid of Mvm more thenne thaym liked.
I was as wise whenne I wente as whenne I came to thaym,
Thay wolde not intremitte of ner nother side,
>   *intervene ; [c] neither*
560 But euer kepte thaym cloos to [cracche] and to mangier,
>   *close ; trough ; manger*
And fedde so the foule flesh that the velle ne might   *skin*
Vnethe kepe the caroigne but yf hit cleue shuld;
>   *scarcely hold in ; flesh ; burst*
And nad the gutte groned there thay gurde were,
>   *groaned ; girt*
Thay had bee sike of swete mete, so me God helpe,
>   *sick ; sweetmeats*
565 For piking of prouendre passing th'assise;
>   *stealing ; provender ; legal amount*
And nadde thay partid with the poure as prestz doon thaire
>   offryng,   *shared ; priests ; do*
That putten alle thaire masse penyes in thaire purses [bottume],
>   *mass pennies*
Thay had be blamyd of Belial for thaire bolde riding   *Belial [c]*
Yn gurdellz of good fold or gilte atte leste.   *belts ; gilt*
Nolite possidere aurum neque argentum in zonis vestris.
570 Thenne woxe I wondre wery of wandring aboute   *grew*
Thorough the wild weyes that I wente had,
Ful woo ; for I ne wiste what was my beste   *very distressed*
Reed – forto reste or rome more at large   *counsel ; roam*
Til I wiste wittrely who shulde haue   *knew for certain*
575 The maistrie, Mvm or the sothe-sigger.
And euery man that I mette mad for my wordes
Wende that I were, wisten thay non other.   *thought ; knew*
And as I stoode staring, stonyd of this matiere,   *stunned*
Mvm with his myter manachid me euer   *mitre ; menaced*

560 cracche] racke.   567 bottume] *omitted.*

580 And cunseilled me to cusky and care for myself,   *submit* [c]
    And leste I soughte sorowe, cesse by tyme.
    I doutid of his deedes, for his delectacion
    Was more in his mynde thenne the masse-bokes,
    And boode til a baron, blessid be he euer,   *waited*
585 (His name is y-nempnyd among the ix. ordres)   *named*
    Sent a saufconduyt so that I wolde   *safe-conduct*
    Maynteyne no matiere to amende myself,   *maintain*; *case* [c]
    Ne caicche no colour [that] came of my wittes,
                    take up; *fictitious argument* [c]
    But showe for a souurayn to shewe hit forth after.   [c]
590 This boldid me to bisynes to bringe hit to ende
                    encouraged; *industry*
    Thorough grace of this good lord that gouuerneth al thing.
    Thenne sought I forth seuenyght and slept ful silde
                    very seldom
    And cessid on a Saterday til sonne roose a-morowe
                ceased; *rose in the morning*
    And burnys and belles ballid to-gedre,   *men*; *bells*; *struck*
595 Momeling on thaire matyns and to the masse after.   *mumbling*
    I satte in a siege my seruice to hire   *place*; *hear*
    Til the prest in a pulpite began forto preche
    The peuple to pees and the peril of synne   *peace*
    And also t'offre as ofte as thaym likid.   *to offer*
f.7b He taughte thaym by tyme thaire tithing to bringe
    Of al manier grene that groweth vppon erthe   *produce*
    Of fructe and of floxe in felde and in homes,   *fruit*; *flax*
    Of polaille and of peris, of apples and of [plummes],
                    poultry; *pears*
    Of grapes and of garlik, of gees and of pigges,
605 Of chibollz and of chiries and of thaire chese eeke,
                chives; *cherries*
    Herbaige and oygnons and alle suche thinges   *herbs*; *onions*
    That growen in thaire gardynes, lete God his parte haue,
    Of hony in your hyves and of your hony-combes,
    Of malte and of monaye and of all that multiplieth,
610 Of wolle and of wexe and [what-]so yow increceth
           wool; *wax*; *whatsoever*; *increases*

588 that] hit.   610 what] *omitted*.
603 plummes] notes.

Or newith yow, the ix partie nymeth to your self,
is renewed; take
And trewly the tithing taketh hooly churche.
And euer I waitid whenne he wolde sum worde moeve
How hooly churche goodes shuld be y-spendid,
615 And declare the deedes what thay do shulde
To haue suche a harueste and helpe not to erie.   *plough*
But sorowe on the sillable he shewed of that matiere,
not a single syllable [c]
For Mvm was a meen and made hym to leue;
intermediary; break off
And as wery as I was yit was I wrothe eeke   *weary; yet*
620 With Mvm, for he made the moppe so lewed   *fool; stupid*
To lene men to lerne the lawe sith he knewe hit.
give permission [c]
Thenne ferkid I forth as faste as I mighte   *went*
Seuene yere sunnedayes and solempne festes,
Sundays; feast-days
Yf prest or prelat or prechour wolde   *preacher*
625 Sey sothe of hymself and serue there-after   *act accordingly*
And teche how the tithinge shuld trewly be departid.   *shared*
But as wide as I wente was noon of thaym alle
Wolde moeve of that matiere more nother lasse.
And why that thay wolde not wol ye gladly wite,
630 Thay haue a memoire of Mvm among alle other;   *memorial*
Ys more in thaire mynde thenne martires of heuene
than; martyrs
That token the deeth for trouthe of tirantz handes.
suffered death; at tyrants'
But here a querele or a question quyk mighte thou make:
objection [c]
Martires had more might and more mynde eeke,   *strength*
635 And couthe more on clergie thenne cunne now a thousand.
knew
But thereto I answere as I am lerid: *instructed*
Thou, lewed laudate, litel witte has.
dull novice [c]*; intelligence*
Hit was for no cunnyng ne clergie nother   *knowledge*
That thay chosid the deeth, but for derne loue *chose; profound*
640 And kindenes to oure creatour that creed vs alle,
affinity; created

And for pure trouthe that thay taught [euer].

Propter veritatem dimittam omnem familiaritatem etc

This made thaym martires more thanne ought elles,

For clercz were not knowe by thaire clothing that tyme,

Ne by royal raye ne riding aboute   *dress*

645 Ne by seruice of souuerayns, so me God helpe,

f.8a Ne by revel ne riot ne by rente nothir

                      revelry; indulgence; income

Ne by thaire double dees ne thaire deupe hoodes,   *dais; deep*

Ne by drynkyng of dollid wyne ne by datz at eue,

                         warmed; dates

Ne by worldly workes of writtes ne seelyng   *sealing wax*

650 Ne by no maniere nicete that thay now vsen,   *foolishness*

But by the deedes that thay dide, I do you to wite.

For I am but lewed and lettrid ful lite,

And yit me semeth the sentence that I shewe couthe   *verdict*

And teche how the tithing shuld trewly be departid,   *shared*

655 For in thre lynes hit [lith] and not oon lettre more.   *lies*

Now hendely hireth how I begynne: *courteously listen*

That ye clepe God-is parte lete God-is men haue hit,   *call*

Reseruyng for yourself sustenance for your foode,

And the ouerplus ouer that for ornementz of the churche.

                        surplus; beyond

660 Though this be shortly y-seide, yit so me God helpe,

Who-so had cunnyng and a clerc were,   *knowledge*

Might make a long sermon of thees fewe wordes,

And though he toke to his theme 'the tresour is among thaym

                         took

And the reuylle of the royaulme and the richesse bothe,' *revelry*

665 He shuld not wende of the waye two whete cornes.

               go; wheatgrains [c]

For thay haue tollid so the tithing thay han the two dooles,

                   taxed; parts [c]

And been so vsid to ease erly and late   *accustomed; comfort*

That thay cunne no crafte saue kepe thaym warme.

Thay bisien more for benefices thenne bibles to reede,

                   busy themselves

670 And been as worldly wise and wynners eeke   *profiteers*

As man vppon molde, and asmuche louen   *earth*

641 euer] were.   655 lith] light.

Mvm and the monaye, by Marie of heuene,   *money*
For mayntenance and mede been thaire two mates.
'Yit wil thou melle more', cothe Mvm, 'thenne hit nedeth.
                                    speak ; is necessary
675 Be stille lest thou stumble, for thou stondes ful slidre,
                                    quiet ; unstable
And thou moeue any more suche maniere wordes.
Thay been not holsum for thy heed ne for thy herte nother,
For thou mos holde with the mo yf thou thy helthe willes;
                                    must ; majority
And so I haue y-tolde the twyes and oones.
680 Thou art mad of thy mynde, and amysse levis
                                    believe wrongly
That Mvm hath a maister there men been of goode;
                                    men are wealthy
For Mvm maketh mo men at a moneth-ende   *more ; month*
Thanne the sothe-sigger in seuene score winter;
For he is priuy with the pruttist and there the price caicchet,
                                    intimate ; proudest ; takes
685 [And] is y-drawe to the deys with deyntees y-seruyd
                                    drawn ; dais ; dainties
Whenne the sothe-sigger dar not be seye.   *dare ; seen*
For and a matier be moeued at mete or at eue
Or in pryuy places there peeris assemblen,   *private*
Mvm musith there-on and maketh many cautelles
                                    muses ; tricks
690 With a locke on his lippe and loketh aboute.
He spendith no speche but spices hit make,   *expends ; bribery*
f.8b Til he wite whitherward that wil doo drawe.
                        knows ; where things are going [c]
But thenne he knittith a knotte and cometh al at ones
And getith hym a greet thanke to go among the beste.
695 Fle fooly therefore, and frendes the make,
And a-rete, I the rede, and rome no ferther,   *stop ; advise*
For thou walkis of the weye forto wynne siluer.
                                    out of the way ; earn
And carpe no more of clergie but yf thou cunne leepe,
                                    speak ; know how to jump

685 And] As.

For and thou come on thaire clouche, thou crepis not thens
clutch ; creep

700 Til thou wite right wel with whom that thou mellys.'
speaks
'I-wis I wil not,' cothe I, 'til I wite more;
indeed
For prestz been not perillous but pacient of thaire werkes,
dangerous

And eeke the plantz of pees and full of pitie euer,
And chief of al charite y-chose a-fore other;
chosen
705 Forto fighte ne to flite hit falleth not to thaire ordre,
dispute ; belongs
Ne to prece to no place there peril shuld be ynne.
urge their way
That proueth wel by parlement, for prelatz shuld be voidid
withdrawn
Whenne any dome of deeth shal be do there,
judgment ; death
Al for cause thaire conscience to kepe vn-y-wemmyd.
unstained
710 A man may saye thaym the sothe sonest of alle,
soonest
Withoute grucche other groyn, but gete many thankes.
ill-will ; grumbling
Thay moste bowe for the beste, God forbede hit elles,
submit
To shewe vs exemple of suffrance euer.'
patience
Sic luceat lux vestra coram hominibus vt videant opera vestra
   bona etc.
'Yee, yit be ware of wiles and waite wel aboute,
aware ; deceits ; watch out
715 For me semeth that thy sight is sumdele a-dasid
somewhat dazed
And al myndelees', cothe Mvm 'and al amysse demys;
mindless ; judges wrongly
For though thou shuldes thy-silf be a sothe-sigger,
Thou has no cleere conceypt to knowe alle thaire werkes.
understanding
And that I pryved by a poynt thou perceipues neuer,
proved ; perceive
720 Al a-tw[art] thy intent and thy tale eeke,
contrary [c]
For Pilat in the Passion among al the peuple
Pilate

720 atwart] tw *and a space left.*

Wilned aftre watre to waisshe with his handes,
asked for ; *wash*

To shewe hym by that signe, of the bloode-sheding
Of Crist that vs creed and on the crosse deyed,   *created*

725 His conscience was clensid as clene as his handes.
Yit was he ground of the grame and moste guilty eeke,
source ; *harm*

For euery man that mynde hath may wel wite
That prelatz aughten haue pite when princz bee moeued,
pity ; *angered*

And reede thaym so that rancune roote not in hert,
advise ; *anger*

730 And ere the grame growe ferre the ground so to wede
damage ; *far*

And amende that were mysse ere any moore caicche
take root

Of man-slaughter or mourdre, as hath many dayes.
murder

For who hath knowlache of a cloude by cours of a-bouue,
sky movement

And wil stande stille til the storme falle,

735 And wende not of the waye, the wite is his owen.
not move away ; *blame*

Though hit heelde on his heede, who is to blame ?   *hailed*
For who hath sight of a showre that sharpely ariseth,

f.9a And wil not caste hym to kepe with couryng abouue
arrange protection ; *shelter*

Til hit droppe al a-dovne and dung-wete hym make,
down ; *soak him*

740 And eeke falle on his frende, in feith as me thenketh,
He is auctor of al the harme and th'ache   *author* ; *the ache*
And so pryuy to the peynes that peeres induren.
party ; *pains* ; *companions*

And also in cuntrey hit is a comune speche
And is y-write in Latyne, lerne hit who-so wil:

745 The reason is '*qui tacet consentire videtur*'.   [c]
And who-so hath in-sight of silde-couthe thingz,   *marvellous*
Of synne or of shame or of shonde outher,   *disgrace* ; *either*
And luste not to lette hit, but leteth hit forth passe,
wishes ; *prevent* ; *allows*

As clercz doon construe that knowen alle bokes,

750 He shal be demyd doer of the same deede.

        judged; perpetrator

And eeke in lond-is lawe I lernyd by anothir: *land-law; from*

Yf a freke for felonye is frayned atte barre

        man; [c]; cross-examined

For traison or for trespas and he a tunge haue   *[c]*

And wil not answere to the deede he is of indited,   *indicted*

755 But stont stille as a stoone and no worde stire,   *stands; utter*

But he be deef or dum to deeth shal he wende,   *go*

As atteynt for the trespas, and is a trewe lawe.   *attaint [c]*

This cursid custume hath cumbrid vs alle;

The grucching of grete that shuld vs gouuerne   *quarrelling*

760 Han y-shourid sharpely thorough suffrance of clercz

        showered; tolerance

That lightly with labour y-lettid thay mighte,

        easily; prevented

The conseil of clergie yf thay had caste for hit.   *devised*

For there the heede aketh alle the lymes after   *aches; limbs*

Pynen whenne the principal is put to vnease   *suffer; distress*

Dum caput infirmum cetera membra dolent

765 (Of sum and of certayn, I saye not of alle,

But of the same seurely that suche maniere vsen.)

        certainly; use

'Now treuly,' cothe I, 'thy talking me pleasith,

For thou has saide as sothe, so me God helpe,

As euer sage saide sith Crist was in erthe,   *since*

770 For thou has rubbid on the rote of the rede galle

        root; red; gall

And eeke y-serchid the sore and sought alle the woundz.

        searched

And yf thou woldes do wel wende to thaym alle   *go*

And telle the same tale that thou has tolde here;

Thou might be man made and mensshid for euer.'   *honoured*

775 'Nay, there I leue the, Lucas, go loke [for] an othir;

        abandon; Luke [c]

For I wil wende no waie but wit go bifore,   *advantage*

No telle no tales for teryng of hodes,   *tearing; hoods [c]*

So taughte me the trusty techer on erthe,

My maister and maker, Mvm that I serue.

775 for] yf.

780 Go walke where thy wil is and waite wel aboute,
　　　　　　　　　　　　　　watch out carefully
　　For thou has sought al a-side with thou begunne
　　　　　　　　　　　　　　by the wayside; since
　　With clercz of Cambrigge and cathedralle churches.
　　Fare forth therefore to finde that thou sechis,　　　　*seek*
f.9b And come not with clergie leste thou a-croke walke
　　　　　　　　　　　　　　crookedly
785 But tourne now to tovnes and temporal lords,　　*turn; towns*
　　There prece is of peuple, and pray thaym to telle　*multitude*
　　Yf any sothe-sigger serue thaym long.'
　　Thenne ferkid I to fre men and frankeleyns mony,
　　　　　　　　　　　　went; free; landowners
　　To bonde-men and bourgois and many other barnes,
　　　　　　　　　　　　　peasants; burgesses
790 To knightz and to comunes and craftz-men eeke,　*tradesmen*
　　To citezeyns and souurayns and to many grete sires,
　　To bachilliers, to banerettz, to barons and erles,
　　　　　　　　　　bachelor-knights; knights [c]
　　To princes and peris and alle maniere estatz;　　*estates*
　　But in euery court there I came or cumpaigny outhir　*either*
795 I fonde mo mvmmers atte moneth-ende　　　　　*more*
　　Than of sothe-sigger[z] by seuene score thousand.
　　For alle the knyghtz of the court that with the king dwellen,
　　For the more partie [yee], mo than an hunthrid,　*indeed* [c]
　　Heulden Mvm for a maister, and more do mighte　*held*
800 With king and his cunseil and al the court aftre.
　　And euery tovne that I trade twelfe moneth to-gedre,　*trod*
　　Mvm was a maister and with the maire euer,　　*mayor*
　　And al of oon lyuraye and looke so to-gedre　　*one livery*
　　That a poure man-is prayer departe thaym ne mighte.
　　　　　　　　　　　　　　poor; separate
805 There was no maner man the maire had levir　　*rather*
　　Bydde of the burnes in benche there he satte　　*invite*
　　As Mvm to the mete among al the rewe;　　*food; row*
　　For he couthe lye and laugh and leepe ouer the balkes
　　　　　　　　　　lie; skip over difficulties
　　There any grucche or groyne or grame shuld arise.
　　　　　　　　　　ill-will; complaint; damage

　　796 sothe-siggerz] sothe-sigger.　　　798 yee] ee.

810 He was ful couchant and coy and curtoys of speche,

                                humble ; *courteous*

And parlid for the partie and the playnte lefte;

                        spoke ; *pleading* ; *abandoned*

The maire preisid hym apert for his plaisant wordes;   *openly*

He was a blessid barne and beste couthe suffre   *man* ; *manage*

Whenne souurayns were assemblid to saye what thaym liked;

815 He toke no maniere travers tenne yere to-gedre,

                              contradiction

Among the comun cunseil lest he caste were,   *defeated*

But euer shewid his seel to sitte among other.

But who-so mvmmeth a mayre to maynteyne his rente,

                           gags ; *income*

Maniere were that the mayre shuld mvmme hym agaynes

                            fitting

820 And yelde hum with a yere-is y[i]fte ere the yere passed.

                   present ; *year's gift*

Mvm with the mayre to the mete wente,   *food*

And euer I after, al vn-a-spied,   *unnoticed*

Forto knowe of my caas couthe I not stynte.   *case* [c] ; *stop*

There shuldrid sergeantz to serue atte mete   *shouldered*

825 For a male ful of misse-deedz that Mvm had in keping.   *bag*

I stoode stille as a stoone and starid aboute

And lokid lightly a-long by the bordes,   *quickly* ; *tables*

Yf any sothe-sigger were sette in the halle.

But sorowe on the shyne I sawe of hym there,   *not a glimpse*

830 But yf he were a soleyn and seruyd al oon,

                  solitary person [c] ; *alone*

f.10a For alle was huyst in the halle sauf 'holde vp the oyles'.

                  hushed ; *flattery*

And forto saye sothe and shone long tale,   *shun*

The sunne and the sergeant[z] my sight so dasid   *dazed*

That I might not eche messe merke as me luste.

                 course ; *mark* [c] ; *pleased*

835 I askid of a eldryn man as I beste couthe   *elderly*

Yf any sothe-sigger sate in the halle,   *sat*

And he answerid sharply that 'the sothe-sigger

Dyneth this day with Dreede in a chambre,

And hath y-drunke dum-seede, and dar not be seye   *dare* ; *seen*

---

820 yifte] yfte.   833 sergeantz] sergeant.

840 Sith Mvm and the mayer were made suche frendes'.
     Thenne waxe I woundre wrothe, as I wel might,   *grew*
     And drowe me to the doreward and dwelled no lenger,
                                     towards the door
     But romed forth reedelees, remembring ofte
                                     devoid of counsel
     That Mvm was suche a maister among men of good.
845 And as I lokid the loigges along by the streetz,   *places*
     I sawe a sothe-sigger, in sothe as me thought,
     Sitte in a shoppe and salwyn his woundes.   *salve*
     Beati qui persecucionem paciuntur propter iusticiam. euangelium.
     Thenne was I ful-come and knewe wel the sothe   *apprised*
     That Mvm vppon molde myrier life had   *merrier*
850 Thenne the sothe-sigger, asay who-so wol;   *examine*
     But the better barne to abide stille
     And to lyve with a lord to his life-is ende
     Ys the sothe-sigger, a-say who-so wol.
     Yit was I not the wiser for waye that I wente;
855 This made me al madde as I most nede,
     And wel fleuble and faynt, and feulle to the grounde,
                                       weak ; fell
     And lay dovne on a lynche to lithe my boones,
                   unploughed strip of land ; relieve
     Rolling in remembrance my rennyng aboute   *running*
     And alle the perillous patthes that I passid had,
860 As priories and personagz and pluralites,
     Abbayes of Augustyn and other hooly places,
     To knightes courtz and crafty men many,   *skilled*
     To mayers and maisters, men of high wittes,
     And to the felle freris, alle the foure ordres,   *wicked*
865 And other hobbes a-heepe, as ye herde haue –
                                yobs ; a-plenty
     And nought the neer by a note this noyed me ofte
                           nearer ; vexed
     That thorough construyng of clercz that knewe alle bokes
     That Mvm shuld be maister moste vppon erthe.
     And ere I were ware, a wynke me assailled,
                        sleep ; overtook me
870 That I slepte sadly seuene houres large.   *soberly ; long*
     Thenne mette I of mervailles mo thanne me luste
                           dreamt ; more

To telle or to talke of, til I se tyme;
But sum of the silde-couthes I wol shewe here-after,
For dreme is no dwele by Danyel-is wordes,
                              dream; illusion; according to
875 Though Caton of the contrarye carpe in his bokes.   *speak*
Me thought I was in wildernesse walking al oon,
f.10b There bestes were and briddes and no barne elles
                                        beasts; birds
Yn a cumbe cressing on a creste wise,
                    valley; broadening; crest-like [c]
Al gras grene that gladid my herte,
880 By a cliffe vn-y-knowe of Crist-is owen makyng.   *unknown*
I lepte forth lightly a-long by the heigges
And movid forth myrily to maistrie the hilles,
                                        merrily; master
For til I came to the coppe couthe I not stynte   *top; stop*
Of the highest hille by halfe [of] alle other.
885 I tournyd me twyes and totid aboute,
                          turned round; twice; looked
Beholding heigges and holtz so grene,   *woods*
The mansions and medues mowen al newe,
                                    houses; meadows
For suche was the saison of the same yere.
I lifte vp my eye-ledes and lokid ferther
890 And sawe many swete sightz, so me God helpe,
The wodes and the waters and the welle-springes
And trees y-traylid fro toppe to th'erthe,   *trailed*
Coriously y-courid with curtelle of grene,   *covered; robe*
The flours on feeldes flavryng swete,   *smelling*
895 The corne on the croftes y-croppid ful faire,
                                fields; cut; neatly
The rennyng riuyere russhing faste,   *running; river*
Ful of fyssh and of frie of felefold kinde,
                    spawn; many different; species
The breris with thaire beries bent ouer the wayes   *briars*
As honysoucles hongyng vppon eche half,   *honeysuckles*
900 Chesteynes and chiries that children desiren
                                chestnuts; cherries
Were loigged vndre leues ful lusty to seen.
                            lodged; leaves; pleasant
884 of] *omitted.*

The havthorne so holsum I beheulde eeke,   *hawthorn*
And hough the benes blowid and the brome-floures;
            beans; blew; broom-blossoms
Peris and plummes and pesecoddes grene,   *pears; peascods*
905 That ladies lusty loken muche after,   *desire*
Were gadrid for gomes ere thay gunne ripe; *gathered*
The grapes grovid a-grete in gardyns aboute,
             grew; abundantly
And other fruytz felefold in feldes and closes; *manifold; fields*
To nempne alle the names hit nedith not here.   *name*
910 The conyngz fro couert courid the bankes
           coneys; shelter; covered
And raughte oute a raundon and retournyd agaynes,
             darted out swiftly
Pleyed forth on the playne, and to the pitte after, *burrow*
But any hovnd hente thaym or the hay-nettes.
           seized; hay-nets [c]
The hare hied hym faste and the hovndes after;   *sped*
915 For kisshyng of his croupe a-caunt-wise he wente,
          touching; rump; in a zigzag
For nad he tournyd twies his tail had be licked,
           had he not turned twice
So ernestly Ector ycchid hym after.   *Hector;* [c] *ran*
The shepe fro the sunne shadued thaymself,   *shaded*
While the lambes laikid a-long by the heigges.   *played*
920 The cow with hire calfe and coltes ful faire
And high hors in haras hurtelid to-gedre,   *stud; galloped*
And preisid the pasture that prime-saute thaym made.
             spirited
f.11a The dere on the dale drowe to thaire dennes,
Ferkid forth to the ferne and feulle dovne amyddes.
         went; bracken; fell
925 Hertz and hyndes, a hunthrid to-gedre,
With rayndeer and roobuc runne to the wodes, *roebuck*
For the kenettz on the cleere were vn-y-couplid;
        hunting-dogs; clearing; unleashed
And buckes ful burnysshid that baren good grece,
         burnished; carried; fat
Foure hunthrid on a herde y-heedid ful faire,   *antlered*
930 Layen lowe in a launde a-long by the pale, *clearing; fence*
A swete sight for souurayns, so me God helpe.

I moued dovne fro the mote to the midwardz
         hill; *middle slopes*
And so a-dovne to the dale, dwelled I no longer,
But suche a noise of nestlingz ne so swete notz
935 I herde not this halfe yere, ne so heuenely [sounes] *sounds*
As I dide on that dale adovne among the heigges,
For in euery bussh was a brid that in his beste wise
Bablid with his bile, that blisse was to hire,   *beak*
So cleerly thay chirmed and chaunged thaire notes,
         chirped; *varied*
940 That what for flauour of the fruyte and of the somer floures,
        scent; *fruit*
The smellyng smote as spices, me thought, *was as pungent*
That of my trauail treuly toke I no kepe,   *notice*
For al was vanesshid me fro thorough the fresshe sightes.
         vanished
Thenne lepte I forth lightly and lokid a-boute,
945 And I beheulde a faire hovs with halles and chambres,
        beheld; *house*
A frankeleyn-is fre-holde al fresshe newe.
       franklin's freehold [c]
I bente me aboute and bode atte dore *turned aside*; *stopped*
Of the gladdest gardyn that gome euer had.   *man*
I haue no tyme treuly to telle alle the names
950 Of ympes and herbes and other feele thinges
       trees; *plants*; *various*
That growed on that gardyn, the grounde was so noble. *soil*
I passid ynne pryuely and pulled of the fruytes
       secretly; *plucked*
And romed th'aleys rovnde al a-boute,   *the alleys*
But so semely a sage as I sawe there
955 I sawe not sothely sith I was bore,   *born*
An olde auncyen man of a hunthrid wintre, *ancient*
Y-wedid in white clothe and wisely y-made, *clothed*
With hore heres on his heede more thanne half white, *hoary*
A faire visaige and a vresse and vertuous to [sene]. *fresh*
960 His eyen were al ernest, eggid to noon ille, *inclined*; *badness*
With a broode besmet berde ballid a lite,
     broad; *broom-shaped*; *beard*; *bald*

935 sounes] *omitted.*   959 sene] seme.

As comely a creature as euer kinde wrought.

He was sad of his semblant, softe of his speche,
　　　　　　　　　　　　　grave ; appearance

Proporcioned at alle poyntes and pithy in his tyme,
　　　　　　　　　　　　　vigorous ; age

965　And by his stature right stronge, and stalworth on his dayes,
　　　　　　　　　　　　　stalwart

He houed ouer a hyue, the hony forto kepe　　*stood ; protect*

Fro dranes that destrued hit and dide not elles;
　　　　　　　　　　　　　drones ; destroyed

He thraste thaym with his thumbe as thicke as thay come,
　　　　　　　　　　　　　crushed

f.11b　He lafte noon a-live for thaire lither taicches.　*left ; evil ; vices*

970　I wondrid on his workes as I wel might,

And euer I neyed hym nere as ney as me ought,
　　　　　　　　　　　edged closer to him ; near

And halsid hym hendily as I had lernyd;　　*greeted ; politely*

And he me grete agayne right in a goode wise,

And askid what I wolde and anone I tolde　　*straightaway*

975　My wil was to wite what man he were.

'I am gardyner of this gate,' cothe he, 'the grovnde is myn
　　owen,　　　　　　　　　　*plot* [c]

Forto digge and to delue and to do suche deedes　　*delve*

As longeth to this leyghttone the lawe wol I doo,
　　　　　　　　　　　pertains ; garden

And wrote vp the wedes that wyrwen my plantes;
　　　　　　　　　　　dig ; destroy

980　And wormes that worchen not but wasten my herbes,
　　　　　　　　　　　slugs ; ruin ; plants

I daisshe thaym to deeth and delue oute thaire dennes.
　　　　　　　　　　　dash ; scoop

But the dranes doon worste, deye mote thay alle;　*die ; may*

They haunten the hyue for hony that is ynne,

And lurken and licken the liquor that is swete,　　*skulk*

985　And trauelyn no twynte but taken of the beste　*not a jot*

Qui non laborat non manducet. Bernardus.

Of that the bees bryngen fro blossomes and floures.

For of alle the bestes that breden vppon erthe　*beasts ; breed*

For qualite ne quantite, n[o] question, I trowe

988　no] ne.

The bee in his bisynes beste is allowed,   *business*
990 And prouyd in his propriete passing alle other,
      proved; natural disposition [c]
And pretiest in his wirching to profite of the peuple.'
      most skilful; work

'Swete sire,' sayde I in slepe as me thoughte,
'The propriete of bees I pray that ye wolde   *property*
Declare with thaire deedes, and of the drane eeke.'
995 'Blethely, burne, thy beede shal bee doo
      gladly; man; request; granted
Yf thou wil tende treuly my tale to th'ende.   *listen*
The bee of alle bestz beste is y-gouuerned
Yn lowlynes and labour and in lawe eeke.

Thay haue a king by kinde that the coroune bereth, *bears*
1000 Whom thay doo sue and serue as souurayn to thaym alle,
      follow
And obeyen to his biddyng, or elles the boke lieth.
The highest hoole in the hyue he holdeth hit hymself,
For there thay setten hym in his see by hym-self oone, *alone*
And maken mansions by-nethe that mervail hit is to knowe
1005 The bilding of the boures that the bees maken.   *chambers*
For the curiousiste carpintier vndre [cope] of heuene
      most skilful; vault
Couthe not caste thaire coples ne cuntrefete thare workes.
      create; rafters; imitate
Thaire tymbre and thaire tile stones and al that to thaym
  longeth,
Thay feycchen hit of floures in feldes and in croftes.
      fetch [c]*; paddocks*
1010 Thayr dwellingz been dyuyded, I do hit on thaire combes,
      partitioned; prove; honeycombs
And many a queynt caue been cumpassid [wy]-thynne.
      elaborate; room; designed
And eche a place hath a principal that peesith al his quarter,
      keeps peace
That reuleth thaym to reste and rise whenne hit nedith, *rules*
And alle the principallz to the prince ful prest thay been at
  nede,   *ready*
f.12a To rere thaire retenue to righte alle the fautes; *muster*

1006 cope] erthe.   *1011* wy-thynne] by thynne.

For thay knowen as kindely as clerc doeth his bokes   *naturally*

Wastours that wyrchen not but wombes forto fille.

                    work ; *stomachs*

Thaire workes been right wondreful wite thou for sothe,

For sum, as thou sees thay shape thaym to the feldes

                  make their way

1020   To sovke oute the swettenes of the somer floures,   *suck*

And sum abiden at home to bigge vp the loigges,   *build*

And helpen to make honey of that thay home bringen,

And doon other deedes thorough dome that is among thaym;

                  regulation

And sum waiten the wedre, the wynde and the skyes,   *assess*

1025   Yf hit be temperate tyme to trauaylle or to leue.

              appropriate ; *cease*

[Thay] eten alle at oones and neuer oon by hymsilf,

Thorough warnyng of thaire wa[r]thour leste waste were

    among thaym.   *watchman*

The bomelyng of the bees, as Bartholomew vs telleth,

             bumbling ; *Bartholomaeus* [c]

Thair noyse and thaire notz at eue and eeke at morowe,

1030   Lyve hit wel, thair lyden[e] the leste of thaym hit knoweth.

              believe ; *language*

The moste merciful among thaym and meukest of his deedes

               meekest

Ys king of bees comunely, as clergie vs telleth,

And sperelees, and in wil to spare that been hym vnder,

              without a sting

Or yf he haue oon, he harmeth ne hurteth noon in sothe.

              no one

1035   For venym doeth not folowe hym but vertue in alle workes,

              venom

To reule thaym by reason and by right-ful domes,

             lawful judgments

Thorough contente of the cumpaignie that closeth alle in oone.

            agreement ; *unites*

And yf the king coueite the colours to be-holde   *wish*

Of the fressh floures that on the feldes growen,

1040   Euermore a-myddes as maister of thaym alle   *in the middle*

1026 Thay] That.   *1030* lydene] lydenys.

1027 warthour] wauthour.

His place is y-properid for peril that mighte falle;

         appointed; *happen*

And yf he fleuble or feynte or funder dovneward,

        weakens; *faints*; *falls*

The bees wollen bere hym til he be better amended. *will*

But of the drane is al the doute, the deueil hym quelle,

         problem; *kill*

1045 For in thaire wide wombes thay wol hide more *stomachs*

Thenne twenty bees and trauaillen not no tyme of the day,

But gaderyn al to the gutte and growen grete and fatte *gather*

And fillen thaire bagges brede-ful of that the bees wyrchen.

         brimful

Quorum deus venter est et gloria in confusione. paulus

But hire hough thay ende with al thaire hole cropping:

      hear; *how*; *whole*; *gathering*

1050 Whenne thay haue soope the swete the soure cometh aftre,

         supped; *sour*

For whenne the bee-is bisynes is bribed fro the hyve

        business; *enticed*

Thorough dranes that deceipuen thaym and doon no thing

 elles,   *deceive*

Thenne seen the bees thair subtilite and seruen thaym there-

 after   *accordingly*

As Bartholomew the Bestiary bablith on his bokes, *speaks*

1055 And of other pryvy poyntz but I wol passe ouer.'

'By this skile,' cothe I, 'there shuld scant hony

        argument; *be little*

Yf euery hyve hurle thus and haue suche a ende'. *contend*

'Be certayne,' he seide, 'that is a sothe tale

But yf the gardyner haue grace and gouuerne hym the bettre

1060 And wisely a-waite whenne dranes furste entren,

f.12b And nape thaym on the nolle ere thay thaire neste caicche;

        hit; *head*; *reach*

For been thay oones ynned his eyen [shal] be dasid

        inside; *dazed*

Fro al kinde knowlache, so couert thaym helpeth.'

'Yit wolde I wite,' cothe I, 'yf your wil be,

1065 Hough to knowe kindely, thorough craft of your scole,

The drane that deuoureth that deue is to other, *devours*; *due*

1062 shal] shald.

By colour or by cursidnesse or crie that he maketh.   *fraud*
Kenneth me the cunnyng, that I may knowe after.'
                                          teach ; knowledge
'Thay been long and lene,' cothe he 'and of a lither hue,
                                                    evil colour
1070 And as bare as a bord, and bringen nought with thaym;
                                                         board
But haue thay hauntid the hyve half yere to th'ende,
Thay growen vnder gurdel gretter than other,   *girdle ; fatter*
And noon so sharpe to stinge ne so sterne nother.'   *severe*
Nichil asperius paupero cum surget in altum. Gregorius.
'Yit I mervaille,' cothe I, 'and so mowen other,   *must*
1075 Why the bees wollen not wirwe thaym by tyme,   *will ; destroy*
And falle on thaym fersly furst whanne thay entre,   *fiercely*
For so shuld thay saue thaym-silf and thaire goodes.'
'The bees been so bisi', cothe he. 'aboute comune profit,
And tendeth al to trauail while the tyme dureth   *attend ; lasts*
1080 Of the somer saison and of the swete floures ;
Thayr wittes been in wirching and in no wile elles   *craft ; else*
Forto waite any waste til winter approche,   *look out for*
That licour thaym lacke thair lyfe to susteyne.   *drink*
But as sone as thay see thaire swynke is y-stole,
                                                labour ; stolen
1085 Thenne flocken thay to fighte thair fautes to amende,
                                            losses ; make up
And quellen the dranes quicly and quiten alle thaire wrongz.'
                                              kill ; requite
'Now wol mote ye worthe', cothe I, 'for your wise tale,
                                        well may you prosper
For hit hath muche menyng who-so muse couthe,   *significance*
But hit is to mistike for me, by Marie of heuene,   *mystical*
1090 So wol I leue lightly withoute long tale.   *leave off ; quickly*
But and ye dwelle, as I dar, derue I you preye   *dare ; boldly*
Oone question to construe that I come fore;   *interpret*
For I haue soughte seuene yere and sum dele more,   *some bit*
And mette I neuer man yit that me wise couthe   *advise*
1095 Cleere to my knowing, clerc nother lewed,
Of the matiere of Mvm that moste me angrith,
That he shuld haue maisters mor than oon hunthrid,
Whenne the sothe-sigger shuld siche his mete.   *seek ; food*
I haue trauailled tenne yere to temporal estatz,

1100 And spied of spirituel and sparid for no wreth
      inspected; *refrained*; *anger*
 Forto wite witterly who shuld haue   *know for certain*
 The maistry, Mvm or the sothe-sigger.
 For alle the foure ordres agayne thaire fundacion *against*
 Prouyd hit ofte by prechement, for peril that myght falle,
       proved; *preaching*
1105 That Mvm shuld be maister and maynteyne th'ordre;
 And alle other estatz euery after other *each in turn*
f.13a Heulden muche more with Mvm thenne with the soth-sigger.
        held; *than*
 And yf ye deme as thay doon, by dere God in heuene,
 By no witte that I wote I wol go no ferther
1110 Forto seke shadue there no sunne apperith.' *shadow*; *appears*
 'Swete soon, thy seching,' seide the freke thenne,
       son; *search*; *man*
 'And thy trauail for thy trouthe shal tourne the to profit,
 For I wol go as nygh the grounde as gospel vs techeth *near*
 Forto wise the wisely to thy waie-is ende. *way's*
1115 For [of] al the mischief and mysse-reule that in the royaulme
  groweth   *realm*
 Mvm hath be maker alle thees many yeres,
 And eek more, [a] moulde, I may wel aduowe;
       pattern [c]; *avowe*
 And principally by parlement to proue hit I thenke,
 When knightz for the comune been come for that deede,
        community
1120 And semblid forto shewe the sores of the royaulme
        assembled
 And spare no speche though thay spille shuld, *perish*
 But berste out alle the boicches and blaynes of the heart
      burst; *boils*; *blisters*
 And lete the rancune renne oute a-russhe al at oones
       anger; *run*
 Leste the fals felon festre with-ynne; [c]; *fester*
1125 For as I herde haue, thay helen wel the rather *heal*; *quicker*
 Whenne the anger and the attre is al oute y-renne, *poison*
 For better were to breste oute there bote might falle
       burst; *remedy*

1115 of] omitted.   1117 a] and.

Thenne rise agayne regalie and the royaulme trouble.
royal prerogative

The voiding of this vertue doeth venym forto growe
absence; causes; venom

1130 And sores to be saluelees in many sundry places   *salve-less;*

Sith souurayns and the shire-men the sothe haue eschewed
since; knights of the shire

Yn place that is proprid to parle for the royaulme
appointed; speak

And fable of thoo fautes and founde thaym to amende.
speak; faults; try

For alle the perillous poyntz of prelatz and of other,

1135 As peres that haue pouaire to pulle and to leue,
power; plunder; make grants [c]

Thay wollen not parle of thoo poyntz for peril that might falle,
speak

But hiden alle the heuynes and halten echone
heaviness; hesitate; each one

And maken Mvm thaire messaigier thaire mote to determyne,
messenger; suit; judge

And bringen home a bagge ful of boicches vn-y-curid,
boils, uncured

1140 That nedis most by nature ennoye thaym there-after.
needs must; annoy

Qui potest contradicere peccato et non contradicit
actor est peccati. Sidrac.

And in al the king-is court there coiphes been and other   *coifs*

Mvm is maister there more thenne men wenen,   *than; think*

For sum of tho segges wolle siche side-wayes,
those; men; seek; crooked ways

Whenne thay witen wel y-now where the hare walketh,
know; enough [c]

1145 Thay leden men the long waye and loue-dayes breken
lead; long way round; love-days [c]

And maken moppes wel myry with thaire madde tales
fools; merry

Forto sowe siluer seede and solue ere thay singe,
[c]; *sol-fa* [c]

To haue ynne thaire harueste while the hete dureth.   *lasts*
Fauor et premium timor et odium peruertunt verum iudicium.
    Canon.

Now feithfully, my ful frende, I wol not feyne to the;   *pretend*
1150 There is no wronge on this world wrought, as I wene,
        crime; committed; think
Treason nother trespas ne trouble that falleth,
Felonye ne falshede ne no faute elles,
f.13b Rancune ne riotte ne reuyng of peuple   *anger; plundering*
Courshidnes ne cumbrance ne no caste of guile,
        cursedness; oppression; trick
1155 That Mvm nys the maker and moste cause eeke.
        is not; greatest cause also
And that shal I shewe the by exemples y-nowe;   *enough*
For Lucifer the lyer that lurketh aboute   *liar* [c]
Forto gete hym a grounde that he may graffe on   *graft*
And to sowe of his seede suche as he vsith,   *uses*
1160 That groweth al to grevance and gurdyng of heedes,
        grievance; beheadings
He leyeth his lynes along that luste may be clepid
        lays; lines; pleasure; called
Of oure foule flessh that foundrith ful ofte,   *founders*
And of gloire of this grounde his griefz been y-made,
        glory; harms
That who be hent in his hoke he shal be holde faste
        caught; hook
1165 Til he [be] caste with couetise or sum croke elles.
        thrown down; crook
Seminator zizanne et agricola diaboli
Thenne fareth he forth felaship to gete,   *goes; supporters*
To holde his opinion ouer alle thingz.
Whenne he is laught on the lyne he can not lepe thens,
        caught; leap
So the cursid couetise cleueth on his herte,   *cleaves*
1170 Or elles dreede forto do wel dulleth his wittz.   *fear*
But seche what he seche wol and asaye eeke,
        seek; examine also [c]
There is no sothe-sigger that wol assent to hym,
But conseilleth hym [the] contrary and construeth the doutes
        explains; difficulties
And poynteth hym the perillz and pleynely telleth   *points out*

1165 be] *omitted.*   1173 the] be.

1175 As a sicour seruant, and sheweth hym the happes.
                                     faithful ; *misfortunes*
He shoneth for no salaire ne soulde that he fangeth,
                          shuns ; *salary* ; *payment* ; *receives*
Ne [for no] likerous lyuelode ne loising of his office,
                                   pleasant ; *food* ; *losing*
That he ne telleth the tirant how hit tourne wol
                                        tyrant ; *will turn*
Hamward by his hows and harme most hymself.
                                           homeward [c]
1180 Thenne fleeth he fro his frend and to his foo tourneth,   *foe*
For til he mete with Mvm may he neuer reste.
He wol abide with no burne that botene hym wolde   *amend*
Ne a-rayne hym arere with reason-is bridel,
                          rein ; *backwards* ; *reason's*
So loueth he go large to lepe where hym liketh,   *freely*
1185 And kiketh faste as a colte that casteth downe hymsilf,
                                               throws
And fondeth forto finde this freeke I haue nempnyd,
                             tries ; *man* ; *named*
That fayne is to folowe hym for fees and robes.   *glad*
Thenne meteth he with Mvm and his matiere sheweth,
That shortly assentith as a shrewed hyne,   *cursed servant*
1190 And spareth for no spurnyng, but spedith the matiere,
And wircheth vp with wiles a walle of deceiptes,
                                       works ; *guile*
Til the fals fundement falle atte laste,   *foundation*
That thay stumblen after stroutyng and stappen no ferther,
                                     strutting ; *step*
But lyen dovne on the diche as well nygh y-doluen,   *buried*
1195 Bothe the maister and his man y-murid at oones.   *imprisoned*
Suche maniere medes Mvm can deserue   *rewards* ; *earn*
Forto mende his maister for meete and for hure,
                                  amend ; *payment*
But by the feith that I finge atte vanstone   *received* ; *font-stone*
f.14a Shal no Mvm be my man and I may a-spie,   *look out*
1120 And namely nygh me but next shal he neuer.   *near*
And therefore I fende the, by feith that thou aues,
                                         forbid ; *owe*

1177 for no] no for.

That thou lieue in no lore of suche lewed gomes
believe; *teaching*; *men*
That fikelly fablen and fals been withynne,
deceitfully; *tell stories*
But sue the sothe-sigger and seche thou no ferther.
follow; *seek*
1205 And though hit tene for a tyme hit tideth wel after
vex; *turns out*
And he that made the molde and man with his handes   *world*
Shal quite the with a quitance whenne querellz been vp
reward; *release from debt* [c]
Of this newe nouellerie that noyeth men ofte.
novelty; *annoys*
Hit is the holsemyst hyne for halle and for chambre
most wholesome; *servant*
1210 To bringe boldely a-bedde the best of the royaulme   *realm*
And arise with the renke, rehershing agaynes   *man*
Salomon and Seneca and Sidrac the noble.
Hit is a sicour seruant forto serue lordes,   *trustworthy*
And to knightz of the cuntre his conseil availleth;
1215 And [thow] he-dwelle with a duc and dide not elles   *duke*
But forto seye hym the sothe in reasonable tymes,
He might serue sum day seuene yeres wages.'
'Grand mercy, gardiner,' cothe I, 'and God the foryelde,
thank you; *God repay you*
For thou has demed deuely the doute I was ynne;   *duly*
1220 But yit wote I not in sothe, ne am not infourmed   *informed*
How to come to the court there the kempe dwellith.'   *man*
'His dwellyng to discryue,' cothe he, 'I do hit on alle clercz
describe; *base*
That I shal teche [the] treuly the tournyng to his place.
truly; *turning*
Yn man-is herte his hovsing is, as hooly writte techet,
house; *teaches*
1225 And mynde is his mansion that made alle th'estres.   *divisions*
In corde fidelis est habitacio veritatis
There feoffed hym his fadre freely forto dwelle,   [c]
And put hym in possession in paradise terrestre   [c]; *earthly*
Yn Adam oure auncetre and al his issue after.   *ancestor*; [c]

1215 thow] do.   *1223* the] hym.

He spirith hym with his spirite that sprange of hymself
                                                        inspires
1230 To holde that habitacion and heuene afterwardes,
     To serue hym in sothenes and no souurayn eschewe
     For dreede of deyeng ne no disease elles.   *dying*
     As wold God that eche gome that gre hath take in scoles
                                          man ; degree ; schools
     Wolde holde that opinion and ouer-lepe hit neuer,
1235 For hit was neuer so nedeful as now sith Noe-is dayes.
                                                   since Noah's
     But Mvm wol be no martir while mytres been in sale,
     And but the sothe-sigger sey the same wordes
     Whenne thou comys to his court, kutte of myn eres.   *come*
     Qui non entrat per ostium in ouile sed aliunde fur est et latro.
        euangelium
     Now I haue y-wised the the weye to his place,   *advised*
1240 Hye the hens to his hows and hippe euene amyddes;
                                   go hence ; hop straight in
     For though his loigge be lite hit is vnloke euer,
                                        lodge ; small ; unlocked
     That thou mays intre eche day bothe erly and late,
     Forto walke where thou wolt wythynne and withoute
     And to moeue of his mote in mesurable tyme
                                     move ; suit ; reasonable
f.14b And haue concours to Criste and come yn agaynes.   *resort*
     For thay been brethern by baptesme, as the boke telleth,
                                                      baptism
     And [he] is y-sibbe to the [sire] abouue the seuene sterres
                                          related ; lord ; stars
     For trouthe and the trinite been two nygh frendes.   *close*
     Yf thou wol folowe this fode, thou mos be faire of speche
                                       man ; must ; gracious
1250 And soft of thy sawys, but souuraynete hit helpe;
                                  gentle ; speech ; authority
     For pouerte hath a pressonere whenne he doeth passe bondes.
                              poverty ; jailer ; exceeds bounds
     And be wel ware of wiles the world is ful of mases;
                                          tricks ; deceits
     And loke wel-a-leehalf lest thou be beguilid,
                                      on the lee-side [c]

1247 he] *omitted* ; sire] fure.

For Mvm hath a man there, and is a muche shrewe,

great rascal

1255 Antecrist-is angel that eche day vs ennoyeth.
He dwellith faste by the dore and droppeth many wiles
Yf he might wynne ouer the walle with a wronge entre.

get ; unlawful entry

He debateth eche day with Do-welle withynne,
And the maistrie among and the mote wynneth,   *lawsuit*
1260 And shoueth the sothe-sigger into a syde-herne

shoves ; obscure corner

And taketh Couetise the keye to come ynne when hym likketh.
Thenne Dreede with a dore-barre dryueth oute the beste,

Dread ; door-bar

And maketh the sothe-sigger seche a newe place,
And to walke where he wol withoute on the grene
1265 Til sorowe for his synnes seese hym agaynes

penitence ; seises [c]

And the tenaunt a-tourne to treuthe al his life.   *turn*
Though thou slepe now my soon, yit whenne thou seis tyme,

son ; see

Loke thou write wisely my wordes echone;

make sure ; each one

Hit wol be exemple to sum men seuene yere here-after.
1270 And loke thou seye euer sothe but shame not thy brother
For yf thou telle hym trouthe in tirant-is wise,

tyrant's fashion

He wol rather wexe wrother thenne forto wirche after.

grow angrier ; work ; accordingly

But in a muke maniere thou mos hym asaye,

meek ; manner ; must ; examine

And not eche day to egge hym, but in a deue tyme.

urge ; appropriate

1275 Do thus, my dere soon, for I may dwelle no longer,
But fare to my good frend that I fro come.
I haue infourmed the faire loke thou folowe after

prosecute [c]

And make vp thy matiere, thou mays do no better.   [c]
Hit may amende many men of thaire misdeedes.
1280 Sith thou felys the fressh lete no feynt herte   *feels*
Abate thy blessid bisynes of thy boke-making

terminate [c] ; *business*

Til hit be complete to clapsyng, caste aweye doutes   *clasping*
And lete the sentence be sothe, and sue to th'ende;
                               judgment; follow [c]
And furst feoffe thou therewith the freyst of the royaulme,
                               enfeoffe; noblest
1285 For yf thy lord liege allone hit begynne,
Care thou not though knyghtz copie hit echone,
And do write eche word and wirche there-after.'
Thenne soudaynly of sweuene and slepe I abrayed
                               dream; started
And woke of my wynke and waitid aboute,   *sleep; looked*
1290 Wondring on my wittz, as I wel aughte,   *ought*
f.15a Where the gome and the gardyn and the gaye sportz   *man*
And alle the sightz that I sawe were so sone voidid.   *vanished*
Hit ferde as a fairye but feithfully the wordes
                         disappeared; enchantment
Were ful wise of the wye in the white clothes,   *man*
1295 And eeke nedeful and notable for this newe world,   *necessary*
And eeke plaisant to my pay for thay putten me reste
                               pleasant; liking
Of my long labour and loitryng aboute.
For he provid by profitable poyntz and fele   *many*
That the sothe-sigger shuld haue the better
1300 Of Mvm, and the maistrie, malgre his chekes.   *in spite of him*
He made Mvm a man-sleer and a-mys thewed
                         murderer; ill-mannered
And likenyd hym to a lorel atte long goyng.
                          rogue; in the long run
And shortly he sheweth right so by thayr werkes
To clercz of conceipte that construen thaire workes.
                             understanding
1305 He chargid me cleerly to change not myn intent
Til the matire of Mvm were made to th'ende,   *matter*
And that I shuld seye sothe and sette no dreede
Of no creature of clay, for Criste so hym taughte.   *earth*
And though sum men of sweuenes sauery but lite,
                               dreams; credit
1310 Yit the lore of the lude shal like me euer,   *teaching; man*
For Daniel in his dayes declarid ful ofte   *expounded*
Dreemes and vndide thaym as deede provid after;   *interpreted*
And Ioseph the gentil Genesis thou saye

(The bible bereth witnesse, a boke of bilieue).
1315 He mette that the mone and elleuen sterres   *dreamt; eleven*
    With the shynant sunne soudaynely at oones

                         shining; suddenly
    A-bowid to his bidding bonairely, hym thought,

                   bowed down; courteously
    And dide hym worship therewith that wroth made after   *angry*
    His brethern that bisied thaym to bringe hym of dawe.

                   busied; kill him [c]
1320 Hit semyd by his sweuene thay sayden tho among thaym,

                             then
    Shuld falle that thayr fadre and thay been fayne eeke

                     happen; glad
    To mete hym with thayre modre in a muke wise,

                 meet; mother; meek
    And pray hym in his pouaire pite forto haue   *power*
    Of thaym and thaym helpe fro hungre and elles.
1325 And so hit feulle sothely thay sought hym thereafter

                   happened; truly
    Ernestly in Egipte or elles the boke lieth,
    For hunger that thay hadde and helpe couthe thay none
    But lowely to loute his lordship to sike,   *humbly; bow; seek*
    Forto graunt of his grayn what hym good likid
1330 That for faute of thayr fode famyne long durid.

               lack; famine; endured
    And so hit semeth in certayne that sum bee right trewe
    And sothe of thees sweuenes of sobre men wittes,   *dreams*
    And prouen ofte to the poynt of pourpoos in deede.   *purpose*
    And therefore my doute and dreede is the lasse
1335 To do that the burne bade, that the bees kepte,
    [Forto saye sumwhat of svth er I passe]   *truth; before*
    How the greete of this ground been y-gouuerned.   *nobility*
f.15b Thenne softe I the soores to serche thaym withynne,   *softened*
    And seurely to salue thaym and with a newe salue

               thoroughly
1340 That the sothe-sigger hath sought many yeres
    And mighte not mete therewith for Mvm and his ferys

              associates
    That bare a-weye the bagges and many a boxe eeke.   *carried*

1336] omitted.

Now forto conseille the king vnknytte I a bagge   *opened*
Where many a pryue poyse is preyntid withynne
                        secret verse; *printed*
1345 Yn bokes vnbredid in balade-wise made,
                           un-opened [c]

Of vice and of vertue fulle to the margyn,
That was not y-openyd this other half wintre.
There is a quayer of quitances of quethyn goodes,
                  quire; *receipts*; *bequeathed*
That bisshoppz han begged to binde al newe,
1350 And a penyworth of papir of penys that thay fongen
                 paper; I.O.U.S. [c]; *receive*
For lemmans and lotebies in thees late dayes,   *concubines*
And lien on the lettrure, for lawe was hit heuer.   *lie*; *learning*
Ve illis qui vendunt peccatum propter pecuniam.
There is volume of visitacion of viftene leves   [c]
How persones and prestis been y-passid ouer
                     parsons; *overlooked*
1355 Thorough fauour of fangyng and no faute amendid,   *bribery*
But liggen in London in lorden courtz   *lie*; *courts of lords*
And pleyen lille for lalle with many levde [kitte].
                 [c]; *ignorant wench* [c]
Thay lusten for to lerne of lettrure no ferther   *desire*
Thenne to the lesson of laudate al thaire life-dayes,   *Lauds* [c]
1360 Forto preche thaire parroisshe how Pernelle is arayed
                   Pernel; *dressed*
And with the tolle of the tithing fetishly a-tired.
              tax; *elegantly dressed*
Thay been losers of the lawe and lewde men maken   *breakers*
The bolder for thaire badnes and breke the tenne hestes.
                  commandments
There is a rolle of religion, how thay thaire rentz hadde
                   incomes
1365 Forto parte with the poure a parcelle other-while,
           share; *poor*; *portion*; *sometimes*
But thay been rotid in a rewe to refresshe greete,
          rooted; *company*; *nobility*
To maynteyne thayre manhode and matieres thay haue to doo
                   lawsuits

1357 kitte] light.

For pleding and for pourchas, to pasture thaym the swetter,
purchase; *sweeter*

So poure thay been and penylees sith the pestilence tyme.   [c]

1370 Yit is there a paire of pamphilettz of prelatz of the royaulme
pamphlets

Yn the bottume of the bagge, how boldely thay ride,

Thees persones and thees prebendiers pluralite that hauen,
parsons; *canons*

[Poperyng] on thaire palefrays fro oone place to an other,
trotting [c]

And lernen to lede ladies and lewed men envien   *conduct*

1375 To do al thing as thay do as by thaire deedes proueth.

Thay autorisen with argumentz and allegen for thaym
authorise; *defend*

That of oon kinde alle came there can no man seye other.
one nature

Thus leden thay thaire lyves in lustes and in sportes,

And spenden on thaire speciales that thay spare shuld
mistresses

16a For pouraile of thaire parroishens and present to be among
   thaym
poor; *parishioners*

Forto salue thaire shepe whenne thay sike were.   *salve*; *sick*

But how shuld a surgean serue wel his hyre   *deserue*; *payment*

That cometh not in seuene yere to se the sore oones,

That they shal not se oon shyne how soutelly thay wirchen.
one glimpse; *subtly*

Ve pastoribus.

1385 I say not but of sum that suche manieres vsen,

For euery wyman that is wise, she wircheth to the beste.
woman

And conseilleth al to conscience leste there come happes.
misfortune

Yit is there a copie for comunes of culmes foure and twenty
items [c]

How sum tellen tidingz at home vppon thaire benches,

1390 Or elles at eue after souper or erely atte nale,   *early*; *ale*

And lyen on the lordz, – lorelles and noon other.
tell lies about; *rascals*

Thaire tales been so trouble that tournen men thoughtz;   *turn*

1373 Poperyng] Properyng.   1377 man] may.

The more that men musen on thaym, the madder thay been
  after.
I mervail but thay mette so how hit might be   *unless; dreamt*
1395 That thay finde fables and been so ferre fro thens   *far; thence*
That though thou ride rennyng, and reste but a lite,   *running*
Fro London forth the long waye to the land-is ende,
And comes right from the king-is courte and his cunseil bothe,
                           council
Fro prelatz vnto peris in pryuete or elles,   *peers; private*
1400 Yit shal tidingz bee y-tolde tenne dayes ere thou come,
That neuer was of worde spoke ne wroughte, as thou shal hire.
                            made
Lesingz been so light of fote, thay lepen by the skyes,
                        lies; foot
And as swifte as a swalue sheutyng ovte at oones
                  swallow; shouting
As falsely forgid as though a frere had made thaym.   *forged*
Rumores fuge ne incipias nouus auctor haberi
1405 That harde happes mote thay haue that Henry so appeiren,
             misfortune; may; injure
Or any lord of this lande that loueth pees and reste,
Though the burne my brother were, I bid hit with my herte.
                         man
Yit wol thay carpe of the coroune as thay of cunseil were,
And ordeyne more in oon houre than other half wintre
                      ordain [c]
1410 Al the king-is cunseil couthe wel bringe aboute.
Thus mellen thay with matieres to moustre thaire wittes,
                interfere; show off
And grucchen whenne the gadryng is that goeth for vs alle.
              grumble; collection [c]
I seye yf hit be sette so and in suche thinges,
Ful ille couthe thay corde with Changwys-is deedes,
              accord; Genghis's [c]
1415 That conquerid many a cuntre as king withynne hymself;
And how he came to his coroune I shal you kenne sone.
                         teach
The greete God of goodnes that gouuerneth alle thingz,
He nempned furst his name to the seuene nacions   *named*
That were wel nygh destrued and disware of thaire lives
                      in despair

1420 And in disease and desperat thorough thaire double intentz.

fraudulent intentions

Thaire diuision dide thaym harme (and so hit doeth
elleswhere),

Omne regnum in se diuisum desolabitur.

That thay were sette in seruitute by souurayns of the marches

slavery

That had y-wonne and y-wastid wel nygh alle the landz.

conquered

The principal[z] of this peuple pryuyly by nightz

leaders; secretly

1425 A voice thaym folowed [in vision] in fourthering of thaymself,

furthering

And bade thaym coroune Changwys king of al thaire peuple,

instructed

A eildren man of aunsetrie that aged was a lite.

elderly; noble ancestry

And so the deede was y-do when day and tyme came after

done

And when this Changwys was y-corouned as cronicle of hym
telleth,

16b And sette in his se with sceptre on his handes,

He stablid two statutz, as storie of hym writeth,   *established*

I herde neuer harder and yit thay holde were.   *held*

The furst that he funded to fele trewe hertz   *test*

And his principal peuple to proue and a-saye,   *examine* [c]

1435 Was that the souurayns of the seuene nacions   *lords*

Shuld sle thayre soones the eldest and thaire hoires;

kill; heirs

The secund that thay shuld eeke sese [hym] in [hire lande]

seise [c]

And yelde hit vp in erniste and yeue hit hym for euer,

pledge; give

To haue and to holde in his high grace.   [c]

1440 And as the king commandid accordid thay were,   *agreed*

Consentyng to his couetise with crie alle at oones.

Thay sparid not to spille blode that spronge of thaymself,

sprang

1424 principalz] principal.   1437 hym in hire lande] thaym in his
1425 in vision] by nightes.   handes.

Ne to lose thayre lordship and lande at his wille.
Now forto telle trouthe, I trowe hit be no lesing,   *lie*
1445 Who wolde haue griefed for a grote he wold haue grucched
    there.   *suffered*; *groat*; *grumble*
Thus preued this prince his [peuple] and thaire hertz,   *proved*
And to feil of thaire fiance ful felly he wroughte;
                   try; *loyalty*; *cruelly*; *behaved*
And [whenne he] wiste that his wil was not encountrid,
                         knew; *contraried*
But that he had thaire hertz al hoole at his wil,   *whole*
1450 He forgafe thaym thaire graunt and goodely thaym thanked.
Thenne clepid he to cunseil knightz and other,
                            called

And wroughte alle with oon wil as wise men shuld,
And wanne wisely ayen withynne a while after   *won back*
The lande and the lordship that thay loste had,
1455 And conquerid cuntrees, as Cathay-is lande,   *Cathay's* [c]
That is the richeste royaulme that reyne ouer houeth.
                         rain; *hovers*
Ecce quam bonum et quam iocundum habitare fratres in vnum.
Now by Crist that me creed, I can not be-thenke
                     created; *think of*
A kindely cause why the comun shuld
Contre the king-is wil ne construe his werkes.
                     oppose; *interpret*
1460 I carpe not of knightz that cometh for the shires,   *speak*
That the king clepith to cunseil with other;
But hit longeth to no laborier the lawe is agayne thaym.
                   belongs; *labourer*
And yit hit is y-vsid with vnwise peuple   *practised*
And a-vailleth not a ferthing, but vireth the hertz;
               helps; *farthing*; *inflames*
1465 That tournen with thaire tales the tente of the lordes,
                     turn; *attention*
That thay leven the labour the londe to defende,   *leave*
To bisye thaym on the bordures to bete oute oure foes,
                     borders
And maynteyne the marches fro myschief and elles.

1446 peuple] pleuple.   1448 whenne he] *omitted*.

Thus clappeth the comun and knocketh thaymself,
> *chatters; injures*

1470 For the [tayl] of thaire talking teneth thaym ofte.
> *conclusion; oppresses* [c]

Thou mays lerne that lesson in the nexte lyne,

For and thy heede be hurte thy [honde] wol apeire;
> *hand; will become weaker*

And who-so hewe ouer heede though his hoode be on,
> *cut; overhead*

The spones wol springe oute and spare not the eye. *splinters*

1475 Thay finde many fautes and faillen moste thaymself

f.17a Of deedes of deuete that thay do shuld. *duty*

Thay shulde loue loyally the lordz aboute,

That thay mighte lerne a lesson of thaire lowe hertz

To reule thaym by reason and by right lawe.

1480 Thay shuld be reedy to ride and renne at thayre heste
> *run; command*

For soulde and for siluer as thay might a-serue,
> *payment; deserve*

And obeye to thayre bidding and bable no ferther,

Potencioribus pares non esse non possumus. Sapiencia.

For suche lewed [labbing] the lande doeth a-peire.
> *chattering; harm*

But God of his goodnes graunt thaym to amende,

1485 To knowe what thaire kinde is and commenche bityme
> *nature; begin; early*

The cunseille of Changwys and construe no ferther,

But loue so oure liege al oure life-dayes

That he may leede vs with loue as hymself liketh.

There is a scrowe for squyers that a-square walken
> *scroll; the other way* [c]

1490 Whenne a tale is y-tolde, yf hit touche greete
> *pleading; concern; nobility*

That piled han poure men of penys and of goodes; *robbed*

Thay wol neghen no neer but yf thay noye thenke
> *approach; give trouble*

And alleigge for the lord and lawe dovne bere,
> *give evidence; bear down*

1470 tayl] tale.   1483 labbing] babling.
1472 honde] hoode.

Leste soulde and thaire seruice cesse al at ones.
            payment; *cease*

1495 Thus poure men pleyntz been pledid ful ofte,   *lawsuits*
For reason-is retenue moste reste nedis   *retinue*
There robes rehercyn the rightz of the parties.   *rehearse*
There is a writte of high wil y-write al newe   *written*; *fresh*
Y-knytte in a cornier of the bagge-ende,   *knit*
1500 And is a courssid couraige and coste-ful bothe
            cursed; *irritant* [c]; *expensive*
That serueth al for souurayns of semblable pouaire;
            serves; *equal power*
For euer egalite errith and stryueth
            equality; *goes astray*; *contends*
More thanne the [mene] man with his more heigher
            lowly; *against his superior*
For whenne a matiere is y-moeved among men of goode,
            men of property
1505 Though there happe no harme saue her[tz] aggreiggid,
            has been no hurt; *aggravated*
They stele into strivyng and strien thaym-self
            steal; *contention*; *destroy*
And stiren so that stuffure and store doon apeire,
            act; *household materials*; *store*
And eeke losen thaire good loos with thaire lewed pride,
            reputation
And annoyen thaire neighborowes nyne myle aboute.
1510 For euery feithful frend wol funde to helpe   *try*
And leue there he loueth, for lothe or elles;
            believe; *has favour*; *harm*
Suche wilfulnes and wisedame wonen a-sunder.   *dwell*; *apart*
Thou mays baathe on a brooke to the breggurdelle;
            bathe; *waist*
But passe not the polle forther for peril that foloweth.
            head

Ira odium generat concordia nutrit amorem
1515 Thus seyeth that oon side, 'Shule [I] obeye
Or make amendes or mukyn myself?   *humble*
Nay, are I worke suche a worke but my witte faille,

1503 mene] more.   1515 I] omitted.
1505 hertz] herg.

Hit shuld stande right straite with stoone of my howses,
For leuer thenne to lowe me while my life dureth   *submit*
1520 I wol do a deede that I dide neuer,
Sille for siluer my sherte and my clothes,   *sell*
f.17b Or borowe til I begge thenne bowe oones.
[And] I were caste in my cuntre and hit knowe were,
                                        defeated; district
I shuld be [eschewid] and ouer-sette ofte.   *avoided; oppressed*
1525 Ney, I wol maynteyne my manhoode, maul-gre that gruccheth,
                                        despite anyone that grumbles
And spare swete spices and spende on my foes'.   *give up*
That other side seyeth right so and the same wordes,
As wilde [and] as wode and as wrothe eeke,   *mad; angry*
And braggeth and bosteth and wol brenne watiers
                                        boasts; burn waters [c]
1530 And rather renne in rede blode thenne a-rere oones.
                                        run; retreat
Ira requiescit non insanitas mentis ac corporis. Salomon
Thus they blowe as a bore til bothe repente.   *huff; boar*
Hit is no witte, as I wene, to waste so siluer
For a woode wil and wretthe in thy herte,
And no harme on thy heede in hande ne in goodes,   [c]
1535 But y-hurte on the hert with a high pride.
For suche maniere medling al to many tymes,
Though hit gaine in the bigynnyng, hit groweth so aftre
That lymes been y-loste and lyfes ful ofte,   *limbs*
Superbia generat omnem maliciam vsque ad mortem. Salomon
And eeke hit is no worldly witte, as me thenketh,
1540 To toille there no trespas is do to a-countz.
                                        contend; offence; property [c]
But hit semeth to a souurayn that ynnesight lacketh,   *insight*
Whenne his mynde is y-moevid to medle in his ire,   *moved*
That though his grovnde be not goode and he gaste were
                                        ground [c]; *if; afraid*
Or feynte forto folowe but fersse to th'ende,
                                        weak; prosecute; fierce
1545 Hit shuld be [aretted] for reprouf whenne hit were rehercyd,
                                        considered; reproach

1523 And] A.   1528 and] omitted.
1524 eschewid] so thewid.   1545 aretted] sette.

And he y-sette the shorter at shire and a-boute.
considered the lesser

Suche cursid construyng accombreth the [peuple].
fabrication of evidence [c]

For [contra] that conceipt I can make a reason,
against ; reasoning ; argument [c]

And a trewe, as I trowe, who-so taketh hede:

1550 Whenne rancune the redeth to reere debatz,
anger ; advises ; raise debates

Or angre at attre arteth thy herte
bitterness ; constrains

Forto commenche a cause not cleere in the winde,
[c]

Bowe ere thou breste whenne thou arte bette y-fourmyd,
submit ; burst ; informed

And revle the by reason and renne not to faste,

1555 But gife hit vp with good wille whenne thy grovnde failleth,

And falle of with fayrenes leste fors the assaille.
withdraw ; grace ; force

For yf thou leue are thou ligge thenne wol thy loos springe,
cease ; overthrown ; praise

But yf thy tale be trewe, to toylle thou hatis.   *contend ; hate*

So wol the worde walke with oon and with other

1560 And cumforte thy cuntre in cumpas aboute   *area around*

To be nere at thy nede a-nother tyme after,   *close*

And bilieue loyally, in lawe yf thou were,

Or medlist with a matiere, thy [mote] were trewe,   *lawsuit*

Elles woldes thou not worche on hit longe.

1565 There is a raggeman rolle that Ragenelle hymself
document ; Ragnel [c]

Hath made of mayntennance and motyng of the peuple,
litigation

Hough thay sheue at sises and sessions aboute,
shove ; assizes

f.18a And halen so the hockerope oon halfe agayne other
pull ; hock-rope [c]

Til the strong steriers and styuest on the heedes
inciters ; strongest

1570 Strifen so and streicchen streight adovne the poure.
contend ; pull

1547 peuple] pleuple.   1563 mote] more.
1548 contra] cuntrey.

(Gold and good thaym glewith so thay wol not go a-sundre)
glue ; separate
Til thay haue haled the howslord oute atte halle-dore
pulled ; house-lord
And drawen hym clene fro his dees ; he dysneth there nomore.
dais ; dines
This same cursid custume the coroune doeth a-peyre   *injure*
575 And bringeth a bitter byworde a-brode among the peuple,
proverb ; abroad
And is in euery cuntre but a comune tale
That yf the pouer playne, though he plede euer
And hurleth with his higher hit happeth ofte-tyme
contend ; superior
That he wircheth al in waste and wynneth but a lite.
works ; in vain ; earns
580 Thus laboreth the loos among the comune peuple
travels ; report
That the wacker in the writte wol haue the wors ende;
weaker ; writ
Hit wol not gayne a goky a grete man forto plede,
benefit ; poor
For lawe lieth muche in lordship sith loyaute was exiled,
maintenance ; loyalty
And poure men pleyntes penylees a-bateth.
penniless ; terminates
585 But Dauid demed not so, I do hit on his bokes.
Munera super innocentem non accipies.
Yit is there a forelle that I forgate that frayed is a lite,
book-cover ; forgot
How the [fleuble] fareth that folowed bee in shires
weak ; prosecuted
Whenne thay griefen greete, though the guilte be lite.
offend against
And he haue any hors or elles hedid bestes,   *horned beasts*
590 He shal be hourled so in high courte and holde so agogge
hurled ; in suspense
That hym were bettre lose his lande thenne long so be toylid;
in contention
Suche crokes been y-courid and coloured vnder lawe,
tricks ; covered ; camouflaged

1587 fleuble] peuple.

To strue a man with [strength] the statu[tz] been so made.
                                                          destroy
For though men pleede and poursuye and in thaire playntz falle
                                              prosecute ; withdraw
1595 And newe thaym aftre nonsuyte[s] nynetene hunthred,
                                              re-open ; non-suits [c]
Withoute grovnde or guilte but forto gete a bribe,
Yit shal thay haue no harme though thay hurle euer.   *contend*
But shuld thay picche and paye at eche pleynte-is ende
                                                        contribute
And compte alle the costz of men of court and elles,   *count*
1600 And taske al the trespas as trouthe wolde and reason,   *tax*
Thay wolde cesse sum tyme for sheding of thaire siluer.
                                                          spending
I seye aswel of simple men that suen ayenst grete,   *sue*
And of the poure proute that peyren ofte thaire better,
                                                  proud ; injure
That causelees accusen thaym to king and to the lordz,
                                                    without cause
1605 As I doo of ducz that suche deedes vsen;   *dukes ; practise*
For lordz and laborers been not like in costes.
Hit wold pese the peuple and many pleyntes bate
                                                  pacify ; abate
And chaunge al the chauncellerie and cheuallerie amende
                                                          knights
And ease be to euery man that been of euene states,
                                                    equal estates
1610 And solas be to souurayns and to thaire seruantz alle,   *solace*
And a miracle to meen men that mote lite cunne,
                                          poor ; can hardly go to law
Were this oon yere y-vsid as I haue declarid, –   *practised*
That of euery writte withoute wronge there were amendes
      made,
f.18b And paye for alle the costes at euery pleynte-is ende
1615 And tolle for the trespas as trouthe wolde and reason –   *pay*
The lawe wold like vs wel, and euer the lenger the bettre.
But pouaire of prerogatife that poynt hath reseruyd
                                          power ; prerogative [c]

1593 strength] lawe ; statutz] status.   *1595* nonsuytes] nonsuyte.

That euery fode haue fredome to folowe vn-y-punysshid.
                                                man ; prosecute
But ciuile seith vs not so that serueth for al peuple
                                                Civil Law [c] *; serves*
1620 That habiteth vndre heuene hethen men and other.   *heathen*
And Crist-is lawe-is y-canonized canon, yf thou loke,
                                                Canon Law [c]
And eeke the glorious gospelle grovnde of alle lawes,
Techeth vs a trewe texte that toucheth this ilke matiere;   *same*
Nullum malum impunitum. euangelium
For in my conscience ne in my credo yit couthe I neuer vele
                                                *conscience ; * [c] *; feel*
1625 But that oure lawe leneth there a lite, as me thenketh.
                                                is biased
There is a librarie of lordes that losen ofte thaym-self
                                                book-collection ; destroy
Thorough lickyng of the lordship that to the coroune longeth,
                                                infringing ; regality
And weneth hit be wel y-do but wors dide thay neuer   *think*
Thenne sith thay gunne that game, I grovnde me on reason.
                                                began
1630 For euery wighte wote wel but yf his witte faille,
That hit is holsum forto haue a heede of vs alle,
That is a king y-corouned to kepe vs vnder lawe,
To put vs into prisone whenne we passe boundes.
For but we had a souurayn to sette vs into reste,
1635 Thees rechelees renkes wolde renne on eche other.
                                                irresponsible men ; run
Thenne of fyne fors hit foloweth, as me thenketh,   *fine force*
That a certayne substance shuld be ordeynid
To susteyne this souurayn that shuld vs gouerne.
And so I wote wel hit was atte furst tyme,
1640 But now hit is bynome hym th'olde and the newe,
                                                deprived him [c]
Not-wi[th]standing statutz ful strattely y-made   *strictly*
To stable many [stablementz] and strong lawes make.
                                                ordinances
But execucion falle what may hit availle

1641 withstanding] wistanding.   1642 stablementz] statutz.

Ne more thenne the mose may or the maij floures *moss*;   *May*
1645 To breke dovne bastiles that beste is y-made ?   *towers*
Hit is as dede as a dore nayle, though the dome come after,
                                              dead; *judgment*
Withoute execucion thees wise men hit knoweth.
Thees knightz of the conseil that nygh the king dwellen,
And eeke lordz y-lettred of oone lawe and other,   [c]
1650 Forto kepe his coroune fro couetous peuple   *protect*
Han pulled thaymself the peres right to the pere stalke,   *pears*
And lickid so the leves he hath the leste dele,   *least part*
For thay holden of his honour halfendele and more.
                                              more than half
This was grovnde and bigynnyng of gurdyng of heedes,
                                              beheadings
1655 And eeke more [of] mourdre and many-folde wronges
                                              criminal acts
That han y-falle for foly withynne thees fourty wintre.
For th'egre enuye that eche had to other   *eager*; *envy*
Dide thaym preece to be pryvy and put aweye the beste,
                                              urge; *secret*
But muche more for the mede to make thaym-self riche
                                              reward
f.19a Thenne to cunseille the king of the comune [wele]
                                              common profit
Or for any deue dome or defence of the royaulm[e].
                                              lawful judgment
This same cursid custume oure coroune hath a-p[ayred],
                                              weakened
And cause is most that comunes collectours haten,
                                              tax collectors; *hate*
For nedis moste oure liege lord like his estat
1665 Haue for his houshold and for his [haynous werres]
                                              heinous wars
To maynteyne his manhoode there may no man seye o[ther],
                                              say otherwise
But of his owen were the beste, who-so couthe hit bringg[e];
                                              [c]; *manage*
To lyve vppon his laboriers, hit may not long indure.

1655 of] and.   1665 haynous werres] *omitted*
1660-2] *margin torn.*

Whenne hit is haled al awey thenne is wo the nexte   *carried*
1670 To you that shullen siluer to solue thenne were tyme.

                                                   owe ; pay

For trusteth right treuly, talke what men liketh,
And wendith and trendith twys in oon wike,   *turn ; twist ;* [c]
And clepith to your cunseil copes and other,   *call ; copes* [c]
And pleyne atte parlement, but yf the deede prouue
1675 That the coroune in his kinde come ynne agaynes,   *nature*
Clene in his cumpas with croppes and braunches,

                                          circle ; foliage

Lite and a lite, right as the lawe asketh,   *little by little*
Wel mowe we wilne and wisshe what vs liketh   *may we want*
And eeke waite after welthe but as my witte demeth,
1680 Oure wynnyng and worship wol be the lasse

                                       profit ; praise ; less

With knight and with comune til the king haue   *commonality*
Alle hoole in his hande that he haue oughte.
There is a copie of couetise, how conscience is revled   *ruled*
Whenne he [hath] gadrid a greete bagge and good at his wil,
1685 And wrongfully y-wonne hit thorough wiles of his hert,

                                       won ; deceits

And is y-runne in riches thorough ryfling of the peuple,

                                       robbing

He maketh maisons deu therewith whenne he may live [no
  len]ger;   *hospitals*
But while he had power of the penyes the poure had but lite.
Hit is a high holynes and grete helth to the soule,
1690 A man to lyue in lustes alle his life-dayes
And haue no pitie on the poure, ne parte with thaym nother,

                                       share

But holde hit euer in his hande till the herte breke.
But thenne he shapeth for the soule whenne the sunne is dovne,

                                       provides

But while the day durid he delte but a lite;   *dealt out*
1695 Now muche moste his merite be that mendeth so the poure,

                                       benefits

That gifeth his good for God-is sake whenne his goste is
  pass[ed].   *spirit ; gone*

1684 hath] *omitted.*   *1696*] *margin torn.*
1687 no lenger] ger.

There is a [title] of a testament that I tolde neuer,
section ; *will*

How pryuyly thay been provid and y-put a-side,
secretly ; *proved*

For so the siluer be y-soluid for the seel of th'office   *paid*

1700 And the feis alle y-funge thay folden thaym to-gedre
fees ; *received*

And casten thaym in a coffre leste thay copied were,

And sith thay seure thaym by thaymself and seyen thees
[wordes]:   *assure*

'Hit is no wisedame forto wake Warrok while he sl[epeth]'
Warrock [c]

For though a quynzieme were y-quethe oon quita[nce shal be
geven]   *fifteenth ; bequeathed receipt*

1705 Though executours after-warde execute hit neu[er],

f.19b [And do noght for] the dede as I do whenne I slepe.   [c] ; *dead*

[And yit] thay seyen for thaymsilf right a subtile reason :
subtle

'[Why sh]uld we dele for the dede ? He dide not while he
mighte.   *dole out ; dead*

[He] made vs in his mynde among alle his frendes

1710 [T]o be his trewe attourneys and treete for his debtes,

[F]or so that they haue halfendele thay mowe thaym holde
content.   -   *half ; must*

[Y]it wol not the good go so ferre so mote we grovnde oure
tale,   *far*

For I wol seye for myself, seye thou whenne the liketh,

Yf we do as he dude, may no man deme vs yuel,   *did ; badly*

1715 Ne rightfully by reason reproue vs here-after.

He was bothe ware and wise while he was on live,   *cautious*

And me lust not be lewed leste I fare the wors.
do not wish ; foolish

His custume was to kepe his good so lete vs kepe hit eeke,

And thenne after oure deeth day lete dele for vs alle

1720 For oure executours aftre vs shal haue the same charge.'
mandate

Thus thay chiden with charite and chacheth eche other,
persecute

That til the day of dome the dele is not parfourmid.

> dole; *distributed*

Yit is there a poynt of prophecie how the peuple construeth
And museth on the meruailles that Merlyn dide deuyse,

> *devise* [c]

1725 And redith as right as the Ram is hornyd,

> *straightforwardly*; [c]

As helpe me the high God, I holde thaym halfe a-masid.   *crazy*
For there nys wight in this world that wote bifore eue
How the winde and the wedre wol wirche on the morowe,

> *behave*

Ne noon so cunnyng a clerc that construe wel couthe
1730 Ere sunneday seuenyght what shal falle.   *week*
Thus thay muse on the mase on mone and on sterres

> *in confusion*; *moon*; *stars*

Til heedes been hewe of and hoppe on the grene,

> *heads*; *cut off*

And al the wide world wondre on thaire workes.
Yit sawe I there a cedule soutelly indited

> *schedule* [c]; *composed*

1735 With tuly silke intachid right atte rolle-is ende,   *red*; *attached*
Y-write ful of wordes of woundres that han falle,
And fele-folde ferlees wythynne thees fewe yeris,

> *manifold*; *marvels*

By cause that the clergie and knighthoode to-gedre
Been not knytte in conscience as Crist dide thaym stable.

> *establish*

1740 For who so loketh on the lawe may lerne, yf hym like,
Thayre ordre and office and how thay [ought] wyrche.
For thay folowe no foote of thaire forne-fadres,
I do hit on thaire deeth-day, and deme no ferther,
For seurly sumtyme I sawe hit not late   *assuredly*; *recently*
1745 Yn cronicle of clercz and kingz lygnees   *lineages*
[H]ow prelatz of prouinces pride moste hatid
[For] the theme that thay taughte was tachid on thaire hertz.

> *fastened*

[Thay] preched the peuple and prouyd hit thaymself
[And w]ere lanternes to lewed men to lyve thaym after.

> *according to their example*

1741 ought] shuld.   1746–51] *margin torn*.

1750　[Thay p]ourchachid no prelacies with prince nother elles
　　　　　　　　　　　　purchased; *church appointments*
　　[Thorough pr]eyer ne povndes but thorough proufe of thayre
　　　workes.　　　　　　　　　　　　*prayer* [c] ; *proof*

THE CROWNED KING

THE CROWNED KING

f.4a Crist, crowned Kyng, that on Cros didest,   *died*
  And art comfort of all care, thow kynd go out of cours,
                                             nature ; *course*
    With thi halwes in heuen heried mote thu be,
                                             saints ; *praised*
    And thy worshipfull werkes worshiped euere,
  5 That suche sondry signes shewest vnto man
    In dremyng, in drecchyng, and in derk swevenes,
                                          nightmares ; *dreams*
    Wherwith that thei ben ware and witterly knowen
                                             aware ; *clearly*
    Of care and of comfort that comyng is here-after.
    This I sey be myself, so saue me our lord,
 10 Be a metyng that y met in a morowe slepe,
                                   dream ; *dreamt* ; *morning*
    Hevy and hidows, y hight you, forsoth,
                                  hideous ; *promise* ; *indeed*
    And the most merveylous that y met euere.   *dreamt*
    And ye like to leer and listen a while,   *learn*
    As y may in my mynde this metynge reherce,
 15 Sekerly and shortly the soth y shall you shewe,
                                            surely ; *truth*
    Of this dredefull dreme – deme as you likes.
                                      frightening ; *judge*
    Ones y me ordeyned, as y haue ofte doon,   *prepared myself*
    With frendes and felawes, [fremde] men and other,
                                                  strangers
    And caught me in a company on Corpus Cristi even

18 fremde] frende.

20 Six other vij myle oute of Suthampton,   *seven*
   To take melodye and mirthes among my makes,

                                                                  companions
   With redyng of romaunces, and reuelyng among.   *revelling*
   The dym of the derknesse drowe into the west,   *drew*
   And began for to spryng in the grey day :   [c]
25 Than lift y vp my lyddes and loked in the sky

                                                           lifted ; eyelids
   And knewe by the kende course hit clered in the est.

                                                             natural ; east
   Blyve y busked me doun and to bed went,

                                                       quickly ; got ready
   For to comfort my kynde and cacche a slepe.
   Swythe y swyed in a sweem that y swet after;

                                                    soon ; sank ; swoon
30 So my spirit in a spaas so sore was y set,

                                                 short time ; affected
   Me thought that y houed an high on an hill,   *hovered*
   And loked down on a dale deppest of othre.
   Ther y sawe in my sight a selcouthe peple –   *strange*
   The multitude was so moche it myght not be [noumbred].
35 Me thought y herd a crowned kyng of his comunes axe   *ask*
f.4b A soleyn subsidie to susteyne his werres,

                                                  extraordinary ; wars
   To be rered in the reaume, as reson requyred,

                                          raised ; realm ; justice
   Of suche as were seemly to suffre the charge;   *bear*
   That they that rekened were riche by reson and skyle

                                                           argument
40 Shuld pay a parcell for here poure neighbowres;   *portion*
   This ordenaunce he made in ease of his peple.   *decree*
   With that a clerk kneled adoun and carped these wordes:

                                                             spoke
   'Liege lord, yif it you like to listen a while
   Sum sawes of Salomon y shall you shew sone,

                                              sayings ; promptly
45 Besechyng you of your sowerainte that y myght be suffred
   To shewe you my sentence in singuler noumbre
   To peynte it with pluralites my prose would faile;   [c]

   34 noumbred] noumbrerd.

To pike a thonk with plesaunce my profit were but simple.'

earn thanks

Than the kyng of his curtesie comaunded hym to ryse,

50 To stonde and sey what hym semed and knele no lenger.

Than he saide, 'Sir, crowned kyng, thow knowest well thyself.

Thiself hast lyfe, lyme and lawes for to keep;   *limb*

Yif thou be chief Iustice, iustifie the trouthe;

And rule the be reson, and vpright sitte.

55 For that is a poynt principall – preve it who-so-will –

prove

To be dred for thy domes [and dowted] for thy myght;

judgments; feared

For ther is neither lered ne lewed that lyveth vpon erthe

learned; unlettered

That [ne] wyssheth after worship; his wit is full fable

feeble

But yif he wite be his werkes he hath well deserued,

unless; know [c]

60 And of his well doyng his dedes to deme the same.

The loue of thi liegmen, that to thi lawe are bounde,

subjects

Take hit for a tresour of hem that are true,

That may the more availl in a myle wey

help; in the long run

Thanne moche of thy mukke that manhode loueth neuere.

wealth

65 The playnt of the pouere peple put thou not behynde,

pleading

For [they] swope and swete and swynke for thy fode;

labour; toil; food

Moche worship they wynne the in this worlde riche,

Of thy gliteryng gold and of thy gay wedes,   *clothes*

Thy proude pelure, and palle with preciouse stones,

fur; cloth

f.5a Grete castels and stronge, and styff walled townes.

strong

And yit the most preciouse plente that apparaill passeth,

plant; surpasses

---

56 and dowted] an dowte.   66 they] the.

58 ne] *omitted.*

Thi pouere peple with here ploughe pike oute of the erthe,

                                                    dig

And they yeve her goodes to gouerne hem euen.

                                    give; *equitably*

And yit the peple ben well apaid to plese the allone.

                                      appeased

75 Suche loue is on the leid of lordes and of lower,   *laid*

And grete is thi grace that God hath the lent.

Thi peres in parlement pull hem to-geders,   *peers*

Worche after wysdom, and worshipe will folowe:

For as a lord is a lord and ledeth the peple,

80 So shuld prowesse in thi persone passe other mennes wittes:

The wittyest and wylyest and worthiest in armes.

                               wisest; *cleverest*

All is but wast wele and he wronge vse,   *idle prosperity*

And vnsemely for a souerain (so saue me oure Lord)

And hevy for his name that hyndren will ever.   *hinder*

85 Sir, thou most be worldly wys, and ware the betymes;

                             guard; *in good time*

And kepe the fro glosyng of gylers mowthes,

                            flattery; *tricksters'*

That speken to the spiritually with spiritual tonges,

[Momelyng] with here mouthes moche and malys in hert,

                           mumbling; *malice*

And of a mys menyng maketh a faire tale;   *wrong*; *meaning*

90 (Vnder flateryng and fair speche falsehede foloweth);

And yif they myght with her moustres to marre the for euere,

                        false pretences; *harm*

With disceit of here derknesse – the deuell hem a-drenche !

                                     drown

Be kende to thi clergi and comfort the pouere: *gracious*

Cherissh thy champyons and chief men of armes;

95 And suche as presoners mowe pike with poyntes of werre,

                           may despoil [c]

Lete hem [welde] that they wynne and worthyly hem thonke;

                                    enjoy

And suche as castels mowe cacche, or eny clos tounes,

                           capture; *walled*

Geve hem as gladly – than shalt thou gete hertes.   *give*

88 Momelyng] Momelyn   96 welde] wilde.

For God in his gospell asketh no thyng elles,
100 But oonly loue for love; and let hym be levest.   *dearest*
Also he that is stronge strokes for to dele,
Make hym thy marchall, and maner his maistre;
                                marshal; habit; master
That for his doughtynesse men mowe hym drede,   *strength*
f.5b And for his wysdom and witte the better to be ware.
105 Knyghtes of thy counseill, [connyng] in armes,   *skilful*
That been seker at asay and sober to thy frendes,
                                trustworthy; trial; respectful
Suche thou shuldest comfort be cours of thy kende,
                                in accordance with your nature
That lede here lyves in labour for thy loue.
Loke thou haue suche a man that loueth not to lye,
110 A faithfull philosofre that flater woll never;   *will*
For he that fareth as a faane folowyng thy wille,
                                weathercock
Worche thou well or woo, he woll the not amende.   *woe*
Lere lettrewre in thy youthe, as a lord befalleth,
                                literature; befits
Whan thou to parlement shall passe there lordes shull pere;
                                appear
115 For to her of thy wysdom they woll awayte after;
                                hear; wait
And though her speche be but small, the more be here
    thoughtes;
For yif thou haue no science to shewe of thy-self,
But as a brogour to go borowe pore mennes wittes,   *broker*
That were most myscheef that myght a lord befalle,
120 Ther as wyse men haue wrapped her wittes togidre.
Sir they it come to the of kynde a kyng to be called,
                                though
Yit most thou know of corage what knyghthood befalleth;
                                temperament; pertains
For he that armes shall haunte, in youthe he must begynne.
                                exercise
Of all artes vnder heven, vse is a maistre.   *use; master*
125 Sir, more-ouere be not gredy gyftes to grype;   *grasp*
Rather thou shalt yeve hem that fele agreved.   *give*

105 connyng] comyng.

So shall thy hawtesse highligh be honoured,   *loftiness*
And prudence in thy principaltee y preised for euere.
For in ensample y shall you shewe that soth is knowe:
130 A kyng shuld not of curtesie couetouse be holde,
                              covetous; *considered*
For ther-as couetyse is knowe in a kynges brest
Ther is corage out of kende when mukke is his maistre.
                              disposition; *nature*
The condicion of a kyng shuld comfort his peple.
For such laykes ben to love there leedes laghen alle.
                              games; *people*; *laugh*
135 My liege lord, of this mater y meve you no more,   *move*
But euere in your mynde haue hym that you made,
And taketh a siker ensample that Crist hym-self sheweth,
                              sure
f.6a Of alle the seyntes in heven that for hym deth suffred,
For his loue thei were so large her lyves they lost,   *generous*
140 And for loue of that Lord aloft now they dwelle
With that crowned kyng that on cros dyed;
Ther Crist in his kyngdom comfort vs euere,
And of his high grace graunte vnto vs alle
Prosperite and pees, pursue we thereafter.'

NOTES AND COMMENTARY

NOTES TO PIERCE
THE PLOUGHMAN'S CREDE

1 Cros is both the cross on which Christ was crucified and the cruciform mark often placed at the beginning of a piece of writing, e.g., at the start of *Sir Launfal* in BL Cotton Caligula A ii. fol.35, cf. *The Kingis Quair*, ed. J. Norton-Smith (Leiden 1981), 90–1: Norton-Smith emends MS + to 'cros'.

5 A.b.c. The narrator is a literate member of the laity; cf. *Piers Plowman* where the priest argues with Piers and is surprised that he is 'lettred a litel' (VII.132). Piers replies that Abstinence the Abbess taught him his a.b.c. (133). In this episode the layman Piers shows a more acute understanding of spiritual matters than the priest. Likewise in *Crede*, both the narrator and Peres are more spiritually aware than members of the institutionalised church.

6 patred None of the readings makes sense. **patred** must have been intended. MED cites a number of examples under 'pateren' – to say the Paternoster. The Paternoster, or The Lord's Prayer, is derived from Matthew, 6:9–13. It was said in the Liturgy before the breaking of the bread.

7–8 The Ave Maria, or Hail Mary, is derived from verses in Luke, 1:28–42. The Creed is the Apostle's Creed, a statement of faith in God the Father, Jesus Christ and the Holy Spirit. It was believed to have been jointly composed by the Apostles. The three texts which the narrator cites are the elementary texts for Christian understanding. The Council at Beziers in 1246 ordered that children attaining the age of seven should be taught the Salutation of the Blessed Virgin Mary, the Paternoster and the Creed.

9 schewen myn shrift The Fourth Lateran Council in 1215 obliged parishioners to make annual confession and receive the Eucharist at Easter.

10 Lent was the traditional time for catechism; the priest's examination of the faith and souls of his parishioners. The narrator fears that his ignorance will result in expiatory fasting.

11–13 Lent traditionally ran from Ash Wednesday to Easter Saturday, forty days of fasting and abstinence. The narrator worries that the priest will enjoin a further forty days of abstinence after Easter, so that he will be unable to eat meat not just on the traditional Friday but Wednesdays as well. **fare** puns on 'state of affairs', MED 7a) and 'provision of food' 8a).

15 cf. John, 3:18: 'He that believeth in him is not judged. But he that doth not believe is already judged; because he believeth not in the name of the only begotten Son of God.'

18–19 **lewed or lered** The narrator is ready to bypass the institutionalised church if an illiterate person who lives the faith can teach him his Creed. **feyneth** recurs at 58, 236, 273 and 487. It is found frequently in Wycliffite texts to connote institutionalised hypocrisy, e.g., Matthew, 20/11–13; *EWS*, I.231/102; Arnold, 110/8; *Lanterne*, 38/15; *Jack Upland*, 64/233.

21–3 suggest the ideal of apostolic poverty derived from Christ's instructions to his apostles when he sent them out into the world to preach, Luke, 10: 1–11.

24 **matter** In the sense of point of law, Alford, p. 102. The examination of faith is couched in legal terminology.

25 **they** One of a number of occasions when the scribe mistakes a 'y' for 'th', e.g. lines 27 and 28.

27 **fraynyng** In the sense of cross-examination, cf. note to *Mum*, 84.

29 The Four Orders were the Franciscans, the Dominicans, the Augustinians and the Carmelites. **frute** puns on the sense of 'spiritual effect', MED 4d) and 'income', sense 1b).

31 **of beleve lyeth** A's reading makes no sense and is obviously corrupt. **lok** puns on the sense of 'key' MED lok n (2) and 'tax' lok n (3) 2c). The line attests to the friars' appropriation of spiritual profits. Christ explicitly entrusted Peter (the Church) with the keys of heaven, Matthew, 16:19; cf. *Pl.Tale*, 65 where the claim of Popes, cardinals, prelates, monks, friars and abbots to keep the gates of heaven and hell is condemned as false. **hondes** alludes ironically to the stipulation in *The Rule of St Francis* that friars should not handle money, cf. *Mum,*

429–30. The Franciscan rule forbade friars to receive money. Wycliffite texts expose the friars' hypocrisy e.g., *Jack Upland*, 68/332–9, and Matthew, 49/29 where the friars are described as using a stick to count out the money.

32 **wende** A's reading appears to be a corruption of 'wittede', (Skeat's reading of A's 'witcede') presumably as a result of confusion with 'wyten'.

33 The Franciscans were known as the Friars Minor because of their claim to humility. St Francis founded the order in 1210. In *Piers*, the two friars whom the dreamer meets are Minorites, VIII.9.

34 **graith** The narrator wants to know the simple truth of Christian belief. Wycliffite texts often state that the plain text of the gospel must be taught as the foundation of belief. Asking a friar for the **graith** is ironic: the friars were often accused of glossing the Bible and/or teaching fables and miracles instead. See *Jack Upland*, 64/233 and Matthew, pp. 56–7; Arnold, pp. 202–3 and *Lanterne*, 55/10ff.

37 **councell** is often used in the legal sense of advice in a legal matter, Alford, p. 38. The Franciscan's response, however, is to defame the Carmelites.

38 The Carmelites took their name from Mount Carmel, the place of their foundation in 1226. The narrator's question allows the Franciscan to slander the Carmelites. The remaining interchanges between the narrator and the friars follow the same pattern. The four orders are so engaged in exposing each other's faults that they lose sight of the narrator's request. The Carmelites' lawlessness is shown by the disregard for the **couenant**, a legally binding agreement, Alford, p. 39, to teach the narrator his Creed.

42 **schulde** The scribe often omits medial 'l'; e.g., 92, 233, 268.

43 **yuguler** has the sense of 'parasite' MED 3) and 'minstrel' 1a). The latter sense puns on the idea of 'joculatores Domini', God's minstrels, the name which St Francis had bestowed on his followers. A Wycliffite text argues that the Franciscans had become 'the deuelis iogelours to blynde mennus gostly eighen', Matthew, p. 99, cf. *Piers*, X.31: 'And japeris and jogelours and jangleris of gestes' where Study states that ribald minstrels are preferred to serious preachers of Holy Writ.

45 **order** appears frequently in Wycliffite texts as part of a

diction which questions the existence of private religions because they were not instituted by Christ. Private orders are contrasted with Christ's orders, e.g., *Jack Upland*, 58/103–6; Matthew, 2/ 6; 51/19; Arnold, 392/3; *EWS*, I.328/59.

46 gestes of Rome, cf. 'Bot thei schulden not preche cronyclis of tho world, as tho batel of Troye, ne other nyse fablis, ne monnis lawes, founden to wynne hom tho money, ffor Crist biddes his clerkes preche tho gospel', Arnold, 147/26–9.

47 i-founded Wycliffite polemics against private religions often use **found** and its derivatives to question the institution of the friars and to assert that their foundation was contrary to Christ's command, e.g., *Fifty Heresies and Errors of Friars*, Arnold, I.367/1–3; cf. Matthew, 51/18–19; *EWS*, I.295/84.

48 Maries men – the Carmelites were often called the Order of Our Lady of Mount Carmel. A Latin poem on *The Council of London* (1382), Wright, I.262, mentions some of the friars' claims to foundation: 'Horum quidam praedicant quod sunt ex Mariae' – certain of them claim that they are descended from Mary – i.e., the Carmelites.

49 juxtaposes the friars' fraudulent claims and their lechery. **lieth** puns on the sense of 'to tell a lie' MED v (2) and 'to have sexual intercourse', v (1) 1b).

50–2 Satire against the friars' lechery is prolific, e.g., Chaucer's *Shipman's Tale*, Friar Hubert in *The General Prologue*, who 'hadde maad ful many a mariage / Of yonge wommen at his owene cost. / Unto his ordre he was a noble post' (212–14); *The Orders of Cain*, which states that a man with a daughter or wife should ensure that no friar confesses them, indeed, says the narrator, if he had a daughter or wife, no friar should come near them unless he were castrated, Robbins, 65/73–96.

54 fynde in the sense of maintain; cf. *Piers*, XX.384, where Conscience envisages a time when 'freres hadde a fyndyng, that for nede flateren'.

58 cf. note to 18–19.

61 All texts have 'But' at the start of the line but the sense requires **And**. I have followed Skeat's emendation.

62 *On the Minorites* alleges that the friars do not know their Creed: 'With an O & an I, Men wennen that thai wede, / To carpe so of clergy that can not thair crede', Robbins, 66/11–12. *PlTale* remarks that 'Suche that conne nat hir Crede/With prayer shull be mad prelates' (413–14).

64–5 puns on **fynden** to question the very foundation of the friars, cf. note to 47. The Pied Friars, or the Friars of the Blessed Mary, were founded in 1257. Their name comes from their habit, black and white like a magpie.

68–9 cf. *The Testament of St Francis* where a friar who is good at flattering or begging is said to have a chamber and jewels fit for a duke, while an infinitely more worthy friar goes naked and suffers misfortune, Matthew, p. 49.

69 felawes often carries the legal sense of accomplice in crime, Alford, p. 57. **good** 'food' would improve alliteration and sense, but as there is no warrant in any version and A's reading is tenable, I have not emended.

70 The transition is abrupt. Skeat queries whether a line is missing between 69 and 70. It is likely that the subject pronoun 'they', to refer to the friars, should be understood, cf. 78.

71 hem ABC reade 'hym' but a plural pronoun is required and I have followed Skeat's emendation. All the texts often mistake singular and plural third person pronouns.

72 Robertes men are rascals or vagabonds, cf. *Piers*, VI.148: 'Ac Robert Renaboute shal right noght have of myne'.

75 put out to ferme MED 'ferme' 3a) is to grant the revenues of something in return for a fixed amount. The friars trade spiritual virtues such as patience.

76–7 refer to miracle plays, in particular, to the play of the nativity. In the N Town play of the nativity there are two midwives who initially doubt the Virgin Birth, one of whom suffers a withered hand for her scepticism, *English Mystery Plays*, ed. P. Happe (Harmondsworth, 1975), 12/249–56.

79 Friars attend miracle plays to persuade women to buy a piece of Mary's smock from them because it will ease childbirth, cf. Chaucer's Pardoner, who dupes the people into thinking that a pillow case is a piece of Our Lady's veil, *The General Prologue*, 694–5.

80–1 Instead of preaching stern Christian doctrine, such as prohibition and penitence, the Carmelites invoke the name of Mary as intercessor to encourage a lax attitude towards sin.

82–3 cf. note to 600. There is a sexual pun on **staues** MED 'staf' 1c.a); cf. *Piers*, Prol.53–4: 'Heremytes on an heep with hoked staves/Wenten to Walsyngham – and hire wenches after'.

84 grete-hedede refers to the large head-dresses fashionable at the time. The Wife of Bath's weighed about ten pounds,

General Prologue, 455. **gold by the eighen** refers to ornamental gold network which was part of the head-dress and covered the side of the face. [cf. *Legend of Good Women*, Prol. G.147–8: 'A fret of goold she hadde next hyre her/And upon that a whit corone she ber'.]

89–94 allude to Philippians, 3:18–19: 'For many walk, of whom I have told you often (and now tell you weeping) that they are enemies of the cross of Christ. Whose end is destruction; whose God is their belly; and whose glory is in their shame; who mind earthly things.'

91 Skeat queries whether MS 'slauthe' ought to be **slaughte** in the sense of 'death'. I have emended to C's **slaughte** because it is closer to the paraphrase of Philippians, : 'whose end is destruction'. It remains unclear how an end can be 'sloth'. Moreover, the **slepe** is clearly a spiritual one, cf. Ephesians, 5:14: 'Wherefore he saith, "Rise, thou that sleepest and arise from the dead; and Christ shall enlighten thee"'.

92 gloppyng B's 'golping' is an attractive reading but I have adopted the reading from C because A's scribe often omits medial 'l', cf. *Piers*, Prol.59 (of the friars): 'Prechynge the peple for profit of the wombe'. On gluttony and drunkenness, cf. the comments in *PlTale*, 144 and 151–6.

95 don betere may allude to the Dowel triad in *Piers*.

103–4 The issue of Apostolic Poverty; cf. note to 21–3, was crucial in the discussion of the friars. The Franciscan Rule stipulated a life of apostolic poverty: the friars were forbidden to receive money and own property. Rather they should go as pilgrims throughout the world in poverty and meekness to the service of God, *The Rule of St Francis*, Matthew, p. 42.

105–111 For the hypocrisy of these claims cf. *The Orders of Cain*: 'Meteles so megre are thai made / & penaunce so puttes ham doun, / That ichone is an hors-lade / when he shal trusse of toun', Robbins, 65/21–4.

113 parteners refer to the lay brethren whom friars invited to participate in their activities. They often charged a fee for their services and issued letters of confraternity. Thomas and his wife in *The Summoner's Tale* are members of a lay confraternity attached to Friar John's convent. Letters of fraternity are criticised in the Wycliffite text, *The Church and her Members*, as a deceitful ruse for the friars to rob the people of their money, Arnold, pp. 377–8.

114–19 The receipt of gifts, money, and building large convents contravenes the regulations of *The Rule of St Francis*, cf. note to 103–4. The Wycliffite commentary on the *Rule* expressly makes this point, Matthew, p. 49.

120–29 Benefactions to the friars were often recorded by inscribing the names of the donors in the stained glass: cf. *Piers*, III.47–72, where, having been fraudulently absolved from sin, Mede agrees to make a donation to the cost of the friar's building. In return, her name will be engraved in the window.

128 noblich The scribe of A misread 'c' for 't'.

132 Ignorance of the Creed incurs a penance. But the friar agrees to overlook it if the narrator will endow his convent; cf. note to 634–6.

136 peine In the sense of punishment imposed after confession; cf. note to 714–15.

141–4 cf. Matthew, 7:3–5: 'And why seest thou the mote that is in thy brother's eye; and seest not the beam that is in thyn own eye? Or, how sayest thou to thy brother: Let me cast the mote out of thy eye: and behold, a beam is in thy own eye? Thou hypocrite, cast out first the beam out of thy own eye; and then thou shalt see to cast out the mote out of thy brother's eye.' This verse is quoted at *Piers*, X.261–2.

149 cf. Exodus, 20:17: 'Thou shalt not covet thy neighbour's house: neither shalt thou desire his wife, nor his servant, nor his handmaid, nor his ox, nor his ass, nor anything that is his.' The narrator mixes his sources. He inserts one of the Ten Commandments into quotations from Christ's Sermon on the Mount.

151 cf. Matthew, 7:16: 'By their fruits you shall know them.' The preceding verse, a warning to beware of false prophets, ravening wolves dressed in the clothing of sheep, is quoted at 458.

152 demest – Christ judges the friars truly in contrast to their mutual slandering. The narrator, a layman, cites scriptural authority to prove the friars' corruption; cf. *The Friar's Answer*, Robbins, 69, where the narrator, who is a friar, is alarmed that 'lewed men' knew the Scriptures because it enables them to expose the hypocrisy of the friars.

153 first is an ironical reference to the Dominican's pride, wealth and learning. They were not founded first.

154 prechoures are the Dominicans. They were famous for their preaching and great knowledge of scholastic theology.

155 Ich A and B's readings are corrupt. I have adopted C's reading.

156 court alludes to the temporal wealth and life of the friars, despite their claim to poverty. *The Lanterne of Light*, 41/7–10 criticises the fraternal orders for building extravagant houses to dwell in like lords of the world.

160–70 The elaborate decoration of the convent alludes to the concern of the friars for outward display rather than inner spirituality. *Vox* criticises the lavish buildings of the friars in a similar fashion, IV.1141–58; cf. *Lanterne*, which states that curious church building was forbidden by the Fathers, and that walls, pillars, glittering gold beams and other ornaments are anti-apostolic, p. 37.

161 knottes suggests the elaborately carved foliage on corbels.

165 The private gates suggest a freedom of movement incompatible with the fraternal vow of obedience and unworldliness.

167 And A's reading is presumably a mechanical copying error, cf. the Wycliffite comment that a simple crucifix allows meditation on Christ's bitter suffering and death, but costly, painted crucifixes, decorated with gold, silver and gems, squander money that could be spent on the hungry, naked and thirsty, *SEWW*, 83/12–21.

169–70 plough-lond is a unit of land which could be cultivated by one plough. The comparison suggests the manual labour conspicuously absent from the description of the friars in the poem.

172–207 This passage is copied into British Library MS Harley 78. Doyle (1959) suggests, p.434, that the subject matter might have had a special interest for the scribe or his director because the description closely resembles the architectural details of the London house of the Blackfriars. See A. W. Clapham & W. H. Godfrey, *Some Famous Buildings and their Story* (London n.d.) pp.254–63.

174 crochetes are small ornaments placed on the inclined sides of pinnacles or canopies. They usually take the form of buds, curled leaves, or animals.

175 cf. note to 120–9.

176–7 There is no holy illustration on the windows. Instead they are scribbled thick with the names of donors, and painted with the coats of arms of benefactors from the nobility and the trademarks used by merchant donors.

180 ragemen is a document recording accusations or offences. When justices heard and determined complaints in the shires, the testimony was recorded on rolls. The seals of the witnesses questioned were attached to these rolls by cutting the bottom edge of the parchment into strips, forming a tattered fringe. The inquisitors who carried these ragged rolls came to be known as 'ragmen' and the term became attached to the rolls themselves and by extension to any document of a similar appearance, Alford, p.125; cf. *Mum*, 1565.

181-8 refer to the friars' practice of burying people in their convents in return for donations; cf.468. *Vox*, IV.734-40 complains that friars demand to bury the dead bodies of those to whom they acted as confessor as long as they were rich and noble. But they make no claim to bury the poor because they gain nothing from it. *The Simonie* describes friars fighting over the corpses of rich men in their determination to secure burial of them (A.181-2).

181 tyld opon lofte The tombs are built on plinths and are therefore raised from the ground.

183 alfor I have emended against the readings of ABC because H's reading restores alliteration. 'clad' is explicable from anticipation of line 185 and explains the lack of 184-5 from A and their later insertion in B.

184-5 are missing in A and H, probably owing to the repetition of **for the nones** and are supplied from C. In B, the lines were originally omitted and inserted later as a correction.

186 seyntes alludes to the worldly motives behind the friars' allotment of burial space and the elaborate tombs.

189-90 tax of ten yer Because they owed their allegiance to the Pope, the friars were exempt from taxation. Nicholas Hereford's 1382 Ascension Day Sermon stated that the king would not need to burden the laity so heavily with taxation if monks, friars and other wealthy clerics were reformed, see Hudson, *Wycliffism*, pp.69-70. In 1380, the Commons clamoured that since the clergy owned a third of the land, they should pay a third of the £1,000 demanded in taxation. There were attempts in 1383 and 1384 to make lay grants conditional on contributions from the church. A year later, *The Twelve Conclusions of the Lollards* demanded clerical disendowment, *SEWW*, pp.24-9. Within three months of their posting, the Dominican, Roger Dymmok composed a refutation of the

Conclusions, his *Liber contra duodecim errores et hereses Lollardorum*; cf. *Piers*, XV.562: 'Taketh hire landes, ye lordes, and leteth hem lyve by dymes'.

191–6 cf. *The Lanterne of Light*, 41/31–34, where the writer states that the church should display no pride in stone, timber, lead or glass.

197 gaynage is the profit derived from agriculture, cf. 169. The necessity of producing from the land is contrasted with the friars' needless opulence.

202 Parlement-hous John Stow notes in his *Survey of London*, ed. C. L. Kingsford (Oxford, 1908), that diverse parliaments and other meetings were held at London, Blackfriars. The most significant large meeting held at Blackfriars in the fourteenth century was the Council of London in 1382 which condemned Wycliff's teachings, see note to 531–2.

204 heygh kinge suggests a confusion of secular and spiritual roles, cf. 210.

215 And othere A's reading arises from reading 'there' separately from **othere**. The line may refer to Anne of Bohemia's huge entourage, cf. note to *Richard*, III.222.

216–18 *Tractatus de Pseudo-Freris* comments that the friars' rich buildings are made by robbery of poor men, Matthew, 321/29–32. cf. *Mum*, 444.

220–26 Satire against fraternal gluttony is common, e.g., the narrator of *The Orders of Cain*, Robbins, 65 states that in all his forty years he has never seen fatter men than the friars, lines 17–20, cf. *The Simonie*, A.154–5. In *The Summoner's Tale*, 1844–50, Friar John pretends he has such a temperate diet that his stomach is ruined. His claim that he could only eat the merest morsels for dinner is clearly satirical, and a pitying plea to Thomas and his wife to feed him up.

228 cf. Friar Hubert in the *General Prologue*, 262–3: 'Of double worstede was his semycope, / That rounded as a belle out of the presse' and *PlTale*, 1003 where the phrase is used of a monk.

229 clene is used three times in as many lines. The outer purity of the habit conceals inner sinfulness, cf. note to 695–6.

230 ground The texture of the fabric, MED 7a). The cloth is so strong that it could be used to make sacks to carry grain.

231 herdeman – shepherd of souls is ironic. The friar's quivering corpulence shows that he cares only for himself.

233 worthely ... wissen The evidence of BC shows A's misreading of individual letters.

239 Austyn The Augustinian friars were founded in 1256.

240 plyght me his treuthe is an act of pledging faith, Alford, p.159, III.B. The friars are unable to keep their own word, let alone God's.

241 sythen A misreads a thorn for a yogh.

242 euelles A misreads 'll' as 'ff'.

246–7 A Pardoner, either a cleric or a layman, was able to transmit **pryuileges** – indulgences – by dispensation from the Pope. The forgiveness of sin required contrition, confession and satisfaction. An indulgence could commute the earthly punishment, the penance, due in this life; it did not secure salvation. Donations towards the work of the church were regarded as an act of penance and could therefore earn an indulgence, which a pardoner could transmit. The system became abused, however, when payment was seen as the *price* of a pardon, not as an act of almsgiving penance for the upkeep of the church. Pardoners are a frequent object of satire for selling pardons as though they remitted the punishment of sin, e.g., *Piers*, Prol.68–77 and *General Prologue*, 669–714. The Dominican in *Crede* sees the pardoner's craft as essentially fraudulent and likens it to the Austins' treatment of penance. They sell pardons and allow sin to go unpunished. The actions of the Franciscan, 135, the Augustinian, 333, and the Carmelite, 394–8 bear out the accusation. The Dominican is too caught up in his own boasting to offer to absolve the narrator, cf.467.

247 proue and asaye The Dominican invites a legal investigation of the Augustinian's treatment of penance. **proue** means to find legal evidence or testimony, MED preven 1c) (cf. note to *Richard*, I.15–18) and **asaye** means to examine a defendant to glean information, Alford, p.10; cf. *Mum*, 1434.

248 cf. *Piers*, XI.55–67 where Coveitise of Eyes tells the Dreamer that he should go and confess himself to a friar. He will court him while he is prosperous, secure him in his fraternity and sue to his Prior for a pardon for him. When the Dreamer falls on ill-luck, however, the friar spurns him.

252 The Constitutions of the Dominicans laid down that they were to be intent on study and teaching, R. Southern, *The Making of the Middle Ages* (London, 1967), p.182. Thomas Aquinas and Albert Magnus were both Dominicans. Famous

English Dominican scholars included Nicholas Trivet, Robert Holcot and John of Bromyard. Cf. *Piers*, XX.273–4 where Envy orders the friars to go to University to learn logic and law, and at XX.296, philosophy.

253 MED does not record this example of **procession**. It is a noun formed from 'proceden' MED (4), 'to undertake legal proceedings against' and means 'proceedings'. **process** also has the sense of legal action, OED 'process' (7). **by processe of lawe** suggests the Wycliffite criticism that the friars were more concerned with worldly learning, such as temporal law, than with Holy Writ, e.g., Matthew, 6/8–11.

254 14th-century Dominican bishops included John Gilbert (Hereford); Thomas de Lisle (Ely); William Bottesham (Rochester) and two of Richard II's confessors: John Burghill (Llandaff and Lichfield) and Thomas Rushook (Llandaff and Chichester), cf. 360–5.

256 Between 1276–1303, three popes: John XXI, Innocent V and Benedict XI were Dominicans.

257 **as godspelles telleth** secures the emptiness of the Dominican's boast since the order was founded some twelve hundred years after the Gospels were written.

261–2 cf. the parable of the Vineyard, Matthew, 20:1–16, verse 16: 'So the last shall be first, and the first last.'

262–3 cf. Luke, 10:18: 'And he said to them: I saw Satan like lightning falling from heaven'. A similar contrast between humility and Satan's pride is made at *PlTale*, 98–100 and 119.

264–5 Matthew, 5:3: 'Blessed are the poor in spirit; for theirs is the kingdom of heaven'.

275 **glose**, cf. 515, 585 and 709, puns on the senses of glossing a text MED glosen 1a), to obscure the truth of a statement, 2a), and flattery, sense 3a), cf. *Mum*, 141, 314 and 388. Scase notes, p.82, how *glose* became a key Wycliffite term to denote false interpretation of texts, e.g., *Vae Octuplex*, where the friars are accused of glosing God's law with contrary laws, saying that God's words must be refuted and newly-founded words substituted, *EWS*, II.376/280–4.

278–9 *Vae Octuplex* argues that the friars have the keys of hell and lock the gates of heaven against themselves and others, *EWS*, II.367/30–2.

287 **peny** A misreads 'e' as 'a'.

288 **cnaue be prest** Skeat reads this to refer to the lad who followed the friars to carry their earnings, citing *Summoner's Tale*, 1754–6: 'A sturdy harlot wente ay hem bihynde, / That was hir hostes man, and bar a sak, /And what men yaf hem, leyde it on his bak.' Skeat thought C's 'name be Prest' 'very absurd', p.41. To my mind, however, it is an attractive reading. It suggests the friars' appropriation of the priest's cure of souls, cf. note to 462. Since AB read in common and the reading is tenable I have not emended.

292–7 The cope is the outer habit. It was forbidden to be more than a moderate width, *Monumenta Franciscana*, ed. J. Brewer (Rolls Series, London 1858), p.575. The cote was worn underneath. It should not have been made of fur. The cope is carefully buttoned so that the transgression is not visible.

295 *The Orders of Cain* comments that the friars trim their garments with many different furs, from squirrel to lambswool, Robbins, 65/49–54.

299–300 *The Franciscan Rule* stipulated that no friar should wear shoes, *Monumenta Franciscana*, p.572; cf. *Mum*, 426–7.

301 *The Orders of Cain* says that the friars carry spices in their purses, Robbins, 65/55–6; cf. *Mum*, 479.

303 her A's reading is a mechanical copying error.

308 Paul of Thebes, d.342, was known as Paul the Hermit, the first of the desert Fathers. The Austins claimed him as their founder to claim precedence for their order, cf. *Piers*, XV.288–9. In C, there is an addition, where Liberium Arbitrium queries the Austin's claim: 'yf frere Austynes be trewe;/For he ordeynede that ordre or elles thei gabben' C.XVII.15–16.

310 lengeden I have followed Skeat in adopting C's reading because it is supported by B. A's reading is a mechanical copying error.

318–20 cf. note to 247.

321–5 cf. the words of the Franciscan, 122–33.

326–7 cf. note to 113. Friar John tells Thomas in *The Summoner's Tale*, 2126–28: ' "Ye sey me thus, how that I am youre brother ?" : / "Ye certes", quod the frere, "trusteth weel; / I toke oure dame the lettre, under oure seel." '

328 A **Prouinciall** was the director of several convents.

333 leue is dispensation from sin, cf. Alford, p.88.

338 Karmes are Carmelites or the White Friars. Friars usually travelled in pairs, according to Christ's instructions to the disciples to go forth 'two and two', Luke, 10:1. The Dreamer meets two Franciscans in *Piers*, VIII.

341 aisliche I have followed Skeat in emending to C's reading. AB's reading is untenable and arises from a simple copying error of an unfamiliar word.

344 lel A's reading is corrupt and easily corrected with reference to BC.

345 hestes I have followed Skeat in restoring medial 's'; present in B, but omitted in the other versions.

350 ABC all read 'For' at the beginning of the line but the sense requires **Yf** and so I have emended. There are other instances of a mistaken function word at the beginning of a line, see 61, 421.

352 The Carmelite is more abusive than the other friars and his insults more proverbial, see 355, 357, 365, 374–5. This either reflects the influence of drink, or the bias against the Dominicans in the poem, see introduction.

354 The Dominicans were satirised as arrogant pedlars of theology, wishing to frequent the tables of the noble, cf. the portrait of the friar in *Piers*, XIII.25–110.

355 digne as the devel cf. the narrator's words at 262.

358 messages were diplomatic notes or official messages from a king or a lord, MED 1b). **mariages** cf. Chaucer's friar who had made many a marriage at his own cost, *General Prologue*, 212–13.

359–60 cf. note to 254.

360 biggeth – B's 'beggen' is attractive as an acute satirical hit at the hypocrisy of the friars' begging while aiming at positions of power, but it is probably a misreading of the less familiar **biggen**.

362–9 Herdforthe alludes to the Dominican friary at King's Langley in Hertfordshire. Richard II was a frequent visitor and held Christmas there in 1392 and 1394. He commissioned new buildings and extensions to those already established. King's Langley was Richard's first burial place, Mathew, pp.32–3.

364–5 In return for the king's patronage, the friars counsel him. Steel notes that Richard maintained an ecclesiastical clique of courtiers, amongst whom were the friars Burghill and Rushook, p. 220. **back claweth** an early analogue to the proverb: 'You scratch my back and I'll scratch yours', i.e. return favours.

365 curry See MED *curreien* (3), to curry favour. I have followed Skeat in adopting the readings of B and C. A's reading arises from misunderstanding or misreading an unfamiliar word.

371 werldliche Skeat did not emend here. From the combined BC reading. I have supplied medial 'l' as elsewhere, the scribe often omits it; cf. note to 42.

375 digne as dich water cf. *Reeve's Tale*, 3964: 'She was as digne as water in a diche.'

377 respondes – a series of verses and responses read or sung alternately by a soloist, and choir or congregation.

383 The Carmelites claimed Elijah and Elisha as their founders, cf. *Summoner's Tale*, 2116 and *The Council of London 1382*, Wright, I.262; others claim, however, that they are from Elijah, cf. note to 48.

394–7 cf. the responses of the Franciscan, 122–33 and the Austin, 324–332.

401 The narrator is an honest labourer in contrast to the idle friars.

405 A common proverb at this time concerned the cat who wanted to eat fish without wetting her paws, e.g., Chaucer, *House of Fame*, 1783–5: 'For ye be lyke the sweynte cat / That wolde have fissh; but wostow what? / He wolde nothing wete his clowes' and Gower, *Confessio*, IV.1108–9: 'And as a cat wolde ete fisshes / Withoute wetinge of his cles'.

409–13 Friars are often presented trying to persuade people to leave them donations in their wills or to be buried at their houses rather than the parish church, e.g., *On the Council of London* which states that if a rich man falls sick, a friar rushes immediately to him and asks him to bequeath his corpse to the friars, Wright, I.257. Fitzralph criticises this practice in *Defensio Curatorum*, p.42; cf. 181–8.

414 vse I have followed Skeat in adopting the combined BC reading. A's reading is a simple copying error. **Anuell** was money given for saying a yearly mass for a departed soul. *The Orders of Cain* states that the friars have become so wealthy from annuals that the monks are not able to maintain their dress, Robbins, 76/141–44 and at 155, that friars have become 'annuel prestes', i.e. in their procuring of annuals, they have usurped the position of the parish priest.

415–17 his I have followed Skeat in adopting the combined BC reading. A's reading is a mechanical copying error. **letteres,**

i.e. letters of fraternisation, cf. note to 113. The Carmelite hopes that the woman will die while she is in mind to bequeath her wealth to them, and that she will die soon because they have issued many letters of fraternity.

419 weren The readings of BC suggest that A's 'werne' is a copying error.

421 I Skeat emended against the evidence of the three versions. I have followed his emendation. 'And' could have been caught from the preceding line, and **seigh** requires a pronoun. *PlTale* contrasts the decadence of the monks against the founding ideals of St Benedict and states that if they had truly followed a religious life 'They must have honged at the plow' threshing and ditching from town to town, with barely enough food to eat (1040–44).

422 cary was a coarse material; cf. *Piers*, V.78 where Envy is clothed in a 'kaurymaury'. The plowman is much more poorly dressed than his namesake in *Piers*, who has patched clothes, but leggings and mittens to protect against the cold, VI.59–60.

426 hokschynes are the sinews just above the heels. The backs of the shoes are so broken down that the hose is exposed to the mud.

430 fen I have followed Skeat in adopting B's reading. A's 'fern' may arise from avoiding repeating a word from the previous line, but it is not appropriate.

431 worthen I have followed Skeat's emendation of AC's 'worthi' to 'worthen' on the strength of B's reading. AC's reading is untenable. Elsewhere, 'worthen' is rendered accurately: 9, 493, 665, 748, 783 and 821. The four heifers may recall the four Evangelists, described as oxen, in Piers's allegorical ploughing, *Piers*, XIX.264–8.

438–9 The couple's children contrasts to the sterility of the friars.

455 A contrast to the friars' determination to strip the narrator of livelihood. **lene** cf. Hunger's advice to Piers to 'love and lene' anyone whom he finds in misfortune, VI.218–21.

446 brother contrasts ironically with the unbrotherly 'freres'.

451 fonded I have followed Skeat's emendation because the reading of all three versions is manifestly corrupt.

452 now my wit lakketh cf. the bewildered and frustrated dreamer in *Piers*, XV.1–3.

457–9 cf. Matthew, 7:15: 'Beware of false prophets who

come to you in the clothing of sheep, but inwardly they are ravening wolves'. This text was often used against corrupt clergy, cf. *Piers*, XV.116 and *Vox*, IV.798, where Gower states that a friar's sheep clothing conceals a hostile wolf. The text is the basis of the Wycliffite tract against the friars, *Vae Octuplex*, *EWS*, II.366/1–4.

460 founded cf. note to 47. *Of the Leaven of the Pharisees* begins with a denunciation of the new orders which were founded not by Christ, but by hypocrisy, Lucifer's pride, and Antichrist, Matthew, pp.2–3.

461 cf. *Jack Upland*, 69/354–65, where Jack asks the friar why it was necessary to encumber the people with so many friars. Christ's ordinance of twelve apostles with a few other priests, was sufficient. The orders of the friars offend against God's harmonious dispensation for the world and obstruct the way to salvation.

462 cf. *Piers*, V.142–5, where Wrath (as a friar) satirises the conflict over pastoral care between the friars and the regular clergy. The decree of the 1215 Lateran Council made annual confession obligatory to one's own priest (*proprius sacerdos*), cf. note to line 9. The secular clergy claimed that this referred to them alone because the power to administer the sacraments was instituted by Christ and transmitted to them directly through the apostolic succession. The friars disputed this claim; they, too, could fulfil the office of *proprius sacerdos* since their power was derived from the pope, earthly head of the church and *proprius sacerdos* of every Christian, see Scase, pp.18–20, cf. *On the Orders of Cain*, Robbins, 65/150–1: '. . . vnnethe may prestes seculers/Gete any seruice for these frers'.

464–6 cf. *Piers*, XV.230–2. Anima says that in St Francis's time Charity could be found in a friar's habit but seldom since.

467 pryuylege cf. note to 246–7.

468 coueten I have followed Skeat's adoption of C's reading. A's reading arises from a copying error. The scribe also has difficulty with the word at lines 149 and 638.

468–71 cf. note to 181–8 and Friar Hubert in *The General Prologue*: 'And over al, ther as profit sholde arise, / Curteis he was and lowely of servyse', 249–50.

468–9 According to the papal bull *Super Cathedram* 1300, friars were to pay to the parish church one quarter of all legacies, bequests and funeral dues received from the laity, Scase, p.20.

473 For the contrast between the hypocrisy of the friars and the true living of Peres, cf. *Tractatus de Pseudo-Freris*, Matthew, p.321/10–12, where the life of a true ploughman or true shepherd is contrasted to the fraudulent blabbering of the friars.

476–8 cf. *Tractatus de Pseudo-Freris*, Matthew, p. 310/ 4–10: if one were to ask a friar whether all the orders were equally good, he would be bound to say that his own order is best because it lives better than the others. Each order has a secret envy towards the others which cancels out the love of God.

479 Thorughe AC's reading is caught from the preceding line. I have followed Skeat's adoption of B's reading to restore sense. **Golias** is *Apocalypsis Goliae*, 12th-century satire on the monastic orders.

480 cf. note to 461.

481 In *Piers*, it is a friar, with authority from the bishop to have cure of souls like a parish priest, XX.325–29, who destroys the Barn of Unity by selling contrition for money, XX.363–380.

486 Wycliffite texts often state that the friars were descended from Cain, the first outlaw. A number of texts use the initials of the four orders to form the acrostic 'CAIM', see notes to *Mum*, 494. Wyclif gives the derivation of the acrostic in *Trialogus*, ed. G. Lechler (Oxford, 1869), IV.33, p.362; cf. *On the Leaven of the Pharisees*, Matthew, 12/8, where the friars are called Cain's brethren and Robbins, 65/109–16: 'Thus grounded caym thes four ordours'.

487 Wycliffite texts often compare the friars with the Pharisees whom Christ denounced as hypocrites in Matthew, 15 and 23, e.g., *On the Leaven of the Pharisees*, Matthew, pp.2–27 and *Jack Upland*, 58/86 where the friars are called 'Caymes castelmakers' and 'Phareseis' who deceive the people.

489 cf. Matthew, 23:28: 'So you also outwardly indeed appear to men just: but inwardly you are full of hypocrisy and iniquity.'

492 cf. Luke, 11:46: 'But he said woe to you lawyers also, because you load men with burdens that they cannot bear and you yourself touch not the packs with one of your fingers.'

493–5 Matthew, 23:29–31: 'Woe to you, scribes and Pharisees, hypocrites, that build the sepulchres of the prophets and adorn the monuments of the just. And say: If we had been in the days of our fathers, we would not have been partakers with them in the blood of the prophets. Wherefore you are witnesses against yourselves, that are the sons of them that killed the prophets.'

498 cf. Matthew, 23:7–8 '[they love] to be called by men Rabbi. But be you not called Rabbi. For one is your master; and all you are brethren.' This passage was often used to satirise the intellectual arrogance of the friars. 'Master' came to signify 'Master of Arts'. St Francis exhorted his followers not to be called masters (see Mann, p.39). In the *General Prologue*, Hubert is 'lyk a maister' (261) and in the *Summoner's Tale*, the friar accepts the title 'deere maister' from the sick Thomas, but when the lord of the village uses the title to him, John quotes Matthew. 23:7–8 to refuse it. Wycliffite texts make extensive use of the comparison, e.g., *Tractatus de Pseudo-Freris*, Matthew, p.306/11–3; cf. *Crede*, 574 and *PlTale*, 1115–24.

499 cf. *Tractatus de Pseudo-Freris*, 306/7–8, that friars worship secular lords to get money from them.

501 beldinge 'tilding', cf. 494, would improve sense and alliteration, but there is no warrant in any version and as the reading is tenable I have not emended.

502 cf. *The Summoner's Tale* where Friar John tries to persuade Thomas to part with his gold to help complete the foundation and the stone flooring (2103–5).

506 paynted cf. Matthew, 23:27: 'Woe to you, scribes and Pharisees, hypocrites; because you are like to whited sepulchres, which outwardly appear to men beautiful, but within are full of dead men's bones and of all filthiness,' quoted by Anima in *Piers*, XV.113 and *Tractatus de Pseudo-Freris*, Matthew, 299/20.

506–14 These lines contradict the wholesale condemnation of the founding of the friars in 486–7. Here the Dominicans alone are founded by the devil, but the original foundations of the other three orders are grounded in the ideal of apostolic poverty, cf. note to 21–3. **ground** is frequently found in Wycliffite texts to sanction behaviour or doctrine supported by the Gospel, e.g., *Lanterne*, 59/8, 65/11.

510 dernlich Skeat read 'derulich' but all three versions have medial 'n'.

515–16 cf. note to 275. The point here is that the friars add unauthorised and misleading commentaries to the gospel for their own advantage. *Vae Octuplex* accuses the friars of ignoring the truth of the gospel and promulgating only those fraudulent unscriptural claims which further their own advantage, *EWS*, II.371/141–77.

520 cf. Matthew, 5:3 and line 264.

522 Skeat reads MS **fell** as 'fele'. BC read 'fele'.

523 cf. note to 253. Peres urges a legal examination of the friars, cf. note to *Mum*, 405.

524–7 The Wycliffite *Fifty Errors and Heresies Against the Friars*, criticises the friars' impatience over reproof, saying that a lord will suffer criticism of a peccadillo more meekly than the friars will tolerate gentle reproof of their heresies, Arnold, 387/25–30.

525 **wexen** I have followed Skeat's adoption of the BC reading. A's 'weyon' is clearly a copying error.

527 **wraththe** I have followed Skeat's adoption of the BC reading. A read 'p' for thorn.

528 John Wyclif, d.1384, philosopher and reformer, dominated the Oxford schools in the 1370s. His teachings on the Eucharist and reform of the church were taken up by the Wycliffites, or Lollards. He originally supported the friars because of the closeness of their founding ideals to Apostolic poverty. But after the friars' denunciation of his views on the Eucharist, he turned against them. In *Trialogus* he bitterly attacks the friars, calling them greedy, idle, blasphemous seducers and hypocrites and forms the acrostic CAIM from the initials of the four orders, cf. note to 486. Between 1382 and 1384, Wyclif waged war against the friars in a flood of pamphlets and sermons, Kenny, pp.93–4.

530 **wikednesse** I have supplied the 'e' omitted in error.

531 **seweden** I have followed Skeat's adoption of the BC reading. A mistakes an 's' for an 'l'.

531–2 The Earthquake Council of 1382 (held at Blackfriars in London) condemned ten of Wyclif's propositions as heretical, including his views on the Eucharist. Of the seventeen doctors of theology present, 16 were friars, four from each order, cf. *On the Council of London*, which sides with Wyclif against the friars, Wright, I.259.

532 Henry Crumpe was a member of the Blackfriars Council. A month later he was suspended from scholastic acts because he called the heretics 'Lollardi', Hudson (1988¹), p.87. **lollede** MED (3) means to accuse of having the beliefs of a Lollard, cf. *Defend us from all Lollardry*, Robbins, 64, which uses **lolle** in a similar fashion, e.g., 81-2: 'And parde, lolle thei neuer so longe/Yut wol lawe, make hem lowte'. *PlTale* describes how the poor wretches who follow a simple faith in contrast to the magnificence of the established church are called 'lollers' (73), cf. *Mum*, 419.

535 myddel-erde I have followed Skeat in adopting the C reading. B's reading suggests that A misread 'herthe' as 'hertes'. **meke** cf. Matthew, 5:4: 'Blessed are the meek; for they shall possess the land.'

540 nemne I have corrected A's simple copying error.

542 cf. *Piers*, V.160-1: 'Of wikkede wordes I Wrathe hire wortes made / Til "Thow lixt!" and "Thow lixt!" lopen out at ones'.

544 knaue The BC reading corrects A's copying error.

545 cf. Friar Hubert in *General Prologue*, 252: 'He was the beste beggere in his hous'.

547 poyntes has the legal sense of accusation, MED pointe (8).

549-52 cf. Matthew, 23:5: 'And all their works they do for to be seen of men. For they make their phylacteries broad and enlarge their fringes'. **chapolories** were scapulars, vestments made of one piece of cloth the width of the shoulders with a hole for the head. They were worn over the habit and hung down back and front almost to the ground, cf. *Jack Upland*, 60/140-3.

554-8 cf. Matthew, 23:6: 'And they love the first places at feasts and the first chairs in the synagogues'.

559 cf. note to 486. Friars' convents are often called Caim's castles in Wycliffite texts, e.g., *Jack Upland*, 58/86, where the occupants of such castles are called Pharisees.

560-3 The secular ornaments are the marks of the wealthy who have endowed the convent. *Tractatus de Pseudo-Freris* remarks that the friars use ornaments in their churches to beguile the people; to feed their bodily eye and rob the eye of the soul, Matthew, 323/7-10.

561 be set I have followed Skeat's adoption of B's reading to restore sense.

564 lym-yerde is a stick smeared with lime for catching birds.

It is often used figuratively to describe devilish ensnarements of the soul, e.g., *Piers*, IX.181: 'For lecherie in likynge is lymeyerd of helle'.

567 cf. Matthew, 23:7: 'And salutations in the market-place, and to be called by men Rabbi'.

568 Lentenes Following Skeat, I have used the BC readings to restore medial 'e' in A.

570–3 Peres accuses the friars of purchasing the bishop's authority to give them cure of souls, cf. note to 481. They then corrupt this office for gain. Unless the people make rich payment for absolution, their penance will fail. Peres quips drily 'May God grant it be a good help [i.e., large sum of money] to guarantee the health of the souls', cf. *General Prologue*, 225–6: 'For unto a povre ordre for to yive/Is signe that a man is wel yshryve'.

574–6 cf. note to 498.

579 A's reading 'wher' does not fit the syntax. I have emended to **Ner** on the basis of B's reading 'Nor'. It suggests that **ner** was the original reading, which was misunderstood in AC and 'wher' was substituted.

580 In B, the original reading for the b-verse was the same as AC. The scribe later inserted a different half line.

581 cf. *Piers*, X.66: 'God is muche in the gorge of thise grete maistres'. There were a number of masters of divinity amongst the friars: the Dominican Thomas Aquinas, who taught at Paris; the Franciscans Roger Bacon, Duns Scotus and William of Ockham, who taught at Oxford; and the Franciscan general St Bonaventure, who taught at Paris.

582 cf. *Piers*, X.99–100, where the rich abandon the common hall and eat by themselves: 'In a pryvee parlour for povere mennes sake, / Or in a chambre with a chymene ...'

585 gloseth cf. note to 275.

586 cf. Friar John in *The Summoner's Tale* who tells Thomas that he has preached a sermon 'Nat al after the text of hooly writ, / For it is hard to you, as I suppose, / And therefore wol I teche yow all the glose. / Glosynge is a glorious thyng, certeyn, For lettre sleeth, so as we clerkes seyn/' (1790–4).

587–90 Peres argues that instead of studying to produce elaborate commentaries on Scripture, they should trust to divine inspiration, cf. Mark, 13:11: 'And, when they shall lead you, and deliver you up, be not thoughtful beforehand what you shall speak; but whatsoever shall be given you in that hour, that speak ye. For it is not you that speak, but the Holy Ghost'.

591-4 cf. Friar John in the *Summoner's Tale*, who tells tales of Cambises (2043) and Cyrus the Elder (2079), and *Piers*, X.71-2: 'Freres and faitours han founde up swiche questions/ To plese with proude men syn the pestilence tyme'.

596 comen The BC reading corrects A's copying error.

597 A lymitour is a friar licensed to hear confession within a certain jurisdiction, Alford, p.89. In practice, 'limitations' were drawn up to enable friars to beg for alms without competition, cf. *General Prologue*, 252a-2b: 'And yaf a certeyn ferme for the graunt; / Noon of his brethren cam ther in his haunt'.

600 cf. Matthew, 10:9-10: 'Do not possess gold, nor silver, nor money in your purses. Nor scrip [bag] for your journey, nor two coats, nor shoes nor a staff. For the workman is worthy of his meat'. Wycliffite texts frequently inveigh against the friars' mendicancy. In *Jack Upland*, Jack asks the friar what law licenses him to beg since begging is utterly forbidden in the Bible, p.66/275-8.

602 cf. Matthew, 6:25: 'Therefore, I say to you, be not solicitous for your life, what you shall eat, nor for your body, what you shall put on'.

603-4 cf. *The Orders of Cain*, where the friars are accused of carrying around different kinds of furs and spices : 'In bagges', Robbins, 65/56.

606-7 Jack Upland tells the friar that it is a sin for anyone to beg who has health and goods, 66/278-81. In *Piers*, begging by the able-bodied is severely criticised, e.g., VI.120-44 and in VII.60-69, where beggars are not included in the Pardon unless their need is genuine. Fraudulent beggars are 'fals with the feend' (68).

608 curious cloth A jibe at the fraternal habit, cf. *Jack Upland*, 60/137-9. Jack asks why the friar wears such fine and precious clothes. The only reason for doing so is vainglory and yet the friars say they are beggars.

609 as lordynges vsen cf. the criticism of the worldliness of the clerics in *PlTale*, 104-9.

610 For the Wycliffite diction cf. note to 45.

612 cf. Luke, 6:21: 'Blessed are ye that hunger now; for you shall be filled. Blessed are ye that weep now; for you shall laugh'.

614 clay Skeat emended to 'clath', arguing that the scribe misread thorn as 'y' in both A and B, and that the friars would not be put in clay when almost dead, only after death, p.50. I have restored the manuscript reading because the friars are bound fast in earth, in the sense of being spiritually dead. **clay** has the sense of 'the earth of the grave' MED clei 2c) and **pottes** the sense of an earthy enclosure. MED potte 2b) cites *The Siker Soth*, 74: 'Deth . . . has . . . put the pouer to the pot and oer him knett his knott. Vnder his clay kist'. The line comments satirically on the friars' separation from other orders of society.

615–19 Once friars are dead, they weep, longing for heaven, and curse the falsehoods formerly committed. But they can pack up their share (**part**) of heaven (**that blissinge**) in a tar pouch. The glossary to the 1553 edition glosses **terre powghe** as 'tar box'. **powghe** is an ironic reference to the wallet in which pardons were kept, cf. *Piers*, A.VIII.178: 'A powhe-ful of pardoun ther with prouincials lettres' (Skeat). Kane reads: 'A pokeful of pardoun there ne the prouincialis lettres' (A.VIII.175). In the C text, Piers's criticism of false priests contains the lines: 'The tarre is vntydy that to the shep by-longeth:/Here salue is of supersedeas in sumnoures boxes', IX.262–3. Pearsall notes that shepherds used tar for the treatment of sheep scab and kept a box of it handy. But today's shepherds [priests] use a substitute made from supersedeas, i.e. letting people off in return for payment. The sense of the line in *Crede* is that the friars can pack up their forfeited share of heaven in the same bag from which, instead of applying tar to wounds (i.e. imposing penance for sin), they dish out easy indulgences in return for money. *PlTale* notes that priests extort money from wastrels with which they 'smere the shepes skall' [skull], 280–2.

618 B originally had 'tree plough' which has been corrected to 'tree pogh'.

619 cf. note to 612.

620–1 cf. the list of deserving poor in *Piers*, VI.136–8.

626 Unless a friar is successful in begging he shall be put to death.

627 He shall be put under the earth, in a tomb, cf. note to 614.

629 blessed All three versions read 'and blessed'. Skeat missed the abbreviation in A. However, since the reading does not make sense I have omitted it. It is possible that the scribe anticipated the words 'and meke', realised from the following line that it would not fit, but forgot to delete the abbreviation for 'and'. As emended, the syntax of the lines is identical to 645–6; cf. Matthew, 5:7: 'Blessed are the merciful; for they shall obtain mercy'. This beatitude is cited at the opening of the Pelican's speech in *PlTale*, 93–6.

631–3 Anyone who criticises a friar found at a brothel and punishes him by whipping will fare as badly as if he had committed an offence against a substantial landowner, cf. note to 675. Wycliffite texts often comment on the friars' intolerance of criticism, e.g., *On the Leaven of the Pharisees*, Matthew, p.18, which states that a friar will offer to fight anyone who reproves him for his sinful life, cf. *PlTale*, 197–8.

634–6 cf. *The Orders of Cain*, Robbins, 65/99–104, where the narrator says that if a man had killed all his family and went to be confessed by a friar, the friar would absolve him absolutely in return for a pair of shoes and say that the sin will never harm his soul.

637–8 cf. Matthew, 5:8: 'Blessed are the clean of heart; for they shall see God'.

637 Crist Skeat adopted C's reading but the syntax of the line was still awkward. The very similar syntax at lines 629 and 645 suggest that the staves have been inverted and the original reading was 'Christ the clene hertes curteysliche blissed.' The corruption could have arisen from attraction to 'Cristes' in the following line. I have supplied the 's' in **curteysliche**.

638–40 These lines constitute a definition of a Wycliffite 'true priest', one who follows fully the apostolic ideal laid down by Christ to his followers, irrespective of whether he is a member of the established clergy.

642 I have supplied **and** from B, which is indicated there by an abbreviation mark. It clarifies the syntax of the line and could have been omitted from the other versions because an abbreviation in the exemplar was overlooked.

643 clene picks up **clene** in 637, but alters the sense from 'pure' to 'completely'. Wycliffite texts frequently satirise the friars' enclosure in their cloisters, cf. *Tractatus de Pseudo-Freris*, Matthew, p.322.

645 cf. Matthew, 5:9: 'Blessed are the peacemakers; for they shall be called the children of God'.

648 wilfulloker I have followed Skeat's reading in supplying the lost 'e' from B's version. C failed to understand the old form of the comparative.

648–9 cf. note to 631–3. Gower compares the friars to stinging bees in the context of alluding to their liaisons with women, *Vox*, IV.878–80.

649 styncande A misread 'c' as 't' and I have corrected from the BC reading.

650 cf. *Jack Upland*, 62/180–1: Jack asks the friar why they have no allegiance to the king, nor owe obedience to bishops. Wycliffite texts frequently criticise a friar's vow of obedience to his order because it takes precedence over secular and ecclesiastical obedience; cf. *Mum*, 431.

651–4 cf. Matthew, 5:10: 'Blessed are they that suffer persecution for justice' sake; for theirs is the kingdom of heaven'. Peres contrasts the friars with those who suffer persecution (Wycliffites, as the succeeding lines make clear). The citation from Matthew suggests that the friars are not part of the congregation of souls destined for salvation. This was the Wycliffite definition of true holy church, cf. note to *Mum*, 516–20.

655–6 cf. *Vae Octuplex*, *EWS*, II.374/241–4, which states that the Pharisees [the friars] pursue [litigate against] true priests who criticise their faults and obstruct their profits. No lawsuit is more full of envy, nor more dangerous, than one conducted by the tricks of hypocrites.

657–62 Walter Brut was a West Country esquire who espoused radical Wycliffite views on the sacraments and the priesthood. He protested against the condemnation of William Swinderby for heresy in 1391 and in October 1393, Bishop Trefnant of Hereford brought him to trial to answer for his views, *Registrum Johannis Trefnant*, ed. W. W. Capes (Canterbury and York Society, 1916), pp.285–358. During the course of his trial, Brut produced a lengthy written statement of his views. The Franciscan friar William Woodford wrote a number of polemical works against Wycliffite teaching, one of which was a response to Brut's defence, see further, Hudson (1988[1]), p.47.

659 hym I have followed Skeat in emending to **hym** against the readings of all three versions. The scribes often confuse singular and plural third person pronouns. Here, the sense requires the singular.

663 cf. Holy Church's comment on chaplains who are unkind to their kin and all Christians, *Piers*, I.193: 'Chewen hire charite and chiden after moore'. *Vae Octuplex* argues that the friars' prosecution of true priests destroys the charity of the church, *EWS*, II.374/232–44.

665 y-worthen A's reading arises from the miswriting of 'y' as thorn.

665–8 Ecclesiastics were forbidden by law to take part in any sentence of death, cf. note to *Mum*, 707–9. Peres refers to the practice of burning heretics and excommunicating them. If the poem is to be dated before 1400, then no Wycliffite had yet been burnt for his views, cf. notes to *Mum*, 165–73.

669 forbadde A misread 'b' as 'l'. I have used the BC reading to correct.

669–70 cf. Matthew, 7:1: 'Judge not that you may not be judged', Matthew, p.311, cf. *Tractatas de Pseudo-Freris* and the identical phrase in *PlTale*, 714.

674 Canon was the title given to secular clergy belonging to a cathedral or collegiate church. The Carthusian monks were founded by St Bruno in 1084 at Grande Chartreuse. The line distinguishes between canons, monks and parish priests.

675 greved carries the legal sense of a wrong or grievance, MED gref, 1d), cf. note to *Richard*, IV.37–8.

677 schamen A's 'schenden' arises from dittography. I have corrected from the BC reading. **schenden and schamen** suggest legal defamation, cf. *Richard*, 74 and *Mum*, 73, 273.

679–80 *Tractatus de Pseudo-Freris* defends its antifraternal criticism by stating that it is one's duty to speak out sharply against the friars' sinfulness. Otherwise innocent people will suffer at their hands. Such criticism should not be undertaken for envy or covetousness, but rooted in charity, Matthew, pp.296–7.

681–6 possessioners were the beneficed clergy and monks who were endowed with lands and goods. The friars, by contrast, were forbidden to own property. The worldliness of monks and parish priests had long been a target of satire, see Mann, pp.17–36 and pp.55–67. Peres's accusation that this worldliness stems from the influence of the friars represents a new stage in anti-clericalism, one which registered confusion between beggars and possessioners and ultimately questioned the right of the church to own property, see Scase, pp.20–24 and cf. note to 462.

684 chesen I have followed Skeat's emendation. None of the three readings is accurate; an infinitive is required. The cluster 'sch' for 'ch' is seen also in **schaf**, 663.

689 The hypocrisy of the friars' habit is a frequent target of Wycliffite satire, cf. *Vae Octuplex*, *EWS*, II.373/199–202 which states that God ordained holiness in soul but the friars claim hypocritically that holiness resides in their habits.

691–2 cf. the vision of the saved in *Apocalypse*, 7:9: 'a great multitude ... standing before the throne and in sight of the Lamb, clothed with white robes, and palms in their hands'.

692 tokens The friars have the outward sign of sanctity and have assumed the robes reserved for those who shall be saved, but they are hypocrites, cf. *Vae Octuplex*, which calls the supposed sanctity of the habit 'feynede signes', *EWS*, II.373/201.

695–6 allude to the dress of the Dominicans. Peres's point is that they do not follow the spiritual significance of their habit; cleanness of soul and penance for sin.

701 fraitour cf. the description of the gluttonous Dominican, 220–30.

703 ho There is no manuscript support for the emendation from 'he' but the female pronoun is required. 'Ho' is used at 411 and 412. It is clear that the scribe of B did not understand the reference. 'Lidgate' is written above the line as a gloss. Hildegard of Bingen (1098–1180) was abbess of the Benedictine community at Rupertsberg on the Rhine. She was a prolific writer in many genres. Between 1141 and 1151 she dictated *Scivias*, a work containing 26 visions, with denunciations of the world and cryptic prophecies of disaster. She predicted the corruption of the monastic orders. Her prophecies are adopted by Wyclif and Wycliffites to refer to the friars, e.g., *Trialogus*, p.338, Matthew, p.11, Arnold, p.413 and p.421. In the last, Hildegard predicts the damnation of the cursed sects for their hypocrisy and deceit. Hildegard's visionary prophecies are discussed in relationship to anti-mendicancy in *Piers* by K. Kerby-Fulton, *Reformist Apocalypticism and Piers Plowman* (Cambridge, 1990), 26–75.

706 belden I have followed Skeat's adoption of the BC reading to restore alliteration and improve sense.

707 **fallynge** 'sellyng' would improve sense and alliteration. The scribes could have mistaken 's' for 'f' (cf. C's reading at 712) but since there is no warrant in any version and the reading is tenable, I have not emended.

709 cf. note to 275.

710–13 Peres accuses the friars of simony, the purchase or sale of an ecclesiastical office or anything annexed to it, cf. Simon Magus's attempt to buy the gift of the Holy Spirit from the apostles with silver, Acts, 8:18–24.

714–15 **a pena ... and a culpa** from punishment and from guilt. Guilt could be forgiven in sacramental confession, and remittance of temporal punishment, e.g., fasting or almsgiving, could be granted by a pardon or indulgence. These indulgences did not secure remittance of eternal punishment however, cf. note to 246–7. Peres accuses the friars of selling pardons as though they granted absolute pardon in order to get more money, cf. *Piers*, VII.3 where Truth sends to Peres a pardon 'a pena et a culpa'.

719 **russet** The Franciscans, or Greyfriars, wore russet habits, cf. *Piers*, XV.165–7, where Charity is said to be as glad of a gown of grey russet, as of a silk jacket of choice scarlet.

720 Russet was worn by shepherds or labourers. Both Knighton, II.184 and Walsingham, *H.A.*, I.324, state that Lollards wore russet garments. Peres contrasts the hypocritical clothes of the friars with the honest garments worn by true followers of Christ.

723 *The Leaven of the Pharisees* states that the friars compete to build the most extravagant houses funded by the poor, Matthew, p.5. **trewe men** is the name which the early Lollards used of themselves, see Hudson (1985), pp.166–7.

724 **biggen** On C's reading, cf. note to 360.

725 I have followed Skeat's adoption of the BC reading to emend A's error of reading 'l' as 's'.

726 cf. *Summoner's Tale*, 1693–6, where a nest of friars fly out of the devil's arse like a swarm of bees. Lawton (1981), p.791 has likened this description to the drones in *Mum*, 1044–50.

729 **furste-froyt** cf. 2 Timothy 2:6: 'The husbandman that laboureth must first partake of the fruits'. The friars corrupt this doctrine, cf. *Summoner's Tale*, 2271–86 where the lord's squire explains to the friar that because of his pre-eminence, he should

first partake of the (first fruyt) of the fart divided amongst twelve.

730–4 cf. note to 626.

734–41 cf. note to 68–9.

738 schon is required by the sense. A omits 'h' and BC's reading stems from misreading 'c' as 't'.

740 cf. note to 69.

744–59 The advancement of the sons of beggars and the corruption of appointments is discussed in *Piers*, C.V.61–82. Will states that only clerics should serve Christ and only those of noble blood should receive the tonsure. Serfs, beggars' children and bastards should labour with their hands and serve their fellow men according to their rank. Now, however, bondsmen's children are made into bishops and bastards into archdeacons. The sons of cobblers have bought themselves knighthoods.

747 alludes to the criticism that friars stole children to boost their numbers cf. *Vae Octuplex*, *EWS*, II.368/48–71.

748–9 Friars recruit the sons of beggars, who are then made bishops, cf. note to 254, and sit alongside the peers of the realm in parliament, cf. Mede's claim in her discussion of the hardships of the Normandy wars, that she would have made: 'The leeste brol of his blood a barones peire', *Piers*, III.205.

750–54 comment on the friars' reversal of natural hierarchy and reflect Wycliffite criticisms that the fraternal orders compromise obedience to secular authority. Instead of ecclesiastics obeying the secular power, knights kneel to the friars, cf. note to 650. The Lollard *Tractatus de Regibus* states that the friars fail in their clerical allegiance to the king because they do not fulfil their spiritual duties, *SEWW*, pp.129–30; cf. *PlTale*, 181–207.

758 Scase notes, pp.69–71 that **faytoures** and **freres** is a frequent collocation in *Piers*, e.g., X.71, with reference to the friars' fraudulent begging. It became a standard formula of antimendicant satire. See also Alford, p.54.

761 cf. note to 554–8.

762–4 cf. Hunger's advice to Piers to feed false beggars with animal feed and beans, VI.212–17.

763 bandes I have adopted the BC reading to restore alliteration.

765–9 cf. note to 50–2. Lechery is linked with drink in *Piers*, V.71–4.

774 cf. note to 254 and 364–5.

781–2 cf. *The Testament of St Francis*, p.47: the friars say that the Pope has dispensed them from their founding role because his authority is greater than that of St Francis. True men say, however, that friars are bound to this rule.

784 worldlyche cf. note to 371.

785 cf. *On the Council of London*, Wright, I.259, where the friars disregard Francis's example of manual labour. They choose to plough another furrow, despite the fact that their rule stipulates manual labour and outlaws begging.

786 cf. the description of the idle labourers refusing to eat yesterday's vegetables, bean bread and halfpenny ale, *Piers*, VI.302–311.

788 wolward wear rough clothing against the skin, cf. *Piers*, XVIII.1: 'Wolleward and weetshoed wente I forth after'.

789 An aunter yif I have followed Skeat's adoption of C's reading. A misreads a 'y' as yogh and alters the spacing.

792 In contrast to the friars the simple ploughman is able to teach the narrator his Creed; cf. *PlTale*, 453–5 which asks what need a ploughman has to know the Pope's name since it is sufficient for him to know his Creed.

794 Peres acts like a Wycliffite true priest. A list of accusations against the Lollards states their belief in one rank of priesthood in the church; that every good man is a priest and has the power to preach the word of God, *SEWW*, 19/16–18. In contrast to the friars, Peres teaches the truth; cf. the end of *Vae Octuplex*, which rejects the dangers of the friars for the truth which God has ordained, *EWS*, II.378/354–7.

798 cf. note to 371.

801 I have followed Skeat's adoption of the BC reading to restore sense. A may have misread an abbreviation.

808 refers to the Harrowing of Hell when Christ fetched out Adam and the patriarchs. The story is recorded in the apocryphal gospel of Nicodemus and is given at length in *Piers*, XVIII.110–407.

810 steigh I have followed Skeat's adoption of C's reading (supported by B). A misread 'e' as 'r'.

817 sacrement I have followed Skeat in adopting B's reading. A misreads 't' as 's'. At this point the printed edition contains 5 lines which are absent from both Trinity and Royal manuscripts:

> The communion of sayntes, for soth I to the sayn;
> And for our great sinnes forguienes for to getten,
> And only by Christ clenlich to be clensed;
> Our bodies again to risen right as we been here,
> And the liif euerlasting leue ich to habben. Amen.

Skeat believed them to be spurious and printed them in brackets and italics. He believed that they were a forgery to cover up the printer's omission of some of the lines on the Eucharist. Skeat notes the absurdity of having 'Amen' in the middle of a sentence and that the lines produce a break in sense, pp.54–5. Dean prints the lines in his edition and Lawton has argued that they are authentic (1981), p.784. I have not included the passage for the following reasons: the 1553 edition is not based on any of the surviving manuscripts, Doyle (1959), p.435; the lines interrupt the sense of the passage, and the fact that the 1553 edition omits lines 818–19 and 823–5 shows that there has been excision and interpolation.

817–18 omitted by 1553 edition. They affirm the doctrine of the Real Presence in the Eucharist, i.e. that Christ's body is fully present in the bread, but cf. the following notes.

819–21 The friars were not the first to raise the question of transubstantiation; it was Wyclif. He argued not against Real Presence but against the doctrine of transubstantiation. He stated that after consecration Christ's body is in the bread, but that the bread still remains on the altar. It is not changed into something else, see Kenny, pp.80–90. *Piers Plowman* satirises the friars' vain and academic questioning of theology, X.71–2. *On the Leaven of the Pharisees* accuses the friars of heresy for saying that the bread seen in the priest's hands is neither bread, nor Christ's body, Matthew, p.19.

821 masedere I have followed Skeat into adopting the BC reading. A clearly made no sense of the text here.

823–5 not in 1553 edition, perhaps for doctrinal reasons, see note to 824–5.

823 Luke, 22:19: 'And, taking bread, he gave them thanks and brake, and gave to them saying: This is my body, which is given for you. Do this for a commemoration of me'.

824–5 cf. *The Plowman's Tale* 1221–4, which also states that it does not matter how Christ's body enters the sacrament. Wawn has noted of *The Plowman's Tale* that this is not an orthodox answer (1972), p.32. Lawton comments that Lollards were condemned precisely for saying that it did not matter how Christ's real presence entered the sacramental elements. The orthodox view was that it did matter because the church doctrine was exact and rigorously articulated (1981), p.782.

825 cf. note to 823. The defence of the Eucharist is evasive because it skirts the crucial question of transubstantiation.

826 cf. *Piers*, X.115–16: 'Swiche motyves they meve, thise maistres in hir glorie, / And maken men in mysbileve that muse muche on hire wordes'.

828 cf. I have followed Skeat's adoption of the BC reading to emend A's copying error.

828–9 cf. Study's criticism of academic questions of theology: 'For alle that wilneth to wite the whyes of God almyghty, / I wolde that his eighe were in his ers and his fynger after. . . . Al was as he wolde – Lord yworshiped be thow – /And all worth as thow wolt whatso we dispute', *Piers*, X.124–5, 129–30.

830–5 cf. *Piers*, X.69–70: 'Clerkes and othere kynnes men carpen of God faste, / And have hym muche in hire mouth, ac meene men in herte'. The lines in *Crede* bypass institutionalised priesthood, cf. note to 794. A true priest is not necessarily a person consecrated by the Church, but anyone who lives a good life and who preaches (835). Preaching the truth was fundamental to Wycliffite thought.

831 cf. *Lanterne of Light*, 5/15–18: 'The apostils of Crist and othir seintis weren not graduat men in scolis, but the Holi Goost sodenli enspirid hem, and maden hem plenteuous of heuenli loore'.

833 cf. note to 498. **ben** A's reading makes no sense. I have followed Skeat in adopting the BC reading.

834 **no** A has reversed the letters and obscured the sense. I have followed Skeat in adopting the BC reading.

837 Peres reveals that he is literate. Literacy was central to the Lollard movement. Lollard texts often emphasise the duty of the literate (not necessarily those considered literate by the church) to teach others. Some Lollard suspects pretended they were not literate to escape detection, see Hudson (1988[1]), p.185.

838 The voice of Peres merges with that of the narrator, and author, cf. note to *Richard*, 79–83 on the distinction between slander and reform.

839 cf. *Tractatus de Pseudo-Freris* which begins with a lengthy defence of reproving the friars. The writer recounts the Bible's mandates to reprove sin and argues that by honest reproof, God may turn the friars to good and keep subjects in God's way who would otherwise tread the path to hell, Matthew, p.296–8.

846–7 modify substantially earlier criticisms which dispute the very existence of fraternal orders and claim that they were founded by the devil, e.g., 483–7, 505–6. This anxiety about writing coupled with a defence of its purpose to reform is found also at the conclusion of *PlTale*, 1357–72.

850 wynnen I have adopted the BC reading. A has simply miscopied the minims.

NOTES TO RICHARD THE REDELESS

Passus One There is no warrant in CUL MS Ll iv 14 for the rubrication 'Prologue' recorded in Skeat and Day and Steele (D&S). There are marginal rubrications for Passus Two, Three and Four, which suggest the presence of a first Passus. Red capitals accompany these Passus markings. In the preceding copy of *Piers Plowman*, red capitals also coincide with the new Passus divisions and rubrication. D&S mark Passus One of *Richard* to begin at line 88 because of the presence of a red capital. However, capitalisation does not always accompany Passus divisions in *Richard*. There are capitals also at I.97 and 136, and at III.37 and 110. Since there is no firm authority for seeing line 88 as the start of a new Passus, and consequently no need to infer the presence of a Prologue, I have marked the start of the poem as Passus One.

1 **And** suggests that a preceding portion has been lost but it is characteristic of the poet to commence a new section or observation with 'And'. See for instance I.27, III.209 and IV.71. The Latin couplet transcribed by Brigham (see Introduction) begins with 'Dum' (while).

2 Bristol may be a reference to the poet's birthplace. His familiarity with topical events centred mainly on London makes it unlikely that he was living in Bristol at the time of writing. Rather like Langland's Malvern Hills (*Piers*, Prol.5), Bristol could be a signature of poetic identity. The town also had an important role in national events. On 28 July 1399, Sir Peter Courtenay, keeper of the castle, surrendered Bristol to the forces of Henry Bolingbroke and handed over Scrope, Busshy and Grene, who had taken refuge there. They were executed and their heads sent to decorate the gates of London (Kirby, p.57).

3–4 Christ Church is, and was, the popular name for the

church consecrated as Holy Trinity. The name suggests familiarity with the affairs of the city of Bristol. The old church,
demolished in 1787, stood in the very centre of the old town at
the crossroads; hence the poet's phrase 'euen amyddes'. The
church was rebuilt in 1790.

8 sidis sets up the rival claims of both parties as if the
narrator were adjudicating a dispute between Richard and
Henry. Henry is reputed to have sent out circulars from Ponte-
fract Castle to all the towns of England, setting out his own case
against Richard, *Traison et Mort*, pp.180–2.

10 the wilde Yrisshe is a phrase used by Richard when
writing from Dublin to the Duke of York in 1395. He remarked
that there were three kinds of people in Ireland, 'the wild Irish,
our enemies, the Irish now in rebellion and the faithful English',
N. H. Nicholas, ed., *Proceedings and Ordinances of the Privy
Council* (London, 1834), I.57–8. Richard made two expeditions
to quell the insurrections in Ireland, the first in 1395, and
the second in 1399 to avenge the death of Roger Mortimer,
Lieutenant of Ireland, who was killed in an ambush on 20 July
1398.

11 Henry landed at Ravenspur on the north-eastern tip of
England on his return to England, probably at the beginning of
July. From Ravenspur he moved through Yorkshire, the Midlands and eventually reached Berkeley Castle in Gloucester at
the end of July. In the course of his progress, he attracted many
supporters, amongst them Henry Percy, earl of Northumberland, Henry Percy his son, and Ralph Neville, the earl of
Westmorland. In the meantime, the Duke of York, whom
Richard had left as Regent, found it difficult to raise an army.
Richard did not leave Ireland until the end of July. He landed
back at Conway in North Wales, where the earl of Salisbury
had mustered an army but desertions were frequent (see notes
to II.6–7). Richard journeyed to Flint with followers who were
continuously deserting. He was either ambushed on the way and
taken to Flint as a prisoner, or, having arrived safely at Flint,
submitted there to Henry. By the end of August Richard was a
prisoner in the Tower of London, while Henry, with his
Lancastrian army, marched into London in triumph at the
beginning of September, L. D. Duls, *Richard II in the Early
Chronicles* (The Hague, 1975), pp.152ff., Kirby, pp.53–59.
entrid is a term of legal diction, meaning the act of taking

possession of lands and also the legal right to do so, Alford, p.51. The term suggests that Henry is the lawful owner of England and thus, the throne. See also notes to III.69.

12–13 The chronicles record warm and enthusiastic support for Henry on his return to England, *Traison*, p.182, *Annales*, p.242 and *Eulogium*, p.381.

13 wronge is a term of legal diction, meaning a criminal wrong, Alford, p.169. Henry received a number of 'wrong's at Richard's hands. In January 1398, Henry presented a petition to Richard accusing Thomas Mowbray, duke of Norfolk, of treason. The matter resulted in a trial by combat between the two men scheduled for 16 September 1398. Before the combatants met in battle, Richard, to the astonishment of the crowd, forbade the joust and imposed a ten-year exile on Henry and life banishment on Mowbray. The *Annales* comments that Richard banished Henry without any legitimate cause and that his action was against all justice, military laws and customs of the kingdom, p.226. In March, after John of Gaunt's death, Richard announced that Henry's sentence amounted to life banishment,and that all the possessions of the house of Lancaster were forfeited to the crown.

14 *The Davies Chronicle* records Henry's promise to redress the wrongs of the people if they lent him their support, p.15.

15–18 The narrator pretends ignorance of the outcome of events here. The use of the legal terms **tales** – the plaintiff's account in a legal suit, Alford, p.151, **priefis** – legal evidence or testimony, MED preven 1c), and **ende** – to conclude a legal case, give judgment, Alford, p.50, suggests he is presiding over a legal dispute whose outcome is not yet known. We know from the beginning of Passus II, however, that the poet must be writing after January 1400 (see notes to II.17) so this ignorance of events is a narrative fiction.

19 they sembled – the antecedent for the pronoun is unclear. The phrase is most likely to refer to the assembly of Parliament in September 1399, which met to depose Richard and accept Henry's claim to the throne.

21–3 The profession of sympathy for Richard's personal plight finds corroboration in contemporary accounts. The *Traison* records mixed feelings in the crowd when Richard was taken to the Tower of London, p.215, and Adam Usk, a man who criticised Richard's rule with candour, visited the former king in prison and records with great sympathy Richard's sorrowful plight, p.182.

24 The MS reading **woll** can be defended. The present tense keeps up the fiction that Richard may regain his crown. Skeat retains the MS reading; D&S emend to 'wolde'.

25 The staves appear to have been inverted in the a-verse and, following D&S, I have reversed their order.

26 There is wordplay here on **hoole** in the sense of 'healthy', MED hole (adj.2) 1, and in the sense of 'undivided, whole', MED hole (adj.2) 5. The narrator's health is dependent on the king's **helthe**. The wordplay demonstrates that allegiance can be due to a king only if he assures his subjects' well-being by ensuring his own.

27 D&S emend MS 'wost' to **wust** following Skeat.

27–36 The narrator claims to be writing a poem of advice to Richard in case God grants him the kingship again. Given the dating of the poem, this must be a rhetorical posture, one which allows the narrator to criticise Richard openly, without slander.

33 Skeat and D&S emend MS 'preise' to **preie**. **preie** makes the better sense. Richard had little to give praise for but much for which to beseech.

37 cf. *Piers*, V.199: 'First I lerned to lye a leef outher tweyne'.

39 Unless the last two words are a line filler, the b-verse suggests that Richard has no hope of regaining the crown.

41 **grèued** MED lists under 'gref' (n) 1d), (law): prejudice or harm, an official complaint of a wrong or grievance. The narrator is defending the legality of his writing, wishing no damage on the king and noting that he himself will be harmed if he inflicts damage on a third party. The b-verse is an oath attesting the truth of his testimony.

42 D&S postponed this line until after line 45 because of the awkwardness of syntax, p.85. However, the remark is clearly an aside and can stand in its assigned place without disruption of sense. The narrator offers his advice in place of a counsellor.

43–4 cf. *Mum*, 1287. As Embree notes (1975), here we reach the true target of the narrator's remarks. The rhetorical posture of addressing Richard II as though he were able to regain the crown has been a disguise to conceal the true direction of the poet's comments, namely an 'advice to princes' written for the benefit of the reigning king Henry IV. Many of the issues which aroused hostile criticism in Richard's reign were also contentious in the reign of his successor. In 1401 Philip Repingdon wrote to Henry IV to warn him about the state of his rule and used the fate of Richard II as a cautionary example, cf. note to *Mum*, 115. In Gower's *Vox Clamantis*, the original praise and cautious optimism for Richard's reign is drastically rewritten and the original version partly reworked to celebrate Henry's accession, VI.545–80. Skeat and D&S emend MS 'grounde' to **croune**, thus restoring sense to the line.

47–8 D&S, reading against Skeat's interpretation of 'the best that I have', gloss **beste** as livestock. The narrator draws an analogy between the way that his body and his livestock owe allegiance to him as his subjects, and the loyalty of his **rede**, his counsel. The force of the comparison is that it is the duty of the narrator to offer up his counsel. The narrator verifies his position with reference to **reson**, the personification of justice; thus claiming high legal authority for his writing.

49–52 The scope of the criticism is extended to include the nobility and **men ther-after** (51b). Skeat and D&S emend MS 'fordyd' to **fondyd** to restore sense to the line. A correction in a different ink marks 'n' above 'r'. In his warning to beware **wylffulnesse** the narrator draws an implicit contrast between the **reson** of the counsellor's good advice and the tendency of those counselled to follow their own wills. Such a course of action may result in **wondris** (52b), a word which recalls the **grett wondir** of line 6. The narrator seems anxious to avoid a repetition of events.

56 **be the rode of Chester** the same oath is used by Sloth in *Piers*, V.460. The cross used to stand on Rood Eye (Cross Island) in the Dee at Chester.

57–58 **fables, frute** and **yffeyned** recall the terminology of allegorical exposition, where the fruit of moral sense is concealed under the feigning literal surface, cf. Henryson, 'And full of frute under ane fenyeit fabill', *The Morall Fabillis of Esope the Phrygian*, 18 in Robert Henryson, *Poems*, ed. C. Elliott (Oxford, 1974). The narrator of *Richard*, however, is concerned only with **frute** and eschews the nut/kernel model of allegorical poetry. His comment is not borne out in practice as there are several allegorical sequences in his poem.

59–60 The narrator invites his audience to engage in the same critical activity as himself. He writes in order to **amende** what is **amysse**. The reader's faculty for counsel, together with clerkly help, must **corette** the narrator's work.

61 secrette suggests that the poem was to be disseminated privately rather than submitted for public copying, possibly as a result of the strictures on writing political poetry, see J. Barnie, *War in Medieval Society* (London, 1974), pp.142–5.

65–8 The singling out of youth for correction is in keeping with the emphasis on the folly of youth at I.176 and III.261–3, especially in regard to the inability of young men to be effective advisers.

71 The systematic and diligent reading of the book by old men contrasts with the youthful browsing which gets only half way through.

72 culorum MED glosses as short for *in saeculum saeculorum*, often used at the end of Psalms or prayers, meaning the substance, gist or meaning. See also IV.61 and *Piers*, III.280: 'The culorum of this cas kepe I noght to shew'. MED records no other examples of this word.

73 apeire hym a peere a proverbial phrase, cf. Hoccleve, *Regement of Princes*, 102 and further references, Whiting, pp.450–1. There is a pun here on **peere** as pear, MED pere (2) and as peer of the realm, MED per 4a).

74 harme nother hurte could be an anglicisation of the legal formula 'damage e huntage' in civil actions where claimants sought compensation for harm and shame, Alford, p.68. The narrator is anxious to avoid the charge of defamation.

77 The **souereyne** in question here must be Henry IV. It would be futile to sue a deposed king for grace and protection.

78 grace in its legal emphasis of 'the power to show pardon or mercy', Alford, p.66.

79–83 entent in the legal sense of 'intentio', Alford, p.74. It shows the narrator anxious to legalise his truthtelling. P. Miller has related the narrator's desire 'not to slander but to correct those whom he censures' to the intention of satire expressed in Latin satirical theory, 'John Gower: Satiric Poet', in *Gower's Confessio Amantis: Responses and Reassessments*, ed. A. J. Minnis (Cambridge, 1983), 79–105, p.86.

85 gouerne him better states that self-government is essential for those who would govern others.

86 blame is not recorded in a legal sense in MED but given the legal tenor of the context, it carries the sense of bringing a charge against, or accusing.

88 Skeat and D&S mark Passus One to begin at this line.

90 Richard's government was characterised by lavish expenditure. The *Eulogium* remarks that Richard was eager to exceed the wealth of all his predecessors (III.384) and records a speech by Richard Arundel which accuses the king of despoiling his kingdom, raising tallages and taxes not for the benefit of the realm, but to satisfy his avarice and display his pomp (III.382). In one year alone, between 1396–7, expenditure on gifts and personal largesse came to £32,231, G. Mathew, *The Court of Richard II* (London, 1968), pp.151–2.

91 Ye were lyghtlich ylyfte i.e., deposed. **lyghtliche** bears testimony to the efficiency with which Henry Bolingbroke defeated Richard in a military campaign, enforced his resignation of the crown and had himself proclaimed king with the assent of parliament all within the space of three months.

94 The a-verse is unusually long. The first two words are possibly scribal. Elsewhere, subject and main verb are not separated between two lines.

95 for euere contradicts the suggestion at I.29 that Richard might be able to rule again. The Latin quotation reads: 'Cupidity is the root of all evils' from 1 Timothy, 6:10.

96 The narrator enumerates a list of crimes which violate the bonds of loyalty between a king and his subjects. The crimes resemble the catalogue of Richard's misdeeds read out after Richard's renunciation of the crown at the assembly of Parliament on 30 September 1399. The 'gravamina', consisted of 32 articles of misconduct, *Rot.Parl.*, III.417–22. The 'record and process' of this parliament was widely distributed by Henry and his supporters as propaganda. It was used by several of the chroniclers. The poet may have had access to it. Adam Usk notes in his eyewitness account of the parliament that all the crimes with which Richard was tainted, were reasons enough for setting him aside, p.181.

98 drede an 'e' is written above 'i' in MS reading 'dride'. The spelling of the verb **drede** at III.339 justifies emendation here. Unlike, Skeat, D&S do not incorporate this correction in their text. The first article of the 'gravamina' relates how Richard intimidated the Justices of the realm with threats of death and violence in order to win their support in the destruction of the Lords Appellant. He menaced the judges into declaring that the acts of the Merciless Parliament of 1388, which had curbed his misgovernment, were illegal. The twenty-second article relates that Richard intimidated his subjects into granting him money and provisions for his expedition to Ireland. The twenty-fourth states that Richard exacted forced oaths of allegiance from his people after the Shrewsbury parliament of 1398. All who had been implicated with the Appellants of 1387 were ordered to seek individual pardons (for which they had to pay) and to renew their oaths of loyalty. It is perhaps with this process in mind that the narrator catalogues Richard's crimes as a lesson of **alegeaunce**.

99 creaunce of coyne The fourteenth article accuses Richard of having raised loans from many of his subjects. He promised to repay them but never did.

100 pillynge . . . peple . . . prynces The first accusation of the 'gravamina' is of Richard's extortions of money from his people in order to gratify his favourites. The twenty-sixth article accuses the king of having appropriated the lands, goods and incomes of his subjects, not because they were legally forfeit, but because it pleased the king to feel that they were at his disposal. Such behaviour is condemned as contrary to the established laws and customs of the realm.

101 wylle were wroughte The articles contain many criticisms of Richard's wilfulness, where the king followed his own inclinations in despite of the law and also where he followed his pleasure in the face of advice. The seventh article narrates that Richard wilfully refused to uphold the legal election of sheriffs, preferring to appoint his own, the sixteenth article states that the king was not interested in maintaining the rights and customs of the realm but only in following his desire, lust and his will. When Justices and members of his council declared to the king that he should maintain the laws and rights of the realm, Richard replied that he alone had the right to change the laws because they resided in his mouth or in his breast. The twenty-third article states that Richard refused to listen to wise counsel offered by the lords of the realm and the justices.

102 without ony werre The fifteenth article states that the king of England should live honestly off the revenues and profits of the realm without burdening his people when there are no costs of war. Richard raised so many grants and taxes on his subjects that he greatly oppressed his people with poverty. The exactions were not used for the profit of the realm but squandered on pomp and vainglory.

103–4 **rewthles routus** probably refers to the private army of Cheshiremen whom Richard retained for his personal protection (see notes to III.317). The fifth article gives a vivid account of the disorderly mob of Cheshiremen plundering and pillaging violently throughout the realm.

106 **loue** is favouritism towards one of the parties in a suit, Alford, p.91, which perverts justice.

107 **endited** means both to compose, MED enditen (1), and to indict, charge with crime, enditen (4), cf. Alford, p.50. The narrator sets himself up as Richard's prosecutor.

109–10 are defective in alliteration. 110 could be lacking 'clere' as a stave before **wordys** in the b-verse.

111 cf. *Piers*, XI.170: 'Lawe withouten love', quod Troianus, 'ley there a bene'.

112 **gylours of hem-self** is an allusion to Richard's favourites in the first half of his reign. The most prominent were Robert de Vere, earl of Oxford, Michael de la Pole, earl of Suffolk, Archbishop Neville of York, Nicholas Brembre, mayor of London, Sir Robert Tresilian, chief justice of the king's bench and Sir Simon Burley. These men were all accused of treason in the Merciless Parliament of 1388 (*Rot.Parl.* III.230–6) for abusing their power by taking advantage of Richard's youth to obtain grants of land from him fraudulently. Tresilian, Brembre and Burley were condemned to death and executed promptly. Neville had his property confiscated and was exiled; de Vere and de la Pole escaped overseas and died in exile. These 'self-deceivers' contrast with the good knights who **knowe well hem-self**, III.200, a reference to the common and important ideas in the Middle Ages of *nosce te ipsum* as a *sine qua non* of commendable public behaviour.

113 **harnesse** The MS reading is to be preferred in the sense of 'armour', alluding to the fact that these men did not exercise self-restraint. This was Skeat's reading but D&S emended to 'harmesse'. The pampered lives of the favourites is attested by Walsingham, who remarks that they were rather knights of Venus than War, more potent in the bedchamber than on the battlefield, *H.A.*, I.156.

116 refers to the accusations of treason against Richard's favourites in the Merciless Parliament of 1388, cf. note to I.112.

117 D&S emend MS 'lordschpe' to **lordschipe** following Skeat.

118 **trespas** means violation of the law, Alford, p.158.

119 **er ye youre-self knewe** cf. notes to I.112. The mention of Richard's coronation invites the reader to compare the promises made at the king's investiture with his actual subsequent conduct. The 'gravamina' in the Parliament Rolls are prefaced by a text of the Coronation oath to demonstrate Richard's violation of his promises. Richard was 10 years old when he succeeded to the throne in June 1377 after the death of Edward III.

120 cf. the description of the bejewelled Mede in *Piers*, II.10–17. Line 10 reads: 'Ycorouned with a coroune, the Kyng hath noon bettre'.

121 The opulence of the coronation is recorded in *Anonimalle*, p.108 and *H.A.*, I.332. The allegorisation of the stones in the king's crown is common; see Kail, XII,64, where the poet states that whoever impedes the law picks the stones out of the king's crown. Gower interprets the king's crown as a symbol of his moral excellence, *Confessio*, VII.1751–82.

122 **vertuous** D&S and Skeat read 'vertus' but there is a correction to the text in the scribe's hand. **vertuous** carries a double sense: natural properties, OED 'virtue' II.9 and moral virtue, sense 2a). In lapidaries, the natural properties of stones are frequently allegorised. This sequence is an example of the poet's use of the natural world as a political exemplum.

123 It is appropriate to begin with a pearl, which Isidore of Seville calls the *prima candidarum gemmarum* (*Etymologiarum*, XVI. x.1; *PL*, 82, p.575).

124 The ruby is traditionally associated with lordship, *English Medieval Lapidaries*, p.21.

129 The diamond is traditionally the hardest of stones, *English Medieval Lapidaries*, p.83.

132 A sapphire is a most suitable stone for a ring to be set on a king's finger. It is associated with 'gentillesse', *English Medieval Lapidaries*, p.22.

133 **pounced** All the lines in this section alliterate regularly on aa/ax and the b-verse is deficient in sense. I have supplied **pounced** from the verb 'pouncen' MED, to emboss, decorate by pricking, because the second sense of the noun 'pounce' given in MED is 'a preparation of finely powdered cuttlefish bone or sandarac, or some similar substance, used to prevent ink from running over an erasure'. This makes sense of **ypouudride** in the first half line. **pounced** could have been omitted because it was

an unfamiliar term, perhaps not legible from the cluster of minims in the middle of the word.

140–2 refer either to outright theft and/or extortion from husbandsmen by the king's retainers, or to the king's right of purveyance when travelling to take goods, food and beasts in return for a tally. A tally was a receipt in the form of shafts of hard wood on which notches were cut to denote particular sums of money. After being split longitudinally, one section was retained by each of the parties to an account, Alford, p.150. **paide** carries a pun on the senses of financial payment, MED paien (3), a beating, and the legal sense of making amends or restitution, Alford, p.107. There is a similar accusation at III.370.

143 pleyne in the legal sense of lodging a formal complaint or accusation, Alford, p.117. The charge that subjects were too afraid to complain about the antics of Richard's favourites finds some substantiation from actual case records. In 1384, for instance, Walter Sibil, an alderman and member of the fishmonger's guild, brought a charge of maintenance against de Vere and was fined 1,000 marks for defamation, *Rot. Parl.*, III.186).

144 dukys carries an attack on Richard's liberal granting of honours often to men whom his critics thought most unworthy. The creation of de Vere marquis of Dublin in 1385 and his subsequent elevation to the dukedom of Ireland in 1386 drew scathing comments from Walsingham *H.A.*, II.140 and 148. At the September parliament of 1397, Richard created five dukes in a single day: Nottingham became duke of Norfolk; Derby (Henry Bolingbroke) duke of Hereford; Huntingdon earl of Exeter; Kent duke of Surrey and Rutland duke of Albemerle. The *Annales* comments that they deserved the title not of 'dukes' but of 'duketti' because the importance of the rank had been diminished by such an excessive act (p.223).

145 huntyd MS reads 'hunyd' but a later hand adds 't'. Hares were proverbially renowned for their speed and fearfulness, cf. Lydgate, *Minor Poems*, II.817.122: 'Men with a tabour may lyghtly cacche an hare.'

146 mendis means reparation for an injury, Alford, p.5.

148 felawis are associates in crime, or accomplices. **felawschepe** means 'a band of fellows, maintenance', Alford, p.57.

151 As a last resort, suppliants who either feared to plead at Common Law, or whose cases had been overturned in Common

Law courts by corruption, took their suits to the chancellor himself in the court of Chancery. There is a repeated pleading in the cases assembled in *Select Cases in Chancery 1364–1471* that the suppliant 'dare not bring suit against malefactors, as the common law demands' e.g., pp.11, 31, 44, 47 and 48.

152 cf. *Mum*, 421, 'For as hit is y-seide by eldryn dawes' which also introduces a proverb. Neither line alliterates regularly.

153 A parallel to this proverb is cited by Whiting, p.3 from *Salomon Seyth* 52.1–2, 'Salamon seyth ther is none accorde / Ther every man wuld be a lord'.

157 As a consequence of Richard's maintenance of favourites by a series of minor grants, the value of the Crown's revenues was steadily diminished and caused royal borrowing on a grand scale. In February 1382, the crown itself, together with other jewels, was pledged to the city of London for £2,000 (McKisack, p.429).

164 In 1388, the Appellants sentenced many of Richard's followers to death or exile, cf. notes to II.57–8. In 1397, the earl of Arundel was arrested and executed, the duke of Gloucester arrested and murdered, Thomas, Archbishop Arundel and the earl of Warwick were arrested and banished. In 1398, the dukes of Norfolk and Hereford were banished after a quarrel. All but Archbishop Arundel were Appellants in 1388.

167 wyteth MS reads 'wyteh' in error and I have followed the emendation proposed by Skeat and adopted by D&S.

170 The scribe writes **clergie** for **clerlie**, the first of a number of occasions.

171 To move a matter has the legal sense to make a plea or put forth a petition, Alford, p.102.

172 D&S, following Skeat, emend MS 'kayseceris' to **kayseris**. Here the poet finally admits to the true direction of the force of his comments, to catalogue Richard's offences to dissuade a future king from the same actions.

176 The men behind these remarks are de Vere, Thomas Mowbray and John Beauchamp from the early part of Richard's reign; in the latter half, his half brother John Holland, earl of Huntingdon, his cousin, earl of Rutland and John, lord Beaumont. The lords who appealed Warwick, Gloucester and Arundel of treason in 1397 were predominantly young men. Besides Huntingdon and Rutland were Thomas Holland the younger, earl of Kent, John Beaufort, earl of Somerset, legitimised son of John of Gaunt and Katherine Swynford, John Montague the younger, earl of Salisbury, and Thomas Despenser, earl of Gloucester. Complaints about the young counsellors around the king abound, e.g., *H.A.*, II.156, *Westminster* p.207 and p.243, Evesham, p.60 and Froissart, p.642.

177 MED glosses 'hurlewain' as a mischievous sprite or goblin, cf. *Tale of Beryn*, 8. This remark is applicable to early favourites such as de Vere or to the trio of hated ministers, John Busshy, William Bagot and Henry Grene. They were the most influential ministers from 1397 onwards despite the fact that they held the rank only of chamber knight. They seem to have been universally despised. Usk describes them as 'the king's most evil counsellors and the chief fosterers of his malice' (p.174); cf. *Historia Anglicana*, II.224, *Annales*, p.209. Gower remarks that all three were odious and unequalled in their ambitiousness, *Tripartite Chronicle*, III.170.

178 Robert Fabyan's *Chronicle* remarks that the chief rulers about the king were of low birth and the men of honour were kept out of favour (entry for 1398), p.543.

183 greues means an official complaint of a wrong or grievance, MED gref 1d).

186 busshinge in the sense of overpowering or oppressing. The verb puns on the name of John Busshy, cf. II.39 and II.152. Richard's 'best frendis' in the poet's view were the Lords Appellant: Gloucester, Arundel and Warwick.

187 a fals colour means 'a fraudulent excuse' and puns on Henry Grene.

189 tale has the legal sense of the plaintiff's complaint in a legal suit, Alford, p.151.

190 cf. notes to I.171.

193 duly means according to due process of law, MED due 2a).

194 that fals dede alludes to the death of Gloucester.

196 brother y-born: cf. *Mum*, 1407. Richard's half brother John Holland was leader of the armed band which seized Gloucester. According to Froissart, Gloucester had plotted with the earl of Arundel to seize the king, but John Holland frustrated the plan by informing Richard, p.639.

199 cas I avowe means to make a statement about a legal case, Alford, p.22 and MED avowen 1a).

201 likens Richard to a horse and his advisers to riders. The advisers spur Richard on with such heedless vigour that both horse and rider collapse, cf. Hoccleve, 'Conseil may wel be likend to a bridil / Which that an hors vp kepeth from fallyng', *Regement*, 4929–30.

Passus Two

2 The Passus contains an extended attack on the vices of livery and maintenance. When a landlord retained a man to serve him, he gave him a retaining fee and a livery with his personal sign or badge. The landlord agreed to maintain his retainer in all his causes, including helping him at law with all the influence and favour that his position could afford. In theory the contract was noble, but in practice it paved the way for all kinds of bribery and corruption and perversion of justice. In 1384 and 1388, the Commons petitioned parliament for maintenance to be abolished. A statute was passed in 1390 to curb some of the excesses, *Statutes of the Realm*, II.74–5, but the petition presented by Thomas Haxey in 1397 repeated the criticism levelled against livery and maintenance in the 1380s, *Rot.Parl*, III.339. In the first year of Henry's reign another statute was passed which outlawed all liveries except those of the king, *Statutes of the Realm*, II.113.

4 The narrator's principal charge is against the excessive granting of liveries by Richard himself. Richard's badge depicted a white hart which may have had its origin from one of the emblems of his mother Joan, countess of Kent. Richard made his first distribution of the white hart badge in October 1390, a month before the passing of the statute which restricted the granting of liveries. Throughout this Passus, the narrator animates Richard's badge of the white hart and discusses the vices of his retainers under the guise of describing the behaviour of natural deer. The deer's antlers suggest the retainers' menacing violence.

6–7 refer to the desertion of Richard's army almost overnight when he landed back at Milford Haven in 1399 to meet the challenge of Henry Bolingbroke. A graphic account of these desertions is given in *Traison*, pp.189–90.

8–9 Henry Bolingbroke's badge was the eagle, cf. *On King*

Richard's Ministers, Wright, I.364, *On the Expected Arrival of the Duke of Lancaster*, Wright, I.368. The **eye** of the eagle refers to the fearsome ability of the eagle to look straight into the sun without blinking, Bartholomaeus, I.603. Bartholomaeus also records that deer stand frozen before any object that startles them before they flee, II.1176, cf. line 8 with *Mum*, 351. The narrator draws an analogy between topical events and the natural properties of beasts outlined in bestiaries in order to show that Richard's actions violated principles of natural law, but Henry's were in accordance with them. Beast lore suggests that it was natural for Richard's supporters to be frightened of Henry. **helpe** refers to the redress promised by Henry on his return for the harms suffered by the people under Richard's reign.

10–16 **mowtynge** Every spring, deer shed their horns, Bartholomaeus, II.1176. In *Richard*, the narrator places this process in summer (14). Bartholomaeus observes that without their horns, deer are 'armureles' and need to find themselves secret hiding places. The deer analogy suggests that the desertion of Richard's retainers was part of the natural course of events. Finding themselves defenceless in the face of a superior enemy, they took the only course of action open to them – flight.

16 **togedir** a later corrector adds 'to' to MS 'gedir'.

17 The retainers had **hornes** (were able to fight) six months after the summer: a reference to the Christmas-tide 1399–1400 revolt against Henry led by nobles who wanted to restore Richard to the throne. They were led by John Montague, earl of Salisbury, Thomas Holland, earl of Kent, John Holland, earl of Huntingdon. The revolt failed, Salisbury and Kent were beheaded by the mob at Cirencester and Huntingdon was executed at Plesshy in Essex.

20 **merke** puns on 'mark' in the senses of provide with a badge MED marken 3e), stain 4b), and strike (10), cf. III.268.

25 MS reads 'Or'. I have followed D&S's emendation to **Of**, which restores sense to the line.

26 The scope of the criticism widens to include the abuses of livery and maintenance by other members of the nobility.

28 **contre** has the legal sense of judicial district, Alford, p.35 and **seruid** of serving a writ, warrant or process, MED serven (14). The retainers corrupted local justice.

29–30 Instead of speaking up in Parliament for the Commons, the retainers voiced only the opinions of the king or the lords who retained them. See further notes to III.317–44 and IV.28–70.

31 reson has the sense of advice in accordance with the principles of justice, Alford, p.134.

32 In a convolution of the allegorical sequence, the oppressed people are described as if they were animals skinned by the retainers.

33–4 describes the direct process of intimidation at law. The threat of recrimination from a powerful noble was sufficient to deter a person seeking redress at law for offences committed against them. **mendes** is a legal term meaning reparation for an injury or crime, Alford, p.5–6.

38 Richard's extravagance in parading his badge of the white hart was matched by some of his supporters. John Holland possessed a livery of the white hart set with three rubies and two sapphires, Mathew, p.27.

39 busshid puns on the name of John Busshy, see notes to I.186.

42 puns elaborately on the senses of **merkyd** noted at II.20 and 'to take aim at', MED marken 10a); **myssed** as 'failed to find', MED missen 1a), and 'failed to hit', 3e); and **schore** as 'twenty', MED 3), 'a total in a reckoning', 2c), and a mark on a tally stick, MED scoren 4c). The wordplay suggests Richard's incompetence and that the granting of liveries was injurious.

43 puns on **hertis** as 'harts' and 'hearts', i.e. loyal retainers.

45 The Great Wardrobe was responsible for the award of liveries. Between the periods November 1390 to September 1392 and September 1392 and 1394, its expenditure doubled because of such extravagant grants, Tuck, p.150.

47 Gower was loyal to Richard at the beginning of his reign but subsequently transferred his allegiance to Henry Bolingbroke. He originally began his *Confessio Amantis* as 'A bok for king Richardes sake' (Prol.*24), but revised it in 1393 as 'A bok for Engelondes sake' (Prol.24). He cut the earlier dutiful remarks about Richard, and re-dedicated the work to 'myn oghne lord, / Which of Lancastre is Henri named' (Prol.86–7).

52 The Latin quotation reads: 'Every kingdom divided against itself shall be brought to desolation' from Luke, 11:17.

53 cf. *Mum*, 652.

55 D&S emend MS 'how' to **what** which restores sense and alliteration.

56 Skeat and D&S supply **ladde** to fill the gap in the a-verse.

57–8 **beganne** A later corrector marks 'a' for MS 'y'. These lines overstate the loyalty shown to Richard before his distribution of the white hart liveries. The Wonderful Parliament of 1386 appointed fourteen Commissioners to amend the administration, and, after a tussle, forced Richard to dismiss his chancellor, Michael de la Pole, earl of Suffolk. In November 1387, the duke of Gloucester and the earls of Warwick and Arundel published an appeal of treason against some of Richard's most stalwart supporters, and Thomas Mowbray and Henry Bolingbroke lent their support. Meanwhile, an army had assembled in Cheshire in support of the king and was marching towards London. It was intercepted at Radcot Bridge in the Cotswolds by the forces of Henry Bolingbroke. Richard's supporters deserted in droves. The five Lords Appellant returned triumphantly to London, where Richard had taken refuge in the Tower. After interviews between the king and the rebel lords, during which Richard may have been temporarily deposed, it was agreed to summon a new parliament for the beginning of February 1388. Known subsequently as The Merciless Parliament, the assembly accused Richard's most prominent followers of treason and secured their executions. Many of Richard's chamber knights were dismissed along with his chaplain and confessor.

58 cf. the similar line at *Mum*, 1480.

60 **lordyns wrongis** refers to treatment of the Lords Appellant. Their treatment of Richard's supporters in the first decade of his reign is omitted.

61 The MS reads **folwyd** but there is a correction above the line to **fayled** which restores the sense.

62 refers back to the desertions of Richard's supporters on his return to England. There is a half-formed image of the Body Politic, a standard metaphor for discussing the affairs of state. The nation is likened to an organic body, with each of its parts representing different classes or groups in society. The image is found in a number of works, including Gower, *Vox Clamantis*, VI.497–8; Hoccleve, *Regement of Princes*, 3933–4. It forms the narrative strategy for the whole of one of the Digby poems, Kail, XV.

64 The MS reads **feble**, which, as D&S observe, is likely to have been caught from the line above. They suggest **wankel** as an alliterating substitute appropriate for the sense.

69 Reson is the personification of justice and his abrupt entry into the poem recalls that of Piers Plowman, who pokes his head without introduction into Passus V.537. The narrator fears that telling the truth to his king might be an act of disobedience. Reason legalises the narrator's criticisms : **reule I alowe**, meaning to uphold a ruling as valid and binding, MED, allouen (2), reule (n), 4d).

70 in dede ne in wordis A common collocation attested by MED dede 8a). The legal context suggests a contrast between 'dede' as written evidence or a document, sense 5c), and word of mouth, i.e. uncorroborated testimony.

72 grauntyd the grace is a legal phrase meaning to bestow an indulgence or privilege as distinguished from a right, Alford, p.66.

74 schewe In the legal sense of laying a complaint before court, Alford, p.143.

76 herte contrasts to the less faithful 'harts' amongst Richard's retainers.

77 The narrator's solution to the problems of livery and maintenance is that it should be abolished and that judges should be provided with a regular salary.

79 apeire is a legal term meaning to harm or damage, Alford, p.7.

81 conscience has the legal sense of the ability to determine right from wrong, Alford, p.34.

82 vnstombled contrasts to the weakness of the king and his supporters, II.62–6 and I.201.

83 leuyd be his owen, of independent means, therefore not likely to be swayed by bribery.

84 mede a bribe or gift, or any payment that is unearned or in excess of merit, Alford, p.98.

85 trien a trouthe be-twynne two sidis means to judge the truth of a dispute between two opposing parties in a lawsuit, Alford, pp.160–1, 159, MED side 8b). Cf. note to I.8.

86 lordschep in the sense of maintenance, the power of a lord, Alford, p.91.

87 pleyned means to make a legal complaint or accusation, cf. note to I.143. **wrongis** are civil or criminal wrongs at law, cf. note to I.13.

89 The only badges to be given are those to reward the proper observance of law. They should be supplemented by a regular salary.

90 contre the judicial district or shire, Alford, p.36.

91 grounde is a legal term meaning good legal basis, MED 'ground' (n) 5c). **so me God helpe** is a legal oath attesting to the truth of one's testimony, Alford, p.146.

92 tente and **entente** (99) have the legal sense of 'intentio', cf. notes to I.79.

93 The MS reads 'and', probably caught from the preceding line. D&S's emendation restores the sense of the passage.

97 Trouthe in the legal sense of 'justice', Alford, p.159. **determyned** in the legal sense of bringing a case to an end, Alford, p.153.

98 rehersid is a legal term meaning to recite aloud a list of charges, a plea or court record, Alford, p.130.

100 A caesura mark after **wene** and an extended number of syllables in the line suggest scribal corruption. Since the line makes sense, I have not emended.

102 sowid connotes the indiscriminate liberality with which Richard bestowed his livery and there may also be a hint of Galatians, 6:8 'For what a man shall sow, those also shall he reap'.

110 deme discrecion to judge your action a sound one. The narrator sets himself up here as judge of Richard's 'intentio'. Rather than criticising the king in terms of moral reproach, he examines his motives from a legal position. **well-doynge** may be an echo of 'Dowel' from *Piers*, cf. *Richard*, IV.93.

111 duble and the play on hart/heart (cf. notes to II.43) captures the senses of 'twice as much, great', MED double (adj) 3a), and 'false, deceitful' 6a); both the increasing numbers of the retainers and their disloyalty.

113 good greehonde There has been some dispute as to whom this refers. D&S collect the various views, p.91, and conclude, quoting from a passage in Adam Usk's *Chronicle*, the greyhound is more likely to represent Henry Bolingbroke. Usk explains how Henry came to be known as the 'dog' as well as the 'eagle': 'by reason of his collar of linked greyhounds; and because he utterly drove out from his kingdom the faithless

harts, that is the livery of king Richard which was the hart',
p.173. He tells the story of how Richard was deserted by his pet
greyhound on his journey to London in captivity. The greyhound found its way unaided across country to Henry, who
welcomed the animal and let it sleep on his bed. When it saw
Richard again, it completely ignored him, having transferred its
affection to its new master, p.196, cf. Froissart p.464. It may be
as a result of this incident that Henry had made collars of linked
greyhounds which he distributed to his supporters. Given the
context of disloyalty and desertions in *Richard* it is possible that
the poet draws on this story and portrays Henry as the greyhound rather than the eagle.

114 **lese** The thong which held greyhounds together, cf.
Lydgate, *Troy Book*, I.8371. There existed a royal office of
being in charge of the king's 'leashe', *Cal.Pat.Rolls. Henry
IV.1405–8*, p.20. The image of greyhounds leashed together
represents the king's supporters. It makes the point that Henry
should have been maintained as their leader.

117 D&S emend MS **thou** to 'you', presumably because of
the address to Richard. But given that the pronoun in the
following line is **the**, this seems unnecessary. **heed-dere** are deer
with horns, see notes to II.128–36.

119 **rascaile** are young lean deer. They refer to the people in
the country oppressed by Richard's extravagance and taxation.

124 **vnduly** not according to due process of law, MED due,
2a), cf. I.193.

124–34 The afflictions of the weather on the deer link the
people's oppression with Richard's disregard for the principles
of natural law. The hailstorms, freezing frost, snows and mists
are not just descriptive of misery; crucially (134), they occur in
summer. The perversion of the natural course of the seasons
mirrors Richard's perversion of the office of protective kingship.

128–36 **hauntelere-dere** These lines refer to the way that
Richard nurtured a group of favourites, cf. notes to I.175–86,
who were often young and of undistinguished birth. When these
friends failed him, he had so oppressed other nobles that they
had no strength to support him. **as a best aughte** (130) accuses
Richard of stunting the true course of nature. These deer ought,
by nature, to have grown a full set of antlers. Bartholomaeus
notes how deer need the sun to make their horns strong and
hard, II.1177. In Richard's 'summer' there has been no sun to

make this possible. **136** D&S are uncertain about the meaning of **leyne**. MED leine (n) 2a) 'a layer, stratum' is appropriate in picking up the connotations of **leyde**. The line means that Richard stacked lordships on his favourites, one after another.

139 mesure is a meri mene, proverbial, Whiting, p.395, cf. Hoccleve, *La Male Regle*, 353–6. The Latin quotation reads: 'God listens to the cries of the poor and judges their cause'. It recalls Psalm 9:38–9: 'The Lord hath heard the desire of the poor . . . To judge for the fatherless and for the humble'.

140 be the rotus Skeat supplies the alliterative stave **rend** in the verse which D&S incorporate. Although **rotus** could mean 'by the depths', MED rote 2d) I have emended in the absence of comparative examples and because the a-verse is shortweight.

141–9 the blessid bredd is Henry Bolingbroke on his return to England in 1399. His maternal protection is in accordance with **kynde** (142). Gower uses a maternal image to describe Henry, *Tripartite Chronicle*, III.138–9. Bartholomaeus notes how hens are naturally protective of their chickens, protecting them under their wings and defending them against kites, I.629–30, cf. II.161. The narrator has foisted onto the eagle the tender maternal instincts of the hen. Eagles, as Bartholomaeus points out, were often quite ruthless with their less accomplished offspring, I.604.

145 D&S, following Skeat, emend MS **Eyere** to 'heyer', glossing it as 'higher' cf. III.74. The MS reading is tenable. MED lists **Eyere** under 'eirer' 1 (n) b), the female of a swan, with this example from *Richard* as a figurative use. The eagle is depicted as a maternal bird in the lines that follow. **Eyere** must mean 'female' in the restricted sense of 'mother'.

146 heruest is a precise time reference to Henry's return in 1399. Richard's distortion of nature is emphasised by Henry's need to protect his people from winter.

147 Henry's concern that the fledglings grow full plumages contrasts with Richard's stunting of the deer's antlers.

148 In contrast to D&S I have emended MS 'y-pynned' to **vn-y-pynned** despite the absence of a correction. The sense of the lines is that the birds are finally released from their bondage and a negative sense of 'pynnen' is clearly required. It would be a simple copying mistake to omit a negative particle.

151 cf. *Piers*, I.148: 'For Truthe telleth that love is triacle of hevene'.

152–92 describes Henry's vengeance on Richard's supporters, especially the hated ministers, Busshy, Bagot, Scrope and Grene, see notes to I.177. The punning on their names is similar to that in *On King Richard's Ministers*, Wright, I.363–6. Busshy, Scope and Grene were executed in September 1399 at Bristol, see notes to I.2.

152 baterid this bred on busshes the execution of John Busshy.

153 gaderid gomes on grene the execution of Henry Grene.

154 schroup sondrid the execution of William Scrope.

155 hand-molde D&S emend to 'hand-melle'. The meaning of this word is obscure. The sense of the line is that Henry crushed, or pounded together (MED mallen a) the metal with the **hand-molde** so that Richard's supporters lost their dearest limbs. The account is obviously not strictly factual since Scrope, Busshy and Grene lost not limbs, but heads. The MS reading may be retained. Under 'molden' (v) 1d), MED lists the meaning 'pulverise' from *Catholicon Anglica* 82a: 'To molde: puluerize'. Thus a **hand-molde** could be some kind of manual implement used to pulverise or crush metals or minerals. This meaning is not listed by MED, which records **hand-molde** under honde (8), glossing it as 'a mould used with the hands'. A crushing implement seems more likely.

156 MS omits **they** which is supplied by D&S, following Skeat.

157 The **faukyn** is Henry Bolingbroke.

158 kuyttis are birds particularly appropriate for Richard's supporters. Bartholomaeus says of them that they are greedy, brave among small birds, but cowardly among great, being keen to kill defenceless chickens. At first there is little apparent difference between kites and other birds of prey, but the older the kite becomes, the more he shows his 'unkynde'-ness. He is sorry if he sees that his own birds are fat and in order to make them lean, beats them with his beak, I.634–5, cf. notes on II.178.

159 raveyne is the criminal offence of taking goods by force, Alford, p.126.

161 Lydgate records the antipathy between eagle and kites, *Fall of Princes*, IV.2952. There is also an obvious contrast between the nobility of the eagle and the miserable characteristics of the kite, cf. notes to II.142–3.

163 The execution of Richard's leading supporters is couched in terms which suggests the natural hunting of prey and carrion by the eagle.

164–76 narrate Henry's treatment of William Bagot. Once news of Henry's return was announced, Bagot went to Ireland to inform Richard. He thus escaped the fate of his former comrades but was eventually captured and tried in parliament for his crimes. He was allowed to go free and went to live in peace on his Warwickshire estate. The *Richard*-poet does not allude to this pardon in contrast to Gower, *Tripartite Chronicle*, III.397–8 and *On King Richard's Ministers*, where pardon is hinted in the penultimate stanza, p.366. In November 1400, Bagot even received a grant of money from the Exchequer, *Cal.Pat.Rolls.Henry IV, 1399–1400*, p.386.

165 **purraile-is pulter** – where the very rags of the poor were often fastened; alludes to Bagot's activities as a member of the council which governed while Richard was away in Ireland. It forced all kinds of fines and exactions upon the poor.

167 MS reads **hadd** but a negative sense is required here. D&S emend to **nadd**.

170 MS reads **hadde** and D&S emend to **ladde**, following Skeat. The emendation restores full sense as well as alliteration and the mistake could have arisen through simple misreading of the initial letter.

176 This description matches the account given by Bartholomaeus of the eagle's hunting habits, I.602.

178 Bartholomaeus notes that the crow is a greedy bird, opposite in nature to the eagle, and terrified of it. The eagle smites the crow with its beak if it should fly too close, I.620–1.

182–6 refer to Henry's treatment of Richard's followers. Apart from the executions of Busshy, Scrope and Grene there was little bloodshed. Many of Richard's followers gave themselves up to Henry. In October 1399 Edward Langley, duke of Albemerle, John Holland, duke of Exeter, Thomas Holland, duke of Surrey, John Montague, earl of Salisbury, and Thomas Despenser, earl of Gloucester were brought before Parliament for trial, and with them Thomas Merke, bishop of Carlisle. Judgment was pronounced on them at the beginning of November. All estates conferred on these lords since 1397 were confiscated, and Thomas Merke was deprived of his bishopric. Roger Walden was deprived of the Archbishopric of Canterbury and Thomas Arundel re-instated, see notes to III.29. **reclayme** is a technical legal term meaning a return to a court when summoned (MED reclaime b) and refers to the parliamentary trial of these men.

191 alludes to the unsurpassed sight of the eagle, see note to II.9.

192 Magpies are proverbially chattering, insignificant birds, cf. note to *Mum*, 152. They contrast with the royal eagle.

Passus Three

1 restore means 'return to the subject', MED restoren e).

2 mater ... meved To move a matter in a legal sense means to put forth a plea or make a petition, Alford, p.102. The narrator shapes his material as though he were arguing a legal case, cf. notes to III.5.

3–4 revert back to the deer analogy to show how the retainers brought ill-health upon themselves. The poem employs metaphors of health to represent a properly functioning realm.

4 axid 'grow towards', see MED asken 8a).

5 schewe The legal sense of this verb is to put up a bill, or lay a complaint before court, Alford, p.143. The narrator 'shows' the 'matter' of the misbehaviour of Richard and his retainers, and tries them for their crimes against the Lords Appellant.

9 Images of natural health signify behaviour in accordance with the principles of natural law. The worst crime is that which contravenes 'kynde'; that is, which is against natural law.

11 clause has the sense of a clause in a legal argument, Alford, p.29.

13 D&S emend MS 'that' to **of**. The scribe may have caught 'that' from the first word of the succeeding line. **of** is required to make sense of the line.

13–36 narrate Richard and his supporters' treatment of the Lords Appellant. The deer behave contrary to their natural properties. In beast lore, when deer become old and their strength begins to fail, they have a natural remedy. They catch an adder and feed on its venom to renew their lives, Bartholomaeus, II.1175–7. Richard and his retainers, however, chose to attack other animals, namely, a horse, bear and swan. Consequently, they failed to renew their lives in the way that nature had provided. In order to narrate the sequence of events in 1397 the narrator puns on the heraldic charges of the badges of the Lords Appellant. This technique is also used in Gower's *Tripartite Chronicle* and the poem *On King Richard's Ministers*.

18 harmen MS reads 'armen' but a later corrector adds 'h'.

26–7 Skeat and D&S emend MS **clergie** to **clerlie**, cf. notes to I.170 and supply **not** in the b-verse. There is a correction 'nat' above the line. These lines refer to the Fitzalan family. Their badge was a horse. The **hors** is Richard Fitzalan, earl of Arundel, one of the original Lords Appellant. The September parliament found him guilty of treason for his part in the 1388 routing of Richard's followers, cf. notes to II.57–8. He was beheaded on Tower Hill in 1397. The **coltis** are his sons Richard and Thomas. After their father's execution, Richard was placed in the custody of the duke of Exeter. He died in captivity. Thomas fled abroad to join Henry Bolingbroke and was one of the small company which landed with Henry at Ravenspur. The **haras** alludes to Richard's brother Thomas, Archbishop of Canterbury. In 1397 Richard deprived him of his see and exiled him.

28 The swan is Thomas Woodstock, duke of Gloucester. He was arrested at his home in Plesshy in July 1397 and taken by Thomas Mowbray to Calais. When Gloucester was ordered to stand trial at the parliament, it was reported that he was dead. He was probably murdered on Richard's instructions. Gloucester clearly commanded public support and to have him stand public trial might have endangered Richard's position. **though it sholle werre** refers to Gloucester's active hostility towards Richard. He appears to have been the chief force behind the events of 1388.

29 The bear is Thomas Beauchamp, earl of Warwick. He was arrested at the same time as Arundel and stood trial in the same parliament. As a result of his confession, Warwick was not executed but was condemned to life imprisonment in William Scrope's castle on the Isle of Man.

30 ny sibbe See III.26 for the treatment of Arundel's sons. Warwick's heir Richard was put in the custody of the duke of Surrey, his father's supplanter at Warwick castle. Gloucester left an underage son, Humphrey, whom Richard kept under close surveillance along with Henry, Bolingbroke's son. Richard took the two cousins with him to Ireland in 1399 and on his return, left Humphrey in Trim Castle. Humphrey died of plague on Anglesey.

31 Prominent amongst the supporters of the Lords Appellant were Sir Thomas Mortimer, an illegitimate son of the second earl of March who was condemned to exile when the parliament resumed in January 1398, and Lord John Cobham, who was banished to Guernsey. Neither of these men **bledd** but the word may be used metaphorically to mean that they sustained injurious treatment.

32 The quotation reads: 'On account of ungratefulness, the free man is recalled into slavery according to the prick of conscience and civil law'. There is nothing corresponding to this in *The Prick of Conscience*. The citation is from the *Institutes of Justinian*, I.t.16.i.

35 suggests that the narration is an arcane riddle, but the badges of these men were well known and punning on heraldic charges was an established technique in the writing of political poetry, see *The Prophecy of John of Bridlington*, Wright, I.126–9.

37–63 form a mini political allegory on the behaviour of partridges to demonstrate how Henry was the natural king of England and Richard the usurper. The narrator praises the properties of the partridge. Elsewhere, however, it is a bird universally condemned for its fraudulence, Bartholomaeus, I.637, Gower, *Vox Clamantis*, VI.143–4. The narrator comes close to scuppering his intended political point by associating a king who deposed his predecessor with a bird known for its deceitful conduct.

41 The first partridge represents Henry Bolingbroke. Recalling the maternal image of II.143–44, he is presented as the natural mother of the birds, the people of England. The narrator emphasises that the behaviour of the partridges is in accordance with **kynde** (40).

42 The MS reading 'heires' is taken by Skeat and D&S as an error for **eiren**, meaning eggs. 'eyren' is used at III.50. In terms of the transferred political significance of the allegory, the eggs are indeed the heirs of the birds but here the sense of the line requires **eiren**.

45 The second, usurping partridge is Richard.

49 MS reads 'cete' but a later correction alters to **sete**. **sesith** is a legal term from seisin, in the sense of taking unlawful possession of a property, Alford, p.141 sense II. The legal terminology implies that Henry was the lawful owner of the people of England.

50 hue is the only example recorded by MED of the 'h' form of the feminine third person singular pronoun in use as a noun to refer to the female of the species. The 's' form of the third singular feminine pronoun is used in a similar way in *The Chester Mystery Cycle*, ed. R. M. Lumiansky and David Mills (EETS SS3 1974): 'Of cleane fowles seaven alsoe / The hee and shee together', III.123–4. Elsewhere, the 'h' form of the pronoun is coupled with the animal, e.g., 'heolomb' or 'hoo-wolfe'. It is possible that **hue** is a scribal error for 'hen'.

55 cometh and crieth A probable anglicisation of the legal phrase 'vint . . . et clama' cited by Alford, p.31. These are the words used to come into court and put forth a claim, which is exactly what Henry did at the parliamentary meeting of September 1399, see notes to III.69 and 92–3. **hir owen kynde dame** states that Henry is the natural mother of the birds.

59 leued destroyed, marred, from MED leven 2e). The hunger of the birds recalls the skinny deer of II.119–20.

60 dewe dame The legal sense of **dewe** suggests that Henry was the rightful owner of the nestlings.

62–7 The abuse of the reader shows the perils of coded political narration. The narrator attempts to clarify his confusing analogy by equating the first partridge with the eagle, Henry's earlier cognomen in the poem.

63 endited cf. note to I.107. The narrator has accused Richard of possessing property to which he had no legal entitlement.

68–9 refer back to I.11 where Henry's return to England is described. As there, the verb **entrid** is used in its legal sense of taking lawful possession. Line 69 stresses the legality of Henry's move with the words **his owen**.

74 hende MS reads 'ende' but an 'h' has been added above the line. Skeat and D&S emend accordingly. The eagle flies higher than any other bird, Bartholomaeus, I.603. Gower alludes to this in *Vox Clamantis*. He uses it to symbolise the king pure in heart, VI.985–6.

75 another pun on Sir John Busshy.

76 beekis connotes physical force in a fashion similar to the

hornes of the deer, II.4 and 17. These lines refer to the massive support commanded by Henry on his return.

77 wrongis in the legal sense, cf. notes to I.13.

78 billis puns on the senses of 'beak' MED bile (1) 1, and a written petition or complaint used to initiate an action at law, Alford, p.16, MED bille 2a).

79 Richard reigned for twenty-two years, 1377–99.

81 Skeat and D&S emend MS 'tymed' to **tyned**. The scribe probably omitted a minim.

81–2 Complaints about excessive taxation were frequent in Richard's reign. In 1377, parliament agreed to the invention of the 'tallage of groats' which was the first of a series of flat rate poll taxes to be paid by all persons over the age of fourteen unless they were genuine beggars. The experiment was repeated in 1379 and 1380. It contributed to the dissent which culminated in the rising of 1381, see notes to I.102.

86–9 Many subjects transferred their allegiance to Henry because of their outrage at Richard's treatment of Gloucester and Arundel. In his *Tripartite Chronicle* Gower writes that a hundred thousand wept because of the departure of the Swan, II.45–6.

88 The MS reads **foole**. **fowle** is written above the line.

90 cf. the similar line at *Mum*, 622.

92–3 suggest that Henry was king by hereditary right. In the 1399 parliament, Henry launched a threefold claim to the throne: lineage, election and lawful conquest, *Rot.Parl*, III.422–3. The conjunction of **hieste of kynde** and **as cronecle tellith** may recall the so-called 'Crouchback legend', according to which, Edmund Crouchback, the supposed second son of Henry III, had really been the eldest but on account of his mental weakness, his younger brother Edward was preferred in his place. Consequently, neither Richard II nor any of the three Edwards ought to have reigned. The rightful king was Henry Bolingbroke, direct heir of Edmund through his mother Blanche of Lancaster. Adam Usk was a member of the commission of lawyers which Henry appointed to examine his claim to the throne using the chronicles. Ultimately it was decided that they supplied insufficient evidence to support a hereditary claim on its own, Usk, pp.181–3; *The Complaint of Chaucer to his Purse*; *Tripartite Chronicle*, III.332–6 and *In Praise of Peace*, 8–14, list Henry's threefold rights to the crown. *Richard,*

III.92–3 suggests hereditary right, authorised by the chronicles. But the partridge analogy legitimises Henry's claim to the throne by lawful conquest and the account of Henry's followers in lines II.83–90 supports Henry's claim to the throne by election.

94 MS reads 'brond' in error for **bond**. One of Henry's first actions was to recall Warwick from exile in the Isle of Man. In the first parliament of his reign he restored all of Warwick's former titles and inheritances.

96 The **berlingis** are Warwick's son Richard and his wife Elizabeth, see notes to III.30.

97 The MS reads 'was' in error for **as**, an emendation proposed by Skeat and incorporated by D&S.

98 Bosse is a nickname for the bear. The precise meaning is unclear. MED boce 3d) glosses **Bosse** as 'a lump of a man', used disparagingly. But the narrator's feelings towards Warwick are hardly those of disparagement. OED Boss 1d) gives the sense 'a bulky animal'. It may refer to Warwick's moral stature.

101 Henry Grene may be singled out because he was one of the property grantees for parts of the Beauchamp estates. The poet seems to have had firsthand knowledge of many of the financial details of the estates of the nobility, cf. notes to IV.7. **gaglide** is a word commonly used of geese, and may simply be a general reference to Henry's supporters. Of these, Westmorland and the Percies were the most powerful.

105–6 The MS reads 'the', which D&S, following Skeat, restore to **they**. In 106, the MS reads 'conude' for **coude** and 'clothed' for **cloyed**. The first two are probably mechanical copying errors. **cloyed** may arise from the substitution of a more for less familiar word, or the misreading of thorn for 'y'. 'Acloy' in the sense of 'laming' is used in *Piers*, C.XX.294. The Earl Marshal was Thomas Mowbray, earl of Nottingham. He was one of the Lords Appellant in the 1397 Parliament which sentenced Gloucester and Arundel to death. The 'stede', Richard Fitzalan, was Mowbray's father-in-law. Froissart narrates that Mowbray bandaged Fitzalan's eyes at his execution on Tower Hill, p.656. Walsingham also records that Mowbray was present at his father-in-law's execution, *Historia Anglicana*, II.225. The narrator plays on two senses of **marchall**: as the political office, MED marshal 1a) and as a horse doctor, sense 4. The sense of the lines is that Mowbray was bad at his craft because instead of healing a horse as a horse doctor should, he lamed it. Thus his behaviour violates natural order.

108 The scribe writes 'venyanunce' in error.

109 The **synffull dede** is the execution of Arundel.

111 poynt in a legal sense means 'charge' or 'accusation', MED pointe (8). The narrator continues his arraignment of Richard. D&S emended MS 'persith' to **passith** but the MS reading can stand in the sense of 'affecting deeply', see MED percen 1b).

112 fynde has the sense of furnishing proof, Alford, p.59.

116 Earlier the poet has criticised Richard for flouting the law, I.89, 106, 193 and II, 26, but here he acknowledges that the king is maker of law as well as its subject. Such a view is a standard tenet of political thought and one enunciated very clearly by Gower, *Confessio*, VII.2704–8, 2714–24.

118 A criticism of Richard's adherence to the foolish counsels of his overdressed young courtiers. **turmentours**: *The Simonie* satirises the costumes of the courtiers and says that: 'Hi ben desgised as turmentours that comen from clerkes plei' (A.285). The line compares the courtiers to the Roman soldiers in the Mystery Cycle play of the scourging and crucifixion of Christ.

119 recalls the image of youth at I.65–9 and the folly which the narrator's own **good rewle** and **resons bookis** seeks to correct.

124–5 D&S, in contrast to Skeat, move these lines to follow after **121**. Whilst there is a change from the third person plural pronoun **they** in 120 to **his** 122, such vacillation in concord is not unusual in the poem, see for instance, III.173 and 175 and 282–7. In line 124, the MS reads 'thynthith' in error. **riall of his ray**: taking the lead from the king, Richard's court was characterised by extravagant fashions of dress. The *Annales* gives a careful description of Richard's dress on the occasion of negotiating his marriage to Isabella of France. On each day, the king and his retinue dressed in a different extravagant costume, pp.189–93.

126 feet in-to chambris suggests promotion to positions of power.

129 The quotation reads: 'Those who are dressed in soft clothes are in the houses of kings' and recalls Luke, 7:25.

130 MS reads 'gyuleris' which D&S emend to **guyleris**.

131 D&S, in contrast to Skeat, move this line to stand at

127. Since the remark is an aside, the MS order makes sense as it stands. Hoccleve's *Regement of Princes* contrasts wide clothes and wisdom. The beggar tells Hoccleve that although he is old and grey, and his gown is not as wide as the poet's, yet his advice is sound and he possesses greater wisdom than Hoccleve perceives, 407–13.

136 D&S, following Skeat, emend MS 'But' to **For**, arguing that **But** has been caught from the preceding line. The sense demands a causative rather than adversative conjunction. The scribe also missed out the 't' from **lyghtly**. The line draws an ironic contrast between the **strouutynge** of line 134 and the leap made by a criminal from the cart which takes him to the gallows. For all the antics of the overdressed courtiers, they will overreach themselves and come to an unfortunate end.

139 chepe is the market held on the modern site of Cheapside. In *Wynnere and Wastoure*, 474, the king ordains the chepe as the most suitable dwelling place for Waster.

140 D&S, following Skeat, reconstruct the second word of the b-verse as **seintis**, meaning 'belts'. This is plausible since the **cheynes** of 139 are probably ornaments for the belts and girdles that were so much in fashion with the new types of gowns worn, see notes to III.152. These girdles were often very long and ornate.

141–2 The courtiers cheapen the currency by exchanging money for such worthless commodities. There is a parallel to line 142 in the poem *On the Times 1388*, 'The ryche make mery, / Sed vulgus collachrimatur', Wright, I.272. In 142 the scribe has written 'pephe' in error for **peple**.

144 cf. *On the Times*, 'Fresche of the newe touch /Incedunt ridiculose', Wright, I.272.

145 lawe of Lydfford Lydford is a village on the edge of Dartmoor. OED cites Thomas Blount's entry for Lydford Law in his *Glossographia* (1656) as 'to hang men first and indite them afterwards'. The narrator's point is that if the courtiers were to be tried by this kind of justice, there would be no hope of escape. **in lond and in water** is a legal formula expressing exclusive jurisdiction, Alford, p.89. The MS reading 'ne' is written over an erasure. D&S, following Skeat, emend to &. The emendation is closer to the legal formula.

147 refers to the extravagant girdles.

150 In *Wynnere and Wastoure*, Winner accuses Waster of being one of the 'poure penyles men that peloure will by' (393).

152 Long and wide sleeves were fashionable at this time. Contemporary comments indicate that this taste was often carried to extremes. The 'houppelande' was a type of outer gown which became fashionable in the 1380s. Its sleeves were funnel shaped, widening from the shoulders downwards and ending in an immense aperture with the lower edge sometimes reaching the ground. These wide sleeves can be seen on the figures of St Edmund and Edward the Confessor in the *Wilton Diptych*. In *Regement of Princes* Hoccleve comments wrily on the nobility's need for such large bands of retainers. Because their arms are so preoccupied with keeping their sleeves from trailing on the ground, they cannot defend themselves from attack, 421–27, 463–71. Further, there is no need to get men to sweep the streets with brooms because the long sleeves can do so, 533–36.

154 The MS omits **but** supplied by Skeat and D&S. Here, the reference is probably to the garment known as the cote-hardie. The sleeves were close-fitting to the elbow and the hanging flap, which became longer and longer during Richard's reign, hung down to the knees or lower. The Squire wears a cote-hardie in the Ellesmere MS of Chaucer's *Canterbury Tales*, illustrating the lines 'Short was his gowne, with sleves longe and wyde', *General Prologue*, 93. There are many references to this excessive fashion during this period, *Parlement of The Thre Ages*, 125, *Wynnere and Wastoure*, 410–14.

155–7 The narrator puns on **acounted** in the sense of 'regard', MED acounten 3a) and in line 157 'to render account for' sense 5. Hoccleve makes a similar criticism, *Regement*, 428–34.

156 Pernell In *Piers Plowman* Pernele is bidden by Reason to put away her fancy trimmings, V.26–7. At V.62 she is associated with Pride, cf. *Mum*, 1360. In *Piers*, C.VI.30 Pernell confesses to being 'Proud of aparyle in port amonges the peple'. **plytis bihinde** cf. *On the Times 1388*, 'They bere a newe fascion, / humeris in pectore tergo', Wright, I.275.

160 Felice in *Piers Plowman* denotes a shrewish wife, V.29. The scribe writes 'ffaunte' which D&S emend as in error for **faute**. Skeat reads the word as 'ffaute'.

162–69 The taste for 'dagging' or 'jagging' the cloth became

widely fashionable from 1380–1400. Almost any border of any
garment was cut into elaborate shapes. These were sometimes
added as appliqué work in overlapping series. 'Dagging' was
especially common on the houppelande, and is criticised in *The
Parson's Tale*, 415–25.

163 y-come now late Skeat and D&S supply 'of' but this is
unnecessary, 'now late' is recorded in *Friar Daw's Reply*, 504
and *Upland's Rejoinder*, 272.

169 The narrator puns on **dere** in the senses of 'expensive',
MED dere 3a) and 'esteemed' 2a).

170 cf. *Mum*, 832. **side tales** has the sense of 'oblique
complaints', cf. the legal sense of 'tale', Alford, p.151.

172 cf. *Piers*, Prol.215–16: 'Thow myghtest bettre meete
myst on Malverne Hilles / Than get a "mom" of hire mouth til
moneie be shewed !'

174 as his statt axith The narrator articulates his belief in a
hierarchically ordered state, where sumptuary laws control
acceptable degrees of dress, cf. notes to III.215.

175 cf. *Mum*, 1690.

176 At Hoxne in Suffolk, a wall-painting dating from
1390–1400 depicts Superbia (Pride) as a young man with bell-
mouthed sleeves. He holds a sceptre in one hand and a mirror
in the other.

178 cf. notes to III.125.

186 beringe vppon oilles means to speak agreeably or flatter-
ingly, cf. *Mum*, 247, 271 and 831. The phrase derives from a
figurative extension of 'oil' as a curative or comfort, MED oile,
5c) e. Gower also uses the phrase in his criticism of flatterers,
Confessio, VII.2192–6, 2580–5.

187 conscience is the ability to judge right from wrong,
Alford, p.34. **assises** are trials in which sworn assessors or
jurymen decide questions of fact, Alford, p.145. The narrator's
point is that liveries are not given for virtuous behaviour but to
reward the kinds of oppression which includes returning
improper verdicts at inquests.

190 MS reads 'clergie' for **clerlie** cf. notes to I.170 & III.26.

193 cf. notes to III.162–9. The **Duche cotis** refer to the
Bohemian influence at court, following Richard's marriage to
Anne of Bohemia in 1382.

194 The MS reads 'scorte' with **scorne** written above. D&S
emend to the correction but the MS reading can stand in the

sense of speaking curtly about these garments, MED short (adv) 2a). There could be a play on the short lengths of the cote-hardies, short (adj) 1a).

195 recalls the description of Patience in *Piers Plowman*, B.XIII.29: 'Ac Pacience in the paleis stood in pilgrymes clothes.'

196 cf. *On the Times 1388*, 'Jerorys han peyntyd slewys / inopes famuli dominorum', Wright, I.273.

197 The narrator digresses from the luxurious fashions to the king's patronage of lawless men.

200 knowe well hem-self a reference to the dictum 'nosce te ipsum', cf. notes to I.112 and 119.

201 The scribe writes 'counude' in error for **couude**, cf. III.219.

203 cf. *Mum*, 39.

206 The image relates moral behaviour to the natural laws which govern the movements of the tides.

207 cf. notes to III.2.

209–10 The entry of Wit is as abrupt as that of Reason at II.69. D&S speculate that a passage describing Wisdom's arrival at court has been omitted, p.101. But the sudden appearances of characters may recall narrative techniques in *Piers*. Wit's **stilleness** contrasts with the strutting courtiers. The wise restraint of his will contrasts with the behaviour of Richard and his nobles, III.119 and 181.

212–15 Wit's **homelich** dress contrasts to the artifice and affectation of the courtiers'. It is old-fashioned but also **holsum** and in accordance with the dictates of the weather, line 215. Wit dresses in accordance with the laws which govern nature and thus represents the principles of natural law.

216 MS reads 'will' with an 'e' written above. Skeat incorporates the correction without comment; D&S emend to **well**.

218 but hales hem helped is a reference to the sheer size and extravagance of Richard's household; a phenomenon which attracted hostile criticism throughout his reign. Hardyng's *Chronicle* provides details of the extravagance, pp.346–7 and Froissart writes that he observed for himself that no king was more extravagant than Richard in the keeping of his household, p.472.

219 The scribe writes 'counude' in error for **couude**.

222 of ladies alle refers to the excessive numbers of ladies maintained at court. These were especially numerous after

Richard's marriage to Anne of Bohemia. The fourth clause of Thomas Haxey's petition of 1397 criticised the excessive costs of the household and mentioned the large numbers of women the commons felt they were supporting, *Rot.Parl*, III.339.

228 cf. the almost identical line at *Mum*, 174, describing the plight of the sothsegger. In *Piers* a similar line describes the treatment of Liar, II.219.

232 There is a pun on **pikis** in the sense of a spiked weapon, MED pike 1a), which is how D&S gloss the word, and piked shoes, MED 5a). These shoes with long exaggerated points became fashionable at around 1395; the higher the rank, the longer the points. A sumptuary law passed in 1363 forbade anyone under the rank of esquire or gentleman to wear shoes with points longer than two inches. Given his status, the porter should not be wearing piked shoes at all. This detail shows both the decadence of court and also its unmannerliness: Wit is actually kicked out. *PlTale*, 930, condemns priests for wearing piked shoes.

235 The fashion of the court at this time was to be clean-shaven. Lack of a beard is also a sign of immaturity, cf. *Gawain*, 'Hit arn aboute on this bench bot berdlez chylder', 280. Significantly, Wit, like the beekeeper in *Mum*, is bearded, III.214, *Mum*, 961.

238 There are similar images of exclusion in *The Simonie*. Truth is forbidden to enter the court of Rome (A.10) and God's religious retinue are forbidden entrance to the realm; indeed, the porter is ordered to eject them (A.143–4), cf. *Mum*, 552.

245–6 Similar sentiments can be traced in the *Digby* poem *Wytt and Wille*, Kail, pp.22–4 and in Gower's poem *In Praise of Peace*, 22–3.

249–53 Society was traditionally divided into three estates: those who fight, those who pray and those who work, corresponding to the nobility, the clergy and the peasants, cf. *Piers*, Prol.112–120. In the fourteenth century this traditional classification was breaking down with the emergence of the moneyed merchant and lawyer classes and the transition from a feudal manorial economy to one that was more urban and cash-based. In *Richard* the traditional threefold division receives altered emphasis. The clergy are omitted and the narrator stresses the proper rule of mature magnates, the fighting strength of men in their prime and the work of the labourers. This classification may be deliberately anticlerical or may simply stress the role of sound government, internal and external, cf. Dan Embree, 'The King's Ignorance: A Topos for Evil Times', *Medium Aevum*, 54 (1985), p.125.

253 cf. *Piers*, VI.272: 'And lerne to laboure with lond lest liflode hym faille'.

254 D&S, following Skeat, supply 'right dome' for the missing stave in the a-verse. I have followed their emendation.

255 longid to his age Another reference which links the proper course of government with natural hierarchy.

256 The stress on the role of good counsel is an emphasis in keeping with the sentiments of contemporary poems, e.g., Gower, *In Praise of Peace*, 141-7; Hoccleve, *Regement*, 4936-49, 4953-6 and Kail, III.81-3.

260-2 Criticism of Richard's youthful counsellors is also seen in Usk's comparison of the king to Rehoboam, son of Solomon, who lost the kingdom of Israel because he followed the advice of young men, p.190. A cow hopping in a cage is an image of distorted nature.

267 cf. *Piers*, B.III.300: 'And make of lawe a laborer; swich love shal arise' and IV.147: 'And Lawe shal ben a laborer and lede afeld donge'. The primary function of a king is to maintain law, a view paralleled in many contemporary political poems: Gower, *Mirour*, 23077-9, 2234-6; *Vox*, VI.613-14 and *Confessio*, VII.2719-24; *Piers*, Prol.141-2: 'Dum rex a regere dicatur nomen habere / Nomen habet sine re nisi studet iura tenere.' Another version of this statement appears at the end of *On the Times*, Wright, I.278.

272 MS omits **not**; a negative is clearly needed to maintain sense. The comparison of Richard to a bat remarks on his unnatural delinquence. Bartholomaeus notes that one of the bat's most salient characteristics is its hatred of light, I.645.

274 wexe is the candle wax kept burning all night in feasting and revelry. Hoccleve warns against the excesses of wine because it causes wit to be buried and counsel to be prohibited, *Regement*, 3830-4, cf. notes to I.90.

279-80 cf. notes to IV.1-15. In 279, the scribe writes **counntis** for **countis**.

281 fynde in the legal sense of 'furnish proof', Alford, p.59.

282 The scribe writes '**What**' for **That**, possibly attracted by the 'w' alliteration, cf. *Mum*, 1512.

284 cf. *Piers*, VI.168: 'And leet light of the lawe, and lasse of the knyghte'.

285–6 This unmerited demand for respect and obeisance finds a parallel in the *Eulogium*'s narration of how Richard ordered a throne to be set up for him in a room so that after supper he could look down on everyone in silence. Whenever he looked on anyone directly, they had to genuflect to him, whatever their rank, p.378. From 282–7, there is some confusion between singular and plural third person pronouns (cf. notes to III.124–5). The narrator vacillates between criticising the king and his courtiers.

293 MS omits **gates**. D&S supply 'gate', citing the parallel to *Piers*, V.594, 'Of almesdedes ar the hokes that the gates hangen on'. I have adopted their emendation, but made the noun plural to match the plural form of the verb.

295 The scribe writes '**kne**' for **knew**. D&S emend.

299 MED glosses **kew-kaw** as 'a turning upside down' and OED has the following citation from the works of J. Taylor, 1630: 'The picture topsie turnie stands kewwaw; The World turnd vpside downe, as all men know'. Line 299 should be punctuated to stand with 298, giving the sense: 'The world always alternates between prosperity and misery; there is always reversal, even at the last minute'.

300 In the MS this line stands at 305 and there is an abrupt break of sense between 299 and 300. D&S, reading **kew-kaw** as 'claw me, claw thee', p.102, read line 300 as an extension of 299. It is more probable that the scribe skipped copying this line because it started with the same words as the previous, and on noticing, slipped it in a few lines further down. The change of focus signalled by the line is not appropriate where it stands in the MS, but is apt at line 300.

301–2 may refer to the sessions courts that were held at different places all over the country, where the King's Justices went to hear criminal pleas. Or there may be a more precise reference to the holding of parliament sessions outside Westminster. The parliament which condemned the Lords Appellant in 1397 reconvened in 1398 at Shrewsbury. The poet appears to have known some of the details of its business, see notes to IV.15–16.

305–16 The narrator turns his attention to the abuses of maintenance in the legal system. The tenor of the complaint is similar to the criticisms of Mede in *Piers*, B.III.153–62.

306–7 **abateth** is a legal term meaning 'to abolish or dismiss a case at law', MED abaten (3). The perversion of justice through bribery is discussed by Gower, *Vox*, VI.43–60, 263–4.

308–11 **weddis** is a legal term meaning a pledge, something deposited as a security for a payment or the fulfilment of an obligation, Alford, p.166. Gower makes a similar point about the effects of maintenance on the efforts of the poor to seek redress through the legal system, *Vox*, VI.265–8, 271–9.

313 Once a case was accepted to be heard in court, a jury assembled to hear the pleading. If the jurors were spoken to, or treated to food or drink by either party, their verdict could be quashed.

315 **reson ... rith ... rehersid** are all legal terms. They mean: 'law', 'justice' and 'to recite aloud a list of charges or pleas', cf. notes to II.98.

316 cf. *Piers*, III.80: 'For thise are men on this molde that moost harm wercheth'.

317–50 A section on the unruly band of retainers which Richard recruited from Cheshire. Richard began recruiting these men in 1387. Throughout the 1390s he built them into a personal bodyguard, decorated with his white hart livery. When parliament opened in September 1397, Richard was protected by over 300 of these Cheshire archers. Because building work was in process in Westminster Hall, the parliamentary meeting was accommodated in a hall newly built for the session. It had open sides. Usk, who was present at the parliament, records that the Cheshiremen were quite visible through the open sides and bent their bows when they thought any quarrel had arisen in the proceedings, p.154. The Monk of Evesham comments that the hall was specially built for this purpose and that the Cheshiremen actually began to shoot but were restrained by the king, p.134. Between January 1398 and early spring 1399, Richard was constantly accompanied by this retinue. Usk cites this as the chief cause of Richard's ruin, stating that these retainers oppressed the king's subjects unpunished, beat and robbed them, committed murders, adulteries and other evils without end. Richard cherished them so much that rather than listen to anyone who had a complaint against them, he would rather treat him as an enemy, p.169–70. See also *Annales*, p.237. The focus in *Richard* is on the way that these Cheshiremen violated the legal system.

318 The ironic use of legal diction shows that the Cheshiremen paid no heed at all to the due processes of law and order. **conceill** is advice or legal counsel, Alford, p.38. **causis** are legal suits or actions, Alford, p.23.

319 The piepowder courts were set up to deal with matters arising out of fairs and markets. Interested parties were often accepted as competent witnesses, and as the courts were only in session for the duration of the fair, judgment was given without delay, see L. B. Curzon, *English Legal History* (Plymouth, 1979), 188–9. To plead **pipoudris** for all **pleyntis** (cf. notes to I.143) is tantamount to disregarding proper legal procedure altogether.

321 cf. notes to I.171. The pleas of the Cheshiremen clearly bore no resemblance to those recognised by any court of law.

322 **fyne** means final agreement or settlement, Alford, p.59.

327 **constrewed quarellis** in a legal sense means to fabricate an accusation, Alford, p.35, MED querele 2b). There is also a pun on 'quarrel' in the sense of 'armed combat', sense c; a pun brought out by the next line.

328 **poyntis** As legal charge or accusation, MED pointe (8), and as the tip of a sword, sense 11a). For the Cheshiremen, swords replaced words.

330 The livery bestowed by the Cheshiremen replaces badges with bruises.

332 **tale** cf. notes to I.189. **harmes** means damages, cf. Alford, p.68.

333 **answere** means a defence in response to a charge or accusation, Alford, p.6.

334–7 cf. Usk's comments in notes to 317–50 above.

335 **mystirmen** are those who follow any calling or profession, cf. *Crede*, 574.

336 MS reads 'lyghliche' with a 't' added above the line.

341 **jewis** is a judicial punishment or sentence, Alford, p.75.

347 There is a break of sense between 346 and 347. Skeat supplied a whole new line, which D&S incorporated. Clearly material is missing but a less drastic revision is to supply **They wrought** for MS 'Of'. In the absence of any other MS witness, it is impossible to reconstruct the original sense.

348 MS reads 'serigauntis' for **sergiauntis**. A sergeant at law was a chief justice, Alford, p.142, sense II.

349 prentise of courte was a law student or barrister of less than sixteen years' standing, Alford, p.8.

350 degonys is a term of contempt equivalent to 'bumpkin', MED cites no other examples apart from *Richard*.

351–70 suggest that God himself took divine vengeance on the misdeeds perpetrated by these Cheshiremen and conflate divine military action with the redress brought by Henry Bolingbroke's 1399 campaign. The *Annales* gives a similarly providential interpretation of these events, pp.240–1.

351 the vijne sterris are the moon, Mercury, Venus, the Sun, Mars, Jupiter and Saturn. Above these were the Fixed Stars, the Primum Mobile and then the Empyrean.

353 mendis means reparation for injury or crime, Alford, p.5.

353 MS reads 'meynteyne it' which Skeat and D&S emend to **meynteyned**.

358 MS reads 'the' which D&S emend to **of. contres** has the sense of judicial shire, Alford, p.36.

359 duke doughty conflates the figures of God and Henry Bolingbroke.

361 Degon and Dobyn names suggesting men of the lower classes, cf. III.350.

362 duke used scathingly of Richard, recalling the jibe at the 'duketti' (cf. notes to I.144) and the partridge analogy where Richard is seen not as the true king but as the usurper (III.37–67).

363 The MS reading, emended by Skeat and D&S, arises from attraction to the preceding line.

365–8 The references to sun, moon and stars may recall the apocalyptic language of political prophecy, see R. Taylor, *The Political Prophecy in England* (New York, 1911), pp.121–7. But given the poet's technique of punning on heraldic devices, there may be allusions to actual historical figures. Henry was known by his badge of the sun, cf. Gower, *Tripartite Chronicle*, I, notes to line 57. The badge of the Percies was a crescent moon, by which they were well known. But this leaves the stars unaccounted for. No nobleman involved in any of the events to which these lines could refer had stars on his arms, cf. notes to *Mum*, 1731–3.

369 felouns are criminals who have specifically committed an act of treason, murder, rape, or theft, Alford, p.57.

Passus Four

2 The king's household was both a domestic organisation and a part of the administrative machinery of the country. Throughout Richard's reign, the Commons attacked the household because of its size and extravagant expenditure. Complaints were fierce in 1381, *Rot.Parl*, III.100–1, and 1386, *Rot.Parl*, III.221. A commission was set up in 1386 to examine all royal revenue and was given wide powers of supervision over the household, including investigation of all the household officers, *Statutes of the Realm*, II.39–43. In 1388, the Appellants took over the royal household, removed some royal servants, arrested others and required certain of Richard's more prominent followers to abjure the court. Between 1390 and 1394, the expenses of the household doubled. In 1397, the household again came under attack in the fourth clause of the petition which Thomas Haxey presented to parliament, *Rot.Parl*, III.339.

4 a **fee-ferme** was a feudal estate in land or tenements held in unlimited tenure, subject only to a fixed annual rent. Here, it means the fixed annual rent paid for such an estate. The **fynys for faughtis** probably refers to the pardons which Richard exacted from his people during 1398. Letters were sent to seventeen counties accusing them of having supported the Appellants in 1387–8. They were forced to buy back the king's pleasure with sums ranging from a thousand marks to a thousand pounds for each shire. The twenty-first article of deposition indicts Richard for this unlawful practice.

5 The forfeiture of properties by the former Lords Appellant is recorded in *Statutes of the Realm*, II.101. Richard also sequestered the Lancastrian inheritance of Henry Bolingbroke after the death of his father John of Gaunt. The twenty-sixth article of deposition accuses Richard of the unlawful possession of other men's lands.

6–7 A nounage is a payment due to the king when an estate fell to a minor. Richard twice received the nounages of the Mortimer estates and twice exercised financial control over the

Mowbray inheritance. Successive earls of March died in 1381 and 1398. On both occasions the king received custody of the Mortimer inheritance because the heir was under age, Tuck, pp.88–9 and p.193. In 1385, Richard distrained the lands of Thomas Mowbray because he had married against the king's wishes. When Mowbray was exiled in 1398, his son was still a minor and Richard sequestered and distributed much of his property, Tuck, p.96, Goodman, p.70.

7 MS reads 'mounbray' in error for **Moubray**.

8 The **issue** (exitus) was the end and object of pleading and the way out into the country where the answer would be found, Baker, pp.67–8. A man found guilty in a case over which the king had jurisdiction had to pay a fine to the king as well as rendering damages to the injured party.

9–16 allude to the Shrewsbury 1398 parliament in which Richard was granted the subsidy on wools, leather and woolfells for the rest of his life. The wording of the statute shows that such a grant was unprecedented: 'they [the people of the realm] have made at this Time of their good Will *more than they have done to any of his progenitors before this Time*, that is to say, the Subsidy of the Wools, Leathers and Woolfells for Term of his Life and a Disme and Quinzime and an half, to be paid in Manner comprised in their said Grant', *Statutes of the Realm*, II.106. It aroused hostility from contemporary chroniclers, Usk, p.164 and *Annales*, p.222 and is alluded to in the nineteenth article of deposition.

13 Adam Usk remarks that in addition to all the other evils enacted at the Shrewsbury parliament in 1398, 'even for his victuals he paid naught', p.163.

14 **poundage** refers to the subsidies on exports and imports. The Commons granted Richard 12d on every pound of merchandise and 3s on every tun of wine entering or leaving the kingdom for the next three years.

17–18 The 'credit' which attracted the curse of the commons may be the series of forced loans which Richard exacted from his subjects between August 1397–8. These totalled £20,000, and most were never repaid.

24–30 The calling of a 'packed' parliament to raise money for the king and his household has obvious reference to the 1398 session, but the chronology of this sequence suggests that such a parliament was called after the grant to the king of the subsidy on wools, leather and woolfells.

25 MS reads 'propffitt' which D&S emend, following Skeat.

26 These closed writs were issued by Chancery and contained special formulas for summoning magnates and clerics to parliament.

28–31 Letters patent were sent to the sheriffs to elect knights to represent the shires in company with the nobility. The narrator is careful to distinguish between the three ranks of the parliamentary assembly: the peers, the prelates who are summoned in their own right, and the Commons who are elected by their communities in order to represent their interests. The shires were supposed to organise elections to choose representatives for parliament. The nineteenth article of deposition accuses Richard of appointing his own sheriffs, notwithstanding the statutes which provided that they were to be nominated to the crown by the ministers, justices and other councillors. **as the charge wold** refers to the legal mandate to elect knights and alludes ironically to the fact that the representatives were not so elected.

30 schewe for the schire means to lodge the complaints of the commons before the court of parliament, Alford, p.143.

33–8 Parliament was customarily opened with a speech from the chancellor, e.g., 'chancellor d'Engleterre, du commandement du Roy monstra & pronunca la cause del sommonce du parlement' *Rot.Parl*, III.347.

36–7 poyntis and **meved** in their legal senses. The chancellor's explanation for calling an assembly of parliament included the reasons for financial exactions.

37–8 glosinge puns on the legal sense of explaining or interpreting, Alford, p.65 (in this instance the chancellor is explaining the nobility's need for money) and on the senses of 'glose' as 'to obscure the truth', MED glosen 2a), and 'to flatter', sense 3a). **greyues** in the legal sense of an official complaint of a wrong or grievance, MED gref, 1d).

39 tale in the legal sense of the plaintiff's account in a legal suit, Alford, p.151.

40 mete puns on the senses of 'come together', MED meten (4) 1c), and 'food', mete (n) 1a), a play which shows how bribery and corruption operated in parliamentary proceedings, cf. notes to III.313.

41 maters cf. notes to I.171.

43 reherse cf. notes to II.98.

45 is ironic given that the speech which follows outlines the ideal conduct of a shire representative.

47 The nineteenth article of deposition states that the people of the realm should be free to choose the knights of the shire for the parliament, those who would air their grievances and seek redress as best as they could for their profit.

50 cf. notes to I.102 and *Mum*, 1667.

51 fyndyth means to support with a salary, Alford, p.59.

53 siphre doth in awgrym cf. Whiting, p.87, who quotes Usk, *Testament of Love*, 72/82–4: 'Although a sypher in augrim have no might in significacion of it-selve, yet he yeveth power in significacion to other'. In *Richard*, the narrator's point is that the representatives mark a place, but have nothing to contribute.

55–6 Symond is the personification of simony, cf. note to *Crede*, 710–13. Here, the secular context refers to the knights of the shire accepting money and obeying the wishes of the king rather than representing the interests of their communities.

58–9 may refer to an actual topical event. In his account of the 1398 parliament, Usk tells of a plot led by the duke of Surrey against Roger Mortimer, the young earl of March, pp.164–5. As a result of this intrigue, Mortimer was summoned from Ireland to take the oath of loyalty. From IV.7, the poet is clearly familiar with details of the Mortimer estates and might have had some connection with the family.

61 cf. notes to I.72.

70 cf. *Piers*, X.54: 'And bryngen forth a balled reson, and taken Bernard to witnesse'.

71–82 The description of parliamentary incompetence and corruption suddenly blossoms into an analogy which makes use of the traditional comparison between a ship and the state. The analogy illustrates the complete lack of harmony in the parliamentary proceedings, how the leader was unskilled at the craft of managing the vessel and how the various members were too stupid to do more than follow their own selfish interests. Gower uses the ship of state image in *Vox* I.1593–2078 to dramatise the danger and confusion at the time of the uprising in 1381.

73 may allude to the speed of the 1398 parliament. The business took just four days.

78 at the monthe-ende The Shrewsbury parliament lasted from 27 to 30 January.

80–2 are either a vivid rhetorical flourish to describe how close the parliament session came to scuppering itself. Or, lowering sails may allude to the termination of the 1398 assembly. Its powers were delegated to a parliamentary commission in order to avoid exposing the king and his council to public criticism.

89 The scribe has written 'owen' for **owed**.

91 hansell is an earnest of good faith or fellowship, Alford, p.68.

93 dukis refers to the 'duketti' created at the 1398 parliament, cf. notes to I.144. **Do-well** is the clearest reference in the poem to *Piers Plowman*, cf. notes to II.110. The rest of the fol.119b is left blank. Only eleven of the customary alliterative long lines have been written. The next five folios are missing and the sixth (fol.126) is left blank.

NOTES TO MUM
AND THE SOTHSEGGER

1–13 The beginning of the poem is lost. The manuscript fragment opens part way through a description of the officers best for a king, see lines 29–30. The narrator warns the king to protect his revenues from greedy nobles and thus prevent the commons from complaining about the burden of taxation. Henry's reign was plagued with financial difficulties, partly because of the unexpected plummet in the volume of wool exports and partly because of the costs of military action against the French, Scots and Welsh rebels. Repeatedly in the parliaments, there were fierce arguments about expenditure and taxation, Kirby, p.127. The image of the unbroken crown represents a kingdom united behind a financially secure king. A similar image is used in Kail, XII.50–55.

1 **couetous peuple** refers to the nobles who supported Henry on his return to England in 1399, especially the Percies. Henry rewarded his supporters liberally and also appeased Richard's by confirming their grants. The *Eulogium* records that in the parliament of 1402 the clergy and Commons were asked for a grant of a tenth and a fifteenth because the king had nothing. The Commons asked what had become of King Richard's treasure and were told that the earl of Northumberland and others had it. The disparity between the king's plea of poverty and the nobles' grants prompted the Commons to ask for an enquiry but Henry refused his assent, p.395. See further notes to 1654–61. Line 1 is repeated at line 1650.

4 The MS reads 'other', presumably caught from the preceding line. The correction marked **grete** suggests the nobles' attempts to bleed money from the crown. **prayer**, MED 1a), has the sense of petition for favour but another of its senses, religious prayer, MED 2a), suggests that the clerics are also being criticised for their financial greed. In the second parliament of 1404 there were proposals to seize the clerical temporalities, but they were eventually dropped, Wylie, I.475–6.

5 **comyn** supplied by the corrector, corresponding to 'commune' – the people of the realm, MED commune 1a).

8 Henry's tax collectors often experienced great resistance against the levies agreed by parliaments and Henry's problems were compounded by the difficulties of actually securing payment, cf. note to 134–9.

9 cf. *Piers*, III.85: 'For toke thei on trewely, thei tymbred nought so heighe'.

11–12 The time references are proverbial; none of Henry's treasurers held office for exactly two years. They all had difficulties finding sufficient income for the king. In February 1402, a King's Council meeting examined the subsidies and grants made at the last parliament. Lawrence Allerthorpe was replaced as Treasurer by Bishop Henry Bowet, one of the examiners. But there was no suggestion of misuse of funds, Kirby, p.143.

13 The duties of the chancellor involved acting as the king's secretary, keeper of the royal seal and chaplain to the king (in

which capacity he was considered to be the 'keeper of the king's conscience'). He sat in the council as an adviser to the king and issued writs for the common law courts. The chancellor also heard proceedings against the crown and petitions of right from those who felt that they had been unable to gain redress in the common law courts, cf. notes to *Richard*, I.151.

16 y-ioyned in the legal sense of appointing as a judge, MED joinen (2) c); cf. *Piers*, C.XVII.125.

17 cf. *Piers*, Prol.212: 'Sergeants, it semed, that serveden at the Barre'.

18 prentys See notes to *Richard*, III.349. **prisist** puns on the senses of 'most praiseworthy', MED prise (adj) a) and 'prise' (n) 1, meaning 'price'.

19 MS omits **not**, supplied by Day and Steele (D&S).

20 pleyntes See notes to *Richard*, I.143.

24 MS reads 'hym', presumably caught from the preceding line. A plural third person pronoun is required. D&S supply **thaym**.

25 In chancery, proceedings were begun not by writ, as in the common law courts, but by the presentation of a bill or petition. The petitioner set out his grounds for complaint and humbly begged for relief. An oral petition had to be transformed into written terms in court. A writ was then issued on the defendant to summon him to court. The narrator urges that the petitions of poor plaintiffs, irrespective of whether they can afford legal fees, be turned into writs and then sealed, so that proceedings can commence against the defendant, Curzon, p.106–7.

28 frounting From MED frounten (v) a) to strike, kick. The violence here is reminiscent of the behaviour of the Cheshiremen in *Richard*, III.319–337.

29 haselle is glossed by MED as 'a retainer, young courtier'. The only examples cited are this line and *Richard*, II.25.

39 cf. *Richard*, III.203.

41 fable used in a positive sense here of speaking the truth, see also lines 140, 145, 1133, in contrast to the words of *Mum*, 264 and 1203, and the rumour-spreading friars of 1395.

42–46 The margin of the manuscript is torn. Reconstruction follows D&S.

42–3 The syntax is awkward. The sense of the lines is that there was no clerk that ever clothed the soothsegger, who clothed him not simply at Christmas (i.e. the season of goodwill) but the entire year following.

44 Saunder the seruiselees This name is an invention of the narrator's, but MED records 'saunder' as a surname of this time, 'saundre' (n) d).

47 A quotation is marked to stand here but with the torn margin the only legible parts are . . . **atem** . . . **atis.**

48 tales in the legal sense; cf. notes to *Richard*, I.189.

49 termes in formal or technical language, cf. Chaucer, *House of Fame*, 857; *General Prologue*, 323, 639.

51-3 Whiting, p.423, cites a number of analogues to the proverb of hitting the nail on the head, among them, *The Book of Margery Kempe*, ed. S. B. Meech and H. E. Allen (EETS 212 1940), p.152/27-8. The metaphor of lancing sores is drawn from the natural world to show the rightfulness of speaking out against corruption, cf. 1122-3 and 1130-40. **poynt** puns on its legal sense as an accusation and as a sharp point, cf. notes to *Richard*, III.328.

55 MS reads 'y-filled'. There is no meaning of this verb recorded in MED which makes sense of the line. The correction to **y-ferked**, understood as 'to drive someone away', MED ferken 2a), gives the sense that the truthteller is trampled underfoot.

56 deceiptz. MED deceit 3b), legal fraud or deception.

57 trauerssid A legal term meaning the formal denial in pleading of some matter of fact alleged by the other side, OED traverse, sense 8.

61 The MS reads 'preynte' with a space following. The corrector supplies **peyntours**. The first two alliterative staves appear confused. Taking their cue from the correction, D&S emend to **peynture**. Understood in the sense of something 'graven', MED peinture, sense e), the line alludes to the impression on the palm of the hand formed by the imprint of a coin. See also note to line 66.

62-69 The grain imagery to describe the false flatterer anticipates the description in lines 176-92. **colour** (lines 63 and 66) puns on the colour of an object MED (2), and as a specious reason, 5b). 'Colour' is a frequently-used word in Wycliffite texts to denote the tricks of the church of Antichrist, see note to 286.

66 the crosse engraved on the back of coins, cf. *Piers*,

XV.542–3: 'Bothe riche and religious that roode thei honoure / That in grotes is ygrave, and in gold nobles'.

71 asserts the resilience of truth, cf. Kail IV. 97–104, especially 101–4: 'And though trouthe a while be slaun, / And doluen depe vnder clay, / Yut he wole ryse to lyue agayn, / And all the sothe he wole say'.

72–95 are a legal defence of satirical poetry. The passage recalls the remarks in *Richard*, I.59–87 and the interchange between Reason and the narrator, II.67–76.

72 cunseil See note to *Crede*, 37.

73 sclaundre A false accusation, Alford, p.140. The narrator is anxious to avoid defamation, cf. *Richard*, I.74.

74 tale in the legal sense of the plaintiff's account in a lawsuit, **tente** in the sense of legal 'intentio', cf. notes to *Richard*, II.79–93.

75 harmed in the sense of legal damage, MED harm 1e) and **serve** in the legal sense of rendering judgment, MED serven (14). The narrator's point is that to bring a false charge against someone renders the plaintiff subject to the same legal process and sentence he initiates.

76 grovnd A common term of authorisation in Wycliffite texts, cf. note to *Crede*, 47. The combination of legal and biblical authority to authorise the narrator's position is seen again at 1594–1625.

77 The injunction to read the Bible for onself can be seen as bypassing ecclesiastical institutions.

79 cf. Matthew, 18:15: 'But if thy brother shall offend against thee, go and rebuke him between thee and him alone. If he shall hear thee, thou shalt gain thy brother'. The Latin citation at line 81 quotes this text. Hoccleve offers similar advice in *Regement* (2486–90).

82 chargeth puns on the senses of 'regard' MED changen sense 3 and 'to impose a tax', sense 8; the latter sense chimes with the pun on **charite** as love, MED (1), and charity, sense 2.

84 freyne to question someone in court, MED frainen 3c), cf. line 752.

85 wittenes continues the legal metaphor; the witness attesting to the good character of the questioner.

86 speke in the legal sense of 'to plead', Alford, p.146.

87–98 The rewarding of a truthteller with **mede** stands in stark contrast to the usual position of sothseggers, cf. Kail, II where the flatterer has plenty of 'mede' while the 'trewe seruant' gets only good thanks. But the sothsegger, like the narrator of *Mum*, states that a wise lord rewards faithful servants: 'Trewe trauayle shal not lese his dede. /To vertuous lord all worship lys. /The trewe seruant is worthy his mede' (38–40).

88 The a-verse lacks an alliterative stave. The corrector marks **soeth**.

90–8 The conjunction of legal correction and penance is reminiscent of Reason's description of justice in *Piers*, IV.134–48.

97 cf. *Richard*, II.89–90.

99–102 mark the beginning of the narrator's quest for the sothsegger, a strategy which recalls the dreamer's search for Truth in *Piers Plowman*. The narrator meets institutions and persons who condemn themselves by their words or actions without authorial intervention.

102 **holsum** The image of health is part of the natural law imagery of the poem. In *Richard*, Wit's dress is **holsum**, III.212.

103 The entry of the nameless clerk into the poem recalls both the entry of Piers into *Piers Plowman* and the sudden speech of Reason in *Richard*, II.69. The clerk undermines himself because he must be one of the **wisemen** who is too astute to be wedded to **suche a simple seruise**.

106 The MS reads 'soulde'. The corrector supplies **mede**, which restores alliteration to the a-verse.

109 cf. line 1016 and *Piers*, V.538: 'I knowe hym as kyndely as clerc doth hise bokes'. The echo of Piers Plowman, an uneducated ploughman, knowing the way to truth as naturally as a clerk does his book, sits ironically in the mouth of a wise cleric who has no knowledge or experience of a truthteller.

115 The corrector adds:
'And souurayns sothely they serue but a whiles
yit shuld hit lengthe thayre lyves and the lawe mende'. There is clearly uncertainty here between the MS and the source of the corrector's emendations (presumably another copy) as these lines also appear at the bottom of the page. Dan Embree has seen line 115 as an example of the topos of the king's ignorance (1985) pp. 122–6. In fact, Henry was not so bereft of truthtelling advice as the narrator suggests. Philip Repingdon, Bishop of Lincoln, wrote to him in 1401, using the fate of Richard II to warn Henry about the state of his own rule. Quoting Proverbs, 27:6, 'Better are the wounds of a friend than the fraudulent kisses of the flatterer',

Repingdon advised the king to take note of the ill-feeling and dissensions in the realm because of the oppression of the people. The letter is quoted in Usk, pp.231–6. *The Davies Chronicle* states that the displeasure with Henry's reign was so strong at this time that the people desired Richard's return as king, p.23.

116 MS reads 'telle'; the corrector amends to **saye** which restores alliteration. At this point the corrector adds four more lines:

> 'thorough mayntenance and mysrewle of maisters above
> And al is consail to the king he knoweth not the fawtes
> For lacke of a loresman that lesinges hateth
> That wold telle hym the trouthe and trippe not aside'.

120 twyes a woke is a rare specific time-reference. It is repeated at 1672. The Long Parliament of 1406 presented Henry with 31 articles of constitutional reform before they would consent to taxation. One of the stipulations was that the king should hear petitions on Wednesdays and Fridays each week in the presence of counsellors, *Rot.Parl*, III.585–8. The quotation is from Psalm 2:10, 'And now, O ye kings, understand : receive instruction, you that judge the earth'.

127 Caution had to be exercised when speaking the truth to one's king. Usk records that a certain William Clerk was beheaded at the Tower in 1401 because he had uttered and written wicked words against the king, p.222. A statute of 1378 stipulated that slanderers against the great men of the realm, mainly the officers of the King's Council, should be imprisoned until the person who first spread the lies was identified, *Statutes of the Realm*, 2 Ric.II. (1378), p.9. See further Simpson, 'The Constraints of Satire', p.17.

133–4 In the parliaments of 1404–6, the Commons urged the king to listen to advice so that he would have sufficient money to live off his income without oppressing his people with taxes, Brown (1964), p.28.

134–9 The margins are torn here, reconstruction follows D&S. In the early years of Henry's reign disaffection with the taxation ran so high that in some areas, especially the cloth districts, it was impossible to collect the taxes. Collectors were driven off, beaten, and in some instances, murdered, see Wylie, I.198.

138 cf. *Richard*, I.60.

141 glose puns on the senses of glossing a text, MED glosen 1a), to obscure the truth of a statement, 2a), and flattery, sense 3a); cf. notes to *Crede*, 275.

144–5 John Cheyne, the Speaker at the first parliament of Henry's reign in 1399, presented a fourfold petition on behalf of the Commons to the king and the lords. The second part stated that no one dared speak the truth at Richard's last two parliaments because of intimidation and violence. Henry granted the petition and, as the *Annales* records, said that it was wholly unreasonable to call those who criticised the bad government of the king traitors, p.303.

147–9 Repingdon (cf. note to 115) contrasts the people's gladness at Henry's return in 1399 with their sorrow in 1401. He singles out as one of the causes for unrest in the realm, oppression of the people by taxation, Usk, p.234.

147–9 At Knaresborough, Henry announced that all taxation would be abolished, McFarlane, *Lancastrian Kings*, p.49. It was an extravagant claim, but some effort was made to mitigate the high taxation demanded by Richard's government. The 1397 parliament had granted one-fifteenth on moveable goods in counties and one-tenth in cities, to be levied annually during the king's life. It added a sum of half as much again, which was to be regarded as a loan, cf. notes to *Richard*, IV.9–16. In the first parliament of Henry's reign (October 1399) the grant was confirmed, but the additional loan, which had fallen due on September 29 1399 was to be remitted, or refunded to anyone who had paid it. Furthermore it was declared that the tax should not establish a precedent, and that the nation should not be asked to pay for wars except by the consent of parliament, Wylie, pp.58–9. The **crosse** of line 148 is likely to have been St Paul's Cross in London. This promise is recalled later in Henry's reign. In 1401, at Norton St Philips near Bath, the dealers in cloth refused to pay the tax on commodities, alleging the king's promise that it should not be re-imposed, Wylie, I.198. In the 1405 rising, the list of grievances posted on the doors of the churches in York stated that Henry promised to abolish the levies of fifteenths and tenths, and the subsidies and customs on wool and wine, but had broken his word, Kirby, p.186.

149 and of coylaige MS omits 'and' which the corrector supplies. I have incorporated the correction because **custume**, in the sense of customs duty on imports or exports (MED custume 6a)) fits the topicality of the remarks.

151 king-is cunseil At the first parliament of Henry's reign, Archbishop Arundel's sermon declared that it was the will of the king to be guided by the advice of honourable, wise and discreet subjects. Petitions presented at the parliament asked that the king's actions should be guided by the advice of his council, including the making of grants, Kirby, p.81. Henry gave a general promise that he would not govern alone, but with the advice of wise councillors, *Rot.Parl.*, III.415. His words were not forgotten. At the 1406 parliament, the Speaker, Sir John Tiptoft, reminded the king of Archbishop Arundel's words, Kirby, p.197.

152–5 D&S read 152 as 'the magpies who once disputed with the parrot', p.32, but it is unclear what **parlid of** means. MED records no examples of 'parlen' as a phrasal verb. Under 'of' (prep) 23a), MED lists verbs denoting speech with 'of' in the senses of 'about', 'with regard to', but in each case an object noun follows the phrasal verb. The absence of a noun in *Mum* makes interpretation difficult. It is likely that either 'of' is scribal, or that a noun or pronoun which should have followed it has been lost. The corrector has made no emendation and as the line stands, it is unclear whether the magpies spoke out against the parrot or alongside it. If the latter, the lines may be a topical allusion to the Cirencester revolt in 1399–1400 (cf. notes to *Richard*, II.17). One of the rebels was Sir Ralph Lumley, whose heraldic charge was three parrots and the **papegeay** might be an illusion to this. The black and white colours of the magpie were sometimes taken to indicate clerical garb (*Brewer's Dictionary of Phrase and Fable*, p.692) and there were a number of clerics among the plotters. They were not executed for their part in the rebellion but were imprisoned for a short time in the Tower of London. This would fit the **caige** of line 153. The magpie and the parrot are often described as idle, chattering birds, Isidore of Seville, *De Etymologiarum*, *PL*, 82, p.462, and Pliny, *Natural History*, ed. H. Rackham (London, 1947), X.59.

157 clamour has the sense of a statement of a grievance or complaint, MED clamour (n) 2b) and **crye** as 'public outcry against a wrong', MED crie 4a).

161 cf. notes to *Richard*, IV.30.

162 so me God helpe cf. notes to *Richard*, II.91.

163 cf. note to line 86.

166 The MS reads 'warne'. The corrector emends to 'mynde' which restores alliteration to the line but it is likely that **mynne** was the original reading, cf. line 285.

165–170 suggest the suppression of religious dissent. The MS reads **y-blent** in line 169 which the corrector alters to **y-brent**. Blinding was not a legal punishment. This emendation, as Lawton notes (1981), p.788, produces a list of punishments very similar to the terms set out in the 1401 act of *De Haeretico Comburendo* which sought to suppress the expression of Wycliffite ideas. These made provision for fines, imprisonment, and in the case of a heretic who refused to abjure or who had relapsed, burning, *Rot.Parl*, III.466–7. The passage in *Mum* is in keeping with the typical account of persecution found in Wycliffite works, e.g., Matthew, 9/27; *Lanterne*, 43/7–15; *Jack Upland*, 65/244–50.

173 principaly of princes The burning of William Sawtre for refusing to abjure Lollard opinions in 1401 preceded the passing of *De Haeretico Comburendo*. It was necessary for Sawtre to be handed over from ecclesiastical to secular power in order for his execution to be effected. In the absence of a statute providing for this punishment his death took the form of a royal edict which applied specifically and solely to his case, McNiven, p.88.

174 The MS reads 'haulid' which the corrector alters to **halowid**. The emendation produces a line identical to *Richard*, III.228 and reminiscent of *Piers*, II.218: 'Over al yhonted and yhote trusse'. In both *Richard* and *Mum* the line describes the plight of a truthteller. In *Piers* it narrates the fate of Liar.

175 harmes cf. notes to line 75.

176 cf. the description of the oppressed people in *Richard*, II.124.

177–92 The imagery is similar to that used in some Lollard texts to describe the suppression of Truth, *EWS*, I.373–7; *Lanterne*, p.126/19ff.

179 The MS reads 'fro grayen' which the corrector alters to 'out of greue'. The apparent dittography can be emended by the simple substitution of **greue** for 'grayne'.

180 The corrector adds 'That droweth all to goodnesse and gouuernaunce after'.

186 graunt in the sense of promise or assurance, MED graunt 1d).

187–9 recall the punishments of lines 165–70.

196 tucke at your tabart To pay one back, see Whiting, p.574, who cites *Tale of Beryn*, 190: 'That I nol touch his taberd, somwhat of his care'.

205 terme of your lifes is a legal phrase meaning life tenancy, MED lif 2b) *Reg.Chichele in Cant.York.S.42* : 'Al my lond and rente I wul that my wyf . . . have terme of hir lyfe'.

206–10 The ordering of the king's household reflects persistent topical criticism. In the parliamentary wrangles over taxation between 1401–6, the expense of the household features as a significant obstacle to the Commons' readiness to agree to a grant. In the 1401 parliament, the Commons demanded that the stewards, treasurer and the controller of the household, all long-standing servants of the house of Lancaster, should be replaced. In 1404, the Commons succeeded in dismissing four prominent members of the king's household, including the king's confessor. In 1406, Sir John Tiptoft, the Speaker of the Commons, demanded that forty-three named aliens be expelled. The running of the household was placed in the hands of the newly-appointed council to reduce extravagance and inefficiency. Further, Henry was persuaded to accept Tiptoft, declared reformer of the household, as keeper of the wardrobe. Nevertheless, Henry maintained high wardrobe expenditure and as late as 1410, there were complaints in parliament about the failure of the household to pay its debts.

209 declarid To declare law or truth, Alford, p.42.

210 Rehershing cf. note to *Richard*, II.98. **rascaille** At the 1406 parliament, the Speaker made the charge that the household was full of 'raskaile' – disreputable persons, *Rot.Parl*, III.577. The poet appears to have known of the business of this assembly, cf. notes to line 120 and **rascaille** may refer to this accusation.

211–22 Criticism of the household concludes with the narrator's pledge of loyalty to the king. The focus on Henry's character asserts his personal right to the crown at a time when rumours were circulating which questioned Henry's claim to the throne, and promised Richard's imminent return, cf. notes to lines 1394–1405.

214–17 As D&S note, p. 109, Henry had won great renown in tournaments and in war. He was one of the leaders of the army which put de Vere to flight at Radcot Bridge in 1387, cf. notes to *Richard*, II.57. He attended the great jousts at Saint-

Inglevert in 1390 where the French agreed that he was the best of the English knights, overshadowing Richard who was also there. Between 1390–3, he went on the expedition of the Teutonic knights into Lithuania and to the Holy Land, Kirby, pp.28–40.

218 of the grettist alludes to Henry's noble lineage, suggesting that he was the rightful king by descent, cf. notes to *Richard*, III.92–3.

220 Of age At the assembly of estates where Henry laid claim to the crown in September 1399, Archbishop Arundel preached a sermon, taking out of their context the words with which God had appointed Saul to rule, 'Vir dominabitur populo', (The man shall govern the people.) (1 Samuel, 9:17). He stressed the word 'man' implying that Richard and other possible candidates were but children, *Rot.Parl*, III.423; cf. notes to *Richard*, I.119.

222 cf. *Piers*, Prol.65: 'Manye ferlies han fallen in a few yeres'.

223 cf. line 1417.

227 cf. notes to *Richard*, II.91.

228–31 The MS is torn; reconstruction follows D&S.

228 knoweth not hymself refers to the notion of 'nosce te ipsum', cf. notes to *Richard*, I.119.

229 is repeated at 765.

232 is Mum's first appearance in the fragment. Although the personification represents more than merely 'keeping mum', it is appropriate that his first words in the poem should be to silence the narrator in mid-sentence. His unannounced entry is typical of the poem's technique. For **matiere**, cf. notes to *Richard*, I.171. The altercation between Mum and the narrator has the flavour of a scholastic dispute. A number of terms from legal diction align the process of truthtelling with legal complaint.

234 not is supplied by the corrector. In the MS, only the first minim is visible.

237 cf. Greene, *Carols*, 401, B.I: 'Some (women) be nyse as a nonne hene', cited by Whiting, p.436.

239 The narrator's embarrassment surrenders narrative authority and allows his interlocutor to condemn himself out of his own mouth.

240 knytte there a knotte means to conclude, MED knitten 1f). Whiting, p.320, cites parallels from *York Plays*, 229/233–4; 'But Judas, a knott for to knytt / Wilte thou to thus comenaunt accorde' and *Townley Plays*, 59.106–8: 'Loke ye do it well in wrytt / And theron a knott knytt'. These parallels bring out the legal flavour of coming to a decision. The phrase recurs in *Mum* at line 693.

242 **disputeson** is a formal debate.

244 The MS reads **fittith**; the scribe has mistaken an 's' for an 'f'.

247 cf. notes to *Richard*, III.186.

250 **saise by the lappe** means to arrest, cf. notes to 127.

253 cf. line 403 and for the b-verse, notes to *Richard*, II.91.

254 **Oon myle and nomore waye** As D&S note p.110, this means 'for only twenty minutes'; cf. Chaucer, *A Treatise on the Astrolabe*, I.16/5: '5 of these degres maken a myle wey, and 3 mile-wei maken an houre'.

256 **contra** means an objection or denial, MED sense c).

259–60 As D&S note p.110, these lines represent a traditional formula; cf. *Wynnere and Wastoure*, 327–8: 'Ne es nothir kaysser ne kynge ne knyghte that the folowes / Barone ne bachelere ne beryn that thou loueste'; *Piers*, A.X.137–84: 'Kynges & knightes & alle kyne clerkis, / Barouns and burgeis & bondemen of tounes' and *Siege of Jerusalem*, 489–90: 'Her nys king nother knyght comen to this place, / Baroun ne burges ne burne that me folweth'.

261 cf. the treatment of Wit in *Richard*, III.209–43.

262 MS reads 'his' but **thy** is clearly required and I have emended.

263 **altercacion** means a charge or argument advanced in a disputation, MED sense b). **answere** has the legal sense of making a defence in response to a charge or accusation, Alford, p.6.

264 **fabelyng** is not used here in a positive sense (cf. notes to line 41) but in the sense of deceitful words. The word **fable** both as a noun and as a verb is common in Lollard texts, cf. *Crede*, 274 and 466; Matthew, 8/24; 16/22; 26/27; 59/11; Arnold, 6/36; 123/15; 274/30; *EWS*, I.557/30; 596/86; 641/61 and *Jack Upland*, 64/233.

266 **kepis the cloos** means to keep secret or hold in confidence, MED closen (v), 11b). The MS reads 'cafting'. As in line 244, the scribe has mistaken an 's' for an 'f'.

267 **putt the in prees** is to take action, bring forth a complaint, MED presse (n) 1a)d. Cf. the petitioning **prece** of line 119 and Lydgate, *Fall of Princes*, III.2644: 'A knyht . . . gan his compleynt for to putte in pres'.

268 passes not the bondes i.e. risk imprisonment for speaking out on the truth, cf. line 1251.

271 The charge places Mum among the **rascaille** of line 210.

272 The MS reads 'caue', presumably the result of a mechanical copying error, which the corrector has emended to **knaue**.

273 MS reads 'yif' which the corrector has emended to **yit**. **shame** carries legal overtones of defamation, Alford, p.68. The narrator argues that the corollary of refraining from possible personal affront is to allow the king to shame himself.

274 The quotation reads 'He who is able to reform [yet] secretly does not bother to reform, shares the blame of the perpetrator'. The saying is attributed in the *Speculum Christiani*, ed. G. Holmstedt (EETS OS 182 1933) to Gregory, see pp.63, 125, 137, 239. **amende** carries legal overtones, cf. notes to *Richard*, I.146.

276 Do Bette the first verbal echo of *Piers Plowman*.

278 mote suggests that the conversation has taken the form of legal pleading answered by counter-pleading, Alford, p.101.

280 opinion is a judgment, decision or verdict, MED opinioun 2b).

281 prouyd in the legal sense cf. notes to *Crede*, 247. **poyntz** in the legal sense, cf. notes to *Richard*, III.328. The corrector has supplied 'and feble' in place of MS y-nowe. Taking the lead from this alteration, D&S emended to [and fele], but the MS reading makes sense without emendation. I have not emended because the correction itself requires alteration to make sense of the line.

283 cf. *Piers*, V.606: 'Thow shalt see in thiselve Truthe sitte in thyne herte'.

286 colourable cf. notes to *Richard*, I.187. This word is found frequently in Wycliffite texts: Arnold, 227/11; 296/34; 305/6/25/28; *EWS*, I.439/34; II.5/99; 51/94; Matthew, 14/5; 74/27; 153/15 and *Jack Upland*, 69/342.

289 The Distichs of Cato were a collection of prose maxims (the *Parvus Cato*) and aphoristic couplets (the *Magnus Cato*) which date from the 4th century A.D. They formed a standard beginner's manual in medieval grammar schools and were studied after the *Ars minor* of Donatus, hence the narrator's reference to **youthe**, line 290.

291 The couplet is from the *Magnus Cato*: 'Rumores fuge, ne incipias nouus auctor haberi, / Nam nulli tacuisse nocet, nocet esse locutum', *Great Cato, The Minor Poems of the Vernon Manuscript*, ed. F. J. Furnivall (EETS OS 117 1901), p.565: 'Shun gossip, lest you start to be thought an originator of it, for it hurts no one to have kept quiet but it can hurt to have spoken'. The first line of this couplet is cited at line 1404. The citation of written authority to support the position of Mum signals the start of an anti-intellectual section of the poem. The narrator uses the trappings of intellectual discourse against itself. Scholastic enquiry either baffles him or provides written evidence to support Mum.

294 double The use of this word as an intensifier recalls *Richard*, I.144. For **doute** see notes to line 360.

295 travers a legal term, cf. note to line 57.

299 rehershyng cf. notes to *Richard*, II.98.

300 the pro and the contra cf. note to line 256.

304–5 cf. *Tale of Beryn* (EETS 105), 2666: 'Seneca & Sydrak & Salamonys sawis'. The reference to Seneca is neither to the Roman philosopher nor to the correspondent of St Paul, but to the author of the moral sentences which were written by Publius Syrus, in use as a school reading-book together with the *Distichs* of Cato, cf. notes to line 289. The reference to Solomon is to the Wisdom literature of the Bible.

308 bablid on thoo bokes i.e. read them aloud to himself.

310 matiere is a legal term, cf. notes to *Richard*, I.171.

311 The MS reads 'yette' but the sense requires 'iette' in the sense of fashion, cf. *Richard*, III.159. Chaucer's Pardoner thinks he rides 'al of the newe jet' (*General Prologue*, 682). The contrast in *Mum* between the new **iette** and the **homely vsage of the olde date** (312) recalls the antithesis between Wit and the courtiers in *Richard*, III.209–43, and anticipates the description of the beekeeper, lines 954–59.

313 recurs at line 377 with **goode** as the first alliterative stave. The corrector supplies **good** in 313. I have followed D&S's emendation.

314 glymsyng on the glose (cf. notes to 141) puns on glossing a text to clarify its meaning, and the practice of 'glosing', i.e. interpreting a text to yield whatever meaning is most advantageous. See further notes to 388.

317 The image recalls lines 52–3.

319 clergie in the sense of learning. This is the start of the narrator's quest to various classes and estates of society in order to determine which of Mum and the sothsegger has the mastery. The device recalls the travels of Will in *Piers*, especially between Passus VIII and XIII.

320 The narrator satirises university learning. The academics are at best incompetent in helping the narrator learn the truth. Wycliffite texts often expose the useless techniques of an academic education and argue that its learning is fatuous, Hudson (1988[1]), pp.225–6; cf. notes to following lines 321–391. **doute** is often used to ridicule university learning. The narrator's trip to the universities to **deme** his **doute** suggests that the premise of his quest is useless.

323 Orleance was famous because of its prestigious Faculty of Law.

324 in scole is often used in denigratory contexts in Wycliffite texts which criticise academic learning, Hudson (1988[1]), p.226.

325 stablid A Wycliffite accusation against the universities was that their establishment was bound up with the temporalities of the clergy, Hudson (1988[1]), p.225.

326–7 These lines are repeated at 396–7.

328 vij sciences i.e. the Liberal Arts. The basic university arts course consisted of two parts: the Trivium (grammar, rhetoric and logic) and the Quadrivium (geometry, arithmetic, music and astronomy). There may be some influence in this passage of *Piers*, X.149–217. **shewed** in the legal sense, cf. notes to *Richard*, IV.30.

329 D&S emend MS **dome** to 'dwere', citing the parallel of Hilton, *Scale of Perfection*, II.xi: 'There-fore fallen some in dowte and dwere'. However, the corrector marks MS 'and' to be replaced by **for**. This produces the sense: 'And how we maintained a decision in the absence of a better solution'. The reading fits the context and avoids conjectural emendation.

330 The root of **Sire Grumbald** is 'grame', meaning 'harm'. MED cites 'gromful' in the sense of 'terrifying'. Hence grammar glowers for anger.

331 congruly has the sense of a logical premise, here used as a term of derision.

332 Music is exempted from criticism. **accorde** chimes on the senses of 'come to an agreement' MED accorden 1a) and 'being harmonious, in tune', sense 5a). The harmony of music is often described as a reflection of God's harmonious creation of the universe, see for instance Chaucer, *The Parliament of Foules*, 59–63. Music and Mum must be contrary of **kynde** because Mum is a cause of disharmony and discord and works to defeat God's created order, see further lines 1111–1217.

334 MS reads 'y'. **the** must be intended though the definite article is redundant. There may be an alliterative stave missing from the b-verse.

336 accumbrid in the sense of 'vexed' MED 1a) and also in the sense of to be perplexed or baffled, sense 3; cf. *Richard*, IV.67 and *Mum*, line 381.

337 The MS reads 'on the skyes' in anticipation of the following half line. The corrector emends to 'with his make'. The preposition **of** produces a better reading and is adopted by D&S, cf. *Piers*, X.155: 'Thanne was I as fayn as fowel of fair morwe'.

338 skyes has the technical astronomical meaning of a sphere of the celestial realm, MED ski(e), 1b). There may also be a figurative sense of being other-worldly, i.e. completely impractical – an anticipation of the later proverbial idiom of having one's head in the clouds.

340 reasons plays on the grammatical sense of a proposition in logic, MED reson, sense 9b) and on the sense of a riddle or joke, MED 8d).

342 subtile shophister i.e. Logic. 'sophister' is always a derogatory term in Wycliffite texts, see Hudson (1988[1]), p.226 and Matthew, 6/8; *EWS*, I.348/77.

343 MS reads 'a' which the corrector emends to **the**, which makes better sense, cf. *Piers*, XII.121–2, 'Forthi I conseille alle creatures no clergie to dispise / Ne sette short by hir science, whatso thei don hemselve'. If the echo is deliberate, it is an ironic recall of Ymaginatif's defence of learning.

345 MS reads 'and couche was he neuer'. The corrector's emendation to **as choghe** makes sense of the line and produces a criticism of Logic in keeping with the narrator's frequent allusions to the natural characteristics of birds. A similar image is used in *Upland's Rejoinder*, where the arguments contained in *Friar Daw's Reply* are described as 'Chiding with blasfemie, on chytering as chowghes' (5).

347 cumpas puns on the sense of a compass for drawing circles, MED sense 5 and 1a), a crafty plan.

348 cf. *Piers* X.181, where Dame Studie tells Will that she taught children how to use measuring instruments, probably a T-square and a plumb line: 'And lerned hem level and lyne, though I loke dymme'. In *Mum* the technical language is used to obfuscate the argument.

351 cf. similar diction at *Richard*, II.8.

354 semely sage is a Doctor of Theology.

359 The comparison of Theology's chair to a throne and the unquestioned obedience of Liberal Arts to Theology in lines 356–8 may reflect the Wycliffite criticism that ecclesiastical obedience compromises allegiance to the secular king, *De Regibus*, p.10; *Jack Upland*, 57/72ff; cf. *Crede*, 650.

360-2 doctour of doutz cf. *EWS*, II.234/38; 'Bysyde lettre of this gospel may men moue doutus of scole; but me thinkuth now it is betture to touche lore of vertewys'.

366 cf. *Piers*, I.5–6: And seide, 'Sone, slepestow? Sestow this peple – / How bisie they ben aboute the maze?' The echo of Holy Church's words belittles the academics by comparing their labours to the general maze of the field of folk.

368 MS reads **better** which the corrector alters to **letter**. The emendation brings out more fully a criticism against the useless knowledge of academic reading. The clerics know the leaves of the book, the letter, i.e. the outward forms, but pass no further through to the spirit, or to the virtue, contained therein.

370 Wycliffite texts often mock speculative enquiries into the precise wording of Scripture which carried literalism to absurd lengths. Hudson (1988[1]) cites a number of examples, p.218–19, including 'what is meant by the words, "days shall come?" – do days have feet?', *EWS*, I.700/21. A Latin quotation to line 370 reads 'Non soli ... sunt ... mens imper ...' (Not only ... are ... mind).

372 The doctor's inadequacy illustrates the failure of academic discourse to answer serious questions.

376 Both the Wycliffites and their orthodox opponents claimed that their arguments were based solely on the true text of the Bible.

381 assoilled puns on absolution from sin MED 1a) and to solve or explain, sense 4a). Speedy absolution anticipates meeting the friars.

383 Sum of this semble i.e. friars. The Dominicans were particularly prominent in the universities, cf. note to *Crede*, 252.

386 wonen with lordes Often in anti-mendicant satire, the friars are rebuked for seeking the company of rich temporal lords; e.g., Gower, *Vox*, IV.829–30, where the friars are said to be able to gain access to the highest houses and where the court so much recognises the friar as one of their company that it renders the decrees of the bishop null and void. See also *Jack Upland*, 64/226–32; Chaucer's Hubert in *The General Prologue*, 215–16, 248; *Piers*, XI.54–8 and *Crede*, 364–9; 770–4. The line may be an ironic reference to Luke 9:2. Christ's instructions to his apostles as they are sent out into the world were taken as a mandate for apostolic poverty. Instead of going out into the world 'to preach the gospel and heal the sick', friars seek the company of rich men, cf. *EWS*, II.9/84ff.

387 croke puns on the senses of a bishop or abbot's crozier, MED crok 2b) and a deception or misleading stratagem 4c); cf.1165 where the crook is likened to the devil's hook. St Nicholas is the patron saint of learning.

388 glose cf. notes to 141 and 376 and *Piers*, Prol.58–60: 'I fond there freres, alle the foure ordres / Prechynge the peple for profit of the wombe; / Glosed the gospel as hem good liked'.

389 plaisance of wordes cf. Hubert in Chaucer's *General Prologue* who is unparalleled amongst the four orders for his 'daliaunce and fair langage' (211).

393 fundament is often used in Wycliffite discussion to question the foundation of the monastic and fraternal orders because they are distinct from the founding of the true apostolic church, see note to *Crede*, 47.

395 frayned cf. note to line 84. The narrator proceeds as though he were prosecuting a case against the friars.

396 For the legal diction, see notes to *Richard*, I.171. These two lines repeat those at 326–7.

397 MS reads 'shotte' which D&S emend to **shorte**. The b-verse at 327 reads: **in fewe shorte wordes** and supports emendation here.

398 couple The friars habitually went about in pairs. In *Piers*, VIII, Will encounters two friars to whom he puts his questions about Dowel. For the legal meaning of **construed**, see notes to *Richard*, III.327.

399 accorded A legal term meaning here to concur in a judgment, Alford, p.1.

402 The friars' desire for extravagant houses (financed by the dues exacted from ministering the sacraments) is a staple of anti-fraternal satire. See notes to *Crede*, 155–219.

405 skiles logical arguments to prove a point, MED skile (5).

408 poynt in the sense of accusation, cf. notes to *Crede*, 547. Thus the four reasons for supposedly exempting the friars from criticism turn into legal charges against them.

408–413 Criticism of how the friars usurped the role of the parish priest in preaching is found in a number of works, e.g., *The Summoner's Tale*, 1715ff; *Vox*, IV.900–910 and Fitzralph, *Defensio Curatorum*, 75/7–18. In 1382 and 1401, legislation passed by parliament required intending preachers other than the priest incumbent in his own parish to obtain a diocesan licence, *Rot. Parl*, III.124 and 467. Wycliffite works attribute the prevention of 'symple prestis' from preaching to the friars, and accuse them either of instituting licences or circumventing the legislation by buying them, *SEWW*, 119/9–11; Matthew, 57/24; 85/11, 106/6ff and Arnold, 375/29–31. These lines could refer to Arundel's *Constitutions* although D&S, p.xxiv and Lawton (1981), p.790 are not convinced of a precise topical referent. Under consideration from 1407 and finally issued in 1409, the first two constitutions stipulated that no one should preach in the vernacular or Latin without a proper licence and that licences were to be given only to those whose orthodoxy had been assured by examination. Anyone admitting an unlicensed preacher would be excommunicated, *Conciliae Magnae Britanniae et Hiberniae*, ed. D. Wilkins (London 1737), III.314–19. Not only were these provisions extremely damaging to Lollard preachers but in March 1409, apparently because of fraternal complaint, Arundel issued a letter to the provincial clergy in which he emphasised that the friars should be exempted from the terms of the constitutions, Wilkins, III.324. **saue seely poure freres** (410) could refer to this exemption; it is a more pointed jibe than saying that the friars instituted preaching licences or were able to buy them. There are Wycliffite criticisms of Arundel's *Constitutions* in *Lanterne*, 17/26; 100/1.

411 The MS lacks an alliterative stave in the a-verse. The corrector supplies **deede**.

413 good in the senses of goodness, MED god n (2) 1a) and material possesions, sense 12.

414 The MS reads 'man is', presumably a mechanical copying error, which D&S emend. A standard criticism against the friars

was that they usurped the role of the parish priest in hearing
confession because the priest alone had cure of souls in his
parish, cf. notes to *Crede*, 462.

416–22 are a textual crux. Lawton (1981) states that their
sense is irrecoverable. D&S emend the MS reading **manieres**
(417) to 'names' following the gloss of the corrector. They
argue, pp.112–13, that the 'sense is clearly that the friars first
gave the Lollards their names and now they must have the same
name given to them'. The corrector has also marked **folowid** for
correction, but his gloss is torn away. D&S interpret it as 'to
give in baptism' from OE fullwian. The lines contain a topical
reference to the hanging of a group of Franciscan friars at
Tyburn in 1402 for their part in spreading treasonable rumours
that Richard was still alive and was returning to wrest his throne
from the usurping Henry, *Eulogium*, III.389–91. *Upland's
Rejoinder* also refers to this event in a passage critical of the
friars, 271–2. **folowid** and **shewed** (418) are used in their legal
senses, to prosecute a case at law, MED folwen 5c) and to
lodge a plea before court, see note to *Richard*, IV.30. Thus the
friars were the first to prosecute Lollard behaviour at law but
since then they have themselves been the subject of a legal plea
before court. The concluding proverb uses the word **dome**,
judgment (422) and states that a judgment passed on the
Lollards has rebounded on the friars' own heads. In 1382, the
Council of Blackfriars condemned ten of Wyclif's propositions
as heretical, cf. note to *Crede*, 531–2. In 1402, the friars were
themselves subject to legal punishment for the crime of treason.

417 Lollardz must refer to the Wycliffites at this date. The
word has a confused history through its closeness to 'loller', cf.
note to *Crede*, 532. For full discussion, see Scase, pp.147–60.

419 cf. *Piers*, XII.190–1: 'That hath take fro Tybourne
twenty strong theves, / Ther lewed theves ben lolled up – loke
how thei be saved'.

421 cf. *Richard*, I.152.

422 MS reads **That the**, which D&S emend to 'The'. Variations on this proverb, that judgment, or cursing, returns to
one's own door, are recorded in Whiting, p.140, e.g., Chaucer,
The Parson's Tale, 619. The proverb appears in English in John
of Bromyard's *Summa praedicantium*: 'Churl yewe then dom/
and efte bi this door ist com' ('Nocumentum', N.IV.), see
S. Wenzel, *Mum and the Sothsegger*, lines 421–, *ELN*, 14

(1976), 87–90. The Latin quotation, 'to suffer the same law which you have proposed. Seneca' is not from Seneca, but from *Little Cato*, cf. *Minor Poems of the Vernon MS*, ed. Horstmann, EETS os 98, p.560. It is also quoted by Bromyard in a development of the passage in which the English proverb is cited. Bromyard also attributes it to Seneca. In *Mum*, the citation is marked to stand at 420. I have placed it at 422 where it more naturally belongs. Some of the letters are illegible because the margins are torn.

423 tale This continues the legal accusation against the friars, cf. notes to *Richard*, I.189.

424 grey freres i.e. the Franciscans.

426–7 cf. *Crede*, 298–300.

429–30 cf. *Crede*, 31.

431 obedience ... ordre are frequent in Wycliffite texts as part of a diction which inveighs against private religions because they were not instituted by Christ, cf. notes to *Crede*, 45. The emphasis on 'obedience' in Wycliffite texts shows that the fraternal orders are more concerned to obey their own rules than to comply with the laws given by God.

434 The sense of **poynt** as a legal accusation is emphasised by **fundid** in the sense of furnishing witness or proof, cf. notes to *Richard*, III.111 and Alford, p.59.

435–41 limitour cf. notes to *Crede*, 597.

437 parcelle-mele has the legal sense of an allotted share, as of an estate, Alford, p.109, but the suggestion that the friars' division of the countryside is legal is ironic.

440 leue has the sense of formal permission MED (2). leue (n) 1a). It jibes at the friars' special laws.

442–3 courtoys is related to the noun **curtesie**, a sum of money or other recompense which is given above the stated terms of a contract or agreement, Alford, p.41. The friars' 'curtesie' is inverted. What is given above the terms of the agreement is given not by the friars, but to them. The friars give one knife and receive two, cf. *The Orders of Cain*: 'For if he give a wyf a knyfe / That cost bot penys two, / Worthe ten knyues, so mot I thryfe, / he wyl haue er he go', Robbins, 65/69–72. The use of the legal terms **courtoys** and **chaungen** in the sense of an exchange of goods for profit, Alford, p.52, serves to define the friars' criminality. Their sense of **charite** has nothing to do with holy love.

444 pille means robbery, Alford, p.115. In legal terms **pille** and **parcelle** are contradictory, cf. notes to 437.

448 with thaire fayre chere cf. *General Prologue*, 211; 253–5 and Gower, *Vox*, IV.1065–8 where the friars are described as colouring their words and stuffing people's ears with the sound of their golden phrases.

451 The friars are often accused of gluttony, cf. note to *Crede*, 220–6.

455 D&S emends MS **Forto** to 'For to'. There is no correction marked at this point and I have retained the MS reading; cf. *Crede*, 216–18 for similar criticisms of the friars' begging.

456 MS reads 'balle his heede'. The corrector has written 'liste balle with hus browe'. Following D&S, I have adopted 'with' and 'browe' from the correction to improve the sense of the line and restore alliteration to the a-verse.

461–5 The sacrament of confession is not questioned. The narrator merely criticises its abuse, cf. *Crede*, 9–10 and 131–3; *Piers*, III.35–64; *Vox*, IV.863–72; Fitzralph, *Defensio Curatorum*, pp.51–3.

465 gouuernen the grete cf. *Crede*, 364–5.

466 tale and **intent** are used in their legal senses, cf. notes to *Richard*, I.189 and I.79.

468 MS omits **for** which the sense requires.

469 The Latin quotation is from Proverbs, 3:9: 'Honour the Lord with thy substance, and give him of the first of all thy fruits'.

473 sauce here as a curative or preventive preparation, in contrast to the **spicerie** of 479.

476–86 The attack widens to include bishops and secular lords.

479 spicerie spices to uses at bribes cf. *Crede*, 301.

482–3 spores puns on the cross shape of the spurs, anticipating **crosse** in the next line as the cross that was engraved on the backs of coins, cf. line 66. **while the crosse walketh** alludes to the Good Friday ceremony of the Veneration of the Cross, cf. *Piers*, XVIII.431: 'And crepeth to the cros on knees and kisseth it for a juwel'.

484–6 accuse the secular lords of abandoning their responsibilities. They interfere in lawsuits and fraudulently acquire wealth through maintenance, cf. notes to *Richard*, II.4ff.

489 cumpaignye has the sense of a band of conspirators or a gang, Alford, p.33, and places the fraternal orders on the wrong side of the law.

490 Martyrdom is encouraged in some Lollard texts, see notes to lines 630–41. The narrator contrasts the friars unfavourably with the Lollards, cf. 415–21. The MS reads 'viij', a copying error for **vij**, cf. 683, 796. Confessors and martyrs are two classes of saints in the Liturgy, cf. quotation of *Piers* at line 830.

491–2 D&S read 'penanche' but the original scribe has crossed out 'he' and inserted 'e' over the correction. MS omits **thay** which the corrector supplies. The charge is reminiscent of the scene in *Piers*, XIII.64–84, where the Doctor of Divinity (who is a friar) exposes his hypocrisy in preaching on penance.

492 MS reads 'not' with a space after it which has been crossed out. **in no** has been added above the line.

493 clothing of conscience A frequent Wycliffite target is the supposed sanctity of the fraternal habit, cf. notes to *Crede*, 549–52 and 608.

494–504 trace the genealogy of the friars back to Cain, the first outlaws, cf. note to 489, and note to *Crede*, 486. Richard Fitzralph, Archbishop of Armagh, was a vigorous opponent of the friars. He linked Cain with the friars in one of his London sermons in 1357, saying that the friars were hypocrites who followed the errors of Balaam and the way of Cain, see Penn R. Szittya, *The Antifraternal Tradition in Medieval England* (Princeton 1986), p.129. Wycliffite texts often cite Fitzralph as a learned authority, or even a saint, e.g., Arnold, 281/13, 412/22, 416/20 and Matthew, 128/26; cf. notes to 1352.

494 fundre see note to 393.

499 withoute titil Here without an abbreviation over the 'y' in Caym to stand for the 'm'. The acrostic must be written out in full.

501 MS omits **for**, supplied by D&S. The following three lines all have **for thees**.

503 The French Dominicans were known as Jacobines because they built their first convent near the church of St Jacobus which had been given to them for their use.

504 The Minors are the Franciscans, so called because of their claim to humility, cf. note to *Crede*, 33.

505 The corrector adds the line 'Hit shal not greue a good frere thogh gilty be amendid'. It is hard to integrate this with the narrator's remarks because the very foundation of the fraternal orders has been questioned.

510 The corrector adds 'of sum and of certayn I say not of alle', cf. 229 and 765. Some of the most radical comments about the friars' existence have been toned down. It is unclear whether this is the poet's retractive work or that of an interpolator who took exception to the stringency of some of the remarks.

511 **deme deuely** judge according to due process of law.

512 The sexual licence of the friars is a staple of orthodox anti-fraternal satire, see *Crede*, 77–85. Because the friars cannot fit into the accepted ranks of society, they are outlaws.

513–15 The MS reads 'iustice' in 514. The corrector alters to **ioustes**, which restores sense to the line. Lollard teaching often maintained that it was unlawful to slay any man in any circumstance because it broke the Sixth Commandment, cf. *SEWW*, 20/37–40. Priests, especially, should not shed blood, cf. notes to 702–13. Lines 514–15, may recall Bishop Despenser's Crusade of 1383, which was attacked with hostility by Lollard sympathisers long after it had ceased to be a topical event. **proue** and **poyntz** are used in their legal senses.

516–20 pass judgment on the friars and sentence them. **declarid** (518) has the legal sense of 'declaring law', Alford, p.42 and **sentence** the legal verdict in a court case, MED 1a). Lollard texts often use **revle** (516) to show that the regulations of private religions are contrary to Christ's rulings e.g., *EWS*, I. 265/38ff. **ordre** (518) is used in Lollard texts with similar import, cf. note to 431. The judgment on the friars is supported by reference to external authorities. The margin is torn and the first letters of the Latin quotations are lost. The second is from Psalm 68:29, 'Let them be blotted out of the book of the living and with the just let them not be written' (a citation used in *Piers*, VI.75–77 of the wastrels). The first is from the hymn for the Vespers of All Saints, 'Placare Christi servulis'. It reads, 'he carries off the treacherous people (Of the believers in the Last Things)'. These quotations spell out that the **oon place** (518) to which the friars are condemned is hell. In light of this, the collocation of **hooly churche ne heuene** in 517 is suggestive of Lollard teaching on grace which maintained that true holy church was not the material church on earth, but the congregation of faithful souls predestined for salvation. The friars are outside the earthly church because they adhere to a rule not of Christ's making, and, as a consequence, they are excluded from the congregation in heaven.

522 'pear' often appears in proverbial contexts to mean 'a worthless item', cf. *Richard*, I.73 and Hoccleve, *Regement*, 2317: 'All thi labour schal nat be worth a pere'.

525 **indifferent to deme the sothe** MED cites a number of legal documents from the parliamentary Rolls, municipal records and court hearings where 'indifferent' means unbiased towards one side or another, e.g. *Proceedings of the Privy Council*, 3:219: 'It semeth expedient that suche were maad shirriefs as were of name and fame true and indifferent between the King and the poeple and alle parties'.

529–30 **alied** is an alliance between parties, cf. *Richard*, III.31, and **partie** is a group of persons involved on the same side in a lawsuit, Alford, p.110.

532 **chalanged** means brought charges against, Alford, p.23.

533 **leste I laught were** either in the sense of being caught in their malicious clutches or as a reference to the friars' propensity for forcible recruitment, a staple of anti-fraternal satire, e.g., *Defensio Curatorum*, pp.55–6 and *Vox*, IV.981ff.

534 cf. note to 442.

535 The corrector adds the following lines: 'Yit gesse I that good men of gray and of blake / And of the white witerly I wote wel been many / But dan conuent the compaignie as my credo techeth / Cunen mo crokes than Crist euer taught.' These lines exculpate the Franciscans, Dominicans and Carmelites from criticism so that only the Augustinians are blameworthy. These lines are unlikely to be the work of the poet, cf. note to 505. D&S note, p.115, that they appear to refer to *Crede* but there, the Augustinians, along with the Franciscans and Carmelites are at one point seen to be less blameworthy than the Dominicans, see note to 506–14.

537 **abbeys of Augustyn** Houses of Augustinian canons.

538 **parfitely y-closid** Given the boorish behaviour of the canons which follows, **parfitely** is ironic. Wycliffite texts state that religious enclosure is contrary to God's law, e.g., *EWS*, I.328/55–9.

542–5 employ diction often used in Wycliffite texts to question the foundation of enclosed private religions, e.g., **fund**, cf. note to 393, and **ground**, note to *Crede*, 506–14.

543 **do beste of alle** is a reference to *Piers*. The Latin

quotation reads: 'They have turned charity into cupidity. Wisdom'. I have not been able to trace any verse in Wisdom which matches this. Given the context in *Mum*, the most appropriate is 19:13: 'For they exercised a more detestable inhospitality than any. Others indeed received not strangers unknown to them: but these brought their guests into bondage that had deserved well of them'. It is possible that the Latin quotation in *Mum* is a very free paraphrase of this verse. Some of the other marginal biblical quotations are paraphrases rather than direct quotations, e.g., 1481 and 1530.

544 MS reads 'of' which D&S retain. The corrector alters 'of' to 'as' which improves the sense of the line. I have followed their emendation of 'fundacions' to **fundacion** because of the singular verb in the next line.

547 A similar charge is made in *Crede* against the Franciscans (123–8) and against the Augustinians (319–27), cf. also *Piers*, III.48–50.

549 MS reads 'sepid' in error for **sopid**.

552 cf. Wit's banishment from court in *Richard*, III.238.

555 **pluralite** was the holding of two or more benefices with cure of souls concurrently by one person. In theory, this pluralism and non-residency was forbidden or restricted by canon law, as in the constitution *De Multa* of the Lateran Council of 1215 and the constitution *Execrabilis* of John XXII (1317), Pantin, p.39. In practice pluralism was widespread, Pantin, pp.35–8 and unless they had papal dispensation, pluralists technically faced excommunication, *Jacob's Well* (EETS 115 1900), p.18/11. A typical pluralist would hold one prebend in a cathedral or collegiate church together with one parish church with cure of souls. Such benefices were 'compatible' and needed no papal dispensation, Pantin, p.37. **prisely** is ironic, cf. note to 669.

556 **questions** has the sense of legal proceedings against, MED sense 5a).

559 **intremitte** in the sense of intervening between two interested parties in a lawsuit, cf. *King Alisaunder*, ed. G. V. Smithers (EETS 227 1952): 4020–1: 'Up stood Sir Mark of Rome / And entremeted of this dome'.

560 MS reads 'racke' which the corrector alters to **cracche**. D&S note, p.116 that 'cracche' is used of a horse's manger in *William of Palerne*, 3233.

565 passing th'assise – above the legal amount, MED, assise, 4a).

566–8 The offering at Mass was supposed to be divided into three parts : for the support of the parish priest ; for the upkeep of the church fabric, and for the relief of the poor, see notes to 657–62. The narrator suggests that priests share with the poor by putting all the Mass offering in the bottom of their purses, i.e. not sharing at all, cf. *PlTale*, 167 where the Pelican accuses priests of excommunicating in order to put pennies in their purses. **bottume** (567) is added by the corrector.

569 The Latin quotation reads : 'do not put gold or silver in your pockets' which is a paraphrase of Matthew, 10:9. The corrector adds 'Matthei 10 capitulo'. The text is part of Christ's apostolic instructions to the disciples whom he sent out into the world to preach. The priests' possession of gold and silver contravenes this injunction. Their riding about has nothing in common with the preaching zeal of the first apostles, cf. 664 and 1371 and *Piers*, IV.124: 'Tyl bisschopes bayardes ben beggeres chambres'. The reference to **Belial** in *Mum*, 568 substitutes a demonic authority for Christ's mandate, cf. the criticism of the priests' riding around in *The Simonie*, A.120–1.

570–5 recall some of Will's bewildered wanderings in *Piers*, e.g., XIII.1–4, XV.1–3, XVIII.1–4.

574–5 recur at 1101–2; cf. *Piers*, XVIII.66: 'Shal no wight wite witterly who shal have the maistrie'.

576–7 cf. *Piers*, XV.3–6: And so my wit weex and wanyed til I a fool weere; / And some lakked my lif – allowed it few – / And leten me for a lorel and looth to reverencen / Lordes or ladies or any lif ellis'.

579 Mum is cast as a bishop, making the point that the authority of the institutionalised church silences truthtelling, cf. notes to 409–10 and 1341–7. **manachid** has the sense of illegal intimidation, cf. 485 and *Richard*, II.337. A Wycliffite sermon interprets the two peaks of the bishop's mitre as the horns of the devil, *EWS*, II.172/148–54.

580 MED records only one other example of **cusky**, *Tale of Beryn*, 423: 'they dronk & made an ende; / And eche man droughe to cusky, to sclepe & take his rest'.

584 a baron i.e. God. A line has been added at line 589 by the corrector, apparently to clarify the identity of the lord : 'The high maker of molde and man with his handes'.

585 among the ix ordres i.e. of angels.

586–90 claim God's protection for the narrator and state that He authorises his words. **saufconduyt, mayntene no matiere, amende, showe, colour, bringe hit to ende** are all terms of legal diction. The narrator claims that the case he is prosecuting is not his own but God's. God's safeconduct prevents him from constructing a case of his own making, or a fictitious argument. Instead God uses him as a mouthpiece to **showe**, i.e. plead for a suitor, Alford, p.144, so that the case can then be laid before court. Observing the correction at 589, D&S emended the first **showe** to 'sende fro'. But the two **showes** can be seen as rhetorical emphasis which makes a legal distinction; the verb is first used to mean to plead for a suitor and then secondly, to lay a case before court, Alford, p.143.

588 I have emended MS 'hit' to **that** because a relative pronoun is required. The narrator is bidden to prosecute God's case, not a fabrication of his own making.

594–5 D&S emended MS **ballid** to 'bablid', but there is no correction marked and the reading is tenable if **ballid** is understood in the sense of 'beat', cf. 456. It describes the sounds of men and bells clashing together. D&S query **belles** as a scribal error for 'burdes', p.116. In Lollard ecclesiology preaching is primary. The saying of elaborate ceremonies such as Mass or matins is spiritually redundant because the ritual is unintelligible, e.g. *Lanterne of Light*, 50/29ff: 'But preiars in the fendis chirche maken miche noise mumling with her lippis, thei reche neuir what, so that men preise fast her feyned occupacioun as Crist seith in his gospel'. **ballid** and **momeling**, together with the conjunction of **burnys** and **belles**, belittle the institutionalised services of the established church.

599–612 The priest's zeal to demand his tithes contrasts strongly with Chaucer's Parson, who is not only 'ful looth to cursen for his tithes', but actually gives money to his poor parishioners, *General Prologue*, 486–90. Sermon writers criticise the diligence of priests in exacting their tithes, see Owst, *Literature and Pulpit in Medieval England* (Cambridge, 1926), pp.249, 253 (n.6), 260–1 and cf. *John Myrc's Instructions for Parish Priests*, ed. E. Peacock (EETS OS 31 1868), 356–59.

601 *Jacob's Well* ed., A. Brandeis (EETS OS 115 1900), lists two kinds of tithes, those from lands and those from possessions, p.37/13.

603 The corrector supplies **plummes** for 'notes' which D&S incorporate. I have followed their emendation because the restoration of an alliterative stave to the b-verse is clearly marked by the corrector.

604 The corrector has added three more lines: 'of lyke and of lynne seede of lambes and egges / of coltes and of calues that the cow lycketh / of benes and of boutre that bele doo make'.

605 cf. *Piers*, A.VII.278: 'Chibollis, & chiriuellis & ripe chiries manye'.

610 MS omits **what**, supplied by D&S on the basis of the corrector's note: 'and . . . increceth : or what so ye wynne'.

612–13 cf. *Jacob's Well*, 37/6–8: 'Ye owyn to tythen of all manere of godys trewly gett; for the tenth part ther-of is dewe to god'.

613–16 cf. the list of food in *Piers*, VI.292–301 where the poor people attempt to poison Hunger. The episode is dominated by ideas of gluttony and shirking, which are relevant to the greediness of the idle priest depicted in *Mum*. Line 616 suggests that the priest gleans where he has not sown. Polemics against tithings are prolific in Wycliffite texts, e.g., Matthew, 57/6–11; 78/6–8, 116/14–16; Arnold, 126/34–6; 176/19–26. One of their central themes is that parishioners have the right to withhold tithes from sinful priests, e.g., Matthew, 132/14–25. This is not stated in *Mum*, but the suggestion that the priest should earn his tithes through his deeds shows a more radical attitude to tithing than that in a manifestly orthodox text such as *Jacob's Well*: 'ye schul tythe truly, for to kepe you sekerly out of the artycle of cursying', 37/5–6. Church law made the payment of tithes obligatory. It was not conditional on the deserts of the recipient, see further Hudson (1988[1]), pp.342–5.

617 sorowe on the sillable MED 'sillable' glosses this as 'to refuse to speak'.

621 D&S read 'leue' for MS **lene. lene** has the sense of 'give permission to' MED lenen (3) v, 1a). The line suggests that canon law is an arcane knowledge which confers power on the clergy because the laity are not able to question it. At line 1621, the narrator cites canon law approvingly, but the apparent inconsistency of criticising canon law, and yet using its texts as authorities, is frequent in Wycliffite texts, see further Hudson (1988[1]), pp.375–82.

622 cf. the similar line at *Richard*, III.90.

623 The corrector adds 'to hire of hire holy nesse for harvest is sake'.

626 recurs at 654.

630–41 Instead of being martyrs for the love of Christ, the priests are allies of Mum. Mum was cast as a bishop in 579 which suggests that martyrs are not to be found in the established church hierarchy in the narrator's own time. **now** in line 635 contrasts the early martyrs of the Christian church with the corrupt practices of the contemporary clergy listed in lines 643–50. Lollard texts often encouraged martyrdom, e.g., *EWS*, I.625/68–9; Matthew, 21/25ff; 452/17; Arnold, 179/25ff; pp.184–5 and *PlTale*, 248, which states that although Christ bade his priests not to slay others, they should not themselves be afraid to die. The emphasis on preaching **pure trouthe** in line 641 is central to Wycliffite definitions of the priesthood, e.g., Matthew, pp.56–7; 111/9ff;188/1; Arnold, 130/16ff; 145/9; 202–3; *Lanterne*, 55/10ff; *Jack Upland*, 64/232ff.

633 querele cf. note to *Richard*, III.327 and **question**, note to 556.

637 laudate The first of the seven canonical Hours was Lauds, which always contained Psalms 148–50, beginning with 'Laudate'. The term means novice, cf. 1359.

639 D&S read 'derue' for MS **derne**. The MS reading has the sense of 'profound', MED derne 2a).

641 MS reads 'were' at the end of the line which makes no sense. The corrector supplies **euer**. The quotation reads 'for the sake of truth, dismiss all intimacies'. This is not an exact biblical quotation but may be a summary of the arguments in Matthew, 10:37–9, where, having given his apostles instructions on their mission, Christ bids his true followers to love him more than any family attachment. He concludes that anyone who does not take up his cross and follow him is not worthy of him, and that whoever loses his life for his sake will find it.

643 Gower criticises the splendid vestments of the clergy in *Vox*, III.1329–30 and in *Piers*, Anima urges the clergy to leave the 'lecherie of clothyng', XV.103.

644 riding aboute i.e. not staying in their parish to minister to their parishioners in contrast to Chaucer's exemplary Parson who: 'dwelte at hoom and kepte wel his folde', *General Prologue*, 512, and cf. the condemnation of the fine horses of the clergy in *PlTale*, 132.

645 cf. *Piers*, Prol.95–6: 'And some serven as servauntz lordes and ladies, / And in stede of stywardes sitten and demen'. In *Vox*, III.137–40, Gower observes that no man can serve two masters yet priests, who are in the service of God, serve an earthly king and wait in attendance on him.

647 double dees Daises raised above the ordinary height. Gower remarks in *Vox*, III.111–12 that priests hold such gluttonous banquets that the huge table is scarcely large enough for their 'moderate' appetites.

648 Gower, in *Vox*, III.104, comments that priests hold the drinking goblet in greater esteem than the communion chalice.

649 Gower contrasts the law of the Gospel with the lucrativeness of ecclesiastical law, *Vox*, III.261–5. In Wycliffite texts, there is frequent criticism of the clergy's involvement in lawsuits, e.g., Matthew, 61/1ff; 63/8ff; 132/1ff; 139/25ff; 182–3; 436/27ff. In *Piers*, Anima notes that whilst charity used to dwell with the priests of Holy Church, now avarice has the keys and: 'kepeth for his kynnesmen / And for his *seketoures* and hir servaunts and som for his children', XV.247–8.

651 Mann notes, p.63, that one of the most prominent themes in estates treatment of priests was that they should set an example by their works, cf. *Piers*, XV.108–110: 'Lothe were lewed men but thei youre loore folwede / And amenden hem that thei mysdoon, moore for youre ensaumples / Than for to prechen and preven it noght'.

652 cf. *Richard*, II.53.

653 sentence ... shewe Having rehearsed a list of charges against the priests, the narrator sets himself up as their legal judge, cf. note to 516–20.

654 cf. 626.

655 MS reads 'light' which D&S alter to **lith**. A verb is required, cf. *Piers*, VII.109: 'In two lynes it lay, and noght a lettre moore'. The narrator pits his 'lewed'ness against the learning of the church and offers his own explanation of how the tithes should be distributed. This recalls the interchange between Piers and the priest, where the 'little lettered' Piers challenges the inadequate teaching proffered by the representative of ecclesiastical authority.

656 hireth The narrator offers a rival sermon to that of the parish priest.

657–62 The division of the tithes seems entirely orthodox, except for the conjunction of **ouerplus** and **ornementz** in 659. According to Lollard teaching, the priest should have no **ouerplus**, let alone **ouerplus ouer**. Many tracts, citing 1 Timothy 6:8: 'But having food and wherewith to be covered, with these we are content', state that any surplus should be given straight to the poor, e.g., Arnold, 475/30. See also Matthew, 132/14–25. Wimbledon's *Sermon* criticises the clergy for wasting in their proud houses 'wagis that were sufficiaunt to hem' the 'ouerplus that nedy men sholde be susteyned by', ed. I. K. Knight (Pittsburgh, 1967), 76/248–55. One Wycliffite text outlines a distribution of tithes similar to that in *Mum*. It includes the provision for 'ornementz of the churche', but the author explicitly states that this distribution is not to be followed because the provision upholds 'mennus law', not 'Goddus lawe', Matthew, 433/5–9. Church ornaments are often criticised in Wycliffite texts *Lanterne* lists ornaments from bells to steeples, 41/31–35 and for other criticisms see Matthew, 69/4–17; 91/27–34; Arnold, 462/22f. *Mum*'s suggestion, to use the surplus of the tithing for church decoration, would have resonated ironically for readers accustomed to Wycliffite thought.

657 God-is men i.e. the poor, cf. *Piers*, III.71: 'Or to greden after Goddes men whan ye gyve doles'.

662 D&S substitute 'lite' for MS **fewe** which is feasible and restores some alliteration to the line. There is, however, no correction at this point and since the MS reading makes sense I have not followed their emendation.

663–4 As D&S note, p.118, there is no obvious source for this text. They cite a possible parallel in Isaiah, 2:7 'Their land is also full of silver and gold, and there is no end of their treasures'.

665 two whete cornes cf. *Pardoner's Tale*, 863: 'the montance of a corn of whete'.

666 the two dooles i.e. both God's share, which should go to the poor, and their own.

668 Gower observes in *Vox*, III.1385–6 that a priest who has advanced in rank through simony having once worn a coat that would not have reached his thighs, is able to wear one that warms his ankles and caresses his feet.

669 The clergy's desire for benefices is seen in *Piers*, C.III.33, where Mede promises the clerks that she will buy them benefices 'pluralite to haue' in return for their support. *Vox*, III.1347–9 states that if a curate cannot live sinfully in one cure then he wants another. Then, having corrupted the first benefice, he proceeds to defile the second. Moreover, priests are more concerned to construe 'mark' as a money rather than Mark as the second Gospel, III.997–8. The precise opposition between benefices and bibles is seen in a Wycliffite text: 'for though thei kunnen not o poynt of the gospel ne whiten what thei reden, yit wolen thei take a fat benefice with cure of mannus soule', Matthew, 153/3. Reading the Gospel is of central importance in Wycliffite thought. It is striking that this is the activity singled out by the *Mum*-narrator as the antithesis of striving after benefices.

673 mayntenance i.e. behave in the manner of secular lords.

675 cf. *The Owl and the Nightingale*, ed. E. G. Stanley (Manchester, 1972) where the Nightingale responds to the Owl's latest charge with the words: 'Thu schalt falle, the wei is slider' (956).

678 cf. *Richard*, IV.86.

681 cf. 844 and *Piers*, III.168: 'Swiche a maister is Mede among men of goode'.

682 men in the sense of 'vassals', Alford, p.96.

685 MS reads 'As' at the beginning of the line, presumably a mechanical copying error which D&S emend to **And**.

687–92 cf. Hoccleve, *Regement*, 2941–7: 'But certes fauel hath caght so sad foote / In lordes courtes he may naght thens slyde; / Who com or go, algate abyde he moote; / His craft is to susteyne ay the wrong syde, / And fro vertu his lorde to devide' / And, for soth sawes ben to lordes lothe, / Noght wol he soth seyn, he hath made his oth'. The poem entitled *Truth is Unpopular*, begins: 'A man that xuld of trewthe telle, / With grete lordys he may not dwelle; / In trewe story, as klerkes telle, / Trewthe is put In low degre' (Robbins, 59/1–4).

692 that wil doo drawe i.e. which way desire will tend. D&S, p.118–19, suggest a possible emendation here, to 'the doo wil drawe', a metaphor from deer-hunting. They cite as analogy, line 1144, 'Whenne thay witen wel y-now where the hare walketh'. The suggestion is plausible but I have been unable to find any comparable construction to support emending the text.

693 cf. note to 240.

694 In *Confessio*, VII.2304–8, Diogenes accuses Aristippus of flattering the king in order to deserve 'Thi princes thonk' (2307).

698–700 may allude to the third of Arundel's *Constitutions*, Wilkins, III.315, which forbade criticism of the clergy in front of a mixed audience. The narrator, as a 'lewed' man, lays himself open to the punishment of the ecclesiastical authorities for undertaking such criticism. The succeeding lines show that the narrator interprets Mum's warnings about the clergy to mean that the Church authorities have the power to put him to death for his activities.

702–6 In *Vox*, Gower criticises the clergy's involvement in military action. Chapters 6–11 of Book III are devoted wholly to the clergy's betrayal of their true office by engaging in warfare. Gower wrote before the passing of *De Haeretico Comburendo*. His comments could not have been seen to voice support for the Lollard sect which he so abhorred. Lollard teaching often maintained that it was unlawful to kill whatever the circumstance because it broke the sixth commandment, cf. notes to 513–14. It is especially unlawful for priests to take any part in death. On the contrary, urges one writer, they should: 'techen lordis and comunes in open sermons and confessions & priue conseillynge the peryl of werris, & namely of wrongful werris, & hou harde it is to fightten in charite', Matthew, 91/ 7–12. Line 705 states that it falls not to the **ordre** of priests to fight or dispute. Order is a term used frequently in Wycliffite diction, cf. note to 516–20, and cf. *PlTale*, 111 which states that priests should not lead men in battle.

703 plantz of pees In *Piers*, Holy Church describes love as 'the plante of pees', I.152, cf. *Crowned King*, 71, and *PlTale*, 245–52. which states that Christ forbade his priests to use the sword but to cherish peace.

707–9 According to the *Constitutions of Clarendon*, the bishops could not, as ecclesiastics, take any part in a sentence of death, R. W. Anson, *Law and Custom of the Constitution* (Oxford, 1922), I.238.

710–11 are ironic. William Sawtre was executed in 1401, prior to the passing of *De Haeretico Comburendo*, and John Badby in 1409, according to its terms. Under ecclesiastical examination both men insisted on the truth of Lollard teaching.

713 The quotation is from Matthew, 5:16: 'let your light shine before men, that they may see your good deeds and praise your Father who is in heaven'.

714 Mum's intervention, that anyone who keeps silent about crime implicates themself in it, is self-condemnatory.

716 demys The legal diction turns the debate between Mum and the narrator into rival cases in a lawsuit.

720 intent and **tale** are to be understood in their legal senses. There is a gap in the MS after *Al a-tw-*. The corrector supplies 'twart' which D&S incorporate into their text, taking 'atwart' as a variant of 'athwart', meaning 'in opposition to'.

721–2 refer to the trial of Jesus before Pilate. Despite his inability to find Jesus guilty of any offence, Pilate delivered him up to the Jews for crucifixion. Before doing so he asked for water and washed his hands so that he was innocent of Christ's blood, Matthew, 27:24.

726 ground For the legal diction, see notes to *Richard*, II.91.

727–42 allude to the disputes between Henry and the Percies which resulted in **man-slaughter** and **mourdre**. The Battle of Shrewsbury in 1403 was the Percies' first armed insurrection against the king. Henry Percy, son of the earl of Northumberland, was killed in battle, and Thomas Percy, earl of Worcester, was captured alive and beheaded. After the uprising in 1405, which was once more orchestrated by Northumberland, Archbishop Scrope was beheaded. Lines 733–40 are especially pertinent to Scrope's involvement. Far from restraining temporal wrath, he encouraged it, and then suffered its consequences. At the Battle of Bramham Moor in 1408, however, where Northumberland was finally put to death, clerics were again amongst the rebels; the bishop of Bangor, the abbot of Hailes and the prior of Hexham.

742 D&S insert 'his' before **peeres**. The addition picks up **his** in 740 but as the line is sufficient without it, and no correction is marked in the manuscript, I have omitted their alteration.

745 The quotation reads 'He who keeps quiet is seen to be in collusion'. This is the only occasion when a Latin quotation is incorporated into the alliterative line; it is underlined in the MS. The same citation appears in the *Coliphazio* play in *The Wakefield Pageants in the Townley Cycle*, ed. A. C. Cawley (Manchester, 1958), lines 143–4. It may have its source in canon law: 'qui non occurrit, consentit erranti', Dist. lxxxiii, c.V., Freidberg, p.294.

752 felonye is a crime of treason, rape, murder or theft, Alford, p.58.

753 traison is any action of deceit or treachery and **trespas** any violation of the law not amounting to treason or felony, Alford, p.157.

755 stille as a stoone A common proverb, see for example, *The Merchant's Tale*, 1818.

756–7 atteynt means convicted, especially for perjury or for giving a false verdict, Alford, p.11. The **trespas** in this line is not the original crime with which the defendant has been charged (line 753), but the trespass of perjury by refusing to answer to the charges brought. The first stage in pleading was the declaration by the plaintiff. Then followed the defendant's reply, his plea. There were three options: denial, admission, or the introduction of new facts. The reply set the remainder of the pleading in motion. If a defendant refused to reply to the charges brought, then the legal procedure could not continue and the process of the court was brought into disrepute, Baker, p.68. Line 756 suggests that this was an offence punishable by death. In fact, this was not strictly true. The punishment for perjury was imprisonment, but in 1407, two thieves, who had refused to answer charges, were imprisoned until they agreed to reply to the accusations. They were pressed down with weights and fed on bread and water on alternate days until they died. However, in 1417, a certain Henry Talbot, who would not answer directly to his indictment, was committed to the Tower without mention of further punishment, *Select Cases in the King's Bench*, p.238.

759 The MS reads **grucching** which D&S emend to 'grucchingz'. Although **Han** in line 760 is plural, the singular **grucching** is required as the antecedent of **hit** in line 762. **Han** picks up the implicit compound subject of 759, the complaining of a number of the nobility.

760–2 y-shourid recalls the weather imagery of lines 733–42 and **showre** in 737. It is a further allusion to the quarrels between Henry and the Percies, cf. notes to 727–42. The syntax of lines 760–2 is contorted. The antecedent of **That** in 761 is the **grucching** of 759. The sense of the lines is that the quarrelling of the nobility has become more widespread as a result of clerical tolerance. The clergy could have prevented such a situation through wise counsel. In line 762 the demands of the alliteration have produced an inversion of syntax. **The conseil**

of clergie is the direct object of **caste**. **hit** is the indirect object, referring back to the **grucching** in line 759. These lines envisage a more positive role for the clergy than elsewhere in the poem.

763 The image of the body politic shows that the quarrelling of the nobility upsets the harmony of the realm, cf. notes to *Richard*, II.62.

764 The quotation is typical of a number of Latin proverbs which state that a diseased head (a bad ruler) results in sick limbs (weak realm), cf, Gower, *In Praise of Peace*, 'Of that the heved is siek, the limes aken' (260) and *O Deus Immense*, 'Quo caput infirmum, nichil est de corpore firmum' (85).

765 **of** is added into the line by the original scribe. D&S treat it as a later correction. Line 765 repeats 229 and the marginal gloss added to 510.

768 The b-verse stresses the legal tone of the debate, cf. notes to line *Richard*, II.91.

770–1 form part of an extended theme of imagery in the poem which compares truthtelling to the lancing of wounds or the healing properties of plants, cf. 117, 316–17 and 729–30.

772 **do wel** refers to *Piers Plowman*.

774 **man** Here used in the sense of vassal or servant. **mensshid** is from 'mensken', to honour. Despite his name and allegorical status, Mum has just enacted in the poem the role of ideal truthteller as outlined by the narrator in lines 31–98. Ironically, Mum's speech is exactly that of a **siker seruant who shuld haue robes** (97).

775 The MS reads 'yf' which D&S emend to **for**. Emendation is necessary to produce sense, though it is possible that a line has been omitted before 776. **lucas** is simply a common name which fits the alliteration. There are no other examples in MED.

776 Mum uses **wit** not in the sense of 'reason', in the traditional opposition between wit and will, but in the sense of 'advantage'.

777 **teryng of hodes** presumably means quarrelling.

778 MS reads **trusty** which the corrector has altered to 'truest'. D&S incorporate the correction into the text. The preceding definite article makes the alteration attractive, but the MS reading is tenable and so I have not emended.

779 **maister and maker** D&S comment that the author has apparently forgotten that it is Mum who is speaking, p.120. There are a number of places where the personification is inconsistent, cf. notes to 1224–32. The lord and servant imagery continues the satire against contemporary malpractices in retaining, cf. lines 1254–66. There may be influence of Holy Church's description of the lineage of Mede, a character whom in some respects Mum resembles, see *Piers*, II.25–7 and Theology's alternative account of her genealogy, II.119–120.

781 sought al a-side recalls 370b.

784 a-croke recalls the pun in line 387.

788 The list is not classified logically and omits distinctions common in estates satire. Whilst there are a number of different ranks of nobility, the commons are represented rather tautologously by **fre men, frankeleyns, bourgois, comunes, craftz-men** and **citezeyns**. A conspicuous absence from this list, and from the poem more generally, are merchants. Lawyers are a curious omission since their profession is satirised so extensively in the poem.

796 The MS reads **sothe-sigger** which D&S emend to **sothe-siggerz** to restore the parallel with **mvmmers** in the preceding line.

797–800 recall lines 115–51.

798–9 The MS reads **ee** in the middle of the line, which D&S emend to **yee**. An identical asseveration is used at 714, though at the beginning of the line. The emendation restores sense to an otherwise meaningless cluster of letters. The breakdown of alliteration in this line suggests serious corruption to 798. The b-verse is exactly the kind of numerical filler that could have been supplied by the scribe. As D&S note, p.120, there appears to be a line missing after 800. In the absence of any further manuscript witnesses, or corrections at this point, I can find no convincing emendation. The scribe may have scrambled a number of lines together.

801–23 cf. *Piers*, III.76–100. The *Mum*-poet emphasises the judicial function of the mayor, a function which Mum corrupts through bribery. In *Piers*, mayors are described as 'menes' between 'The kyng and the commune to kepe the lawes' (76–7). As Bennett notes, p.137, n.87, the mayor's chief role was as a magistrate responsible for fair trade practices. Line 803 in *Mum* states that Mum and the mayor corrupt the legal system by wearing the same livery. Such maintenance excludes the poor from the due processes of law. The emphasis in *Piers* is rather different. The mayor disadvantages the poor by corruptly patronising retailers (87–90). But just as the mayor is Mum's puppet, so too in *Piers* is the mayor Mede's.

806 The MS reads **he** which the corrector alters to 'thay'. D&S incorporate this emendation into the text, but the line makes sense as it stands.

807 The satire focuses on the corrupt practice of entertaining interested parties in a lawsuit to lavish meals. The account recalls *Richard*, IV.40. See further notes to 821ff.

808 leepe ouer the balkes means omit a stage or part of the legal process, MED lepen 9a). Mum trims the processes of law to his own advantage.

810–11 speche ... partie ... playnte all carry legal senses. Mum speaks only for the interested party, in disregard for the due process of the lawsuit.

815–16 travers means the formal denial in pleading of some matter alleged by the other side, cf. notes to line 57. Mum never spoke against a cause in case he were contradicted or defeated. For **caste** (i.e. forfeited because of the process of law) in this context, cf. *Alphabet of Tales*, ed. M. M. Banks (EETS OS 126 1904), 73/29: 'The parties put forth her cawsis & ... he that gaff hym the ox was like to be castyn'.

817 Mum avoids committing himself to a position in the lawsuit by showing a sealed document which allows him to sit apart from proceedings.

818–19 The word-play of **mvmmeth** and **mvmme** captures the reciprocal bribery between Mum and the mayor.

820 MS reads 'yfte' and D&S supply 'i'. Cf. *Piers*, III.93–100 where a text from Job 15:34 is quoted, 'fire shall devour their tabernacles, who love to take bribes' to warn mayors and those who maintain the laws what will happen to them if they desire 'Yiftes or yeresyeves because of hire offices' (100).

821–34 dramatise the corruption of local administration. The judicial system is made to serve the interests of the rich. The sergeants hope to obtain business from the list of criminal offences which Mum has collected (825). The passage is reminiscent of the Franklin's portrait in *The General Prologue*: he rides in the company of the Serjeant of Law (331) and his table, ready to be laid with food, is juxtaposed with his office of presiding over court sessions (354–5). Both Chaucer and *Mum* link hospitality with the corruption of the law.

822 al vn-a-spied cf. line 540. In both instances, the humble status of the narrator is used to highlight the position of the poor in a system where money and patronage hold sway.

823 caas used here in the sense of lawsuits. The line is a grim comment on how the ordinary person finds it impossible to gain legal redress. D&S emend MS **forto** to 'For to'. There is no correction marked and I have retained the MS reading.

824 MS originally reads 'a sergeant' but the scribe crosses out 'a' and adds 'z'. D&S incorporate the alteration. **shuldrid** conveys a sense both of the numbers of sergeants and their eagerness for business; cf. *Piers*, Prol.211–13: 'Yet hoved ther an hundred in howves of selk – / Sergeants, it semed, that serveden at the Barre, / Pleteden for penyes and pounded the lawe.'

829 cf. notes to 617.

830 The solitariness of the sothsegger indicates his independence from patronage and maintenance. The account of the penitent thief in *Piers* contains a description of the distinct positions of the guests at a feast, according to their rank, XII.200–201: 'As tho that seten at the syde table or with the sovereynes of the halle, / But sete as a beggare bordlees by myself on the grounde'.

831 holde vp the oyles cf. notes to *Richard*, III.186.

832 cf. *Richard*, III.170.

833 The MS reads 'sergeant'. A plural form is required and D&S emend accordingly. There was such a swarm of sergeants that they blotted everything else out of sight; cf. the description in *Money, Money!*, Robbins, 51/41–4: 'In westmynstre hall the criers call; / The sergeantes plede a-pace; / Attorneys appere, now here, now there, / Rennyng in euery place.'

834 implies that each course is plentiful and that there are many of them, cf. *Wynnere and Wastoure*, where the opulence and extravagance of Wastoure's banquet is linked to power and patronage (325–65). Line 356: 'Iche a mese at a merke bytwen twa men' prices each course at about two-thirds of a pound, see Trigg, p.40. **merke** (834) puns on the senses of 'coin', MED merke (n) 2a) and 'to observe', merken 8a).

835 anticipates the ancient wisdom of the beekeeper (956).

838 The private room in which the sothsegger dines alone contrasts with the public festivity of the feasting hall.

839 dum-seede appears to be a potent drink which induces speechlessness. I have found no comparable expression. The phrase seems antithetical to the description of the **sauce** of **the sothe-sigger** in line 473.

841–4 recall episodes in *Piers* where Will reels away from a series of conversations or encounters with little sense of what to make of them or where to go next, e.g., XV.1–12; XVIII, 1–5.

844 recalls *Piers Plowman*; cf. notes to 681.

847 Truthtelling is often associated with lancing wounds or healing them; cf. note to 770–1. But speaking out truthfully is so far banished from the realm that the sothsegger is left licking his own wounds.

847 The side note is from Matthew 5:10, 'Blessed are they that suffer persecution for justice' sake'; cf. *Crede*, 653–4.

849–53 cf. note to 687–92.

857–65 cf. note to 841–4.

866 cf. 349.

869–70 The dream-vision prepares for a revelation of higher authority than any that can be granted to the narrator in his waking life. The episode resembles the inner dreams in *Piers*, XI.32off. and XVI.2off., where the dreamer's quest gains new momentum from a deeper level of conscious experience and the explications of sanctioned authority figures.

874–5 The citation of Cato and Daniel in defence of the authority of dreams recalls Will's discussion on the matter in *Piers*. VII.149–67. At line 150, Will notes that Cato counsels against interpreting dreams ('Take no account of dreams [for while asleep the human mind sees what it hopes and wishes for]', *Distichs of Cato*, II.31). The same authority is quoted by Pertelote in *The Nun's Priest's Tale*, 2940–1. In *Piers*, Will counters this with Daniel's true interpretation of the dream of Nebuchadnezzar.

876 cf. *Piers*, B.Prol.12: 'That I was in a wildernesse, wiste I nevere where'.

877–943 Descriptions of the natural world appear in *Morte D'Arthure*, 920–32; *Wynnere and Wastoure*, 32–44; *The Parlement of the Thre Ages*, 1–46; *Death and Liffe*, 22–79. D&S regard this passage in *Mum* a piece of nature appreciation, p.121. But there is a precise allegorical significance. The scene is closest in temper to the landscape in *Death and Liffe* and the panoramic vision of the natural world granted to Will in Passus XI of *Piers*. The narrator glosses the significance of the scene at line 931: 'A swete sight for souurayns'. The scene presents a picture of the healthy plenitude of nature and provides a moral speculum of the art of government following the traditions of Aquinas and Giles of Rome, who urged in their respective *De Regimine Principum* that man should learn the art of government from the examples seen in nature, see Aquinas, *Selected Political Writings*, pp.66–71 and Giles of Rome, *De Regimine Principum*, Bodleian Library MS Digby 233, fols.132b–36b.

877 Man's absence from the natural world is significant. It recalls *Piers*, XI.323–70, where Will is shown a panoramic vision of the natural world in which Reason follows and rules all beasts except 'man and his make' (370).

878 on a creste-wise i.e., broadening out in the shape of a crest, presumably a bird's crest.

879 For the first time the narrator derives comfort from his experiences. It indicates that there is a deeper meaning to be drawn from the scene.

883 In *Piers*, the narrator is led to the top of a mountain called Myddelerthe (XI.323). In *The Crowned King*, the narrator is 'high on an hill' (31).

884 The MS omits **of**, presumably a mechanical copying omission, which D&S supply.

888 From the mown meadows (887), the reaped corn (895) and the grapes (907), the **saison** must be harvest, symbolising a healthy, prosperous kingdom.

889 cf. *Crowned King*, 25.

896–7 A river is part of the natural scene in *Wynnere and Wastoure* (41), *Morte D'Arthure* (920), and *Death and Liffe* (26). *Death and Liffe* refers twice to 'ffishes of the fflood' (113 & 197), but only in *Mum* is there the emphasis on the life-generating properties of water as part of the description of the scene: '*Ful* of fyssh'. The poet appears to be influenced here, and in other lines, e.g., 898, 908–9, by the idea of the 'plenitudo Naturae', the fulness and fecundity of the natural world when left uncorrupted by humankind, see Alain of Lille, *The Plaint of Nature*, ed. and trans. J. J. Sheridan (Toronto, 1980), pp.108–112 and *Death and Liffe*, p.23.

898–907 The hawthorne (902) appears in *Death and Liffe* (31) and *Wynnere and Wastoure* (36), but none of the medieval nature descriptions cited include berries, honeysuckles, chestnuts, cherries, beans, broom-flowers, pears, plums, peapods and grapes. The list resembles the produce that the folk bring to appease Hunger in *Piers*, VI.292–300. Amongst the food are peapods (292), beans (293) and cherries (294).

904–5 an anti-feminist comment. Pears are associated with female sexual appetite in a number of Middle English works: e.g., *I have a new garden*, Davies, p.158, where the pear-tree is used as a symbol of illicit sexual intercourse; the comparison of Alison in Chaucer's *Miller's Tale*, to 'the newe pere-jonette tree' (3248) and the denouement of *The Merchant's Tale*, where May's desire for 'the smale peres grene' (2333) facilitates the consummation of the lovers in the pear-tree. Burrow, p.260 notes that **pesecoddes** carries a pun on 'scrotum' and compares Touchstone's speech in *As You Like It*, II.iv.43–52.

913 hay-nettes are for catching wild animals, especially rabbits. *Mum* is the only poetry example in MED and the only instance where 'hai' and 'nette' form a compound word.

915 a-caunt-wise i.e., in a zigzag fashion. MED compares OF *cant-on*, a corner, angle. *Mum* is the only citation in MED.

916–17 The natural world is not idealised. Rabbits and hares are in danger here. The scene is not a political utopia; rather, it stresses the ordinances and hierarchies of the natural world which rulers should imitate.

917 Ector is the name of a hound. There are no citations of Hector as a common name in MED.

922 prime-saute i.e., spirited, precipitous from OF *prin-sautier*, MED 'prim-sautier'. *Mum* is the only citation.

925–30 Reindeer and roebuck are coupled together in the *Morte D'Arthure*, 922 and the chasing of deer by **kennetz** forms the opening description of *Somer Soneday*, 5–13.

928–9 contrast with the deer described in *Richard*, II.117–34; cf. *Gawain*, 1326: 'Gedered the grattest of gres that ther were'.

934–9 The charms of birdsong form part of the nature description in *Death and Liffe*, 74, 112–14; *The Parlement of the Thre Ages*, 14–15, and *Wynnere and Wastoure*, 37–40.

935 The line in the MS ends with **heuenely**. I have followed D&S in supplying 'sounes' because the b-verse is deficient in both sense and syllables.

939 The MS reads 'cleerly' which D&S emend to 'cheerly' to restore the alliteration. At 1305, the corrector alters MS **cleerly** to 'cherely'. Given that elsewhere the poet alliterates [k] with [tʃ] (204, 1414, 1426, 1429, 1486), emendation is unnecessary.

941–2 cf. the 'floury flaght' of *Pearl* (57) which is redolent of spices (35–44).

946 Frankeleyn means a landowner, see Alford, p.63. **Freholde** is the first of a number of terms drawn from land law. It means a land held by fees or in term of life. The possession of the land is not temporary, nor at the will of an overlord, but in consideration of specified payments or services. The only other example from poetry cited by MED is from *Destruction of Troy*, 7858: 'We are folke full fele in this fre holde / Of lordis and Ladies and other lesse pepull'.

948 The image of the garden is without the obvious influence of the biblical tradition of Eden, the *hortus conclusus* from the *Song of Songs*, or the gardens in dream-visions inspired by *The Romance of the Rose*. The closest analogue is Passus XVI of *Piers Plowman* where Anima explains that the Tree of Charity 'groweth in a gardyn'. . . . 'that God made hymselve; / Amyddes mannes body the more is of that stokke. / Here highte the herber that it inne groweth, / And Liberium Arbitrium hath the lond to ferme, / Under Piers the Plowman to piken it and weden it' (13–17). The lines are altered in the C text, XVIII.1–7.

957 wisely y-made contrasts with the clothing of the clergy, 643 and 647; cf. the garments of the courtiers in *Richard*, III.118–243.

959 The MS reads 'seme' at the end of the line. D&S emend to **sene**. The beekeeper's virtue is not in doubt. The scribe made a mistake in copying the minim.

961 MED glosses **besmet** as the past participle of the verb 'besmen', to sweep or brush, and gives the meaning 'shaped like a broom or besom'. There are no comparable examples. This is the meaning suggested by D&S, and gives more plausible sense than 'besmet' as the past participle of 'bismitten', to soil, or corrupt, given that the beekeeper is presented as a paragon of virtue.

962 as euer kinde wrought means either: as Nature ever made; or, as was ever naturally made. Both senses stress the innate propriety of the beekeeper; cf. **Proporcioned at alle poyntes** in 964, which suggests natural measure and regularity.

963 cf. the description of Wit in *Piers*, VIII.120: 'Sad of his semblaunt and of a softe speche'.

966 kepe has the legal sense of guard or protect, Alford, p.77, cf. notes to 987. The introduction of a beekeeper to the political exemplum of a hive of bees is unique.

976 D&S emend MS **gate** to 'garth'. But the MS reading can stand in the sense of 'furrow', 'track to be ploughed', MED gate (n) 2 1c). The gardener / beekeeper explains the digging and delving of his plot of land.

978–81 cf. *Piers*, XVI.17, where Piers pikes and weeds the land which Liberium Arbitrium farms; cf. also notes to 948. In Passus VI, Piers sets the workers to task and 'Dikeris and delveres digged up the balkes' (107). But he has also to deal with the scroungers who 'wasten that men wynnen with travaille and with tene' (133), a contrast which may inform the description of the drones in *Mum* (967, 985) and the slugs (980).

978 stresses that the beekeeper's activities are in full accordance with the law. The treatment of wastrels is extremely harsh and simplistic compared with the tortuously drawn-out discussion of the problem in *Piers Plowman*. See M. Godden, 'Plowmen and Hermits in Langland's *Piers Plowman*', *RES* (1984), n.s. 35, 129–63.

982 **doon worste** is a negative inversion of the Dowel triad from *Piers*.

985 The quotation is attributed to St Bernard. It is from 2 Thessalonians, 3:10, 'If any man will not work, neither let him eat.' The quotation also appears as a gloss to *Piers*, B. Prol. 39 in MS Oriel College 79 and CUL Ll.4.14. The letter MS contains *Richard*.

987 The exposition of the habits of bees as a model for human society has a literary tradition which goes back to Virgil's *Georgics*, Book IV. The beekeeper gives as his source Bartholomaeus Anglicus (1028 and 1054). See Bartholomaeus, I.609–14. Aquinas singles out bees as the political model for man to follow in his *De Regimine Principum*, ch.12; likewise Giles of Rome, *De Regimine Principum*, fols.132b–33; cf. Shakespeare, *Henry V*, I.ii.187–204.

988 The MS reads 'ne' for **no**, presumably the result of scribal attraction to the preceding negative particle. D&S correct.

989–91 The bees' zeal for common profit is stressed by Bartholomaeus, I.609/24 and 610/7–10, 32–36.

990 **propriete** picks up the title of *De Proprietatibus Rerum*; cf. 993.

992 cf. Will's request that Holy Church explain the meaning of the mountain and the dungeon, *Piers*, I.11 and I.58–60.

993 ye The narrator respectfully addresses the beekeeper with the polite second person pronoun. The beekeeper replies using 'thou/thee'. Mum and the narrator use 'thou' to each other.

998–9 stress the natural lawfulness of the bees.

1000–1 cf. Bartholomaeus, I.610/18–21: 'Ande though they ben iput and iset vndir a kyng, yit they beth free and loueth hire kyng that they maketh by kynde loue and defendith hym with ful greet diffens and holdeth feire and worshipe to perische and be isplit for here kyng'.

1002–4 cf. Bartholomaeus, I.611/20–2: 'And first they bigynneth to make hous that the kyng shal wony inne; thanne thay maketh othir houses for othur been that kepith the hyue'. **setten in his see** (1003) adds a more legalistic tone to Bartholomaeus' description.

1005–11 extend and elaborate the description of the skill of the bees in Bartholomaeus, I.609/27–9. **countrefete thare workes** stresses the wonder and skill of the natural world which humankind ought to imitate.

1006 The MS reads 'erthe'. A correction supplies **cope** which D&S adopt.

1009 feycchen carries the legal sense of recovering what is rightfully one's own, Alford, p.56, II.

1011 The MS reads 'by thynne' in error for **wy-thynne** which D&S correct.

1012–15 A description not found in any bestiary. The closest analogue in Bartholomaeus is I.612/17–19, where the bees are described as fighting those who would plunder the hive when honey-levels are low. The emphasis on the **principal** who pacifies the community under his jurisdiction mirrors concern about the behaviour of contemporary nobles; cf. notes to 727ff. and 1650ff.

1016 cf. 109 and note thereon. The bees' knowledge of the wasters is as natural to them as clerics' knowledge of books.

1019–25 cf. Bartholomaeus, I.610/33–611/1: 'somme beth besy aboute mete; and somme aspyeth comynge of rayne; and somme byholdeth concours and metyng of dewes; and somme maketh wex of floures; and somme maketh celles, now rounde, now square, with wondir byndynge and ioynynge and euenes'.

1023 dome gives a distinctive legal emphasis to the natural behaviour of the bees.

1026 MS reads 'That' in error for **Thay** at the beginning of the line. D&S correct. Bartholomaeus mentions common food, p.610/7–8.

1027 MS reads 'wauthour' in error for **warthour** which D&S correct; cf. Bartholomaeus, p.613/11–14: 'And yif a man leueth to ham moche hony, thay worchith nought moche theraftir; and yif he leueth to lyte, thanne thay waxith slow to worchen hony. Therfore the wardeyne schal leue hem hony as the multitude of hem is mothir lasse'.

1028–30 The reference to Bartholomaeus is curious. The only buzzing which he mentions is the noise bees make with their wings, p.613/22–4. The attribution of a common language to the bees emphasises their transferred political significance.

1030 MS reads 'lydenys' which D&S emend to **lydene. hit** requires a singular antecedent.

1031–7 cf. Bartholomaeus, p.610/24–7: 'And been chesith to her kyng thilke that is most worthy and noble in hugenes and fairenesse and most cliere in myldenesse, for that is chief vertue in a kyng, for though this kyng haue a stenge, he vsith it nought in wreche'. Hoccleve notes that the king of the bees is without a sting, *Regement*, 3375–77.

1036 cf. 1479 where the sentiment is applied to the subjects of the kingdom. There is no legal emphasis in Bartholomaeus.

1037 that closeth alle in oone cf. Giles of Rome, fol.132b: 'For as it is kyndeliche that multitude cometh of oon, so it is kyndelich that it be reduct in-to oon and be i-rewled by on'.

1038–43 cf. Bartholomaeus, p.612/22–3: 'The kynges beth nought iseye withoute the huyues allone but they haueth many been aboute hem, and the kyng is in the myddel' and p.611/32–3: 'And whan here kyng may nat flee, thanne a companye of been bereth hym', cf. note to 1012–15.

1044 The corrector adds an 's' to **drane** and supplies a different b-verse, 'that deye mote they alle'. D&S incorporate the plural inflection on **drane** and substitute the third person plural pronoun **thaym** for MS 'hym'. But emendation is not necessary. **The drane** is to be understood generically. At 997, the poet refers to **The bee** as a species and then uses the plural pronoun **Thay** in 999.

1045–55 expand Bartholomaeus' account substantially. **brede-ful** (1048), the description of the false beggars in the Prol.40–3: 'Bidderes and beggeres faste aboute yede, / Til hire bely and hire bagge were bredful ycrammed, / Faiteden for hire foode, foughten at the ale. / In glotonye, God woot, go thei to bedde'. **cropping** in 1049 recalls the wastrels in Passus VI of *Piers* and cf. *Crede*, 726–9, where the gluttonous friars are likened to drones.

1048 The quotation is from Philippians, 3:19: 'whose God is their belly and whose glory is in their shame'. This is quoted by Thought in *Piers*, IX.61a and cf. *Crede*, 89–92.

1059–61 The precise allegorical significance of the beekeeper's actions is unclear. His defence of the hive intrudes on the symbolism of the bee-community because it creates a king figure outside as well as inside the hive. **grace** (1059) suggests that the guardian/gardener assumes a Providential role. The political vision presents the state as a political community which can work for good, but **gouuerne hym the bettre** suggests a wise ruler figure who knows his own actions; cf. *Piers*, XVI.40–52. Piers explains to Will that the devil often tries to steal his fruit and flowers before his very eyes. Sometimes, Liberium Arbitrium, his lieutenant/guardian, allows it. But when the world, the flesh and the devil threaten to steal the fruit, then: 'Liberium Arbitrium laccheth the thridde planke / And palleth adoun the pouke pureliche thorugh grace / And help of the Holy Goost – and thus have I the maistrie' (50–2).

1062 The MS reads 'shald' which the corrector alters to 'shal be dasid'. D&S emend accordingly.

1063 **kinde knowlache** recalls *Piers* and suggests that the beekeeper recognises the most effective form of government by natural instinct. But once he admits destructive forces into the community, he will be blinded to his own nature. It is a comment applicable to the relationship between the king and his nobles.

1064–8 cf. Will's questions to Holy Church in *Piers*, I.81–2, 138–9 and II.4.

1066 **deue is to other** places the drones on the wrong side of the law.

1069–1086 do not derive from Bartholomaeus.

1070 cf. the proverb in *The Floure and the Leaf*, ed. D. Pearsall (London, 1962), 58–9: 'As plain as a Board'.

1074 The quotation reads 'Nothing is as harsh as a pauper when he is raised to prosperity' and is attributed to Gregory. D&S, p.122, note a parallel in Claudian, *In Eutropium*, ed. M. Platnaeur (London, 1922), I.181: 'Asperius nihil est humili, cum surgit in altum'.

1088–9 cf. *Piers*, Prol.209–10 where the narrator refuses to explicate the political significance of the rat fable.

1092 question to construe returns us to the narrator's prosecution of his suit, cf. note to 556, and for **construe** cf. 398 and notes to *Richard*, III.327.

1094 The failure of the narrator's search is a satirical indictment of his contemporary society.

1096 matiere cf. 232 and note to *Richard*, I.171.

1101–2 cf. 574–5 and note thereon.

1103–5 cf. notes to 393 and 431.

1106–7 There is a folio missing between these two lines, but it must have been missing from the original quire. There is no disjunction of sense and the scribe writes the beginning of line 1107 as a catchword at the bottom of fol.12b. Similarly, at the bottom of fol.4b the scribe writes the beginning of line 370 before commencing a new quire.

1108 deme The narrator asks the beekeeper to judge his case.

1110 cf. the similar proverb at *Richard*, II.134.

1111 sone the Doctor of Philosophy also addresses the narrator as 'soon', cf. note to 366.

1113 the grounde as gospel Wycliffite texts often collocate 'ground' in its legal sense (cf. notes to *Richard*, II.91 and *Crede*, 506–14) and 'gospel' to show the primacy of the Bible as the source of truth. The highest voice of authority in *Mum* belongs to a layman who nevertheless authorises his discourse with appeal to the Bible.

1115 MS omits **of** which D&S supply.

1117 MS reads 'and moulde' which makes no sense. **moulde** must be understood in the sense of 'pattern or model', MED 3, moulde (n). I have emended 'and' to **a** to give the sense that Mum is indeed a model for all the mischief and misrule that has plagued the realm. A similar syntax is seen at 1549. **aduowe** means to make a statement at law. See MED avowen 1a).

1118–33 cf. *Richard*, IV.46–52. The imagery recalls lines 117, 317, 730 and 770ff. The parliaments of Henry's reign, especially up to 1406, saw stormy discussions over taxation, the affairs of the king's household, and clerical temporalities. Line 1128 shows that the focus of the poet's remarks is on the risings that occurred between the Cirencester revolt of 1399–1400 and the Battle of Bramham Moor in 1408. Instead of resolving grievances through parliamentary channels, disaffected members of the community such as the Percies and Glendower chose armed revolt.

1120 shewe cf. note to *Richard*, IV.30.

1121 speche cf. note to line 86.

1124 There is a pun on the senses of criminal, MED feloun (1) and suppurating sore, MED feloun (2).

1130 cf. similar diction at lines 1381–3.

1132 cf. note to *Richard*, IV.47. *PlTale*, 677–84, states that Parliament should take heed of the misfortunes of the people and bring them to the attention of the king.

1134 poyntz cf. note to *Richard*, III.111.

1135 pulle means to cheat out of possessions, MED pullen 1c) and **leue** means to authorise grants, MED 3.leuen (vb) 3a).

1138 mote to determyne cf. note to *Richard*, II.97.

1141 The quotation reads: 'He who is able to contradict sin and does not contradict [it] is a perpetrator of sin.' It is attributed to Sidrac but as D&S note, it is not in the common text of Sidrac, p.123. They cite a parallel from Matthew Paris's account of the last words of Bishop Grosseteste: 'Qui ergo potest contradicere et non contradicit peccat & videtur fautor esse, secundum illud Gregorii, Non caret scrupulo societatis occultae, qui manifesto facinori desinit obviare', *Historia Anglicana*, ed. F. Madden (London, 1869), III.146; cf. note to line 274.

1141 king-is court is a royal court of justice, e.g., the King's Bench, Common Pleas or Exchequer, Alford, p.79.

1144 where the hare walketh alludes to the proverbial madness of the hare, anticipating **madde tales** in line 1146; cf. *The Friar's Tale*, 1327: 'For though this somonour wood were as an hare'.

1145 leden men the long waye means to mislead. Neither MED nor Whiting cites any parallels to the phrase. **loue-dayes** are formal meetings to settle disputes out of court (often by leave of the court), Alford, p.92. In *Piers*, Mede is accused of leading the law as she pleases by making love-days (III.158). In Passus X, Study criticises those who aspire to land and lordship rather than true speech. Those who corrupt the law, or manage love-days so that justice is impeded, are called to be members of council for their skills. They lead the nobles with lies and contradict truth (17–22).

1146 tales Here used in its legal sense of proceedings in a law case.

1147 sowe siluer seede To take bribes, the only example in MED. **solue** is from 'sol-fa' to practise singing the notes of a scale; cf. *Piers*, C.VII.31: 'Yut kan ych nother solfe ne synge'. **solue ere thay singe** is equivalent to the proverbial phrase 'run before they can walk'. Such behaviour is that of an upstart.

1148 haue ynne thaire harueste cf. *Richard*, I.166. The side note reads: 'Patronage and fear, reward and hatred pervert true justice'. It is a summary of a chapter in canon law, *Decreti Secunda Pars*, Causa xi. Quest. III.c.lxxviii, Freidberg, I.665. The chapter discusses the ways in which justice may be perverted by fear, remuneration, hatred and favour.

1154 cf. line 12.

1156 shewe the by exemples legal diction, cf. note to 401.

1157–65 link Mum directly with Lucifer the Liar. Lucifer is called a liar because of his fraudulent claim to the souls of mankind. He gained possession by his fraudulent conversation with Eve; cf. *Piers*, XVIII.403: 'And for thi lesynge, Lucifer, that thow leighe til Eve'. Mum's self-interest is linked with three of the deadly sins, lust (1161), pride (1163) and covetousness (1165). The imagery casts Lucifer as the antithesis of the gardener/beekeeper; cf. the passage on the indestructability of Truth, 176–92.

1160 grevance cf. note to *Richard*, IV.38. A number of the leaders of the rebellions in Henry's reign were beheaded, including Thomas Percy, earl of Worcester and Archbishop Scrope.

1165 MS omits **be** which the corrector supplies and D&S incorporate. There is a pun on **croke** in the senses of 'hook' and 'criminal act'; cf. note to 387.

1166 felaship is a reference to illegal maintenance; cf. note to *Richard*, I.148. The quotation reads 'the sower of tares and the farmer of the devil'. D&S suggest that it might be a reference to Matthew, 13:24–30; 36–43, especially 38–9.

1170 forto do wel recalls the Dowel triad *Piers*.

1171 asaye means to examine a witness or defendant for the sake of information, Alford, p.10.

1172 assent has the sense of two parties coming to an agreement, MED assenten 2a).

1173 MS reads 'be' which the corrector alters to **the**. D&S adopt the emendation; cf. *Tale of Melibee*, 2385: 'swich folk as conseille yow a thyng prively and conseille yow the contrarie openly'. **construeth the doutes** carries a legal sense; cf. 294 and note to *Richard*, III.327.

1174 **pleynely telleth** cf. lines 49–51.

1175 cf. line 97.

1176 **salaire** cf. note to *Richard*, IV.47.

1177 MS reads 'no for' which the corrector alters to **for no**, an emendation which D&S accept.

1178–9 **hit tourne wol / Hamward by his hows** is a figurative expression meaning 'rebounding on his own head'. There is no equivalent phrase in MED or Whiting. The corrector adds a Latin quotation: 'Iuris consultus / Cicius debet homo omnia mala pati quam malo consentire'. 'The lawyer Cicius ought, as a man, to suffer all evils rather than consent to evil'.)

1182–85 cf. the image in *Richard*, I.200–1.

1185 cf. *Guy of Warwick*, ed. J. Zupitza (EETS ES 42 1883), 5709–10: 'Than lopen about hem the Lombars / As wicked coltes out of haras'. In *The Miller's Tale*, May is compared twice to a colt, 3263 and 3282.

1187 contains a contrast to the sothsegger, who ought to have robes (line 97), but who does not. See also 288.

1188–91 The legal terms **matiere, sheweth, assentith, deceiptes** show Mum's corruption of the law.

1191–2 anticipate the analogy in 1224–66.

1193 cf. *Richard*, I.201 and III.134.

1195 **man** in the legal sense of retainer, Alford, p.96. A further attack on the corruption of maintenance.

1197 cf. line 22.

1201 The command takes the form of a legal injunction. **fende** is an apheticform of 'defenden' in the sense of to forbid or prohibit, Alford, p.44.

1206 cf. note to line 584.

1207 **quite the with a quitance** means to pay a sum to make amends, Alford, p.125. In *Piers*, Christ uses the verb 'quiten' to state that he will make amends for what was lost through man's sin, XVIII.341. **whenne querellz been vp** has a legal sense; cf. note to *Richard*, III.327. It refers to the treatment of the narrator at the Last Judgment.

1208 cf. 311 and 375. **nouellerie** is a term used frequently in Wycliffite texts to denote practices contrary to Christ's ordinance, e.g., Matthew, 2/29; 3/1; 50/34; Arnold, 170/30; *EWS*, I.252/14.

1209 cf. 102 and 206 and the **holsum gyse** of Wit in *Richard*, III.212.

1210 **the best of the royaulme** is the king.

1212 see note to 304–5.

1213 cf. lines 97 and 1175.

1214 **cuntre** in the sense of shire; cf. note to *Richard*, II.28. Representatives of the shires should speak up truthfully in parliament.

1215 MS reads 'do' which the corrector alters to **thow**. D&S incorporate the correction.

1216 I have retained the MS reading **reasonable** despite D&S's attractive emendation to 'seasonable' because no correction has been marked.

1219 **demed deuely the doute** casts the beekeeper as an honest judge. Reward from God is his only payment (1218b).

1221ff. cf. two episodes in *Piers*: the pilgrims' wish to be directed to Truth and Piers's subsequent exposition of the route, V.510–629, and Wit's description of the dwelling of Dowel in the 'Castle of Caro', IX.1–59.

1221 **court** in the sense of noble household, MED 3. At line 1238, it is a court of law, MED 8a). Apart from *Siege of Jerusalem*, 1328, where it means 'man', **kempe** elsewhere means a fighting champion or athlete.

1223 The MS reads 'hym' which D&S emend to **the**. Since the beekeeper is addressing the narrator's request, the second person pronoun is required.

1224–30 **Yn man-is herte** cf. Piers's description of the dwelling place of Truth: 'Thow shalt see in thiselve Truthe sitte in thyn herte / In a cheyne of charite, as thow a child were' (V.606–7). The legal allegory in *Mum* is convoluted. The poet attempts to equate truthtelling with Eternal Truth. Truth has been granted possession by God of an estate where he is entitled to two dwelling places, man's heart and man's mind. Truth has also been put in possession of Adam and his successors in the earthly paradise. Through the inspiration of the Holy Spirit, Adam is entitled to possess earthly paradise and afterwards, heaven. The sequence suggests that God has naturally endowed mankind with rational behaviour which directs him to good and, ultimately, to heavenly reward. The Latin quotation reads

'The dwelling place of Truth is in a faithful heart'. The beekeeper calls on Holy Writ to authorise his exposition in 1224. D&S compare Proverbs, 14:33: 'In the heart of the prudent resteth wisdom', but the correspondence is inexact. The quotation recalls *Piers*, V.606 but 1224 explicitly mentions **hooly writte**. There is no biblical text identical to the quotation.

1226 feoffed means to put in legal possession, Alford, p.57.

1227 possession has the sense of 'seisin'. Possession of the estate gives Truth physical occupation of the estate, i.e. mankind, but not ownership (cf. Curzon, p.313). Ownership of the estate rests with God and thus the poet avoids stating that man is self-sufficient for good.

1228 issue has the sense of legal successors, Alford, p.74.

1230 holde in the sense of holding an estate from a feudal lord, MED holden 7b).

1231 God is depicted as a feudal lord whom man should obey in just the same way as he obeys his temporal **souurayn**.

1233–4 cf. the description of friars in 510–11.

1236 A reference to the simoniacal appointment of bishops, cf. 579 where Mum menaces the narrator with his mitre and also notes to 634–41. There is wordplay on **martir/mytre**. The Latin quotation reads: 'He who does not enter by the door into the sheepfold but from another place, is a thief and a robber', cf. John, 10:1. The gloss refers to the simoniacal bishops. Gower cites this same text to make an identical criticism, *Vox*, III.1005–8.

1238 Bennett notes, p.91, that 'worth bothe his eres', *Piers*, Prol.78, may allude to cheats or their accomplices losing their ears in the pillory. **kutte of myn eres** is an oath which invites the beekeeper's words to be examined for fraudulence. The beekeeper is confident that he has spoken the truth.

1240 The quest is now internal, in the narrator's heart, and by extension, the hearts of humankind in general. **euene amyddes**, cf. *Richard*, I.3.

1241 The constant and free access to the heart contrasts with the narrator's attempt to gain entry into the monasteries, 550–2. In *Piers*, V.601–4 entry to the heart requires 'Amende-yow' to unlock the gate.

1244 The legal diction suggests that humankind should follow its heart by prosecuting the case of the sothsegger abroad.

1245–6 suggest the sothsegger is akin to God.

1247 The MS omits **he** which D&S supply and which the singular verb **is** requires. **sire** is supplied by the corrector for the meaningless MS 'fure', D&S emend; cf. *Richard*, III.351.

1248 cf. *Richard*, I.46.

1249–50 recall the description of the ideal truthteller in lines 72–98.

1251 A poor man ends up in jail if he dares overstep the limits by drawing attention to corruption; cf. 268 where the narrator criticises Mum's self-interest in not daring to go beyond the bounds in order to speak out truthfully. The personification of poverty anticipates the allegorical sequence of lines 1251–66. The description recalls the siege of the barn of Unity in *Piers*, XX.53–373.

1253 **a-leehalf** cf. **alee** *Richard*, IV.74. MED records no other instances of 'a-lee'.

1254 MS reads **and** which D&S emend to 'that'. The relative pronoun makes smoother sense, but a conjunction is not impossible. **man** in the sense of retainer, cf. 774.

1255 Other instances of 'angel' in MED denote a servant of God. The mention of Antichrist is without apocalyptic overtones (in contrast to the siege of Unity in *Piers*). Mum is in the service of the leader of vice.

1257 **wronge** has the legal sense of crime, see Alford, p.169. There is a misprint in D&S. The terminal 'ge' of 'wrong', and **entre** are omitted.

1258 **Do-welle** the most explicit recall of the Dowel triad from *Piers*.

1261–6 established that the combined forces of sin commit a crime against God's act of tenancy. The truthteller is dispossessed from man's heart because Mum's servant commits an act of unlawful entry, covetousness gains the key by fraud and dread evicts the rightful tenant by criminal force.

1261 **taketh** has the sense of 'appropriate unlawfully'; cf. OED 'take' 19. 'coveitise' is one of the assailants of the Barn of Unity in *Piers*, XX.297.

1262 cf. *Sir Beues of Hamptoun*, ed. E. Kölbing (EETS ES 46 1885), 43–4: 'The dore barre he toke yn honde / And slewe all that he there fonde'.

1265 In *Piers Plowman*, it is the sale of contrition which finally brings down Unity, XX.365–74. In *Mum*, penitence allows the lawful keeper of the place to regain possession. **seese** is from seisin, to put in legal possession, Alford, p.141.

1266 al his life recalls the legal phrase 'terme of your lifes' at 205 to indicate life tenancy.

1269 exemple puns on the senses of model of virtue, MED 4a) and exemplar of a book 4b).

1270–4 recall 72–81.

1273 asaye cf. note to 1171.

1277–87 The beekeeper's instruction to the narrator to make a book of his criticisms takes the form of a legal injunction. MED records no legal senses in the entry for **infourmed**, but under 'informacioun' 1c), the sense of legal counsel or advice is recorded. The beekeeper has given the narrator advice fully in accordance with legal procedure. **folowe** in its legal sense; cf. note to 417.

1278 make vp thy matiere cf. note to *Richard*, I.171. The b-verse recalls the Dowel triad from *Piers*.

1279 cf. *Richard*, I.38 and *Mum*, 81, 92, 274, 527.

1281 Abate cf. note to *Richard*, III.306–7.

1283 sentence cf. note to 653. **sue** in the legal sense of pursue at law, Alford, p.148, cf. 1602.

1284 cf. note to 1226. **freyst** i.e. the king.

1285–8 The beekeeper hopes that the king will read it first and then the nobles will copy his exemplar both in word and deed.

1287 cf. *Richard*, I.44.

1289 cf. *Piers*, V.3: 'Thanne waked I of my wynkyng and wo was withalle'.

1296 cf. *Pearl*, I: 'Perle, plesaunte to prynces paye'.

1298 provid . . . poyntz cf. note to 492.

1303 The corrector alters MS **he** to 'hit' and D&S emend accordingly. But the MS reading is intelligible.

1304 workes may have been caught from the preceding line. D&S note that it should probably be 'dedes', p.125.

1305 cf. note to 939. MS **cleerly** is superior in sense to the corrector's alteration to 'cherely'.

1308 creature of clay i.e. a mortal man; cf. *St. Aug. Contemptu Mundi*, 374: 'thou art a man . . . made of clay-molde' cited in MED.

1309–36 repeat the substance of 874–5, see note, but in a more expanded form. The narrator adds Joseph's dream to his authorities and summarises the story from Genesis, chapters 39–45. In *Piers*, the dreamer also includes Joseph in his defence of dreams, VII.160–67.

1314 cf. *Piers*, VII.152: 'Ac for the book Bible bereth witnesse'.

1315 The corrector alters to 'the seuene sterres' to restore alliteration. But in Genesis, 37:9, there are eleven stars, cf. *Piers*, VII.160–1. 'And Joseph mette merveillously how the moone and the sonne / And the ellevene sterres hailsed hym alle'.

1319 bringe hym of dawe (day) means put to death; cf. *W.Palerne*, 3817: 'Mani a bold burn was sone brought of dawe' and *Pearl*, 282: 'I trawed my perle don out of dawez'.

1326 The same b-verse is used at *Piers*, III.251 to back up a biblical citation.

1336 This line is supplied by the corrector and included by D&S. **passe** is crossed out and 'lafte' substituted. Elsewhere, the narrator uses 'pass' to describe his movements, e.g., 353, 536, 859 and 952, but not 'lafte'. I have included the correction because a line is needed before 1337.

1338–9 for the imagery cf. note to 51–3.

1341–7 represent a new narrative device to separate the narrator from his criticisms. He is not the author of the comments which follow, merely a bibliographer of other people's writing. Mum has twice earlier been cast as a bishop 579 and 1236. His theft of the bag of books may allude to Archbishop Arundel's *Constitutions*. These measures were concerned with the suppression of heretical ideas. The sixth sought to ban heterodox books. All books had to be examined prior to use by twelve persons from the universities of Oxford and Cambridge who had been approved by ecclesiastical authority, Wilkins, III.318. Many of the comments which follow in *Mum* are anticlerical. In this context, the narrator's resort to suppressed books mirrors ecclesiastical censorship of written material.

1343 forto The original scribe adds **to** to **for**. Opening the bag to counsel the king is an activity compatible with Wycliffite sympathies: *Tractatus de Regibus* and *The Thirty Seven Conclusions* offer political advice from Lollard positions.

1345 vnbredid is glossed by D&S as 'unrolled'. From the comment at 1347, it is more likely to mean 'unopened'; cf. MED breden v (2) 'to open a book'.

1348–9 receipts of goods which the bishops have caused to be bequeathed to the church; cf. *Piers Plowman*, XV.138–9 where the bishops are said to regale themselves with the property of anyone who dies intestate.

1350 papir has the legal sense of a written promise to pay a debt, an IOU, Alford, p.108. The lines criticise bishops for receiving bribes to ignore immorality; cf. *Piers*, Prol.68–79; *The Simonie*, A.90–91, and the Summoner in *The General Prologue* who teaches that people will be punished for their sins only by having to bribe the archdeacon, 653–7.

1351 cf. *Piers*, III.149–52 where Mede blesses ignorant bishops, provides prebends for priests and supports them : 'To holde lemmans and lotebies alle hir lif daies / And bryngen forth barnes ayein forbode lawes'. There is a correction 'now' written after **leotbies** but the line is sufficient as it stands.

1352 The quotation reads 'Woe to those who sell sin for money' and is attributed to Bishop Grosseteste. Grosseteste, along with Fitzralph, was a favourite authority with the Wycliffites, see Arnold, 459/1; 467/17; Matthew, 112/20; 92/13. Grosseteste is sometimes canonised, e.g. Arnold, p.420/17.

1353–6 visitacion is the visit by the bishop or archdeacon to examine the state of the diocese or parish. The narrator complains that officials of the archdeacon's courts were open to bribery with the result that the visitation failed to report malpractices. Instead of being punished, the priests are overlooked. They desert their parishes and live promiscuously in London in the households of nobles; cf. similar criticism of the visitation in *Piers*, II.172–8, and V.411 where Sloth the priest lies in bed at Lent with his sweetheart in his arms and *The Simonie*, A.72–77 which complains of priests abandoning their parishes once they have milked them for all they can gain, and then spending their time (and their profits) with wenches.

1356 D&S read 'at' for MS **in**.

1356 cf. *Piers*, Prol.85–6 where parish priests plead to the bishop to have official permission to dwell in London and sing masses for simoniacal payment.

1357 lille for lalle MED records no other examples of this phrase. It presumably means 'play amorously'. The MS reads 'light' which the corrector has altered to **kitte**. D&S emend. The phrase 'lewd kitte' is used in *The Tale of Beryn*, 443 and 1011 and 'kitte' is used to signify a lecherous woman in *Piers*, C.VII.304.

1359–60 The ignorance of priests is criticised in *Piers*, XI.296–316. Sloth the priest would rather hear obscene stories than any of the Gospels, V.409. See also *The Simonie*, A.97–108. For **the lesson of laudate** cf. note to 637.

1360 Pernelle cf. note to *Richard*, III.156.

1361 cf. notes to 657–62. In *Piers*, IV.117–19 Reason says that he will have no pity on Mede until lords and ladies put Pernell's trimming in their trunks, and clerics become covetous to clothe and feed the poor.

1362–3 Priests break the law and set a bad example to the laity. In Passus XI of *Piers*, Trajan is astonished that bishops 'Maketh swiche preestes that lewed men bitrayen' (302).

1364–9 accuse monastic foundations of spending their income from **rentz** (endowments, Alford, p.132), on themselves and the rich. Instead of feeding the poor, they engage in expensive lawsuits and buy land. **1364 A rolle** is a scroll containing legal documents and records of various sorts, Alford, p.138. Here, presumably the charter of endowment or account of bequests.

1365 parcelle cf. note to 437. A portion of the monks' endowment ought to be given to the poor.

1366 rewe is used at 807 to describe the corrupt burgesses who sit down to feast with Mum; cf. *Piers*, XV.341–2: 'Ac religious that riche ben sholde rather feeste beggeris / Than burgeises that riche ben, as the book techeth'. In *Vox*, Gower contrasts the founders of monastic houses who sold ornaments from their altars in order to distribute food to the needy with the selfish monks of his own time. He comments that it is not permissible for members of religious orders to hoard goods of the Church when they see need, IV.229–30.

1367 cf. the description of the monk in *The General Prologue*, 167: 'A manly man, to been an abbot able'. **matieres** carries the sense of lawsuits.

1368 pourchas means to acquire land by money or gift, Alford, p.123. Through lawsuits, the monks acquire more land and property for their affluent lives; cf. *Piers*, X.303–6: 'Ac now is Religion a rydere, a romere by stretes, / A ledere of lovedayes and a lond buggere, / A prikere on a palfrey fro manere to manere, / An heep of houndes at his ers as he a lord were'. This is altered and transposed in the C text: Passus V.157–60. For Wycliffite criticisms of the involvement of the clergy in lawsuits, see references in note to 649. **pasture thaym the swetter** puns on the senses of acquiring land and feeding gluttonously. Gower describes the avaricious monk who sneaks away from the cloister as a bull in the fields ruminating on the grass, IV.213–14.

1369 is ironic. The b-verse is a conventional phrase in complaints on the times, echoing the opening sentence of the Statute of Labourers 1350, Alford, p.115. Since the plague, there have been fewer people to give the monks money; cf. *Piers*, Prol.83–4: 'Persons and parisshe preestes pleyned hem to the bisshop / That hire parisshes weren povere sith the pestilence tyme'.

1371 **boldely thay ride** cf. note to 644.

1372 **pluralite** cf. notes to 555 and 669.

1373 MS reads 'Properyng' which the corrector alters to **poperyng**. The reading is adopted by D&S and recalls *Piers*, A.XI.213: 'Poperith on a palfrey fro toune to toune'. This reading is not in B or C; cf. note to 1368.

1374–7 invert the standard precept that priests should provide a model of virtuous behaviour for their parishioners to follow. Mann, pp.63–5, traces the tradition in estates satire; cf. *Piers*, XV.108–10: 'Lothe were lewed men but thei youre loore folwede / And amenden hem that thei mysdoon, moore for youre ensaumples / Than for to prechen and preven it noght – ypocrisie it semeth!' In *Vox*, Gower says that the priest is not better than the layman unless he live better, III.1022–30. *Mum* links the idea of the exemplary nature of priests to their preaching that all people are of a common descent (1377). The latter doctrine is orthodox in itself; cf. Trajan's speech in *Piers*, XI.198–201: 'For alle are we Cristes creatures, and of his cofres riche, / And bretheren as of oo blood, as wel beggeres as erles. / For at Calvarie of Cristes blood Cristendom gan sprynge, / And blody bretheren we bicome there, of o body ywonne'. In some contexts, however, the doctrine licensed dissent. In 1381, John Ball preached a sermon to the rebels on Blackheath, taking as his text, 'When Adam delf and Eve span / Who was then the gentleman?' In *Mum*, the notion of common kinship licenses the clergy to ape the immorality of the laity.

1377 The MS reads **may** which D&S emend to 'man'. **may** suggests that no woman can contradict this; cf. note to 1384–7.

1379 cf. Gower's complaint that priests amass worldly

wealth which women then extort from them in return for sexual
favours, III.1525–48.

1380–4 The biblical imagery of the shepherd and his sheep is
prominent in discussion of the clergy, e.g., Chaucer, *The General
Prologue*, 505–6: 'Wel oghte a preest ensaumple for to yive, / By
his clennesse, how that his sheep sholde lyve.' Mann, pp.56–60,
illustrates the range of the conventional image. Closest to *Mum*
is the 13th-century French poem, *Roman de Carite*, which links
the sheep metaphor with physical sickness: 'The shepherd keeps
his sheep healthy and if one falls sick, he cures it. But the
hireling says "He's coughing a lot – who cares if he dies or is
dragged away by the wolf?"' (CXXII.1–4, translated in Mann,
p.57); cf. the criticism of hirelings in *PlTale*, 425–8.

1384 The Latin quotation reads 'Woe to the pastors' and is
taken from Jeremiah, 23:1. The verse continues 'that destroy
and tear the sheep of my pasture'. It is marked to stand at 1383,
but I have placed it at 1384 where it more naturally belongs.

1384–7 D&S state in error that two folios are missing at this
point but fol.16a follows straight on from fol.15; the two folios
form the central opening leaves of the quire. D&S appear to
have confused this section with the lost folio at the beginning of
the quire; cf. note to 1106–7. The switch to criticising women
rather than the priests (1384) is abrupt and perhaps a line or
two has been lost. The sense of the sequence is tenable, however,
if the criticism of women stems from the **speciales** of line 1379;
women encourage the wantonness of their priestly lovers. In
Chaucer's *Nun's Priest's Tale*, women's advice is satirised and
at 3256–66, blamed for the Fall.

1388–1404 concern the spreading of persistent seditious
rumours against Henry by the friars, see notes to 416–22. In
May 1405, the council instructed the sheriffs of all the counties
of England to make proclamations against the circulation of
lying rumours against Henry, *Cal.Close Rolls 1402–5*, p.515. A
petition presented by the Prince of Wales to the Long Parliament
of 1406 criticised those religious who persisted in sowing
dissension amongst the king's subjects by spreading rumours
that the late king was still alive, see McNiven, p.101, and for
rumours persisting into 1407, pp.145–6.

1388 culmes from Latin 'culmus' meaning a stipulation, or
item in a narrative.

1390 cf. the labourers singing over their ale rather than working, *Piers*, VI.115–16.

1397 land-is ende Rumours that Richard was alive often claimed that he was in Scotland.

1403 The swallow derives its name from 'crienge' and is noted for its swiftness, Bartholomaeus, I.631–2.

1404 frere See notes to 1388–1404. The Latin quotation reads : 'Shun gossip lest you start to be thought an originator of it'. The continuation of this couplet from Cato's *Distichs* is cited at 291. The corrector adds after the quotation : 'But caton is all contra and his consail bothe'. It is another instance of toning down anti-fraternal comments ; cf. note to 505.

1407 Though the burne my brother were cf. *Richard*, I.196.

1409 The narrator believes in maintaining the strict hierarchical ordering of society. **ordeyne** means to make a law or decree, Alford, p.106. Its use is ironic, demonstrating the commons aspiring to a function beyond their powers.

1411 matieres alludes to petitions brought by the commons to parliament to alleviate the burdens of taxation.

1412 gadryng is taxation. For the tussles over this in Henry's reign see notes to 134–9 and 147–9.

1413–56 The story of Genghis Khan is taken from Mandeville's *Travels*. As D&S note, p.xxiii, the choice of story may reflect topical interest in Genghis Khan. In July 1402, Timur, or Tamburlaine, said to be his descendant, defeated the Turks at Angora and gained control of all Western Asia. In the winter of 1402, an English Dominican friar called Greenlaw, who held the title of Archbishop of Ethiopia and the East, and acted as the intermediary between the courts of Europe and the Eastern potentates, came to England with letters from Timur. These informed Henry of his victory over the Turks, and offered welcome and protection to English traders. In February 1403, he returned with letters from Henry to Timur, Wylie, I.312–21. Citations from Mandeville's version of the story are noted from C. W. R. D. Moseley's translation into modern English, pp.146–7 of the French version contained in MS Egerton 1982.

1414 Changwys-is Genghis Khan (Changuys Chan in the French version).

1417–18 The seven nations of the people of Tartary were Tartar, Tangut, Eurac, Valair, Semok, Menchy and Tobak. **He**

nempned furst his name refers to God's choice of Genghis Khan as emperor of the seven tribes.

1417 The line repeats 223.

1419–22 alter the details of the source. Mandeville relates that the seven tribes had been in subjection and bondage to other nations around them and makes no reference to internal division and dissent amongst the people of Tartary. The inclusion in *Mum* of this detail reflects the political situation in England, most especially, the quarrels between Henry and the Percies, see notes to 1626–65. The Genghis Khan story is used as an exemplum to encourage fractious nobles, such as the Percies, to bind their allegiance to the king.

1420 double cf. use at 294 and 555 and *Richard*, II.111.

1421 and so hit doeth elleswhere is an allusion to the internal dissensions during Henry's reign. The Latin quotation reads: 'Every kingdom divided against itself shall be brought to desolation' from Luke, 11:17. The same quotation appears at *Richard*, II.52.

1422 souurayns of the marches This does not appear in Mandeville. The narrator anglicises his source, to suggest a parallel with the rebellious Scots and Welsh, see note to 1466–7.

1424–6 principalz MS reads 'principal', but the pronouns in 1425–6 require a plural subject. **principalz** is used at 1014 to refer to the loyal nobility represented by the bees. See also 1434. The narrator omits the first dream in Mandeville, which is granted to Genghis himself, and concentrates on the second dream, which appears to the people of the seven tribes. **bade thaym coroune** may refer to Henry's mention of election in his claim to the crown, see notes to *Richard*, II.92–3.

1425 in vision is supplied by the corrector and incorporated by D&S. The MS reads 'by nightes'. The correction restores the importance of dream-vision to the story.

1427 omits Mandeville's references to Genghis's former strength and lack of wealth to focus on his age, cf. note to 835.

1430 sette in his se cf. 1003.

1431 Mandeville describes many of Genghis's statutes and laws. The narrator focuses on the last two and reverses their order.

1434 proue and a-saye cf. notes to 515 and 1171 and *Crede*, 247. This legal emphasis is not in Mandeville's account.

1436 hoires not in Mandeville.

1437 sese hym in hire lande is the corrector's alteration, adopted by D&S. The MS reads 'sese thaym in his handes'. The copyist must have failed to perceive the legal meaning of **sese** (cf. note to 1265), thinking it meant 'to seize' and altered the pronouns and indirect object.

1438 erniste means a legal pledge, MED ernes (n) 1. **for euer** is used in grants of land, associated with unconditional possession, Alford, p.61. Again, this legal diction is not in Mandeville.

1439 to haue and to holde is a common phrase in conveyancing, derived from the 'habendum et tenendum' of the old common law, Alford, p.69.

1441 couetise is not in Mandeville. The exemplum is concerned to uphold the behaviour not of Genghis himself, but of his exceptionally loyal subjects.

1445 griefed for a grote cf. *Richard*, IV.38. The word-play is ironic. Taxation causes suffering; execution and dispossession only grumbling. Thus the line implies that contemporary complaints over taxation are trifling.

1446 peuple MS reads 'pleuple' in error. D&S emend.

1448 whenne he is not in MS, supplied by D&S.

1449 hertz al hoole cf. *Richard*, I.26.

1450 graunt means conveyance of land, or property, Alford, p.66. Khan's remission is not in Mandeville. Once he is sure of his subjects' loyalty, Khan orders them to follow his banner. He then reconquers all the neighbouring lands.

1451–2 In Mandeville there is no calling of council. The addition provides a closer parallel with the English parliamentary system; **clepid to cunseil** is used at 1461 with reference to the knights of the shire.

1455 Cathay-is The region approximating to China.

1456 cf. *Piers Plowman*, III.208: 'That is the richeste reaume that reyn over hoveth'. Mandeville comments that China is the richest of all lands, p.149.

1457 The Latin quotation reads: 'Behold how good and how pleasant it is for brethren to dwell together in unity' from Psalms, 132:1.

1458 The commons' carping offends against the naturally ordained structuring of society.

1464 cf. *Piers Plowman*, V.558: 'I nolde fange a ferthyng, for Seint Thomas shryne!'

1466–8 refer to the insurrections in Scotland and Wales. In the summer of 1402, the Scots made several incursions into the north of England, culminating in the Battle of Homildon Hill, September 1402, where they were defeated. The Scots remained a threat throughout these years. Many of Henry Percy's followers in the Battle of Bramham Moor were Scots. Led by Owen Glendower, the Welsh maintained a series of raids into England from 1400–9. The Percies were important in the defence of these areas. In 1399, Northumberland was made keeper and warden of the West March, and his son Hotspur, warden of the East March and constable of Cheshire and justiciar of North Wales. Yet after quarrelling with Henry in 1403 over remuneration for these duties, they joined forces with Glendower and Mortimer, see further, notes to 1654–61.

1469–70 connect the neglect of the defence of the realm with the disaffection of the people, see notes to 147–9.

1470 The corrector alters MS 'tale' to **tayl** which D&S adopt. 'Conclusion' makes better sense here than 'cause of complaint'. **teneth** has the sense of being oppressed by fines or legal suits, Alford, p.153; cf. *Richard*, III.79. The commons' grouchings about taxation cause heavier fiscal penalties to finance the suppression of civil disobedience.

1472 The corrector alters MS 'hoode' (caught from the following line) to **honde**. D&S emends accordingly.

1473–4 is a contemporary proverb, see Whiting, p.272.

1475 finde many fautes is used ironically in its legal sense to indicate the commons' usurpation of function.

1479 cf. the description of the bee-king, 1036.

1480 reedy to ride i.e. in defence of the realm; cf. *Richard*, II.58.

1482 The Latin quotation reads: 'We are not able to be equal with the more powerful. Wisdom'. It is a paraphrase of Ecclesiasticus, 8:1: 'Strive not with a powerful man lest thou fall into his hands'.

1483 The corrector alters MS 'babling' to **labbing** which D&S incorporate to restore the alliteration.

1484 cf. 224–5.

1485 kinde cf. note to 1458.

1489–97 criticise squires who provide supporting evidence to acquit nobles accused of robbing the poor. The squires' concern to safeguard their positions as retainers leaves the poor unable to gain legal redress against theft.

1489 a-square i.e. at a distance, cf. *Tale of Beryn*, 585–6: 'He stappid oppon a bronde all vnware, / That hym had been better to have goon more at vn-a-sware'.

1493 alleigge means to cite evidence, Alford, p.3.

1496 reason-is retenue The servants of equity, or justice, Alford, p.134, are contrasted with the perversion of justice by retinues of the nobility.

1497 robes are judges who have been bribed with the rewards of expensive garments; cf. 97. **rehercyn** cf. note to *Richard*, II.98. **rightz** is used ironically in the sense of a just or legally enforceable claim, Alford, p.137. **parties** cf. note to 529–30.

1498–1564 criticise nobles of equal rank who litigate against each other not for a just cause, but because of rivalry. The narrator criticises both the nobles and the legal system for allowing such conflict to expand unchecked.

1498 writte of high wil is a legal document which initiates a criminal action.

1500 couraige is a water-pepper (OF cu[l]rage). MED cites from *Piers of Fulham: Remains of the Early Popular Poetry of England*, ed. W. C. Hazlitt (1886), p.133: 'An erbe is cause of all this rage, / In oure tonge called culrage'. The use in *Mum* suggests an artificial and unnecessary anger.

1503 MS reads 'more', caught from later in the line, which D&S emend to **mene**. Parties of equal rank frequently engage in litigation. By contrast, prosecutions by a person of lower rank against a superior are rare.

1505 harme in the legal sense of damage; cf. note to line 75. There has been no legal transgression, only ill-feeling. MS reads 'herg', presumably a mechanical copying error. The corrector alters to **hertz** and D&S emend accordingly.

1506 stele has the sense of taking feloniously, Alford, p.147. It suggests the nobles' misappropriation of the legal system.

1507 stuffure and store i.e. waste their estates.

1511 leue there he loveth i.e. believe in one or other party out of favouritism, Alford, p.91.

1512 cf. *Richard*, III.282.

1514 The Latin quotation reads: 'Wrath generates hatred, agreement nourishes love' and is taken from Cato, *Distichs*, I.36; cf. note to 291. The corrector adds 'Cato'.

1515–27 The direct speech impersonates the motives of the opposing parties for continuing the law-suit.

1515 MS omits I which D&S supply.

1516 amendes in the legal sense of reparation, cf. note to *Richard*, I.146.

1523 MS reads 'A' which D&S emend to **And**. The following line requires a conditional conjunction. **cuntre** in the sense of judicial shire.

1524 MS reads 'so thewid'. I have followed D&S's emendation to **eschewid** to restore sense.

1528 MS omits **and** which the corrector supplies. D&S emend.

1529 A brenne-water is a nickname for a blacksmith who plunges hot iron into water, cf. *Swarte-smeked smethes*, 22: 'May no man for brenwateres on night han his rest'. The image in *Mum* likens rage to the steam and spluttering caused by immersing hot iron in water.

1530 The Latin quotation reads: 'Wrath may not rest in a sound mind or body. Salomon.' It paraphrases Ecclesiastes, 7:10: 'Be not quickly angry, for anger resteth in the bosom of a fool'.

1531 A boar is a proverbially angry beast; cf. *Song of the Husbandman*, Robbins, 2/51 and *Siege of Jerusalem*, 781.

1534 in hande D&S emend to 'in lande' arguing that there seems no reasonable sense in the MS reading unless it means 'in person'. Although it spoils the alliteration, there are many lines in the poem which read aa/xx, p.128. The MS reading can be defended in the sense of 'owning property'; cf. MED honde 2b). The line would thus mean 'and no injury to you either in terms of property or goods'.

1538 The Latin quotation reads: 'Pride generates all malice, even unto death'. This recalls Ecclesiasticus 10:15: 'For pride is the beginning of all sin: he that holdeth it shall be filled with maledictions and it shall ruin him in the end'.

1540 trespas Used here in the legal sense. **a-countz** is glossed by MED as property recorded in an account, 'account', 2b).

1543–46 In order to avoid dishonour, a foolish noble can be so angry that he prosecutes his case to the bitter end, even if his cause is not good. **grovnde** used here in the sense of legal justification for action; cf. note to *Richard*, II.91.

1544 folowe in the legal sense of prosecute; **th'ende** the end of the proceedings; cf. note to *Richard*, II.97.

1545 MS reads 'sette' which D&S emend to **aretted**. There is no correction marked but it is likely that 'sette' has been caught from the following line. **aretted** restores alliteration and gives the sense 'considered dishonourable'. **rehercyd**: The nobleman is more concerned with the rehearsal of charges against him outside the court than the lawful recital of accusations within it.

1547 construyng Used in its legal sense of fabricating evidence to highlight the wrongfulness of such a course of action; cf. note to *Richard*, III.327. MS reads 'pleuple', a mechanical copying error which D&S emend to **peuple**.

1548 MS reads 'cuntrey' which the corrector alters to 'cuntre'. D&S incorporate this correction. It should probably read **contra**. The narrator counters the false reasoning by offering his own **reason**, i.e. a speech putting forward a ground or cause, Alford, p.135. At 1560, the corrector needlessly alters **cuntre** to 'contre'. It is likely that this correction should have been marked for 1548.

1552 commenche means to commence an action at law, MED commencen 2b). **not cleere in the winde** means not sound. In *Troilus*, 'cler in the wynd' means 'safe from discovery', III.526–7.

1553 y-fourmyd Used in the legal sense; cf. note to 1277.

1555–64 The narrator counsels quarrelling nobles to abandon their cases once they see that they have no ground for dispute. Unless their complaint is just, they should spurn litigation, so that if in future they are involved in a protracted lawsuit, the district will be more inclined to support their cause.

1559 i.e. so that word and deed match up, cf. 142.

1563 MS reads 'more'. **mote** restores sense to the line.

1565 raggeman rolle cf. note to *Crede*, 180. **Ragenelle** is a devil; cf. *Patience*, 188: 'Ther Ragnel in his rakentes hym rere of his dremes' in *Pearl, Cleanness, Patience, Sir Gawain and the Green Knight*, ed. A. C. Cawley and J. J. Anderson (London, 1978).

1565–73 criticise the unfair interference in lawsuits through maintenance. Householders are dispossessed from their estates.

1568 halen so the hockerope 'Hok' is the second Monday and Tuesday after Easter, a period in which merrymakers stopped travellers on the road, bound them with a rope and exacted contributions from them. The description in *Mum* conflates this custom with an image of tug-of-war whereby the stronger party wins the dispute by sheer brawn.

1569–73 **strong** is the MS reading. D&S emend to 'strongest' but the line does not require two superlatives. The corrector's insertions in these lines suggest that the text is corrupt and that lines may have been transposed. At 1570, the corrector inserts: 'Han halid oute the hows lord oute at his halle dore'. On the basis of this, D&S move line 1572 back to stand as 1570. At line 1573, the corrector writes: 'Til thay han drave hym fro his dees he disneth there nomore'. D&S emend line 1573 accordingly. Neither of these alterations significantly improves the sense of the lines. The MS order is tenable. The confusion arises from the poet's extension and mixing of the original hockrope metaphor. Pulling on a rope gives the idea of dragging a householder away from his lawful property. The muscular effort required suggests the idea of the rich bearing down on the poor. Two parties pulling on the same rope suggests the indivisibility of gold and unlawful tussling (1571).

1576–85 Maintenance at law favours the rich and oppresses the poor; cf. *Piers*, III.159–62 where Mede: 'doth men lese thorugh hire love that lawe myghte wynne – / The maze for a mene man, though he mote evere! / Lawe is so lordlich and looth to maken ende: / Withouten presents or pens he pleseth wel fewe' and 168–9: 'And alle that maynteneth hire men, meschaunce hem bitide / For povere men may have no power to pleyne though thei smerte'.

1582 cf. *Piers*, XI.307–8: 'So is it a goky, by God! that in his gospel failleth / Or in masse or in matyns maketh any defaute'.

1585 The Latin quotation is modified from Psalms, 14:5, 'do not accept bribes against the innocent', a text quoted in *Piers*, III.241. Alford notes that it is used as a proof-text against excessive legal fees, p.124.

1586–93 outline the problems of the poor when the rich prosecute them for trifling offences. It is better to submit than suffer the injustices of the law.

1587 The MS reads 'peuple' which the corrector alters to **fleuble**. D&S emend accordingly.

1593 MS reads 'lawe' followed by a blank space. The corrector supplies 'strenght' [sic] which D&S incorporate, emending to **strength**. MS reads 'status' which the corrector alters to statutz.

1594–1616 criticise the loophole in the legal system which allows both rich and poor to continue to resort to law, even if the plaintiff has brought an action wrongfully. In order to amend the system, anyone who brings an unlawful action should pay costs at the end of their case.

1595 nonsuytes are failures of a plaintiff to prosecute his claims or to provide sufficient evidence, MED 'non-suit'. D&S emend to 'nonsuytes'. The phrase 'nineteen hundred' requires a plural noun and I have followed their emendation.

1602–3 depart significantly from the customary defence of the poor in literary criticisms of the legal system.

1604 causelees means without ground for a legal action.

1606 The corrector adds 'yf this were y vsid and y holde lawe'.

1608 chauncellerie i.e. Chancellor's court, or chancery; a court of equity which served to correct the injustices of common law in individual cases.

1617–25 prerogatife is the special right granted by law to allow individuals who felt that they had been treated unjustly by common law, to take their cases to the equitable court of chancery.

1618 folowe vn-y-punysshid To prosecute at law without penalty.

1619–20 ciuile Roman law. The *Digest* or *Pandects* of Justinian sets out those who are prohibited from prosecuting a case at law, for example, minors, those serving in the army, magistrates, convicted criminals and women, Scott, *The Civil Law*, XI.18–19.

1621 Crist-is lawe-is y-canonized canon i.e., ecclesiastical law, as laid down in the decrees of the popes and statutes of councils, specifically, Gratian's *Concordia discordantium canonum* or *Decretum*, Alford, p.21. A passage in the *Decretum* stipulates that clerics should neither bring proceedings in secular law courts nor be tried in them, Causa XI, Quest 1 c.xlvii, Freidberg, I.641.

1622–3 In 1 Corinthians, 6:1–8, Paul chastises the people of Corinth for going to law in the secular courts and bringing lawsuits against each other.

1623 The corrector adds a Latin gloss from Innocent, *De*

Contemptu Mundi, III.15, 'nullum malum impunitum euange-lium' (No evil should go unpunished); cf. *Piers*, IV.143–4. The attribution to the Gospel may be to Matthew, 16:27 or 25:31–46. I have incorporated the quotation because it is clearly signalled by the preceding line, but it is not the citation that one would expect to support the narrator's case; cf. note to 1622–3.

1625 **conscience ne in my credo** i.e. the faculty which applies the general principles of moral reason to specific circumstances (Alford, p.34) and the narrator's belief.

1626–82 concern the appropriation by the nobility of rev-enues due to the king and which are needed for good govern-ment. *The Simonie* criticises the nobles for despoiling the king with the result that he makes exactions from the poor (A.331–5).

1627 **lordship,** i.e. the estates belonging to the king.

1629 **grovnde me on reason** cf. note to 1548.

1631–35 affirm the narrator's belief in a hierarchically ordained society in which the law is upheld and the nobles are prevented from fighting each other. cf. Gower, *Vox*, VI.469–70: laws were established for the transgressor so that each person receives his due reward. Strife grows out of injustice and ultimately threatens the kingdom (486–90) and Kail, I/63: 'And law be kept, no folk nyl ryse'.

1637 **shuld be ordeynid** i.e. voted in parliament, cf. note to 1409.

1640 **th'olde and the newe** are the regular revenues of the Crown, and the taxes and subsidies voted by parliament. See Jacob, p.77. Since the reign of Edward III, parliamentary grants of taxation were made with regularity and the king was granted the customs as a matter of course. But these subsidies still remained grants of special grace, dependent on the goodwill of the Commons. Henry was never denied these subsidies, but in his reign the Commons made unprecedented demands before granting them. In 1401, they asked for a reply to their petitions before they made their grants, but were answered that such a step was without precedent. In the 1406 parliament, the Com-mons presented the king with 31 articles which he had to accept before taxation was granted.

1641–2 MS reads 'wistanding'. I have followed D&S and supplied **th** in the middle of the word. The **statutz** are the 31 articles drawn up in the 1406 parliament, which sought to regulate the business of the king's council. Those nominated to serve on the council had to swear a solemn oath to be bound by these new articles. The principal concern was to regulate grants and financial favours granted by the king and thus ensure that revenues were being properly assigned for the effective running of the household, *Rot.Parl*, III.585. In 1642 MS reads 'statutz'. I have emended to **stablementz** in the sense of an ordinance, enactment. 'Statutz' repeats the previous line tautologously and could have been copied through eyeskip, especially because of the similarity of **stablid** and **stablements**. The sense of the passage is that extra ordinances have been necessary in order to uphold the statutes.

1646 dede as a dore nayle cf. *Piers*, I.187: 'And as deed as a dorenail but if the dedes folwe'.

1648 knightz of the conseil The 31 articles make it plain that the commons thought that members of the council were using their position to obtain grants and favours from the king.

1649 of oone lawe and other are the bishops, learned in both Canon and Civil Law; cf. *Piers*, VII.13–14: 'Bysshopes yblessed, if thei ben as thei sholde / Legistres of bothe lawes, the lewed therwith to preche'.

1650 repeats line 1. The comments in this section of the poem repeat the substance of lines 1–8 and 132–4.

1651 peres The corrector substitutes 'pure', but the MS reading is tenable.

1653 holden of his honour The nobles have more than half of the king's lands and revenues.

1654–62 refer to the Percies. When Henry came to the throne he rewarded the Percies lavishly for their loyal support. But he was unable to meet the demands of the Percies completely and in 1403, Northumberland wrote to Henry telling him that £20,000 and more was owing to them, Kirby, p.154.

1654 gurdying of heedes After the Battle of Shrewsbury in which Henry Hotspur was killed, Thomas Percy was executed. Both their heads were placed on public display. Northumberland was killed in the Battle of Bramham Moor in 1408.

1655 MS reads 'and', which D&S emend to **of**. **mourdre** may continue the reference to the Percies, or allude to the death of Archbishop Scrope in 1405.

1656 fourty is a formulaic number which fits the alliteration.

1657 enuye may refer to the relationship between the Percies and Ralph Neville, earl of Westmorland. In 1399, the Percies had been given a monopoly of border offices, but Henry subsequently advanced Westmorland's responsibilities on the border, possibly as a check on the power of the Percies.

1658 put aweye the beste i.e. cream off the best of the revenue.

1660–3 The margins are torn and reconstruction follows D&S. **1660 cunseille the king** When military duties allowed, the Percies served on the king's council. All three were present at the council which sat in February 1402. The line may have wider reference to the role of the council in advising grants; cf. note to 1648 and 1672. D&S supply **wele**. The bottom of two minims is visible, the margin of the MS is torn.

1661 deue dome One of the 31 articles stated that no warrants or grants were to issue from Chancery which would not pass 'droit ne loy' (right of law), III.587. **defence of the royaulme** Before their rebellion, the Percies were active in the defence of the realm; cf. note to 1466–8.

1662 a-payred supplied by D&S. The margin of the MS is torn. The line repeats 1574.

1663 cf. note to 8 and 132–4.

1665 Haue for his houshold cf. note to 1641–2. **haynous werres** is supplied by the corrector on a blank left in the MS. The drain on finance because of war was expressed in the chancellor's speech to the Hilary parliament of 1404, quoted in Jacob, p.74.

1666 other As D&S, margin torn away.

1667 of his owen A plea expressly made in the second parliament of 1404 was that the king should live off his own. Additional subsidies should be raised only for war and for no other purpose, *Rot.Parl*, III.546–9; cf. *Richard*, I.102.

1668 lyve vppon his laboriers The subsidies granted by the Commons; cf. notes to 1, 8 and 132–4.

1669–70 If the nobility siphon off the king's revenues, then the king cannot pay his debts. In order to meet the demands of government, Henry borrowed heavily. The subsidies granted to the king could be assigned to pay off the creditors, but often they had been assigned elsewhere, Jacob, p.74.

1671–82 state that despite the provisions to safeguard the king's revenues, the country will not be prosperous unless these measures are actually kept and the king has sufficient funds.

1672 twys in oon wike cf. note to 120. As a result of the 31 articles in 1406, Wednesdays and Fridays were assigned for the reception of petitions, and it was stipulated that only on these days should members of the household make requests for grants, Jacob, p.84.

1673 copes were the long garments worn by clerics.

1674 pleyne atte parlement refers to the appeals made by the commons for the proper use of taxation; cf. note to 1640.

1676 cf. lines 1–4 and the description in *Richard*, I.128–32.

1683–96 criticise those who make large fortunes at the expense of the poor. They give away nothing while alive, but make provision for hospitals in their will.

1684 hath is supplied by the corrector and D&S incorporate.

1687 no lenger The MS is torn away with only **ger** visible. D&S reconstruct.

1690 cf. *Richard*, III.175.

1692 holde hit euer in his hande A legal formula indicating possession; cf. note to 1534.

1695–6 In *Wynnere and Wastoure*, Waster says to Winner that making donations after his death will not profit him: 'A dale aftir thi daye dose the no mare / Than a lighte lanterne late appone nyghte' (305–6).

1696 The margin is torn away and the addition of 'ed' to **passed** follows D&S.

1697–1723 criticise fraudulent executors who appropriate the bequests of the wills they prove.

1697 title of a testament MS reads 'lite' which D&S emend to **title**. I have not retained their addition of 'z' to 'testament' because the text does not always preserve a strict grammatical relationship between noun and subsequent pronouns, cf. note to 1044. **testament** is a document recording a person's wishes on the disposition of his personal property after death, Alford, p.153.

1699 seel of th'office A will was authenticated with an official mark or seal, cf. Alford, p.142.

1700 feis are those paid to the lawyers to prove the will.

1702–5 The margin is torn and the additions to the end of lines follow those suggested by D&S.

1703–20 cf. *Piers*, XV.140–3, where the bishop who appropriates the goods of a man who has died intestate has the following speech : 'He was a nygard that no good myghte aspare / To frend ne to fremmed – the fend have his soule ! / For a wrecchede hous he held all his life tyme, / And that he spared and bispered, spende we in murthe !'

1703 cf. *Tale of Beryn*, 640: 'The warrok was a-wakid' where warrok is a savage dog, restrained by a clog round its neck, but which does not prevent him from biting the pardoner in the thigh. Line 703 gives an alliterative rendering of a common proverb; cf. *Troilus*, III.764: 'It is nought good a slepyng hound to wake'.

1704–5 Even if a whole fifteenth is bequeathed and a receipt given, the executors keep the donations for themselves.

1706–12 The margin of the MS is torn and the insertions follow those of D&S except 1706 where they read 'Ne do not for the dede', rather than **And do noght for the dede** – 'and do as much for the dead as I do when I sleep', i.e. nothing.

1710 attourneys are persons formally appointed to transact official business, here, the administering of a will.

1711–12 Only half the money will be distributed because they will say that there is no more to be had. **grovnde oure tale** ; the legal diction highlights the illegality.

1713–20 Since the deceased kept all his goods to himself when he was alive, the executors should follow his example and do likewise. In *Wynnere and Wastoure*, Waster criticises Winner for hoarding all his life and making bequests only after his death : 'Thi sone and thi sektours ichone slees othere / Maken dale aftir thi daye for thou durste neuer' (302–3).

1715 reason reproue means accuse according to the law.

1723–33 criticise those who try to interpret the topical significance of old prophecies. In 1402 and 1406, acts were passed to prevent their dissemination because they were regarded as a highly effective means of fostering dissent. A forecast of the future could reflect dissatisfaction with the past and/or present. The 1406 law accused the Lollards of publishing false prophecies which predicted the overthrow of the princes and lords temporal and spiritual (*Rot.Parl*, III.583ff.).

1724 meruailles that Merlyn dide deuyse Geoffrey of Monmouth's 'Book of Merlin' (Bk VII of his *Historia Regum Britanniae*) was the source for most of the prophecies composed in England for the next four centuries. Some are direct translations, some use its conventions, some simply use the name of Merlin for authority. A poem known as the *Six Kings to Follow John* was often attributed to Merlin and was circulated by the supporters of Glendower, Mortimer and the Percies, Scattergood, p.32. The Merlin prophecies are discussed in R. W. Southern, 'Aspects of the European Tradition of Historical Writing: History as Prophecy', *TRHS*, 22 (1972), 159–60 and R. Taylor, pp.1–47.

1725 as the Ram is hornyd i.e. a reading process as convoluted as the horns of a ram are curly. It alludes to the way that prophecies make coded references to people under the guise of narrating the behaviour of animals; cf. Lydgate, *Ryght as a Rammes Horne*, MP, II.461–3. The techniques of encoding are discussed in *The Prophecy of John of Bridlington* (Wright, I.124–7).

1727–30 Those who attempt to interpret old prophecies are foolish since no one is able to predict tomorrow's weather.

1731–3 Caroline Eckhardt has argued that these lines contain a reference to the executions of the Percies since their heraldic sign was a crescent moon. See for instance, Gower, *Tripartite Chronicle* I, note to line 55. She notes that this leaves the **sterres** of 1731 unaccounted for, p.497. **sterres** could refer to a marvellous comet which appeared at around 1402; *The Dieulacres Chronicle* says that the 'stella comata' was a prognostication of the Battle of Shrewsbury, p.175. But the moon and the stars might allude more simply to the characteristic language of prophecies; for example, the closing passage of Monmouth's *Book of Merlin* refers to the moon and the stars in an extended astrological circumlocution. In *Dives and Pauper* there is a discussion of the evils of astronomy in which the collocation 'moon and sterrys' is frequent; cf. I.118/31–3.

1734–51 criticise further the shortcomings of the clergy, especially the relationship of the spiritual and temporal powers.

1734 cedule A brief document attached to a roll or enclosed in a letter and usually containing a list of names or bill of particulars.

1735 OED gives as the second sense of 'tuly' the colour red or crimson; cf. the description of lead in *Bartholomaeus*, II.867/5: 'tewly reed'.

1737–42 cf. the echo of *Piers* at 222. The use of **ordre** and **office** in the context of Christ's institution of the clergy (1741) suggests that the spiritual and temporal powers are confusing their functions. They are knit together not in conscience, but in concern for temporal wealth. They have abandoned the example of apostolic poverty set down by their **forne-faders**.

1740 the lawe is the Bible. The clergy have departed from Christ's ordinances; cf. note to 431.

1741 MS reads 'shuld' which the corrector alters to **ought**. D&S emend.

1746–51 The margin is torn away. The emendations follow those of D&S.

1748 cf. the Parson in the *General Prologue*: 'That first he wroghte, and afterward he taughte' and note to 1374–7.

1749 Mann, p.62, notes how the example that the clergy should set their parishioners was often expressed in imagery of light, see *Vox*, III.1070–80. *Lanterne of Light* is used as the title of a Wycliffite criticism of the contemporary church and *PlTale* 969–70, states that priests' deeds should be as bright as a star and their form of living a light to ignorant men.

1751 preyer puns on the sense of 'prayer to God', MED preiere 2a) and 'petition for favour' sense 1a).

NOTES TO THE CROWNED KING

1 cf. *Death and Liffe*, 1: 'Christ, Christen King that on the crosse tholed'.

2 thow kynd go out of cours There are references to the 'kynd cours' at 26 and 107, and to 'kynde' at 28, 121 and 132. The course of nature provides a pattern which man's political nature ought to follow; cf. notes to *Mum*, 931. Christ offers comfort if nature is deflected from its true course.

5 implicitly claims high authority for the dream which follows. It is a **sondry signe** from Christ himself and thus assumes the status of a revelation.

9 The b-verse attests to the truth of one's testimony; cf. note to *Richard*, II.91.

16 puts the reader in the position of judge of the dream. Evasion of authority is a common narrative technique, cf. *Piers*, Prol.209–10: 'What this metels bymeneth, ye men that ben murye, / Devyne ye – for I ne dar, by deere God in hevene', *Richard*, I.57–60 and *Mum*, 1087–9.

18 MS reads 'frende' which Skeat emends to **fremde** – 'unknown people', hence 'chance acquaintances, companions to whom one is not related', p.531. Robbins retained the MS reading in the sense of 'intimate friends', p.386. Since the line already contains **frendes** in the a-verse and the miscopying of a minim is a common scribal error (cf. 105), I have emended to **fremde**.

19 In 1415, Corpus Christi Eve fell on 29 May.

20 Henry V set out from London on 18 June 1415 to wage war against the French. He set sail from Southampton in August. The poet could have lived at Southampton. The variation between **kynde** and **kende** in the poem, e.g., lines 28 and 26, is characteristic of Hampshire, *LALME*, III.154. But **kende** is recorded in most of the counties south of a line drawn from Gloucester to Norfolk, *LALME*, IV.204.

22 The company which devotes its time to revelry and reading of romances may owe a literary debt to Chaucer's *Canterbury Tales*.

24 is deficient in alliteration. Robbins suggests '(it) began (to dawn), p.386. Skeat glosses the line: 'The night receded and dawn began', p.525. Possibly the subject for **began**, such as 'glemes' – gleams of light – has been lost from the a-verse.

25 cf. *Mum*, 889.

26 The description of the time of day is not mere decoration. The narrator goes to sleep at dawn, just as day is beginning. The sun follows its natural course but man is out of step with it. He is awake **reuelyng** during darkness and asleep when it is light; cf. note to *Richard*, III.272.

29 Robbins reads 'swer' and emends to **swet**. MS and Skeat read **swet**.

30 cf. *Pearl*, 61: 'Fro spot my spyryt ther sprang in space'.

31 cf. *Piers*, Prol.13–18:

> As as I beheeled into the eest an heigh to the sonne,
> I seigh a tour on a toft trieliche ymaked,
> A deep dale bynethe, a dongeon therinne,
> With depe diches and derke and dredfulle of sighte
> A fair feeld ful of folk fond I ther bitwene –
> Of alle manere of men, the meene and the riche.

And cf. Will's vision of the workings of Nature from the top of the mountain of Middle Earth, XI.320–67.

33 Robbins reads 'sere couth' and emends to 'selcouthe'. Skeat and MS read **selcouthe**.

34 MS reads 'noumbrerd'; a copying error which both Skeat and Robbins emend.

35 Robbins misreads 'comounes' for MS **comunes**; cf. the sudden appearance of the king in *Piers*, Prol.112: 'Thanne kam ther a Kyng: Knyghthod hym ladde'.

36 On 19 November 1414, Henry exacted from parliament a very large grant of two tenths and two fifteenths. Although war had not yet started, it was understood that this grant would support the costs of French invasion, *Rot.Parl*, IV.35. **soleyn** refers to the unprecedented nature of the grant. In the previous parliament, eight months earlier, Henry had stated that the usual grants of a fifteenth and a tenth would not be imposed, *Rot.Parl*, IV.16.

37 **reson** has its legal sense of justice, see also line 39; cf. note to *Richard*, II.69. Ironically the narrator appears patriotic, but the tenor of lines 61–5 suggests that he is critical of the king's fiscal policy.

39 **skyle** has the sense of a legal argument; cf. notes to *Mum*, 405.

40 **parcell** has the legal sense of an allotted portion; cf. note to *Mum*, 437.

41 **ordenaunce** has the legal sense of a decree; cf. note to *Mum*, 1409. This line also has ironic undertones.

42 cf. *Piers*, Prol.123–4: 'Thanne loked up a lunatik, a leene thyng withalle / And knelynge to the Kyng clergially he seide'. In *Crowned King*, the clerk begins with the polite 'you' form of address (43). Once the king has granted him permission to speak, the clerk uses the more familiar 'thou' form (51). This

reflects the directness of his speech, see lines 46–7. The clerk reverts to the 'you' form when he takes his formal leave of the king in line 135.

44 cf. *Piers*, III.93–4: 'Salamon the sage a sermon he made / For to amenden maires and men that kepen lawes'. cf. *Mum*, 304 & 1212 and Lydgate, *Ballade to King Henry VI*, 51–2: 'First of alle thy staat to magnefye, / With Salamons souerain sapyence'.

46 **shewe** in the sense of putting forward a complaint, Alford, p.143 and **sentence** as judgment; cf. note to *Mum*, 516–20 and 653. The clerk frames his speech as though he were putting forward a case at law. He licenses his right to make criticism and offer advice.

47 The clerk professes to shun rhetoric; cf. the description of the sothsegger in *Mum*, 49–51, who cannot speak in **termes** and always hits the nail on the head. His claim is not strictly true, as he talks not in **prose**, but in verse, and his speech employs figures and tropes. For **pluralite** MED records the senses of 'more than one' and 'an expression in plural number'. This example from *The Crowned King* is not listed. Given the context, **pluralites** here must be a term for words and phrases with a double meaning, equated with flattery. Hence, **pluralites** may also have the sense of 'duplicity' – in contrast to the **singuler noumbre** of line 46.

48 The only profit the clerk wishes to gain by his speech is thanks. He is not interested in financial reward; cf. *Mum*, 87 and 1218 and the flatterer's words to the truthteller in the Digby poem *Mede and Muche Thank*: 'Thou getest the thonke with spere and launce, / Ther-with thou might the clothe and fede; / I gloser will stonde to my chaunce, / And mayntene my men al with mede' (Kail, II.45–8).

51 refers to the dictum 'nosce te ipsum'; cf. *Richard*, III.200 and note to I.112. The Digby poem *Loue god, and drede*, includes the lines: 'Drede god, and knowe thy selue, / That ouer puple hast gouernaunce', Kail, I.9–10.

52 cf. Kail, XII.105–6: 'Eche a kyng hath goddis power, / Of lyf and leme to saue and spille'; cf. *Richard*, III.116.

53 cf. Kail, III.11–15: 'Iustice in goddis stede is dight. / Do euene lawe to fooll and wyse. / Set mesure in euene assise, / The righte weye as lawe ges. / And lawe be kepte, folk nyl not ryse', and Hoccleve, *Regement*, 2514–16: 'A kyng is made to kepen and maynteene / Iustice, for she makith obeisant / The mysdoers that proude ben & keene'.

54–6 cf. *Piers*, IV.136–42: '"Ac I may shewe ensaumples as I se outher, / I seye it by myself" quod he, "and it so were / That I were kyng with coroune to kepen a reaume, / Sholde nevere Wrong in this world that I wite myghte / Ben unpunysshed in my power, for peril of my soule, / Ne gete my grace through giftes, so me God save!"'

54 cf. *Mum*, 1036, 1479 & 1554.

55 poynt has the sense of point of law, MED **preve** in the sense of furnishing evidence; cf. note to *Richard*, I.17.

56 MS reads 'an dowte', which both Skeat and Robbins emend to **and dowted**.

58 I have supplied a negative particle before **wyssheth** to restore sense to lines 56–60: there is no one alive who does not desire honour. He is feeble-witted unless he know that he has deserved well on account of his works. Skeat and Robbins retain the manuscript reading. Lines 57–60 are an incentive to the king to gain worship through his own **well doyng**, i.e. the tough administration of justice; cf. Hoccleve, *Regement*, 2885–89: 'Thus, my gode lorde, wynneth your peples voice; / For peples vois is goddes voys, men seyne. / And he that for vs starf vpon the croyse / Shal white it yow, I doute it noght certeyne; / Your labour shal naght ydel be, ne veyne;'

60 well doyng may recall the Dowel triad in *Piers*.

61 cf. *Richard*, III.354–5.

62–4 cf. *Piers*, I.135: 'Whan alle tresors arn tried, Truthe is the beste', repeated at I.207.

65 The e of **behynde** is scarcely visible; cf. Kail, XIII.43–44: 'Youre tenauntes playntes ye mot here, / Ffor they kepen all youre tresour.'

66 MS reads 'the', which Robbins retains in the sense of 'for thee'; subject (they) of 'swope and swete' omitted (as commonly), p.387. However, in line 67, the pronoun 'they' is used alongside 'for thee'. Skeat emends 'the' to **they**, which gives a more straightforward reading of the line.

69 cf. Mede, dressed in **pelure**, fine clothes and decked with **preciouse stones**, *Piers*, II.9–16.

71 cf. *Piers*, I.152: 'And also the plante of pees, most precious of vertues' and *Mum*, 703.

73 Robbins reads 'goddes' for MS **goodes**; cf. Kail,

XIII.49–52: 'Lordis that han castels and toures, / Alle folk stonden of yow awe. / The puple is goddis, and noght youres. / They paye youre rente, to gouerne lawe.'

74–6 cf. Kail, I.89–94: 'Why pore men don riche reuerence, / Two skylles y fynde therfore : / To tyrauntes don hem greuaunce, / To rewe and agen restore, / Goode men for loue they worshipe more, / That don hem good, and help at nede.'

77 cf. image of the crown in *Richard*, I.131.

78 cf. Kail, III.81–2: 'What kyng that wol haue good name, / He wol be lad by wys counsayle'.

79–81 cf. *Mum*, 211–220, and *Tractatus de Regimine Principum*, written for Henry VI, ed. Genet, p.55, where it is stated that the virtues of a prince are a pattern which the people must follow.

82 Robbins reads 'waste' for MS **wast**.

84 Robbins reads 'hyndred' for MS **hyndren**.

85–92 Warnings against flatterers are prolific in works concerned with rulers, e.g., Gower, *Mirour*, 26545–7; *Vox*, VI.545–80; *Confessio*, VII.2165–2694; *On the Times*, Wright, I.270–81; Robbins, 49/29–32 and Kail, II and IV.93–6 and Chaucer, *The Merchant's Tale*, 1478–1518.

88 MS reads 'momelyn'. Elsewhere in the poem, the 3rd plural present ends in -e (e.g., 66) or -en (e.g., 134). Line 88 is the only instance of -yn-. A present participle seems more appropriate here than the simple present. The scribe could have simply omitted the final 'g' by a mechanical copying error and therefore I have emended to **momelyng**.

88 maketh probably ought to be 'maken' or 'make' because the subject is the **gylers mowthes** of line 86. It is possible that the order of 88 and 89 has been reversed. I have not emended because strict grammatical unity is often lacking between lines of alliterative verse.

90 Robbins reads 'mame' for MS **marre**; cf. *Piers*, XIII.360–1: 'And awaited thorugh wittes wyes to bigile, / And menged his marchaundise and made a good moustre'.

93 Robbins reads 'clergie' for MS **clergi**. Amongst the advice given to Henry V in Hoccleve's *Ballade* on the king's return to Kennington is : 'Be holy chirches Champioun eek ay' (22).

95 Robbins explains **poyntes of werre** as warlike exercises, p.387. Under 'pointe' 9b) MED gives the meaning 'feats of arms'.

95–7 Letters written to Thomas Tunstall, Nicholas Colnet and Thomas Morstede in 1415 promise a share in the profits of war: prisoners, booty, money, gold, silver and jewels, Rymer, *Foedera*, IV.116–17, ix.233–9.

96 MS reads 'wilde' which Robbins retains without commenting on the unusual form. I have followed Skeat in emending to **welde**.

97 cf. *Piers*, C.III.250–2: 'And that is the kynde of a kyng that conquereth on his enemys, / To helpe heyliche alle his oste or elles graunte / Al that his men may wynne, do therwith here beste'.

99 Robbins reads 'nothyng' for MS **no thyng**.

100 cf. John, 13:34: 'A new commandment I give unto you: That you love one another, as I have loved you, that you also love one another'.

102 The Earl Marshal was the chief political officer of the realm; cf. note to *Richard*, III.105–6. **maner his maistre** is obscure. Robbins, following Skeat, suggests 'and let use be his master' or 'let habit guide him', p.387. The uses of **maistre** at 124 and 132 suggest that this is the sense intended; that if the Marshal make a habit of dealing out strong blows, then the people will fear him for his strength.

105 MS reads 'comyng'. The sense requires **connyng** and both Skeat and Robbins emend accordingly. The importance of wise counsellors is a frequent theme in poems on kingship. Gower's remarks provide a summary: '... for ther is nothing / Which mai be bettre aboute a king, / Than conseil, which is the substance / Of all a kinges governance' (*Confessio*, VII.3887–90).

107 The b-verse states that it is the king's natural office to cherish the knights of the council.

111 cf. Kail, II.57–8: 'I likne a gloser, in eche weder / To folowe the wynd, as doth the fane'.

116 The line lacks an alliterative stave in the b-verse. Skeat comments: 'The writer had no business to link "speche" with "small" (thus alliterating "sp" with "sm") and then leave out the chief letter,' p.523. A word such as 'sotil' may be missing after **more** though this still produces rather rough alliteration.

118 cf. *Piers*, II.66: 'And as a brocour broughte hire to be with Fals enjoyned'.

120 cf. *Richard*, I.169 & III.122.

121 cf. *Richard*, III.92 and *Mum*, 999. Henry is king by virtue of his birth but he must still learn the craft of kingship, cf. Hoccleve, *Regement*, 3963–6: 'O worthi Prince! I trust in your manhode, / Medlid with prudence and discrecioun, / That ye shulle make many a knyghtly rode, / And the pride of oure foos thristen adoun.'

125–6 cf. Kail, I.145–8: 'Who that taketh fro pore to eke with his, / Ffor that wrong is worthy wo; / Another, richer than he is, / Of the same shal serue hym so.'

126 cf. *Piers*, III.209–10: 'It bicometh to a kyng that kepeth a reaume / To yeve men mede that mekely hym serveth'.

130 cf. Hoccleve, *Regement*, 4012–15: 'And if a kynges honour schal be queynt / With a foul and a wrecched couetise, / His peples trust in hym schal be ful feynt; / A kyng may naght gouerne hym in that wise'.

135 The narrator returns to the formal mode of address. **mater y meve** carries the legal sense of putting forth a case; cf. note to *Richard*, I.171.

137–44 To his subjects, a king should represent the qualities of the Christ, cf. Hoccleve, *Regement*, 2409–2412: 'And syn a kyng, by wey of his office, / To god I-likned is, as in manere, / And god is trouthe itself, than may the vice / Of vntrouthe, naght in a kyng appeere'. The closing lines of the poem, particularly line 138, view kingship from a much more overtly religious perspective than either *Richard* or *Mum*. The clerk urges the king to follow Christ's example of selflessness and that of subsequent martyrs for his love. The lines exalt death in the sense of religious martyrdom, not glorious death in battle.

142 cf. *Piers*, Prol.105: 'There Criste is in kyngdom, to close and to shette'.

144 Prosperite; and pees The linking of prosperity with peace at the close of a poem written in the context of the start of a military campaign is striking. The poem concludes on a note of Christian pacifism.